THINK OF AN ELI

CW00919374

THINK OF AN ELEPHANT

COMBINING SCIENCE AND SPIRITUALITY FOR A BETTER LIFE

PAUL BAILEY

WATKINS PUBLISHING

LONDON

This edition published in the UK in 2007 by
Watkins Publishing, Sixth Floor, Castle House,
75–76 Wells Street, London W1T 3QH

10 9 8 7 6 5 4 3 2 1

Designed and typeset by Jerry Goldie

Printed and bound in Great Britain

British Library Cataloguing-in-Publication Data available

ISBN: 978-1-905857-17-3

www.watkinspublishing.com

CONTENTS

For numbered text reference notes and glossary go to
www.thinkofanelephant.com

A NOTE ON NOTES

All the numbered notes in this book would have taken up a good thirty pages of valuable paper, and therefore the loss of countless trees. To avoid this unnecessary consumption, you will find a glossary and all the numbered supporting notes – sources, comments, case studies and further information – on the *Think of an Elephant* website:

www.thinkofanelephant.com

ACKNOWLEDGEMENTS

Kristina Cabala – My loving partner, for enduring those endless long years when I was totally immersed in the book. Only a writer's partner can know the isolation and frustration involved. The reality check provided by my two stepsons Greg and Max, along with your love, affection and wise counsel have helped keep life in balance.

Albert Bailey – my father, whose love and compassion to his fellow man was never restricted, in spite of his horrendous war experiences. **Elvie Bailey** – my mother, a woman who encouraged other ways of seeing and being; a woman who forever practised and promoted compassion, care and a free spirit; the person who first extended my boundaries beyond the norm and allowed unlimited possibilities. **Fran Bailey** – my sister-in-law, who gave time selflessly, converting my initial tapes and jottings to first manuscript stage. **Family** – particularly brother-in-law Rod, sister Jen and my mother – for their unwavering faith and encouragement.

Tony Hanly – for friendship, constant encouragement and generous support. **Richard deSauty** – for friendship and motivation.

This book has gone through redrafts too many to mention. Key in the end stages of this process has been **Julie Ganner** – whose consummate professionalism, determined and gifted editing – along with the ability to really hear me – helped bring structure and polish to the final story. Finally, thanks to the team at Duncan Baird/Watkins for their editorial support, guidance and feedback – publisher **Michael Mann**, publishing manager **Penny Stopa**, and editor **Peter Bently**.

The mind is where tomorrow's victories will be won.

This book is dedicated to the world's children.
May its story empower each of us to leave our small
planet a little better for them, in perpetuity.

To Joseph, my son, through whose death I learned
that there is never a perfect time to love, so reach
out with kindness and love now.

To Lillian, my daughter, whose resilience and bright
spirit are an inspiration to so many.

Introduction

As we watch the way the world is changing and evolving around us, most of us worry about what is driving today's environmental, political and social upheavals. We also wonder how we, as individuals, can ever reach out effectively and positively impact these global problems from the local landscape of our daily lives.

September 11, in particular, highlighted a global spiritual crisis, propelling many of us into a deeper spiritual search and personal introspection. It is as if we have entered a 360-degree war zone. Meanwhile, global warming has snapped our attention towards an environmental crisis rapidly developing worldwide. Environmental and political instability is everyone's concern, while global poverty and corporate collapses have highlighted cruel social and economic inequities.

With our social, political and environmental worlds becoming increasingly chaotic and uncertain, it is not enough to wonder how we can halt the crises we see unfolding around us. Before we have any hope of resolving these increasingly urgent problems, we need to address a deeper, underlying issue: the extent to which these ecological and social crises reflect on our progress and direction as a species, on our personal behaviour, and on our spiritual evolution.

How can a highly evolved species such as ours, with its natural instinct for happiness and hope, stop doing some of the things we do and turn the tide to create a better future? Our world has evolved to a point where one animal, the human species, has the power to influence the evolution and destiny of the planet, for better or worse. Put simply, the future direction of life on Earth is now in human hands. What happens from here depends on the choices we make personally *and* globally.

The spiritual progress of humanity has come to an exciting highpoint. At last we are beginning to realize how science, religion and spirituality can work together to enlighten us about reality and creation – and where our life fits in to it all. With the mounting scientific evidence of the extent to which observation and mind affect reality in many ways, science is about to take a momentous step: an acknowledgement that the 'hard sciences' (physics, chemistry and so on) and the 'soft sciences' such as psychology and philosophy are not only interrelated but in fact inseparable. Our quest is to balance what science is telling us today about the nature of physical reality, biological evolution and life in general with what religion and spirituality have been teaching throughout the centuries in their calls to eternity, 'divine' experiences, and life beyond ourselves.

Although these two positions have traditionally been presented as mutually exclusive, people of all persuasions and times have suspected that not only is reality bigger and vastly more wonderful than we can grasp with our limited senses, but also that it is something all of us are already influenced by and part of. *Think of an Elephant* establishes that the traditional positions of science and religion are *profoundly intertwined*, and that there are more dimensions to reality and spiritual maturity than most of us ever realized.

This book sets out to explain these connections and discover how they can be applied to our day-to-day lives.

We might think we live in a three-dimensional world of space plus time, but science today tells us there may be ten or more dimensions to greater reality. My graduate studies, archival research, professional observations and personal experience have led me to the conclusion that most of us live parallel lives – presently unbalanced – between forces of separation and isolation on one hand, and forces of connection and unity on the other. Our spiritual search remains the life-long quest to balance these two realities in our lives.

This spiritual quest is in itself part of our personal and collective evolution. Life has so far evolved through several transitions on its way from simple bacteria to more intricate organisms, and then on to human consciousness and our recent large-scale complex societies. Now another major transition is underway, a spiritual awakening that involves the development of 'breakthrough' or spiritually holistic consciousness.

On a physical level, our network of connections is being expanded everywhere by new technologies. The World Wide Web – with its bulletin boards, blogs, and other arrays of online networks – points to a globally interactive world where physical space is now interchangeable with cyberspace to create a new and extended self. The Internet, in particular, is becoming our external brain – an extension of our consciousness, and as much a key to the evolution of thinking as the grey matter of our own brain. Embraced by most who experience it, the ultra-connectedness of Internet technology and telecommunications is being matched within our own biology by the enhanced connections of our evolving (yet rudimentary) psychic intelligence and our emerging creative abilities.

While challenging the bedrock of many belief-systems, *Think of an Elephant* joins the momentum of the human potential movement and its literature. This is a book about discovering deeper connections within our physical, psychological and spiritual worlds, about the evolution of the human soul as we begin to understand the full impact our psychic separation is having on us and the way we live, our spiritual fitness and our world. These discoveries do not come with a formula or an instruction sheet; rather, this is a process of gradual enlightenment that will unfold throughout these pages. You will be presented with some astonishing ideas that challenge everything you think you know. Although some of these ideas may seem difficult, they are worth following, as they offer us the key to unleashing the full power of human potential.

This book is written in defence of the best in human consciousness, and the best within the spirit of modern civilization. The book not only distils the evidence for multiple realities within an infinity of higher connections, but also explains the steps that will take us further towards our evolving spiritual maturity by putting our personal search for meaning into a scientific framework designed to be understood by the layperson. As well as identifying the different levels of personal spiritual development in today's global context, this book provides insights into the converging forces operating within the fields of science, health, the environment and psycho-spiritual evolution. It takes the reader on an exploration of our most profound possibilities, uncovering our personal power and indicating how we can make an immediate, real and significant difference. We can do this by using the capacities each of us has within us today, irrespective of where we are or what resources we *think* we have or haven't got.

In addition to the body of scientific research supporting these arguments, *Think of an Elephant* also addresses a number of questions to which there are no readily agreed answers. The idea here is not to argue the finer points of any single theory, but merely to make us think, inquire, debate and wonder; to find significant answers we first need to challenge our assumptions about what we think we know, about what is important, and about the limits of what is possible. Cynicism before investigation is one of the surest ways to kill creativity and inhibit exploration and discovery. To make any material or spiritual progress we must first learn to open our minds to new ideas, possibilities and choices.

At every moment of our lives we are choosing between safety and growth – a profound moment that registers a planetary turning point within each of us, a time either to stay locked into fear and distrust or to open up to our spiritual maturity and global stewardship. In choosing to open ourselves to deeper insights and personal transformations, we recognize that there is more to living than mere existence, and more to life than mere survival.

Human consciousness has been grasping for a central truth ever since our brains became sufficiently evolved to do so. Achieving this is humanity's promise and our personal responsibility. It is also the possibility reflected in the insights of the scientists, philosophers, artists, politicians, religious teachers and writers quoted in this book. The next great wave of human potential is beginning to take shape. We are equipped with a consciousness capable of registering the most subtle connections, intangible relationships and multi-dimensional networks. More and more of us realize that only by understanding the true nature of the universe both scientifically *and* spiritually can we can get to see where we fit into it all, how we each affect everyone and everything around us, and how we can make a significant difference. This understanding is the key to personal responsibility for change and also, ultimately, to our lasting happiness and fulfillment.

The best of human experience is just beginning.

Section One

ISLANDS OF SEPARATION

CHAPTER 1

Your part in the scheme of things

The most beautiful and most profound ...
experience is the sensation of the mystical.
And this mysticality is the power of all true
science.

Albert Einstein[1]

I t is a characteristic of human nature that from an early age we start questioning everything, making the word 'why?' a fixture of our conversation. Across history we have been seeking answers to the most fundamental questions about the nature of the universe and how we fit into it – a desire to understand the connections that make us who and what we are today.

Yet here we are in the 21st century, still unable to agree on how these questions should be answered. While we yearn for intimacy, recognition and a sense of meaning, many of us feel disconnected from our planet, our work, our community, our partners, and even ourselves. Many of us want to make a positive difference but don't know where to start…

If we were to look for one universal feature spanning all cultures and times, we would certainly uncover humanity's hunger for a meaningful existence. Yet in our hostile world of factions and frictions, life so often becomes a spectator sport. Populist ideas and theories are kicked around without result. It remains very easy to merely theorize about spiritual connections and the meaning of life yet still not change the way we live. Ours is a spiritual search for meaning and unity, a quest that is in itself part of our evolution. No matter what our apparent differences, this fundamental hunger is one we all seem to share.

In our search for higher meaning, we have founded an almost endless array of religions and spiritual traditions down through the ages, while science has more recently begun probing for answers to big questions as well. Most religions search for their highest meaning in a unifying heavenliness and an ultimate godliness, while science similarly sets its sights on what it calls 'the unifying theory of everything'. This 'Holy Grail' of physics is what Einstein said would allow us to 'read the mind of God'. Apparent opposites, yet remarkably similar, the evolving positions of science and religion are bringing prayer and pragmatism closer together.

The current crises we are seeing in the world – ecological, social and religious – cry out for us to think and act in new ways. This is sometimes described as linked-up thinking, and it begins right here, by recognizing that science and religion have more in common than meets the eye. One cannot work in isolation or be excluded from the other; they are co-dependent, with each having part of the answer. What we are missing is a level of insight and experience that takes us beyond the boundaries separating the here and the hereafter – that captures both the world of science and the world of religion without collision or contradiction.

For as long as either science or religion excludes the other, or is taken up in isolation, then we will always miss the point. Certainly, scientists who believe in God – as do 15 per cent of scientists in the US National Academy of Sciences – find no contradiction in their dual position. In a similar way, scientific discoveries awaken in us a sense of mystery, if not the mystical. The spiritual heart of religion and life, and the factual understanding of the physical as it supports the spiritual, are entwined. In this combination we can find a true account of the world and how it works.

The liberating insight we need to help us grasp fully the true significance of our life can only be gained by what history tells us is the most life-changing personal breakthrough: enlightenment, or what I call in this book 'the unifying *experience* within everything'. Find our way to this experience within ourselves and we will have found the equivalent of the philosopher's stone: a way of being that transforms lives, generates happiness and allows us to unleash the full force of human consciousness dormant in so many of us.

When we experience true unity in this way, we no longer see reality as something independent of us that we receive from the outside, but rather a phenomenon continuously changed by our perception of it. When we 'get' this point about co-creation, our relationship with the world is transformed forever – from the way we look at our personal and spiritual health to how we begin to solve the social, political and ecological problems of our time. In our fragmented world we find it easy to be dismissive and disparaging of one another, yet unity of experience need no longer be thought of as some armchair discussion among the intellectual elite, nor as an exercise for philosophy classes. It has direct, daily relevance to our lives.

From the burnings of the libraries of the ancient world to the enraged medieval purges of Europe's teaching monasteries, history shows that much has been learned and lost, much done and undone. And still we hunger. In early societies, people saw spirits and mystical meaning in almost everything, including the wind, forests, water, rocks, clouds, plants and fire. The human mind has designed everything from the dastardly to the divine. It was not until the ancient Egyptians created the 'unknowable' god Amun that we had an early version of unity under one god.[2] Since then, each religion's assumption of superiority and preoccupation with exclusivity has slowed our spiritual progress and hastened separation and sectarianism while neglecting higher connections and the spirit of unity.

In more recent times, science has looked for unity in more measurable things, finding links between different types of energy (Faraday) and matter (Lavoisier), and finally the connection between matter and energy (Einstein). Science has also questioned the logic behind the concept of a personal God, wanting an answer in the form of a mathematical equation, such as Einstein's famous quest for 'a unified theory of everything'. However, just as science has been seeking a unified theory and can't quite get there, so too religion in general has been seeking the unified experience of God and the divine, yet can't quite agree on how to get it.

This failure is because the search for universal truth by both science and religion is fundamentally flawed.

Scientists forget that any 'unified theory of everything' needs an observer positioned outside the theory (and outside of everything) to validate the theory's claim that it embraces everything. But this ultimate point of observation, by its very existence as external adjudicator, forever escapes the theory and so invalidates the theory. This inability of a theory to capture its own ultimate act of observation means that science can never attain its unifying Holy Grail.

Similarly, religion and spirituality have largely depended on attaining and holding onto unity and eternity as their own – an impossibility when infinity and eternity have no boundaries and no circumference, yet almost all our thinking is restricted to the finite and measurable. Furthermore, while many religions claim an infinite unity with God, they are invariably diverted by having to defend their own claims of exclusive access to the divine and the superior, squandering energy on arranging the exclusion of those who do not follow. In this state of mind, any God can only ever remain an enthusiastic idea at best, never truly and directly experienced.

However, in the following pages we will be finding the ways to resolve this double conundrum and get beyond the divisions of the ages. Along the way we will uncover our most powerful abilities, as well as the dormant connections deep within each of us – connections that maintain us while interweaving our lives with a profound sense of purpose and meaning. Eventually we gain enough insight to arrive at the ultimate breakthrough in understanding, the ultimate unifying experience. And in that moment our life blooms into full significance.

**Our scientific power has outrun our spiritual power.
We have guided missiles and misguided men.**
Martin Luther King Jr

To begin our quest into this overarching unity, we need an initial appreciation of what holism is and a little background to our present emergency. There have been two emergencies in the evolution of the human race. The first was the need – shared by all life – to ensure the survival of our species and the protection of our personal boundaries during life's early evolution. To do so, we developed internal (immune) and external (social) systems to protect, support and defend us as we extended our sphere of power and control into a hostile environment. Accompanying this biological mechanism of self-protection is an entrenched and primitive psychology of separation, a mental instinct for self-preservation still underpinning our outlook and much of our behaviour in the world. Our five senses have been crucial in this successful survival strategy, keeping us in touch with the changing environment around us and alerting us to 'risk and reward' situations.

We have learned to cooperate to overcome common enemies. The fact that we have become the dominant species demonstrates the effectiveness of our particular brand of cooperative aggression as a survival tool. This first emergency – physical survival – remains ongoing, with our aggressive immune system forever on the brink of being overwhelmed by opportunistic invaders such as bacteria and viruses. However, the question now is whether survival into old age is enough to call a life 'well lived'. This book is written from the understanding that life invites a legacy from each of us that involves more than merely getting to death safely.

The second emergency, which we are now facing, is the environmental crisis threatening our planet. Paradoxically, although aggressive cooperation has made our species the most successful survivors, we have now overused that aggression to the point of destroying the environment on which we depend for our continued survival. What we have made our greatest advantage has now become our greatest handicap: we have been so successful that we are literally 'improving' our planet to death.

In order to confront this new emergency, we need to start looking at a better model for our existence. The standard model of evolution focuses on survival of the fittest – a good model, except that this type of fitness favours the physical, with survival focused on the individual. The scope of Darwinian evolution is fundamentally mechanistic, and without the addition of spiritual experience Darwinian evolution misses the *impetus* of life – which, as we will see, is the creation of whole-health as something more than mere individual survival.

Although aggressive cooperation – uniting against a common enemy or for a common benefit – is not necessarily wrong (and forms the basis of most social evolution), something more is needed if we are to find a better way of dealing with the complexity of problems around us. This will require from us a higher range of adaptive skills, so that we can finally evolve from being merely successful at survival and go on to reach the higher state of becoming spiritually *significant*. The only way to achieve this is with what I call 'breakthrough consciousness' – a level of personal awareness that extends our take on reality beyond the separate, the singular, and the self; a conscious perception of the complete and undivided whole that takes our attention beyond space, time and matter.*

An integral part of this new, higher 'spiritual' outlook is a deeper understanding and experience of holism: the capacity to sense that we are an inseparable part of the larger whole and it a part of us, and that when we harm our environment – whether ecological or social – we are in fact harming ourselves. Our spiritual immaturity shows up in our psyche as a mentality of separateness – a mental zone of separation that secures our sense of separate self while reinforcing our instinctive suspicion of strangers and our assumption of distance and separateness from almost all other people, places and things. With this un-evolved spiritual outlook, both our activity and identity remain biased towards things physical and formed.

Spirituality – and let us be clear about this – is different from religion, because spirituality is a purely private experience, whereas religion also involves public ritual. In this book, the term spirituality is used to describe the process of looking into our deepest internal resources – the divine experience within, and our deepest connections – rather than devotion to a figurehead or deity. We all share the same spiritual potential – the same possibility for enlightenment and breakthrough consciousness – but our spiritual capacities are different, depending on our degree of accumulated spiritual development and experience.

With a less developed outlook, all we see are those things that we observe from the outside. However, when we develop a holistic outlook we are also aware of every whole that we are a part *of*, rather than only seeing those things we are apart *from*. In effect, we get to see some things from the inside.

The holistic outlook dissolves unnecessary boundaries, makes molehills out of mountains and takes the sweat out of the small stuff. What

* While quantum physicists and mathematicians chide that there is nothing beyond reality, there is acknowledgement that an infinite field of energy in perfect balance 'exists'. It is impossible to consider the vastness of the infinite whole from within created reality without reference to notions contrasted against time and place. Where this book uses phrases such as 'beyond time and place', in this context the use of 'beyond' is my attempt to invoke a sense of infinity that is, by definition, impossible to grasp completely.

begins as a state of mind becomes a force for holistic healing and ultimately the ability to 'see' beyond or through boundaries – 'seeing beyond everything'. Holistic thinking and holistic healing go hand-in-hand. Holistic thinking is linked-up thinking. Discovering holism is about the progressive discovery of not-so-obvious links and deep connections. The facility to see beyond all forms and structures – which are themselves the final result of networked links between smaller contributory parts – is a healthy part of breakthrough consciousness. Health is a relationship, an outcome, an indication of 'whole' or unbroken networks. Every biological network can be measured for its healthiness against its degree of wholeness.

Increasingly, many research scientists are realizing that we cannot effectively study any part without studying the whole. Life itself gathers together the right mix of inanimate molecules, and presto! – this collection of assembled parts begins behaving in ways no study of their separate properties could have predicted. In the same way, mainstream health professionals are realizing that our health is the result of many contributory causes. Accordingly, doctors are becoming more concerned about treating the whole person rather than just the symptom. Western medicine is coming to recognize that health, wellness and disease are entirely communicated conditions, passed on by a complexity of culture, environment, genetic transferences, family and upbringing, state of mind and personal attitude, as well as by life's experiences in general.

More and more scientific papers on holism are being presented and accepted at orthodox medical conferences, indicating the rising tide of change as doctors shift their outlook from the tradition of reductionism (reducing everything to its smallest part) to the science of holism.[3] Living systems are far too complex and integrated to be studied in isolation: the secret of birdsong is not discovered with the vivisectionist's scalpel.

This expanded definition of health – as something operating for the better of the whole and extending beyond the parts while at the same time including them all – is one entry-point we will take on our path to ultimate recovery. While doctors confidently describe disease, they have no agreed definition of health; doctors are unclear about just what full health and wellness are, and the modern art of healing (as practised in the West) has not had a really significant breakthrough for decades. Recent discoveries show that good health is not guaranteed or even controlled by any one single factor such as diet, exercise, sanitation or environment. The path to good health extends beyond the physical, and in this book I take you beyond the limits of personal health, and show you how to combine the spiritual with the physical to create whole-health.

The common-sense view of how the world works is that things are assembled, bolted together, pulled into place, pushed around and manipulated. Yet this 'assembly line' world-view is inadequate to explain the existence of consciousness, choice, creativity, or life itself. From this limited outlook, creativity is not seen as a strong force or field but more as a leisure activity, a soft option, an add-on. But creative genesis and sparks of creative insight represent forces bigger than art, allowing the instantaneous effect of transformational change to exist in the world alongside the mechanics of assembly and reaction.

Holism – where the integrated whole is greater than the sum of its parts – means that all parts are creatively integrated. The holistic age is upon us, where the forces of creativity and transformation emerge to create connections that surpass the era of mechanical assembly, cause, effect and disassembly. Holism, which has its origins in religious belief,[4] is now progressing simultaneously in religion, science, business, education and training, and the environmental movement. Multi-denominational conferences are becoming a theme within mainstream religions worldwide. Ethical businesses attract strong investor interest along with enthusiastic consumer support, and have begun including workers in decision-making and problem-solving. Urban recycling of household waste is another indicator of growing community awareness of holistic environmental issues. In some countries, forestry management is slowly yielding to international pressure to introduce sustainable harvesting techniques.

However, the absence of an overarching holistic outlook is a symptom of our fragmented times, affecting everything from our psychological outlook, our nutrition, our health, our relationships, politics, and even the architectural harmony of our city skylines. Buildings consume 30 per cent of the world's energy output and need to be integrated into the whole symphony of city life as well as the city skyline. Where architectural design has paid attention only to its one particular structure and not to how that design integrates and harmonizes within the surrounding cityscape, we see ugliness. It takes a better architect to see and create unbroken harmony between a stucture and its surroundings. As with architecture so too with life: in any whole system, parts positioned in the wrong place affect the integrity of the whole.

As we are beginning to see, holism and the spirit of integration affect all aspects of life. Tens of thousands of symbiotic relationships have been studied in detail, and it has been found that without these mutually beneficial relationships most life would cease.[5] From our first breath to our last, we are all connected through one atmosphere to the environment. All people in a room are intimately connected – after 20 minutes, each person has absorbed the DNA of every other person in the room through their sweat and breath.[6] In this way, our shared breath blurs the boundary between 'self' and 'other', weaving us into the ecology through the filaments of our lungs. Our unseen connections also extend deeper and wider than this. For example, increased anxiety in a pregnant mother can raise her cortisol levels, which then crosses the placenta into the unborn, leading to the increased likelihood of childhood depression.[7] Even too much cleanliness is a bad thing for an infant – our immune system needs exposure to certain combinations of bacteria if it is to form robustly and protect us fully.

As we evolve, we come to realize that everything forms an integral part of one dynamic whole, which then forms another integral part within an even larger dynamic whole and onwards, ad infinitum. This system of overlapping, interdependent, integrated networks is the fabric of holism, woven around our personal interests, influences, hopes and aspirations. Understanding this system is key to our personal experience of a fully integrated, 'spiritual' and balanced life. In this sense, integrity's reach extends way beyond issues of personal honesty; integrity, in the form of integration extending seamlessly through us and including the whole of creation, goes to the heart of our mature spiritual life.

While an integrated outlook knows no bounds and is alert to the highest connections, a *disintegrated* outlook misses the connections that form whole-health networks, leaving us fragmented in mind and body. An outlook of separation and disintegration is ultimately unhealthy.

Nature abounds with instances of group behaviour revealing networks that are often complex, sometimes astonishing. For example, the Portuguese man-of-war (a jellyfish) appears to be one individual but is in fact a conglomerate of tiny, single-celled creatures living in delicious cohabitation as one super-organism. What strategic mechanism provides the template for this gelatinous association of parts? And what mystifying network orchestrates the blueprint of the termite mound, or the symmetry of the beehive, so that all players know their part? One of reality's riddles is that while every identifiable form or entity is no more than the sum of its component parts and contributory causes, it also stands alone as uniquely different from any one of those parts.

In reality, *everything is a network*. Any whole, from you to the entire universe, is the inter-relationship of its components, the interconnected network of its contributory causes. There is more to networks than mechanical connections and solid structures; networks are relationships of parts, often arranged symmetrically, but always engaged to form a larger entity. Matter is a fuzz of organized energy, and reality is an energy network. Our so-called spiritual life, and the path to uncovering life's meaning, involves us in the unifying experience of higher networks. Higher networks increase our range of opportunity, with the velocity of opportunity in our lives depending on the scope of our networks.

The science of networks is gaining momentum and, as the first big idea of the 21st century, is poised to provide the discipline for a new world-view. The study of networks – what they are, the way they influence us and how we can better access them – is uniting science, philosophy, religion, psychology, sociology and other disciplines. Our increasing knowledge of interconnectivity is key to understanding how the world *really* works. Though many networks have no detectable mechanism for their existence (which might make their existence questionable), science already accepts uncertainty in fields such as psychology and astrophysics. The study of networks and network transference are candidates for an entirely new group of subjects without tangible structure, mechanism or medium.

As will be discussed in this book, it is vital to recognize the nature and extent of the networks in which we live in order to understand our significance within them. Networks and higher connections give significance to life itself.

Just as 'wars begin in the minds of men', peace
also begins in our minds. The same species who
invented war is capable of inventing peace.
The responsibility lies with each of us.
'Seville Statement on Violence', 1989.[8]

When we change ourselves we change the world around us, and in these troubled times, everyone must take some responsibility for how that change is brought about. Many are already active on the frontlines, selflessly donating time, money and expertise to build a better world. Yet the rest of us cannot afford to keep procrastinating. If we continue to deny this moment of personal responsibility, the crises now afflicting us and our planet will deepen. To borrow from Dickens, it is the best and worst of times.

Only when we make progress by breaking down the barricades of our psycho-spiritual isolation and experience the other dimensions of ourselves as the fully integrated beings we are becoming, will we rediscover the personal power and joy of life on this beautiful, fragile planet. Only when we fully understand and value *who* we are, will we value *where* we are.

Humanity is now poised to enter the next exciting breakthrough in spiritual evolution – a shift of emphasis away from separation, conflict and competition and towards connection, communication, the forces of creativity and positive transformation. Already we are seeing a convergence between the fields of science, psychology, religion, philosophy and environmental studies. Welcome to the age of evidence-based spirituality, the age of spiritual rationalism. This is the age in which science, spirituality and religion become mutually inclusive, evolving to inform and create a healthier, happier and more spiritually mature world.

CHAPTER 2

Looking after Number One

Most men live lives of quiet desperation and
go to the grave with the song still in them.

Henry David Thoreau

The search for immortality is a growth industry. There have been about 3,000 supposed cures and treatments for the ageing process, with more than 300 in vogue today. Yet although we may rail and struggle against the inevitability of death and ageing, for many of us the real human tragedy is not the fact of dying, but of not having fully lived. And to live fully we need to be fully integrated, mind and body, within ourselves; connected to our environment in its entirety, and spiritually awakened to the wholeness of creation. However, many of us remain numb to higher connections, anaesthetized against pain but, in the process, unable to feel much at all.

We hold onto life, fear death, and seek out how we can live longer because we rate our separate existence so highly. There is more to the art of living than learning social skills, avoiding loss and accumulating wealth. As we evolve spiritually and learn to let go of our limited way of looking at the world, we uncover more of the connections that exist between us and our world rather than continuing to see everything as separate from us, or 'other' than us. Along the way, even the fear of death is overcome as we rekindle some bone-deep memories and come to see the meaning of life-beyond-life and the limitations of self-absorption.[9]

Whatever the reason, humanity's search for spiritual links and higher connections has been a work in progress for 40,000 years at least. In that time, the structures and rituals of religion have evolved a long way – from cave paintings to cathedrals, from sacrifice to supplication. Now we are ready to supersede our reliance on these forms and connect directly to the personal spiritual experience. Spirituality no longer needs to be riddled with mysterious, unanswerable questions. Spirituality is evolving beyond the limitations imposed by formal religious practice, so that religious devotion is no longer needed to create the spiritual experience.

Evolution also reflects the nature of this spiritual progress; as we will see later, survival of the strongest and fittest is yielding to survival of the healthiest, the most interconnected and the most whole. If we merely concentrate on issues of personal health and wealth, we miss the point, which is that each and every individual affects the collective whole, and the whole affects the individual, because each is part of the other.

The real issue is not how to live longer, but how to live. With this approach, our life becomes a quest for spiritual connections. We can choose to stay locked into the limited outlook where everything is viewed as separate from ourselves and where we maintain a world of separation and division. Alternatively we can open ourselves to the spiritual panorama of connection and discover new links, paths, answers, possibilities and freedom.

Although we all suffer in enclosures, many of us still choose to live like caged animals, chasing elusive securities – the comforts of predictable food, shelter and mateship – that never completely compensate for a life caught up in the economic grind. Our 'separation identity' drives a wedge between nations, religions and families as we arm ourselves with our different values and barricade ourselves with our different beliefs. Many of us postpone our dreams, reaching mid-life only to realize we have spent too much time concentrating on *how* and *what* we have been doing, while neglecting to question *why* we have been doing it. This is why mid-life is less a crisis and more a wake-up call, a reorienting of priorities and a discovery of greater possibilities.

Preoccupied as many of us are with the specifics of our lives and the drama of our personal existence, we fail to see our two selves clearly – the biological, individual self, and the so-called spiritual or connected self. These are the two intermingled aspects of us, two cross-networked dimensions creating one whole life.

Enough for me the mystery of the eternity of life,
and the inkling of the marvellous structure of
reality, together with the single-hearted endeavour
to comprehend a portion, be it ever so tiny, of the
reason that manifests itself in nature.
Albert Einstein

Creation is almost certainly made up of more dimensions than we realize. If we are to gain a better understanding of how 'separation' and 'connection' underwrite both our existence and our day-to-day behaviour, we need first to understand where everything comes from and how the reality we see around us was created. To do this we begin with a look at the Big Bang – an amazing set of cosmic events that includes the original creative burst of energy or inflation that subsequently transformed into matter, galaxies and the universe as we know it.

That the Big Bang was a genuine event (rather than mere theory) has been confirmed by the existence of residual microwave radiation left over from that first electromagnetically charged 'fireball' of original creation, radiation that has been detected and measured.[10] Further confirmation comes from studies showing that the universe is still expanding and accelerating.[11]* In addition, only 10 per cent of the total helium in the universe can be accounted for from those nuclear furnaces we call stars – the other 90 per cent is left over from the Big Bang blast. After the Big Bang there was a 400,000-year period of darkness during which the original hydrogen froze as snow, only thawing when the first starlight appeared.[12] The ever-expanding Big Bang remains visible today in some of the off-channel 'snow' or haze on your television; look at that and you are looking at the Big Bang.

It is important to realize that before the Big Bang there *was* no 'before', because there was no time as we know it. And there were no atoms or

---

* Our universe is still expanding everywhere today – the expansion that began with the Big Bang continues, though much slower, cooler and lumpier in parts now that galaxies and planets have formed. It should be noted that it is space itself that is expanding, rather than the 'local' distances within space. Neighbouring galaxies can still collide; we are actually moving closer to the nearby Andromeda Galaxy, with collision approximated to be three billion years away.

molecules; no space, no time, no matter of any kind – a total absence of physical existence and its dimensions. The universe did not begin as a shrunken entity surrounded by space, into which it inflated after the Big Bang, as is commonly imagined, because *there was no time or space until the Big Bang* – just what science calls 'an infinity of energy in perfect balance'. In other words, infinity is neither a location nor a fiction; it is an energetic state. Space, time and matter first appeared in the same instant that the universe began to expand – and continues to expand today.

To see how all of this is relevant to our understanding of who we are, and how we fit into this universe, begin by picturing *two* realities, one created, the other uncreated or original.

Created reality is everything that we see around us. This is the reality we are born into, and where we are today, with our five senses developed to keep us informed about our world and our existence in it. This view of reality is what our brain registers to give us the sense of ourselves as separate individuals, contained within our bodily cocoon, looking at the world as if it was a picture-perfect impression of a reality that exists outside us and all around us. This created reality brings with it the appearance of distance, separation and distinct differences. This is where we see causes and their effects, and where events appear to unfold consecutively. Later we will see how the appearance of depth, distance and separation is as much a creation of our mind as our mind is a creation of this reality. Our created world of familiar observations is where the laws of causes and their effects operate – Isaac Newton's fundamental laws of the physical universe.

The other reality – *original reality* – is more mysterious. This is the reality we are born *with*, the reality we arise *from*. This original reality, the 'infinite field of energy in perfect balance', provided the 'background' to the Big Bang – and perhaps of many Big Bangs other than the one that created our particular universe. It still exists in spite of creation, and is referred to generally as 'infinity'. The infinity remains intact, *co-existing* with and supporting created reality, but unaffected by the Big Bang that has exploded in its midst. Though hard to grasp, this original, timeless state of reality remains forever present everywhere, yet invisible. This reality is the source of creativity and spontaneity and concurrence, the source of instantaneous or timeless transformation, a reality only vaguely explained through the mathematical language of theoretical science.

These two realities continue to coexist. Though they also coexist in the roots of our attention, we are much more conscious of created reality than the infinite original. With right teaching and right practice, these two realities – the one we are born *into* and the one we are created *with* – emerge into joyful and liberating co-existence within our conscious attention. All unhappiness and hurt arises from the imbalance of these two realities within us. To live a significant, healthy and happy life, we need to bring these two realities into balance.

Think of the original reality as a never-ending, invisible force-field that (paradoxically) does not come into anything like existence as we know it until disturbed (by a Big Bang). Then, with one creative pulse, the Big Bang (silently) interrupts the field; but the interruption is localized and cannot possibly break the infinity that is the force-field. (A bit like a small hole appearing in a windscreen that leaves the rest of the glass clear and unaffected – except that a windscreen is flat and what we're talking about here is a field infinitely large and everywhere, without circumference.) After a cool-down period, the disturbed energy at the interruption site converts into cosmic 'condensation' that evolves into spiral galaxies, suns, and in fact every atom of everything around us. Meanwhile, the infinite energy of original reality – because it is *infinite* – remains unchanged, a forever-present background to everything everywhere.

Somewhere within the intermingling of both realities – which still coexist today – life was created, and our life depends on a continuing collaboration between them both. Yet when theoretical physicists speculate on other likely dimensions and possible parallel realities, they often miss the fact that *we are actually already living right now within at least one other dimensional level: infinity.*[13] What is missing is our conscious experience of it.

The argument that the existence of other dimensions is not just science fiction is supported by studies in astrophysics: observations of gravity and some of the workings of subatomic particles at the minutest levels suggest that our own universe may in fact be a black hole* with not four but five

* See the glossary on the book website (www.thinkofanelephant.com.au) for an explanation of black holes. Quantum 'string' theorists propose at least six dimensions beyond our four dimensions of space and time. Light may occupy a constant 'space' or 'zone' linking two or more dimensions. Exciting research into locating evidence for other dimensions is concentrating on the 'area' around the smallest of subatomic particles.

dimensions.[14] Although there is some dispute about whether or not black holes actually exist, their presence is generally agreed by science based on specific distortions and other phenomena that have been detected in outer space. The exciting part is that these extra-dimensional effects can occur only where time and space are broken through or suspended – and the non-existence of time and space is exactly what we would require of any concept of original infinity. In other words, astrophysicists now have strong evidence to suggest that infinity measurably exists and influences our reality.

How does this affect us? Does this mean that at some level we have direct personal access to the same original infinite energy that gave rise to all creation and inspired religion for centuries? With infinity intermingling and merging everywhere with created reality, every point anywhere (including where you are at this very moment) is also a position directly linked by infinite reality to everywhere else. In this way every single, solitary point can also be seen as a point of 'super-connectedness', where 'single' no longer simply means the individual or local but also refers to the interconnected whole of which the individual is part.

As a result, we can say that *everything in existence is in a condition of separation within a unified field of infinity*. Everything in creation – including us – is in direct and inseparable contact with the original energy. This infinity of energy in perfect balance is the first and ultimate background. Therefore, like everything else, we are linked to it, participate within it, cannot exist without it and will return entirely to it. Though there is a lot of reality beyond us, at some level none of it is absolutely and entirely separate from us.

Yet despite this intrinsic interconnectedness of all things, we mistakenly see everything as existing completely separately and distinct from its background, because at first view this is how reality appears. But what we are seeing when we look at something is only ever its surface, forming the boundary at which it ends and something else begins, the interface between one thing and the next. (For instance, the surface of this page is where the paper meets the air, and so the paper and the air begin and end at exactly the same point, with the beginning of one marking the end of the other.) Every idea, outlook, attitude or action also has defined points of separation, and every cause appears separate from its effect. However, when you look at the outer surface that everything has, you're not just looking at the edge of that object. As strange as it may seem, you're also looking at part of the cooled-down edge of the Big Bang.

Let me explain. The Big Bang not only gave rise to the atoms and physical make-up of all separate 'things', but also their *state* of separateness – the Big Bang was the point at which not only substance but separateness itself, *as a dimension*, came into being. Everything that we see existing today is bounded by an outer limit that gives it a state of separateness and the appearance of being forever disconnected *from everything else.*

So we have one deep, uncreated and original reality that has no separation, and also a created reality within which everything is defined by its surface appearance and maintained in a state of separation. It is important to realize that physical reality is seen by us as a surface, or reflected reality, picked up and detailed by our five senses. We cannot see 'into' anything with these senses; when we break open anything in an attempt to look beneath its surface, all we see are more surfaces. This applies right down to the smallest indeterminate subatomic particles of matter. Because our normal five senses by themselves never let us get beyond surface appearances, we are left with a life of mere impressions with no real depth of understanding or insight. Any insight we gain through experience needs other capacities, additional levels of perception.

The reality of separation and distance is necessary for our existence, but it is only one side of the coin. The other, less familiar, side is the state or dimension of wholeness and deep connection. This deeply connected aspect of life is something we have relegated to religion (where it is shrouded in mystery), elevated to the impossible, or excluded completely from our one-sided existence. This is the original state, arising within the perfectly balanced field of infinite energy that accompanied creation and still supports our existence today. Creation and original reality are not two separate states; they exist together, back to back, two sides of the same coin. Reality has two sides, and it is the uncreated one that we are missing in our lives. And just as a one-sided coin can't possibly exist, a one-sided hold on reality is equally incomplete. Such a shortsighted outlook is predestined to disappoint, to fail us in any search for meaning in our lives. It has proved dangerously misleading, leaving us today with a sense of spiritual emptiness and dislocation – and with a planet out of control.

We are all meant to shine as children do.
We are born to manifest the glory of God that is
within us.
It is not just in some of us; it is in everyone.
Marianne Williamson [15]

What is needed is a balance between separation and connection. Crucially, as life evolved and human consciousness developed, separation became part of our intrinsic psychology, with the result that we are most comfortable treating all objects and individuals as 'other' – as entities separate from ourselves and each other, rather than as being part of the whole *of which we are also a part*. Everything exists in separation's shadow – from the smallest atom or germ of an idea, to the largest galaxy or grand vision. Our innate psychology of separation, whereby we view all things only as separate from one another, gives our created reality its necessary framework; it is as if, from where we stand, separation originated as some kind of porous membrane keeping all things simultaneously intact yet apart.

In this dimension, life at base level is a competition, a struggle for energy and resources. Staying alive was our first emergency in the primal age where life faced constant risk from predators, ice, fire and famine. Without our habit of viewing all things as separate – a habit so much a part of our hold on reality that it passes largely unnoticed – we would not survive. As much today as then, our ancient psychology of separation acts as a shield to protect us from physical danger – whether predators or a speeding bus. Yet this protective barrier can itself become a force for destruction, since in distancing ourselves from danger we also tend to eliminate any perceived threat to our survival. Indeed, our psychology of separation has been such a necessary and successful survival strategy for life in general, and for our species in particular, that we have little time for alternatives. As a result, we have now separated ourselves from the very things that sustain us: our loved ones, our communities and our environment.

As we will see in the following chapters, the paradox is that if we remain locked within the mentality of separation, we actually risk our survival by creating a fragmented future on a planet that we have rendered unfit for our children. Therefore, if we are to evolve beyond the limitations set by our outlook of separation, we must find a way ahead that includes seeing beyond the psychological 'edge' of separation that gives everything its definition. Original separation, by flooding our reality, gives the objects of our attention the appearance of permanence in time and space, obscuring the fact that unseen connections and esoteric relationships are much more than fantasy or cultism. In order to get back in touch with our spiritual capacity and understand the significance of our lives, we need to rediscover our first, primal nature: our connectedness to the whole of life and the whole of reality, including the seen and the unseen, the created and the uncreated.

In our day-to-day lives, we are more familiar with separation than with any real and heightened experience of brotherhood and connectedness with all things in creation; these are ideas that sound more like clichés than common sense. We more readily engage the psychology of separation, with our present sense of individual existence requiring that we mark a point of separation between everything that is mine and yours, past and present, here and there, good and bad. Locking into our usual outlook, any conscious experience of original reality as being part of us is extremely rare and considered dubious, most often getting lost in religious or spiritual metaphor. However, holistic consciousness, as described in the previous chapter, provides the possibility of ultimately developing a vantage point from where we can experience core reality beyond space, time and the limited four-dimensional universe – a vantage point that is infinitely vast: the infinite viewpoint of 'super-consciousness'. Our search for higher meaning is, in some way, the search to recognize and experience this original reality.

Yet we know that something about our lives is out of balance and that we need to address this imbalance, now. This is where our creative powers come in. Separation, which we have indulged to such excess that it has become our disease, came into being at the same time as its cure: the power of creativity. Creative power was originally revealed the very instant separation appeared. This same creativity, now within us, allows us to rediscover and reactivate our own more esoteric connections.

When there was only an infinite field of energy in perfect balance, causes and their effects did not exist. The Big Bang emerged within this infinite field of energy in perfect balance to give us our first evidence of creativity, being the necessary accompaniment to original creation. But what is creativity exactly? We need not trouble ourselves to answer, but merely note that as there was a creation, therefore there is creativity. Creativity exists as an accompaniment to all of reality, and on the evidence of its first appearance with the Big Bang, creativity possesses the significant capacities of spontaneity and instantaneous transformation. Coming *directly* from infinity, which is timeless and formless, creativity can bring about change instantaneously, as it did with the Big Bang. Today, being mostly reflected *indirectly* through our created world, we only catch glimpses of it in such situations as human creative insight and inventiveness, and as it appears before us filtered through the fog of cause-and-effect reactions and sidelined in the physical world of assembly.

Creative power is more directly seen in the mother's womb. There, none of our body-parts are assembled; we just simply and wondrously manifest, cell by cell – a process of prolonged yet spontaneous transformation only measurable after the event. In contrast, assembly is measurable, takes time and has a beginning and an end. Life is lived between these two positions, where the dimensions of separation and creation conjoin.

Creativity as a force cannot be quantified, yet it is something we all share in common; creativity is *not* a rare thing restricted to artists and the gifted. Indeed, any outstanding creative work also reflects the accumulation of a long series of insights, of which any one of us is capable. Creative sparks of insight manifest from beyond time and place to sever time and space; creativity is a transformational force that transcends known dimensions or definitions. Without the transformational power of creativity, our abilities are restricted to activities such as controlling, protecting, defending, resisting, convincing, manipulating, forcing and withholding our energy and effort. With this approach to life, where we see ourselves as fundamentally separate from everything else, the best we can do to influence the world around us is to add something to it, subtract something from it, hold something or avoid something. To help us decide which of these options to use at any one time, we become judges, critics and evaluators of our surroundings, and completely neglect the possibility of becoming conscious creators of something entirely new.

As we have seen, the Big Bang marks the point where original reality and created reality intermingle and remain conjoined forever – the point at which eternity meets modernity. That bond, or adherence, between the formed and the unformed is the original state of connection, destined to remain forever intact around every particle, atom, object, attitude and outlook in the created universe we live in.

This original point of conjunction remains in existence everywhere, as part of everything. Through this original creative adherence, everything everywhere connects into its background and context, seamlessly becoming part of a progressively larger whole. This includes us, so that whatever we are doing right now unavoidably affects everything around us, all the time. When we fail to see this point of universal connection, we fail to see both our responsibility for the way things are and our opportunity to change them for the good. Yet when we do acknowledge the existence of the whole, and the power of our position within it, we realize that even one idea can inspire a group with enthusiasm, adding to a momentum that can lead to change on a global scale. We each contribute to the whole, just as it contributes to us.

We live a multi-layered existence rather than a singular experience, drawn between points of separation and the power of connection. When we say we need balance in our lives, what we really mean is we need to balance the two realities – original and created – in our lives: the realities of connection and separation. This unified or total reality is the original seat of holism, the root of all connections.

This book is about a search that is as old as time, the search for original connection. Although here we are less interested in cosmology than in consciousness, the two intertwine. And while consciousness may have appeared in evolution a long time ago, a new era has now begun, affecting our attitudes, our outlook and our reality. Minds are on the march. Welcome to the age of possibilities where everyone is affected. The human spirit is about to bloom.

CHAPTER 3

What's the environment got to do with me?

Human beings and the natural world are on
collision course. This environmental crisis
offers both a mirror and solution to our
spiritual crisis and our need for original
balance. Human activities inflict harsh and
often irreversible damage on the
environment and on critical resources. If not
checked, many of our current practices put
at risk the future we wish for human society.

**'World Scientists' Warning to Humanity', *Union of Concerned
Scientists*, Cambridge, Massachusetts. 18 November 1992.**

aving begun to understand what we mean by the psychology of
separation and connection, we can go on to look at the implications of our current outlook: in other words, the negative impact
our current way of life is having on our social and physical environment.

The damage we are causing both to our planet and, ultimately, to ourselves is brought about by our fragmented view of the world around us.
This dislocation occurs not only at an ecological level, but also in our
business, social and personal relationships. In order to halt, and even
reverse, this damage, we need not only to understand the consequences of

our behaviour, but also to recognize the harm we are causing ourselves in the process.

Nearly 25 per cent of the Earth's land surface is now cultivated; in fact, humanity's ecological footprint now exceeds the Earth's regenerative capacity by about 20 per cent, as a conservative estimate. And while food production has doubled in the last 25 years, much of the water needed for this increase has been drawn from unsustainable, limited underground reserves.[16] Yet it is not just our numbers that are the problem – indeed, if all six billion of us were gathered together and given 1m² to stand in, we would occupy an area only of 80km², with room to spare. The heart of the problem lies in our levels of consumption, and we are only just beginning to recognize the extent of our global impact and its consequences. According to the Millennium Ecosystem Assessment – the first-ever global inventory of natural resources – the environmental systems most at risk are those that support life (such as water and air purification systems); weather and temperature patterns; and the complex ecological arrangements that support plant pollination cycles and their dependent animal and insect breeding patterns. Though all of these natural systems are essential to human health and wellbeing, 90 per cent are being dismantled, degraded or used unsustainably, largely due to deforestation, chemical fertilizers and fossil fuel pollution.[17]

Put another way, it currently takes about eight hectares of farmland to support one citizen in almost any industrialized country, and it would take almost six planets to provide each person alive today with that same standard of living.[18] The global dream of independent, personal, high-consumption material wealth for everyone can never be fulfilled – there aren't the living systems and other resources on the planet to support it, using our present methods and mindset.

Our great-grandchildren will almost certainly inherit a planet with less than 20 per cent of ancient forests intact. Indeed, the consequences of what happens when we damage a single forest provides a good example of the devastation that occurs when we humans mess with life's support systems. While some see a forest as just a bunch of trees, others recognize it as a living thing, whole in itself, and know that any living thing will die when too much of it is cut away. The regrowth of vegetation after any logging operation may still look like a forest – after all, the same number of trees may have been replanted. But a forest is essentially a single living organism kept alive by supporting the microscopic life forms that live there – the spores, mosses, fungi, insects, and all the micro-life that lives in it, on it, under it and around it. Indeed, we now know that a minimum of 50,000ha is required to support larger animals and also be capable of self-regeneration.

A healthy forest regulates local temperature and rainfall by a complicated interaction within itself that still remains a mystery. Logging companies cannot recreate the natural order of connections and communications with which the original forest evolved its survival. So what is lost is the complex interaction of micro-climates in the tiny places, the essential pollination cycles, the moisture and temperature changes, the nutrients, the seeds, and the minute nooks, crannies and breeding places. And when these connections are lost the mysterious whole is lost, and all life is diminished.

This 'whole forest' system directly affects our health. Japanese researchers have discovered that diabetic patients have improved sugar levels after breathing forest air.[19] Researchers working in the Sierra Nevada woodlands of California have discovered many previously unknown atmospheric chemical compounds in the forest air. The significance of these findings is clear: by saving old growth forests, we are ultimately saving ourselves.

Our strongest connections are often invisible.

The entire range of living matter on Earth, from whales to viruses and from oaks to algae, could be regarded as constituting a single living entity capable of maintaining the Earth's atmosphere to suit its overall needs.
James Lovelock[20]

In any fully integrated 'whole', even the smallest changes in any part affect the whole system – size doesn't matter. One small pill can help return the ill to health, while one drop of poison can kill its victim. So too with the living environment. One striking example of how even the smallest change can wreak havoc on a holistic system is seen in the function of the minute fig wasp of Central and South America. In times of drought and seasonal cycles, figs offer the only food-source for many of the forest birds, insects and animals. If fig wasps were removed, there would be no more figs, because the wasp is the only pollination source for the fig. The minute size of the wasp conceals the enormous significance of its place in the forest's relationships and interconnections. The fig wasp is a keystone species, and when we remove keystones, the whole pyramid of life is endangered.

On the other hand, pathogens that may be harmless or controlled in their original setting often turn nasty when released among previously unexposed and unprepared hosts. Today, various fungi and other minute moulds, viruses and bacteria are being inadvertently translocated, only to decimate an assortment of bird species, wildlife and forest timbers world-wide. The problem of invasive species of all shapes and sizes is so vast and out of control that it is estimated to cost the global economy $US 400 billion annually (and growing).[21]

In his 1979 book, James Lovelock gave the name *Gaia* to the living entity inhabiting the surface layer and atmosphere of planet Earth. His insight that all life and its surrounding environment is one self-organizing system runs counter to Darwinian theories of evolution. In the Darwinian view, organisms merely compete for independent survival and may only *adapt* to environments rather than permanently change them. Yet the havoc to be wrought by failing to see the global environment as a single, inte-grated bio-system – one whole, interconnected, living organism – has already begun. With each square metre of the planet's surface absorbing about 1 watt more heat than it can release,[22] global warming – now known to be due in large part to human activity – is causing chaotic changes worldwide.[23] The widespread thawing of the Siberian permafrost risks the imminent release of 'catastrophic' amounts of ozone-depleting methane into the Earth's atmosphere.[24] Major ocean currents, a critical part of temperature and weather regulation around the world, are showing signs of slowing down.[25] Our atmosphere operates as an engine, and that engine is overheating and beginning to race erratically. Some biologists are warning of a global ecosystem that is blended into a puree of misplaced

- One quarter of Europe's 1.6 billion km² of forest is sick or dying. The major cause of this death-rate is industrial emissions, with sulphur dioxide and nitrogen dioxide the major pollutants and cause of acid rain. (*New Scientist*, 9 October 2004.)
- In the industrialized economies, each dollar we spend produces more than one kilo (two pounds) of atmospheric carbon. (www.abc.net.au/science/features/greener.)
- In the year 2000, farmers used 13 times more energy in terms of fuel, food, fertilizer and other such resources to produce only 2.5 times more food per hectare since WWII. In other words, farming worldwide has become five times *less* energy efficient. (Calculated by author from various sources.)
- Today we produce about 2 billion tonnes of food annually, of which 50 per cent is spoilt in production and 25 per cent wasted or lost before it reaches any human household (after which a further 5 per cent is discarded from our tables). (Calculated by author from various sources.)
- Fishing catches are not limited by the number of fishing boats but by the diminishing number of fish – cut the world's fishing fleet by half and the same amount of fish could still be caught. (*New Scientist*, 4 September 2004.)
- The deadliest predator in our seas is not the shark or killer whale but the plastic shopping bag. (www.pbs.org/odyssey/odyssey/index.html)
- Half the world's hospital beds are taken up by people suffering from diseases they drank. (U.N. Commission on Sustainable Development, April 2004.)

parts, broken, no longer holistic, and stripped of its key checks and balances. Our oceans now support fewer fish, smaller fish and hungrier fish as the oceanic systems are stripped and thinned to their tipping point. The Icelandic ice sheet, containing enough ice to raise sea levels by 11m, is suddenly and unexpectedly slipping into the sea at an accelerating rate; and the carbon dioxide we are streaming into the atmosphere is also changing the chemical composition of the oceans, putting complex marine eco-systems at risk as our oceans become more acidic.[26]

All these are examples of where undiscovered feedback loops and

- By 2030, two-thirds of us will be living with water scarcity. (*New Scientist*, 16 October 2004.)
- Approximately 10 billion animals, birds and fish are killed each week for human consumption – almost two per person per week. This number is increasing. (Calculated from Robert Lawrence interview data in *New Scientist*, 14 August 2004.)
- For every rubbish bin of waste produced by the average modern household, 500 more are produced on our behalf by the very economy that supports our lifestyle. (Calculated by author from various sources.)
- The western world spends more on pet food annually (about $20 billion) than would be needed to provide basic health and nutrition for every person on the planet (about $15 billion). (Calculated from *Worldwatch Institute* figures and others: www.worldwatch.org.)
- Our ability to pollute has even reached beyond our planet. There are millions of pea-sized bits of space junk, and the United States Space Command tracks more than 9,000 man-made objects that create an extraterrestrial obstacle course. Scientists at NASA's Johnson Space Center in Houston are now speculating that the proliferation of such garbage may have become so widespread it may even threaten the viability of satellites and the safety of future space missions. (*Guardian Weekly*, 3–9 February 2006.)

unforeseen convergences generate huge and violent weather spasms, sudden climate instability and other unexpected repercussions. When enough eco-systems become dysfunctional, the natural equilibrium that supports human existence will be permanently forfeited. Until our personal and collective actions are driven by the deepest personal experience of the spirit of holism and integration, we will continue dismantling nature's web as we 'improve' the planet to death.

The natural environment has become the amphitheatre in which the consequences of our addiction to separation and fragmentation are being dramatically played out. Even the health-conscious and herbal are unwitting contributors to the carnage, with between 4,000 and 10,000 traditional medicinal species endangered worldwide through excessive harvesting. The ancient wisdom of our traditional elders advised us to walk lightly on the earth. Now our gentle footprint is leaving a giant crater.

If present trends continue, economic disparities between industrialized and developing nations will move from inequitable to inhuman.

United Nations Development Program Report (2003)

For all the good we have achieved in many areas, there is a cruel – and some say self-destructive – legacy looming over us from some of what we do: pollution itself has become a weapon of mass destruction. With a public ignorant of the linked-up nature of the world, discussions about the effects of climate change too easily concentrate on the inadequate regulation of industrial emissions or the price of waterfront real estate at the new high water mark. However, no matter how we barricade our personal security, no one is left unaffected by climate change. The roll-on effects of pollution in a linked-up world can work like this: I pollute, therefore the planet gets warmer; this over-heating changes local environments worldwide and creates millions of climate change refugees who must move because of rising sea levels, droughts or floods; now I am directly affected, because the displaced population needs new places to live, and that means coming to my place or a place near me. In today's interconnected world, *every* doorstep is the doorstep next door.

This sequence of events reveals the underlying problem with the way our world is currently run as a series of self-serving and separate nation-states: when each country looks out for its own economic interests above all others, this is often to the detriment of the whole.[27] As a result, many governments continue to pursue national and regional interests ahead of a global outlook because that is all they are designed to do. The responsibility lies with all of us to put pressure on our governments to represent our collective interests, whether at the ballot box or in the environmental courts of the world.[28]

Although the health of our life-support systems in the natural environment is vital to our survival, it should also be remembered that the *social* environment is as important to our wellbeing as nature is. Indeed, imbalance in the social environment can bring disruption and chaos as severe as any imbalance in the physical environment. Unlike past civilizations that could rise and fall in relative isolation, today's interlinked and globalized village ensures that no society is immune from another's problems, and all individuals are affected sooner or later. The disconnections we set up in our social environment are as much a cause of dysfunction as our treatment of the natural environment.

The more stuff we own and surround ourselves with, the more we feel momentarily secure, except that now there is more we have to defend. The human male has learned to do this better than any other species alive. Traditionally expected to build safety, status and security for themselves and their 'close ones', men have ended up owning about 90 per cent of all global assets. However, while human males have learned to be physically very successful in the competition for energy, their failure to grasp the linked-up nature of nature has perpetuated a cycle of domination, power and control that now extends to a natural environment heading out of control.

In a 'man's' world, power and status are traditionally identified with an individual's physical strength and wealth. Aggressive ownership, along with control over knowledge and information, are used to decide who eats, who is sheltered, who travels and is educated, where we draw the line between good and bad, and whose side God is on. In effect, the human male has so far stopped at nothing to assert dominance and ownership of the planet, with most other desirable species ensnared into providing food, clothing and shelter. However, we have missed noticing that our economy is totally dependent on the ecology, and that our blundering disregard for ecological connections has caught humanity up in an environmental demolition of our own making.

And that's not all, because the financial divide has become as cruel as the natural one. Worldwide, wealth has increased by more than 50 per cent in the last 30 years, and global GDP is set to quadruple by 2050. Yet everywhere the poor are increasingly separated from the wealth of their nation: every year about 35 million men, women and children die of hunger worldwide, while the 500 richest individuals have more wealth than the poorest 3 billion of us.[29] Similarly, at a national level, rich countries' demands for debt repayments cripple the economies of many developing countries: in 2003, for example, worldwide debt exceeded global assets by a whopping 300 per cent.[30] Capital doesn't corrupt us; we corrupt capital, and create an economic velocity of opportunity for a few at the expense of the many. Globalization of capital without a corresponding globalization of consciousness limits the world to nothing more meaningful than a marketplace, and accelerates the global division into bigger winners and ever more resentful losers.

In a survival-of-the-fittest evolutionary model it would be enough to say that some win, some lose, and so what? That's life! However, in the linked-up world we are now uncovering, we are learning that what goes

As part of a test to expose the provocative truth about whether or not society (i.e. our collective mindset) is fundamentally aggressive or peace-loving, in some of my workshops participants are shown two pictures. The first, taken during the Vietnam War, captures the moment a handcuffed Viet Cong prisoner was publicly shot by a senior police officer. The second is a Japanese erotic etching depicting a close-up of a man and woman's genitalia during sex. Participants are asked to choose which picture is most suitable for public access, which is more obscene and offensive, and which they would prefer to participate in personally. Invariably, the violent picture is chosen for public release, while the erotic scene is the choice for participation – even though it also causes the most offence. This exercise, as provocative as the truth it exposes, provides an example of how, by keeping our public and private positions separate, we suppress our personal instinct for harmonious connections and (as any newspaper headline will confirm) allow our fixation on brutality and aggression to flourish in the public domain.

around comes around; the massive imbalances and widening disparaties imposed by our excessive consumption return a measurable cost to our health, if not our security. At this moment, while 8 per cent of the world's population are literally dying of starvation, another 16 per cent are dying of obesity[31] – and not just in the West. While 30 per cent of Americans are overweight or obese, so too are 20 per cent of adults in Latin America and 12 per cent of the population in China's cities, the nation with the fastest growing incidence of obesity and diabetes.[32] This epidemic of obesity and its related illnesses tells us a lot about the relationship we have with our environment. In the survival stage of our evolution, when the food supply was often uncertain, fat genes developed as a survival mechanism in times when food was scarce – storing extra fat often made the difference between death and survival in lean times. However, although our evolution into complex societies has resulted in a stable supply of food (with more than enough food in the world for everyone), our old survival mechanisms still lead us to hoard food – both in our bodies as fat, and in silos as food surpluses. This is to the detriment of both our personal and global health. Our instinctive insecurity drives a gluttony that makes it possible for many of us to keep producing, buying and eating far more than we need, and to hang onto supplies we cannot use rather than share them with those millions of people in the world who are still in desperate need.

Hunger is a sign we all recognize, an urgent need for nourishment. However, at this stage of human development we need to realize that hunger can be spiritual as well as physical. The hunger that many of us experience today has nothing to do with bodily needs, but results instead from a spiritual deficit. Not only are many of us suffering from an excess of edible food, many are also suffering a lack of soul-food. Failure to recognize this imbalance is what keeps us trying to satisfy a base survival instinct for physical nourishment that is already provided for, when instead we should be trying to satisfy a higher need for spiritual nourishment. It is this failure of basic understanding that has us suffer an unnecessary self-inflicted injury – eating, working and shopping ourselves to death in the name of progress.

Faced with a spiritual vacuum, intense consumerism is becoming the preferred escape, with modern urban life risking a dispirited existence where aspirations plateau at a comfortable numbness. We suffer what has

been called 'affluenza' – the disease of over-consumption and conspicu-
ous affluence – anaesthetized against the loss of deep, personal happiness
and our lack of spiritual nutrition.[33] As spirit develops, consumerism is dis-
closed more and more as an empty shelter.

The negative warning signs we are now receiving from both the environment and global society are placing humanity on notice that it's time
for us to change our ways. We can take what is happening either as a cue
for the wringing of hands and knee-jerk reactions, or as a goad into
positive and personal plans of action.

The good life can no longer be linked to unrestrained consumption,
just as it cannot be left to the winner-take-all endgame of global free trade
and the present momentum of the global economy. The debt burden of
the world, along with the deteriorating support environment and the
effects of global warming, show that this particular commercial model of
social organization is not working. Although there is a crying need for
equity and fairness to bring about a redistribution of resources across the
great divide, this needs to be underwritten by a deeper awareness if any
change is to last. The situation calls for us to recognize the fundamental
interconnectedness woven through absolutely everything. As we will see,
the power of connectivity is emerging as a new evolutionary drive beyond
separation and survival, a power that energizes unseen networks and
higher connections.

Such is the world's great harmony, that springs
From order, union, full consent of things!
Where small and great, where weak and mighty, made
To serve, not suffer, strengthen, not invade...
Alexander Pope

With our growing awareness of how the forces of connection and
separation shape our world, it is worthwhile taking a brief look at
the commercial world, because the business of business affects us all.
Commerce, like everything else, exists in a context, a larger background

environment. As a result, businesses do not exist in isolation; they have an impact at a wider level that ultimately has a worldwide effect. This greater reach also brings with it greater responsibility; in today's global village it is business that drives global outcomes, creating futures that affect all of us.

We all live on environmental welfare. We run our world like an economy, not a community. We understand prices but not costs. Adding the true environmental cost to present economic activity (including travel and transport) would increase all prices by at least 40 per cent (100 per cent by some estimates). However, the old economic model that has largely ignored any cost to the environment in the first place is not working, and the old ways of doing business must yield. Many fine minds are working right now on developing a sustainable model. Let's pay attention to them. Businesses worldwide can no longer be allowed to distance themselves from the social and ecological consequences of their actions while retaining all the benefits. For example, the chocolate we all love may be enjoyed in New York, produced for a corporation based in London, made from cocoa beans picked in West Africa by one of the world's 20 million debt slaves,[34] and wrapped in paper from old-growth rain forest logged anywhere from South America to Indonesia. The conventional business model is based on two assumptions: all business prefers a monopoly, and all businesses aspire to growth without end, while assuming that we live in an environment with unlimited resources, and that our 200-year love affair with fossil fuels can be maintained indefinitely.[35] However, unlimited growth is also the operating principle of the cancer cell, which eventually kills its host as well as itself. In the industrialized world, the business of business presently releases in excess of 1kg (2 pounds) of carbon into the atmosphere for every dollar we spend living our lives. Already governments are requiring that businesses (and residents) clean up their own mess. There are ways to create sustainable, prosperous communities without blowing out prices, choking the atmosphere and dismantling the environment.[36]

Prosperity cannot be enjoyed for long in a dangerous, depleted, poisoned and bankrupt environment. Material wealth will be of little use to the wealthy in an unsafe, violent and resentful world in which almost 3 billion people live on less than $2 per day.[37] If we trade unfairly and impoverish others in the process, we are also harming ourselves in the long run. If we organize the world in such a way that many people cannot afford our products, then eventually we also stand to lose everything by our own selfish actions.

An alternative business model is needed, one that includes the cost to the environment and the value to the wider community. Then, rather than seeking growth (and profit) without end, profits become sufficient to maintain the healthy life of the corporation and its interconnected community of 'stakeholders'. Such a model recognizes that unbridled efficiency can prove destructive and unhealthy.[38] The purpose of an economy today should be to connect a nation's population to the wealth and resources of the country for the benefit of all. Mere assembly-line efficiency alone cannot aim this high or see this far. Business can be profitable without profit being its overarching and only purpose.

New business knows that if the extended population is poor and desperate, then the rich are at risk too. New generation leaders are aware that the physical and social environment, along with climate change, global warming, the corporation's carbon footprint and other effects, must be taken seriously as part of the new business bottom line. New generation corporate leaders, connected to the bigger, holistic picture, know that they have a responsibility not only to their shareholders and the corporate profit margin, but also a responsibility to provide a safe, secure and sustainable community within a healthy environment in which the shareholders can enjoy their corporate wealth. Similarly, a 'new' leader values the unseen network of contacts surrounding all employees, knowing that an employee's *net worth* includes their extended *network* of business and other contacts. New business leaders know that the front-line employee is the corporation's bottom line, and if the workers are poorly rewarded, poorly managed, poorly motivated and without any sense of meaningful work, then the bottom line is at risk.

Companies based on the old win-lose scenario still seek to retain all the benefits of doing business while separating themselves from the costs, leaving governments and other institutions to pick up the environmental and social tab. However, new ethical companies know that corporate citizenship also requires them to accept responsibility for their indirect costs. Corporate harm-minimization now extends beyond reactive spin-doctoring and brand-name protection to include pro-active involvement in social issues as well as accepting environmental responsibility for corporate activity.

Environmental impact has become a key calculation on the invisible balance sheet of new business. Global disgust at the corruption behind high-profile, international corporate collapses has also put corporate ethics and values under the spotlight. Extraordinary teams only happen because of extraordinary individuals and outstanding leadership. In this age of climate change that accompanies global warming, enlightened business leaders are employing senior environmental officers to advise on the company's long-term carbon footprint and strategies for change on many fronts. Only when environmental responsibility is recognized as an investment in the future rather than an attack on today's bottom line will businesses become sustainable in the long term.

The first priority of all political systems and every leader should be to ensure there is food on every table and a roof over every head. These are bedrock issues for every business, political party, ideology, religion or election slogan wanting to prove its worth in the 21st century. Only a leader with a closed mind, a heart unopened and a view disconnected could allow war and weapons of mass destruction. Though defence is necessary, fighting for peace is like sex for chastity. We have a hunger that commerce alone cannot satisfy. A community is more than an economy, and for as long as our leaders equate life with commerce we will be dissatisfied, because they are missing this basic truth. The global economy does not exist in isolation, any more than anything else in our universe does. Today's global economy has evolved by exploiting the ecology, at the expense of our planet. This reality confers a new level of responsibility on our economic decision-makers. Indeed, since ecologists offer economists a more complete account of the impact of economic activity on the world, any economist who doesn't study ecology should be considered guilty of professional misconduct.

The illiterate of the future are not those who cannot read or write, but those who cannot learn, unlearn and relearn.
Alvin Toffler

There is still time, if we take action now to change the way we see the world and act in it. The environment is our miner's canary – a warning that something is going terribly, terribly wrong, a warning to all of us that our present way of being and of seeing the world isn't working. We can only inherit our significant role as planetary managers when our spirit is fully awakened. Otherwise, if we miss this opportunity, all that will happen is that another combination of genes – another life-form – will evolve to pick up life's relay baton and assume our role as planetary managers.

The evidence is now conclusive that home-made atmospheric pollution has made planet Earth a dangerously hot spot; if we fail to act, there will be abrupt, widespread, catastrophic and irreversible changes to Earth systems. Already, present extinction rates are estimated to be running up to 10,000 times higher than natural extinction; some species are only 1.2 generations from completely disappearing. We are dismantling nature's web of life and support.[39] Now even our regional climates face extinction. The long-term changes have begun, and if we don't do something to reverse this process, these changes will be as devastating to humanity as they are becoming to many species around us.

Previous global environmental collapses have not been driven by human negligence, but this one is. The collapsing environment is life's next emergency, a crisis that, like the first, threatens our survival. In this generation we will witness a turning point: either a spiritual breakthrough, or environmental breakdown that leads to social chaos and global resource wars. This new emergency can be resolved only by using resources we develop within ourselves across all areas of our life: in our mind, body, spirit, family, society and work. This is not a new idea: such concerted change across whole communities has already been shown to work in the past. For instance, Professor Jared Diamond has shown not only how societies can self-destruct, but how some have chosen to reverse their self-destructive trends, defy their traditions and take a new path to environmental health, with encouraging results. One example is Japan – a country whose natural environment was severely depleted during the Tokugawa period (1603–1868) but has rebounded to be almost 80 per cent forested today.[40]

So there is hope – if we act now. To survive as a species we will need to develop a wider and deeper sense of reality and of who we are, in order to be able to understand and protect what is sustaining us: the planet and our connections to it. As we will see, the first step towards changing the way we choose to live is to uncover what it is in our nature that *causes* our self-destructive behaviour in the first place. Discovering what ails us gives us not only the chance to treat the symptoms, but also the hope of finding a lasting cure.

CHAPTER 4

When enough is too much of a good thing

To be shaken out of the ruts of ordinary perception, to be shown for a few timeless hours the outer and the inner world not as they appear to someone obsessed with words and notions but as they are experienced directly and unconditionally by mind at large – this is an experience of inestimable value to everyone.

Aldous Huxley

Have you ever walked in the bush and been startled by a small animal suddenly darting from its hiding place? The animal's fear gave rise to a sudden need for more distance between the two of you, but the little creature's solution – quite instinctive – exposed it to the very risk it sought distance from. So too with us: as we saw in the last chapter, our instinct for survival has made us so successful at creating distance between ourselves and everyone and everything around us that we are now generating more problems than solutions, exposing ourselves to more risks than rewards.

Yet, from life's beginning to its end, separation remains key to survival. Survival is our top priority – life's first ongoing emergency – and without any form of separation we have no protection from harm. A newly conceived embryo's continued development in the womb depends on cells separating, dividing and multiplying; and, eventually, mother and unborn child must soon separate if life is to be renewed at birth. At the same time, however, our early instincts include attachment and connection. From our first contact with our mother's breast we grasp and suck, pulling what we want towards us and holding our desire close. Soon after, we begin consciously to influence people within our family circle and close support-environment. We use smiles, tears, tantrums and touch to discover the reactive world of cause and effect, especially our ability to cause the effect: objects fall when we pull them over, the cat scratches us if we annoy it, and we find it easier to dismantle a toy than to assemble it. As we gain more experience and skills, we learn to camouflage intention and dress up our behaviour while continuing to pull the objects of our desire towards us and hold on to them. Even as adults we remain reluctant to let go, making sharing difficult.

Spiritual evolution involves developing a balance between both separation and connection to fulfil our various needs from moment to moment. At any one time we are using a mixture favouring either separation or connection, though the less developed we are the more we restrict ourselves to separation while remaining ignorant of deeper connections. As a spiritually immature species, we use force and aggression in various guises to great effect, to get our own way and successfully defend our separate positions in the world. Indeed, we are born with only two fears – the fear of falling and the fear of loud noises. We quickly learn more, but these first two fears reveal our instinct for self-preservation. This instinct is good, because without this inborn urge to avoid pain and separate ourselves from risk, we would be extremely vulnerable and soon suffer. However, although our use of aggression to secure our survival is sometimes necessary – from swatting a malarial mosquito to resisting an assault – so too are *connections*, from the ones that establish the help, support, love and approval of those closest to us, to those that link us to the many aspects of human creativity and better living.

If we are to understand ourselves fully, we need to understand what fundamentally motivates our behaviour, beginning with the early days of our evolution and later as individuals. Early in our lives we become aware of our own separate existence, a life distinguishable from its environment and from others. In our minds we create a world-view with ourselves at its centre, always fearful and on the defensive against imminent attack. We have learned to defend ourselves well, but perhaps too well. Approximately 1 per cent of the human population – about 60 million people worldwide – are employed on defence – either full-time, part-time, paramilitary or ancillary support, with about 20 million in uniform.[41] In contrast, only 0.2 per cent of our blood cells – the white cells – are devoted to our internal defence. This means we use five times more 'units' defending our *external* territory than our blood supply has needed to evolve for the defence of our *internal* territory; our conscious defences are five times more aggressive than nature deems physically necessary![42] Our self-protective instinct that has learned to see reality from the viewpoint of distinct opposites (good and bad, high and low, bright and dark), combined with an outlook that discriminates between insider and outsider, means we are out of balance in favour of separation. We have taken self-preservation too far and become our own worst enemy – we have gone on the offensive to become the very threat we fear.

The cost of learning to survive and succeed in an uncertain, unpredictable world has been billed against our creativity. As freely creative children, we horrify our parents and endanger ourselves by putting all manner of disgusting things in our mouths while playing with the live power cable, but we also charm our carers with our spontaneity, openness, innocence and natural insight. However, soon this creative vulnerability and innocent curiosity begins to change. We begin learning the tactical importance of the word 'because', practising and embracing its principle of cause and effect as soon as we understand it. Indeed, we eventually learn *to be* a cause, ultimately spending the rest of our lives manoeuvring causes and managing effects, designing inputs and expecting results.

At about the same time that we learn to be a cause, we also begin hearing the word 'no'. This is a formative point in our childhood, because the moment our understanding of the power of cause and effect is combined with 'No, because…', our innate creativity and its transformative power immediately launch into a dive. Our inborn creativity is quickly suppressed while we learn the rules of life's game and gain the skills we need for survival in this potentially dangerous world.

We have paid a high price for the methods used in a socializing process that teaches us survival skills and a range of limitations and boundaries on the way to achieving status and acceptance. We do this through learning to balance a sense of cooperation with competition in a high-risk world. Along the way we pull together a sense of who we are, what we should be doing and what we are capable of. On average, children are criticized and corrected eight times more than they are praised and encouraged, and much low-level depression in adults stems from a negative self-concept and world-view accepted in the formative years.[43] As pre-schoolers, we are 95 per cent creative, but this figure drops by 40 per cent in the next two years, and continues down to its lowest point in early adolescence.[44] Many of us never rediscover this original creativity, and its lack remains a lifelong hunger. The suppression of our inborn creativity and insight has helped psychiatrists define more than 400 ways for us to become mentally unbalanced.[45] Paradoxically, if we choose to reawaken our childhood power of creative transformation, visualization, fearlessness, enthusiasm, curiosity, play, innocence and spontaneity by re-contacting our creativity now that we are more mature, we can use it wisely and safely without putting our very existence at risk as we did in our early days.

This personal evolution from infancy to maturity has a parallel in the biological evolution of our species. Physical safety and survival were evolution's single, direct and overarching pre-occupations until about 10,000 years ago, when we began securing ourselves and supporting one another within the first towns and cities. Later came buildings that supported a growing spiritual awakening – structures such as Stonehenge and the Great Pyramids – as we went about creating advanced societies and complex religions. Cave paintings, monuments and the traces of lost civilizations all point to the emergence of a conscious drive towards higher meaning that supplements our need for self-preservation while also surpassing it – the exploration of mysterious, unseen connections that today we call the spiritual life.

The impetus of our life – our personal challenge and responsibility – is towards maturing life's hugely creative consciousness. As we will begin to see in the later sections of this book, the full awakening of consciousness, along with the tremendous power for spontaneous, transformational change that already lies dormant within us, is a breakthrough that we can make moment by moment, at any time we choose, once we make the connection between this power and our ability to unleash it.

I am a part of all that I have met.
Alfred, Lord Tennyson

To help us make these connections, we need to know more about who and what we really are. What is it that links all our parts together? Who are we preserving? What exactly is 'self'? Are we just a skin bag full of flesh and bones, or are we spirit that has taken form? Are we consciousness and nothing more, with all of reality either a hologram or a mere afterthought? Is there a soul, or something else? What maintains our physical shape and repairs us back to that same shape whenever we are cut or damaged?

Some wondrous power still unknown to science maintains our bodies in their variety of human shapes, heals wounds with neat precision, keeps each of us intact and whole and prevents us from disintegrating. As for us having completely conscious control of anything, neuro-scientist Benjamin Libet of Harvard University was the first to find that any conscious decision to act comes *after* our brain has already begun the process of choosing.[46] Somehow, somewhere, our brain – informed by our total body chemistry, sensations and other influences – begins processing the outcome *before* we consciously give the go-ahead. A moment later, when the conscious mind kicks in, we may decide to veto or amend the initial choice, but choice begins somewhere beyond the conscious self in a brain that appears to have a mind of its own. Libet's work confirms that important decisions are being made earlier, at levels of mind other than the conscious. The conscious self is not the actual creative point at which our decisions begin; while the conscious level is where the decision is articulated, the choice actually happens *outside of consciousness*. Indeed, choice is not a single, separate activity, but is connected to everything else that is going on in us, and is influenced by everything going on around us.

One of the most obvious yet intangible connectors we use is electricity, yet electricity itself remains a mystery. We don't know exactly how or why subatomic electrons move or why electricity happens. Yet we each live an electrical life: an atom is the smallest electrical circuit in the universe, and atoms contribute structure to the universe, including your body. Life – indeed, all of physical existence – is an electrically charged event. Each atom in creation is made up entirely of various types of subatomic particles. Moreover, none of these individual particles appears 'solid': each subatomic particle within any atom behaves more like *a particle of power* than a piece of matter. Even this may be an inadequate view of what reality is made from because the various types of subatomic particles popping in and out of existence display qualities that make them more like concentrated *information* than a concentrated formation. Once we get smaller than atoms, individuality disappears, with each subatomic particle indistinguishable from any other – quarks indistinguishable from other quarks, electrons from electrons; at this quantum level of reality, existence is revealed as a completely integrated energy *system* rather than a parade of distinct particles.*

Importantly, just as there is no definite point of separation between the different colours of the rainbow, so too there is no definite point at which quantum non-reality ends and physical reality begins. Energy and existence are inseparably entwined. All created reality is in fact a vast, supercharged powerhouse of dynamic energy, an infinite field of energy-circuits and connections where spontaneous transformation emerges. Some of these connections are active within us right now, at the heart of our physical and spiritual circuitry, whereas others exist as potentials – inactive links that are waiting to be reactivated.

Virtually all matter in the universe is magnetized. Some local magnetic fields can even be stronger than the prevailing gravitational force (a child's toy magnet is the simplest example, being able to 'lift' small objects). Indeed, this electrical charge, which helps bond the universe, has helped structure reality since the Big Bang. We live on a spinning planet cocooned in its own electromagnetic field as it rotates within masses of larger, cosmic, electromagnetic fields.[47]** This is exactly how electrical motors and

---

* The exception is the neutrino which, though subatomic, has mass.

** Plasma (a gaseous, electromagnetized 'mass' of ions and electrons) is the dominant state in the universe as a whole. Almost all cosmic plasmas carry electrical currents, and all electrical currents have magnetic fields.

generators work: magnetic fields rotating within magnetic fields. Electrical frequencies and energy-waves have been discovered to roll across our head and throughout each and every organ of our body, exciting the research of a new breed of theological scientists. There is even an interactive circuit of nerves towards the front of the brain that, when stimulated, induces mystical, transcendental experiences and supernatural sensations.[48] Could this collection of circuitry, commonly referred to as the 'God-spot', be causing hallucinations that feel good but serve no other useful purpose, or are they a system of receptors for cosmic or divine connections, as many believe? Either way, whether or not we discover a gene specifically tuned in to God or other creative forces, we are certainly shaping up to be more than skin, flesh and bones, much more than a chemical set of nerves and messy bodily functions.

I find the question, 'why are we here?' typically human. I'd suggest, 'are we here?' would be the more logical question.
Mr Spock, *Star Trek*

Spock might have added, 'Where is "here"? What is real?', because the fact is that almost all of reality escapes our senses. Once we understand our physical make-up and the instincts for separation that drive our never-ending quest for survival, we start to see that our usual perception of ourselves and our surroundings is essentially flawed.

Indeed, our usual view of reality is way past its use-by date and needs upgrading. What we see and sense in the world around us does not enter our head as a picture-perfect impression of what reality really looks like. Scientists tell us that our five senses are selective and that we build our sense of reality from as little as one two-billionth (1/2,000,000,000) of the energy in the known universe. However, the energy making up our known universe is only a tiny fraction of all the energy released with the Big Bang. Most reality disappeared into 'dark matter' and 'dark energy' long before we appeared, so our normal senses never get to sift through very much at all!

Though more than 10,000 papers have been written about 'dark matter' and 'dark energy', we still know almost nothing about them. Scientists estimate that at the exact instant of Big Bang the universe was filled with 25 times more energy than we can now observe and account for. So-called 'dark energy', 'dark matter' and 'black holes' feature in explanations of the missing material, with dark energy generally held responsible for the acceleration of the universe's rate of expansion. All the mislaid matter and energy is certainly not to be found within the dimensions of time and space, because we've looked there quite thoroughly. While it has now been proven that all matter can be made to revert to energy[49] (the thrust of Einstein's famous equation, $E = mc^2$), astrophysicists have no good and accurate explanation for where all the missing matter has gone.

Using data from NASA's Wilkinson Anisotropy Probe satellite, launched in 2001, astrophysicists calculate that 73 per cent of the Big Bang's aftermath is dark energy and 23 per cent is dark matter, leaving only 4 per cent to become light-emitting atoms and familiar forms of energy. In other words, the approximately one trillion, trillion, trillion, trillion, trillion tonnes of material in the universe – stars, galaxies, atmospheres, you and me (as well as other known energy) – is only 4 per cent of what originally came out of creation. The other 96 per cent of created matter and energy has disappeared into the infinite territory around us. Because we already know that our senses pick up on a mere two-billionth of the remaining 4 per cent, a quick calculation shows that our senses keep us in touch with only about one fifty-billionth (1/50,000,000,000) of total reality. Any statistician would reject such an absurdly small sample as being too unrepresentative of the whole to be meaningful!

To see just how imperfect our senses are, consider the mechanics of sight. If we think our eyes pick up a perfect impression of an ordered reality, we are wrong. In fact we don't actually or directly 'see' anything at all. Our brain composes an image of the world from a bombardment of subatomic light particles striking the back of our eyes. These assembled images are then transferred to another part of the brain where their emotional significance is calculated and our actions decided upon. Our other four senses use a similar process, whereby whatever we know about reality only reaches us after going through the filter of our sensations and the processing plant of our brain.

Our brains are incredibly creative. In the colourless, silent world in which we have evolved, our amazing brain adds colour and sound in response to bioelectrical stimuli triggered by signals from the surrounding field. Without our act of observation, these important parts of reality cease to exist. We will see later just how important observation and conscious-ness are to reality at many levels. Consciousness contains a multi-faceted amalgam of sensations and processes, a mass of mind-parts. In effect, our five senses are composed of 21 'mini-senses' working within the main senses to glean and pass on information for further processing. What's more, the attention we give our five senses is active and selective, not passive and indiscriminate: we seek, filter and assemble information from the sur-rounding field, then pay selective attention to some of it while ignoring the rest! We don't ever see what we don't pay attention to.

Our attention is itself a mystery, a selective and mobile point within our mind, not located at any one place in our brain. While attention anchors the outlook of our conscious mind and our attitudes, it is best described as a point *affecting* our consciousness – something like the cursor on a computer screen. What's more, we pay selective attention by focusing only on small parts of the already microscopic fragment of energy we let pass for reality, and ignoring the rest. Our grip on reality is then further affected by genetic and cultural variations that make us all sense the world differently.[50]

At this point, who can say what reality is, when everyone's reality is truly different from everyone else's?

Whatever reality is, our view of it is proving to be little more than a con-vincing mirage of colour and form – a hologram – created in the mystery that is our mind. When we dream, for example, the images seem real. However, when we wake from the night's dreams we find that the people, places and events were not real after all. Yet how do we know that our morning state of wakefulness is anything more than another level of dreaming? Even when we bump our head and the throbbing bruise feels real enough, can we wake up beyond this and look further?

Perhaps so, because during the assembly phase of 'reality' – after our five senses have picked up their initial samples – we can still make mistakes. Consider pain. Our body doesn't have specialized pain paths. Instead, pain is something we assemble in our head from multiple fragments of chemical information communicated through our nerves.[51] Neuroscientists report surreal distortions of the senses, such as amputated 'phantom' limbs causing real pain; cases of synaesthesia, where patients with tangled senses see sounds in colour and hear shapes;[52] and clinically 'blind' people being able to correctly report movement because one or more of the 30 sight centres in the brain is still active, though isolated.[53]

As if all this evidence of slippery reality isn't unsettling and humbling enough, dogs hear better and goldfish see better than we do – some goldfish can even see the infrared beam of your television remote control. We cannot see ultraviolet light, but exposure to it can blind us. Radio waves surge through us, recognized only by our radio or TV set. There is a lot we miss out on, even though it connects to us and sometimes passes right through us. All this is happening to us because we are alive in an infinite field of energy in perfect balance.

Part of why these things remain a mystery for us comes from the fact that we live in dual realities. One reality (which I have earlier called 'created reality') anchors reality as an imperfect three-dimensional picture in our consciousness. The other, 'original reality', is the perfectly balanced state of infinity, without origins, anchors, circumference or blemishes (infinity, by definition, can have no origins). As we saw in Chapter 2, the created reality that we see and interact with is the seat of all separation from everything, including separation from our source in original reality.

The historically recent rise of religions, along with our global interest in spirituality, suggests that, though inactive, our direct connections to original reality are beginning to resurface and reactivate. We have mastered one view of reality – the created reality of *separation* – in order to survive. But ultimately this is not enough if we are to continue to develop spiritually. Now it is time to consciously engage with the other, original reality; it is time to master *connection*. The simultaneous experience of both original and created realities is an intermingling of energies into what we may refer to as the experience of 'super-reality'. This higher experience is what we are calling 'super-consciousness'.

James Jeans, the British astronomer, said that the universe has begun to look more like a great thought than a great machine.[54] Current scientific evidence points to one startling conclusion – our reality is nothing more or less than our personalized, highly complex and creative interpretation of the infinite energy field around us.

We might say, 'But I know what is real. When I close my eyes the world doesn't disappear, and it exists whether I think about it or not'. Yet even this 'absolute certainty in knowledge' is itself another event of mind, rendering unanswerable the question of whether or not reality exists separate from mind. Objective reality is hypothetical, and the consideration of its existence pointless; we can have no objectivity, since we can never escape the confines of our own minds. There cannot be any evidence of reality *outside* of mind, because evidence *requires* mind; any speculation on reality can only be just that, speculation that uses the unavoidable mind.

Grasping this difficult concept does nothing to limit or diminish reality, but does a lot to expand and empower the scope and reach of mind. Our consciousness is inseparable from reality itself, and with consciousness and reality intermingled in this way, both are better spoken of in one breath as 'reality-consciousness'. We have already mastered the reality of separation, now we are beginning to grapple with the deeper reality of unseen connections. Because of the severe limitations our five senses place on our way of viewing life and the universe, our present grasp of reality is about as reliable (and makes about as much sense) as trying to scoop a cloud into a butterfly net.

> In our endeavour to understand reality we are
> somewhat like a man trying to understand the
> mechanism of a closed watch. He sees a face and
> the moving hands, even hears ticking, but he has no
> way of opening the case. If he is a genius he may
> form some picture of a mechanism which could be
> responsible for all the things he observes. But he
> may never be quite sure his picture is the only one
> which could explain his observations. He will never
> be able to compare his picture with the real
> mechanism and he cannot even imagine the
> possibility or the meaning of such a comparison.

Albert Einstein[55]

So if reality is not what we think it is – if reality cannot be defined or limited by our extremely narrow experience of it – then what is it? Recent scientific discoveries confirm that mind and matter intermingle, and that our four dimensions of space and time are avoidable, making common reality unreliable.

In fact, reality is a lattice of many dimensions. In the last decades, the quantum discoveries made in particle physics laboratories worldwide have reached some mind-altering conclusions. Even our assumptions about reality are being challenged, along with the precepts of how we live our lives. One of the most amazing of these challenges is the discovery that just by looking at things, we affect them in some weird and wonderful way.

Though some details are better left until later in the book, it is important to outline here the most significant of these discoveries. Science has now proven that matter is something more than just a solid array of atoms. Matter:

- *can be physically affected without any known mechanism for the change.* In 1964 physicist John Bell of CERN, the European Laboratory for Particle Physics, proved that there is 'influence at a distance' working in nature – whereby something can directly influence something else in another place without there being any detectable way for the effect to happen.

- *is changed by observation.* In 1922 Walter Gerlach and Otto Stern found that the spin of an electron changed depending on whether it was being observed or not. This proved what quantum physics had theorized – that the act of observation changes the original state of the electron in a specific way. This phenomenon has been routinely verified since then, and with entities larger than subatomic particles.

- *can be in two places at once.* Physicist David Wineland and fellow researchers at the National Institute of Standards and Technology in Boulder, Colorado, caused a single atom in a vacuum to be in two positions – a superposition – at the same time. More recently, Wineland's team has transferred the substantial features of one ionized atom (such as its energy, motion and magnetic field) to another ionized atom. At this level of reality, features are the same as substance, so by transferring the atom's features, Wineland was effectively transferring parts of the atom itself. The extrapolation of these experiments is that the building blocks of our universe (atoms) are capable of multiple existences simultaneously, and that within physical existence we have the potential for teleportation.[56]

- *can exchange information instantaneously (timelessly).* In 1997, Nicolas Gisin and others at the University of Geneva sent bonded pairs of photons to different locations several kilometres apart. Using fibre optic cables, Professor Gisin and his team were able to alter the spin and angle of axis of one subatomic particle and see the effect instantaneously mirrored in the other at the distant location. Gisin's research confirms that influence can transfer from one point to another instantaneously – as if beyond the reach of time – as well as allowing communication over long distances with no known mechanism. This also means that even when matter appears separated by large distances, it may still be inextricably linked.

- *can move through other matter, like ghosts through walls.* In 1995, physicist David Pritchard of MIT in the US led a team that built a machine to pass one portion of a sodium atom through assorted grids and then recombine and reassemble it as the same measurable and original atom on the other side of the grids. This experiment effectively moved matter through other matter.

- *can move from the classical (real) state to the quantum (immaterial) state and back again.* In 2007, Caslav Brunker and Johannes Kofler at the University of Vienna, Austria, showed that the assumed boundary between the quantum (weird world) state and our level of reality does not exist, and that the quantum world and our world are intermingled. The researchers found that there is no point at which an object fails to follow the laws of quantum theory, which means that there may be a point at which the world as we know it fails to follow the laws of matter.[57]

An unavoidable conclusion arising from these revelations is that through the power of observation (mind) and these 'miraculous' workings of the quantum world, all matter interconnects across space and time, as well as interconnecting and interacting with mind. This leaves no actual point of separation to ultimately differentiate the three. Mind, matter and the quantum world are revealed as parts of one and the same thing, three aspects of some mysterious whole. With observation being inseparable from what is observed, and because we need to be conscious in order to make observations, it therefore follows that our *conscious* mind influences whatever we are conscious of! Mind itself contributes some reality to reality. Moreover, even though we know we are conscious, we now realize that consciousness has no beginning or end point that separates it from our observed world and the world of the unbelievable. This explains why consciousness has not been specifically located or defined – a problem that has led some researchers to conclude mistakenly that consciousness does not actually exist at all. Our knowledge of consciousness and how it works are appallingly primitive.

This irrefutable fact of linkage between mind and matter now makes consciousness a far greater power to be reckoned with, rather than merely being thought of as some inaccessible abstract state, as it has in the past. The point where mind and matter merge is also where we come into being and continue to exist. These conclusions are significant, since they direct us to reformulate our view of the world and our conscious behaviour in it. We can no longer allow ourselves to be deceived by external appearances. We need to create a new world view, one that inspires us to harness the full transformative power of mind.

However, it would be a mistake to doubt that created reality exists. Created reality is something substantial, intricate, puzzlingly precise, and observable. The roots of material existence are seemingly beyond our direct conscious manipulation, yet obedient to objective laws of physics to a degree that our minds can only marvel at. However, while this phenomenon called mind is not material, remember that it is also part of reality, and even has the ability to use itself to think about and observe itself. Mind can observe mind.

Moreover, in the same way that inside and outside can be seen to intermingle at a sub-atomic level, so too reality informs our feelings just as feelings inform our reality. Reality is not only what we sense on the outside, but also *our reaction to it*. Research by Professor Stephen Kosslyn at Harvard University has shown that when we imagine any scene, we activate parts of the brain's visual cortex in exactly the same way as when we see it in 'real' life. Our brain uses the same circuitry for imagination and reality. Brain activity in video-game players shows the brain reacting as if the violence was real.[58] Mental rehearsal – active visualization – is used by most top-ranking sports champions today to measurably improve their performance. Even professional musicians use it to practise their instrument before a performance without actually playing. This suggests that our brain, *as a processor*, cannot tell the difference between imagination and the real world. The brain does not treat them separately – both get processed in the same place, using the same perceptual paths, and produce the same feelings. Similarly, actors construct imagined reality by using their own personal memories, feelings, attitudes and experiences to reproduce emotions appropriate to the scene and character they are playing. Our mind is very creative and inseparable from reality. Indeed, every one of us is really only alive because of a string of creative flashpoints and transformational moments originating at the beginning of time.

The first spontaneous, creative flashpoint was the genesis for the whole universe, while the second spontaneously created life. The third flashpoint is within us now, existing as our capacity for creative genesis inspired by personal flashes of insight.

Just as the Big Bang was accompanied by the impulse of creative genesis that allowed it, and just as our personal existence is due to the pulse of creative genesis released at our own conception, so too our creative consciousness is capable of generating spontaneous and instantaneous transformations. The creative potency within us is not only capable of producing good ideas, great art or many languages, but it is also capable of illuminating the connections between the individual and the whole of creation. We are always changing physically, psychologically and emotionally, and some of these changes are changes we choose. Spontaneous transformation at the personal level is already an ongoing reality.

While the first creative impulse happened in timeless infinity (as space and time began), the last happens within the inner space of our own psyche. Remember that the astronaut's deep space, along with the psychological space of our creative mind and the original infinity of energy, all share an original connection that continues unbroken. While creation's first flash generated all separation, our personal creativity has the power to see beyond separation and supersede it.

The interconnectivity uniting all of reality may be easier to access than we think. Just as it takes only ten numerals in different combinations to connect all the telephones on the planet, so too our brain cells have the potential to make more possible combinations of connections than the number of atoms in the known universe.[59] Our brain has so much capacity for multiple levels of connections that the experience we seek most deeply – a true and honest grasp of reality – may be accessed using no special powers beyond those we already possess, which is the creative capacity already potent within us. Indeed, the convergence of religion, philosophy and science is not just an abstract idea or intellectual theory. The experience of the unity of the spiritual and the physical is emerging at this very moment, both in the laboratory and within each and every one of us.

CHAPTER 5

Spiritual freedom is a journey, not a destination

Eternity has nothing to do with the hereafter....
This is it.... If you don't get it here, you won't get it
anywhere. The experience of eternity right here
and now is the function of life. Heaven is not the
place to have the experience; here's the place to
have the experience.

Joseph Campbell (*The Power of Myth*)

O n the face of it, it would seem that science and spirituality target different realities, with science concentrating on the universe *since* the Big Bang of original creation, and spirituality concentrating on the situation *before or outside* that original creation.* Yet all forms of science, religion and spirituality have one thing in common: they look at reality and attempt to explain it. As we have seen earlier, while the Big Bang gave us our material world along with the physical dimensions in which we live – science's 'created reality' – there also exists a meta-reality

* Along with the word 'beyond' defined earlier, the phrase 'Before or outside' is the best term for identifying the state of infinite energy. As mentioned in an earlier note, while quantum physicists and mathematicians chide that there is nothing beyond reality, just as there is nothing 'north of north' and that if we keep walking we go south again, there is acknowledgement that an infinite field of energy in perfect balance 'exists'. The great Steven Hawking himself describes infinity within a timeframe by using the phrase 'the infinite past' ('Decoding the Afterglow', *New Scientist*, 9 October 2004, p.15). Hawking's statement confirms the difficulty we

of pure energy and perfect balance. This is the 'original reality' that philosophers contemplate and the religious seek.

However, it has been humanity's perennial mistake to view these two realities as different entities to be considered separately by different disciplines. The infinite power of religion's metaphysical God and the infinity of science are the same infinity. Religion and science meet at the point where the infinity and the divine intermingle; the divine is looked for inside us, while the infinity is projected outside. To reach eternity we must go beyond any particular religious space and any particular scientific speciality. Indeed, the convergence that is currently developing between science, philosophy and religion is witness to their common ground. What religion generally calls 'God', science calls 'infinite energy in perfect balance', and spiritual philosophy calls 'enlightenment'. Though using different starting points, they are all chasing the same universal truth. There is one well with many buckets. As the Hindu tradition says, 'The ways to enlightenment are as many as the minds of men.'

It is becoming clear that spiritual evolution is *a state of mind*. Somewhere in our brain we have a supremely powerful combination of connections available. This powerful position of mind grants us access to such vast reaches of reality that most of us either recoil with disbelief or are too afraid (or indifferent) to really look. Call it enlightenment, heaven, wishful thinking, or merely the activities of the brain's excitable neurons, most of us settle for the merest fragments of reality and truth. Yet human consciousness is evolving, and along with it our spiritual consciousness. We are moving on, somewhat haltingly, from bronze-age spirituality with its personal gods and competitive theologies, passing through the 'new age' with its metaphysical mysteries and fairy dust, and emerging now into the era of informed spirituality. It is here that science and psychology meet and realities combine in one seamless experience of truth.

---

confront when trying to consider the vastness of the infinite whole from where we are, within created reality, without reference to notions identified with time and place. While at times within this book it has been appropriate to use phrases such as 'beyond time and place' or 'without recourse to time and place' or 'independent of time and place' or 'without relying on time and place', these terms are intended to identify a state rather than a location. They are my attempt to invoke a sense of something that is, by definition, infinite and therefore impossible to grasp entirely.

Have you ever felt you knew what to look for but went looking for it in all the wrong places? A friend of mine – a devout Buddhist – went on a pilgrimage to the actual Bodhi tree under which Buddha is said to have sat and reached enlightenment 2,600 years ago. I asked him what he found there. His reply: 'Only a tree!' Any pilgrim site is just that – a site. If the healings and miracles at all the pilgrim sites on Earth were caused by the site itself, everyone who visited these sites would be healed. Yet in January 2006, more than 350 Muslim pilgrims died in a stampede during their *hajj* to the holy city of Mecca. Every year Hindus drown during devotions at the Ganges, and thousands are injured at the Khumba Mela ceremonies.[60] Untold numbers have become sick at pilgrim sites all around the world, picking up diseases and infections from the water or other pilgrims. The power of healing is in the pilgrim, not the place. Inspired by their sense of location, it is pilgrims, making a powerful inner journey, who find within themselves the connections and spiritual circuitry to heal their own diseases. Indeed, all healing, including spiritual healing, involves some measure of self-healing. At some level, all healing involves the collusion of either biological or psychological powers operating within the patient.

Churches, mosques, synagogues and temples all claim to be God's one true home. But just suppose that any one of these religious buildings was no more God's house than any other. What if no single place or designated day was any better or worse for true prayer and spiritual experience than any other? If God is accessible through your thoughts and prayers at any time, as well as when you are in God's house, which place is the more heavenly: the mind or the mosque, the consciousness or the cathedral?

Specific places and icons help us remember our belief, often acting as a substitute for what is missing from an incomplete existence, and doubling as an *agent* for our desires, needs and dreams. When we are crippled or lame we need crutches and require help to move around the smallest obstacles; take away our crutch and we are lost. But when we are healed and whole we have no need for crutches and can walk a direct path, unaided. Those who only have beliefs need sacred sites, while those who have direct experience do not. For them, every site has the same powerful connection, and all places are equally sacred. Wherever you are is holy ground. The world is our monastery, and our whole life is our prayer, our mantra, our full spiritual expression.

Ever notice how devout Christians report visions of Jesus rather than Muhammad, and Muslims in deep prayer often see Muhammad but rarely Jesus? Buddhists don't get images of Hindu gods, while Jews at prayer don't see Buddha. Whatever vision we favour rises from the range of our beliefs, the horizons of our hopes and the extent of our experiences. To say there is no other way to the one God than through a particular religion is to contradict ourselves, to put limitations and boundaries on something we otherwise claim is boundless. If God hasn't designed us with built-in compliance and conviction, why do the pious take it upon themselves to insist on it, as if they know more about God than God does?

To get to God, we must get beyond our sense of an exclusive self and an absolutely separate 'other', beyond concerns about where God is or is not, and beyond the competition over whose version of the universal truth is right and whose is wrong. As we have already seen, our grip on reality is so flimsy as to be almost non-existent. This alone will make any search for God's whereabouts always incomplete, as we are unable to offer an access-all-areas map of reality to use in our search. Nor are we allowed any observable hold on objective reality, caught as we are within the subjective confines of our own minds. This leaves our spiritual experience ultimately dependent on our own actions and insights, not someone else's, however inspiring their life or noble their efforts on our behalf may be.

Tribalism and the tribal mind have been developing in humans for more than 100,000 years, yet civilization and civilized thinking for only 10,000 years. Through this somewhat recently civilized mind, spirituality then began finding expression in the first organized religions, which were a mix of this earlier tribalism and more advanced spiritual insight. Now evolution is urging us towards a more personal and direct experience of the infinitely divine state beyond houses of worship, sacred sites and authority figures. By keeping God at a distance – and at last count there were almost 7,000 different gods and goddesses being worshipped around the world – we remain self-serving; there is no better way to avoid real, direct and personal spiritual experience than by keeping the spiritual destination at a distance. Keeping our distance is a survival tactic originally designed to keep us physically intact. Yet complete spiritual freedom requires we go beyond this assumption of primal distance and allow ourselves direct and instantaneous connection to dimensions and experiences beyond separation.

Man is quite insane. He wouldn't know how to create a maggot and he creates Gods by the dozen.
Michel de Montaigne

The early monotheistic religions, by offering a belief system based on one God, attempted to look beyond polytheistic myths and superstitions in search of a more durable answer to the human quest for origins, unity and insight. These monotheistic systems sought paradoxically to provide the unified experience of *everything* while achieving this through a *separate* being – God – which not only failed to make the experience a unified one, but even itself became the source of much disunity *between* religions. All major religions have the same essential narrative: the capacity of the individual to transcend ego and personally experience the infinite divine. However, this universal aim is often lost within arguments about whose narrative is better. In both East and West, religions have generally claimed the divine space exclusively; they have sought territory, found enemies, and self-righteously fought for the high moral ground while at the same time failing to focus honour towards the living, instead reserving reverence almost exclusively for the dead. In the separation between religious demand and the spiritual desire for eternal life, life has been the least respected.

The God business is no different from every other business whose fundamental drive is to increase growth without end – to monopolize. Turf wars are as fundamental to institutional religion as they are to business, with both business and religion seeking to control territory while resisting any competition. If God is one, then God cannot be one-sided. However, over the last two or three millennia, during humanity's most intense and prolific church-temple-mosque-synagogue phase of supposed spiritual development, each major religion has more or less marketed itself as the one true faith (with the exception of Buddhism, whose essential teachings identify it more as philosophy than religion). Even within each major religion, rival 'brands' have arisen, with such names as Catholic, Baptist, Lutheran, Shia, Sunni, Theravada, Mahayana and many more, each brand claiming superiority over the others. Again we see our addiction to separation break the whole into segments, with our wisdom falling through the gaps.

Values, beliefs and ethics are insufficient without a greater vision to transform them. Great religions are initiated and progressed by the insights of inspired individuals such as Muhammad, Christ, Krishna, Buddha and countless other prophets and sages. Rather than become mired in division and exclusivity over whose inspiration is the correct one, we should aspire to follow the example of these inspiring people, and find our *own* inspirational inner vision, our own in-sight.

Yet one exciting fact is that the world's religions are more similar than we might think, and our spiritual evolution more advanced than some recent cruelties suggest. The word 'Islam' is derived from the consonant root *slm*,

- When Jesus said, 'The kingdom of heaven is through me', Christians interpreted this in a way that gave them a monopoly, finding exclusivity by emphasizing the word 'me'. From this interpretation, the kingdom of heaven could be accessed only through Jesus – and, of course, his agents. But suppose that Jesus meant us to emphasize the word 'through' instead. Now we see a completely different meaning, something like: 'As a teacher I'm showing you a doorway of perception that takes you to the direct experience of God. Please go through this doorway and get the experience. But whatever you do don't cluster around my feet, making a fuss and worshipping me. I am not the destination, merely the light for your journey. Just follow my personal example, and access God directly. God is an immediate experience, not some distant idea. Make a *direct connection* by living with kindness, compassion, and selfless love.'
- Jesus, Buddha, Muhammad and the many other great prophets and teachers should not be regarded as special – on the contrary, they set the benchmark for what should be considered normal. Yet we set them up as superior beings so that we can continue doing less than our best, scraping by on spiritual welfare. Devotion is an easy way to excuse our spiritual immaturity; being devoted to any spiritual messenger can hold us back from achieving our own direct, heavenly experience.

meaning 'peace' or 'safety', also seen in the word 'salaam' meaning peace; the meaning of 'Islam' is that we submerge ourselves in peace as we surrender and submit to the will of God. The Hindu Vedic culture's most important mantra is *Loka Samastha Sukhino Bhavantu* – let the entire world be happy. The Jewish Torah can be understood within the words, 'Keep our neighbour in good health and happiness; care for all others'. The Dalai Lama has succinctly summarized Tibetan Buddhism with four words: 'Help others. Be happy.' And through Christianity, Jesus urges believers to experience forgiveness by loving the enemy as well as the neighbour.

A desire for peace and happiness is a key feature of the major religions, along with belief in God. Yet, by itself, belief in God is not enough to guarantee even basic human values and decency – Heinrich Himmler demanded belief in God as a prerequisite for officers in the murderous Nazi SS. The pain and suffering spread by religious wars throughout history show that when we concentrate on a distant heaven we create hell here on earth. God can't do it alone. Hell is born in our anger and fear, heaven in our compassion and kindness. Just as the womb is the incubator of our life on earth, this world is the incubator of our heavenly experience. Within our mind we have the instrument to transform hell into heaven. Inequality can only be remedied by inner quality.

From a spiritual perspective there are three levels of energy we need to be aware of and tune in to if we are to gain full spiritual insight: the all-embracing infinite energy in perfect balance ('the infinity') through which all things have arisen; the 'physical' energies released by the Big Bang and existing now to form our reality within time and space; and the creative energy, which first appeared with the Big Bang, then supported the creation of life and is now re-emerging through creative consciousness. The development of our spiritual capacity is marked by the degree to which each of these revealed energies – the infinite, the material and the creative – becomes consciously accessible, to be expressed through the quality of our outlook and the mix of our actions in the world. At present our mindset has us ignore the infinity, compete for energy in the world, and more or less confine creativity to leisure activities or a range of professional specialities.

These energies, intermingled and expressed in potentially any combination, flow through us to any purpose we set our mind on. The more selfless we are, and the more focused on the welfare of others we are *by free choice* at any moment, the more spiritual capacity and potency we express. On the other hand, the more self-absorbed and less spiritually integrated we are at any moment, the less spiritual capacity we are capable of expressing, and the more we are left grasping at shadows and echoes and calling them real. By the simple act of looking upwards to the sky and beyond, we may be inspired with a momentary sense of something wonderful also within us yet dormant and hidden; look down and we may sense within the common objects at our feet something of the power within creation holding every insignificant thing in place and intact. The difference in what we see in any direction is all a matter of shifting our spiritual horizon, our outlook, our spiritual line of sight rather than merely shifting our eyes. Being able to see within – our *in-sight* – is the spiritual way.

Happiness is as a butterfly, which, when pursued, is always beyond our grasp, but which, if you will sit down quietly, may alight upon you.

Nathaniel Hawthorne

While any idea of God that we support may benefit ourselves personally, there is no measure of the worth of our experience except as it translates into the *goodness of our behaviour* here on Earth. Good and bad behaviour is something the human race hasn't really sorted out yet, though we easily recognize them both. We see good when it comes in big lumps like battlefield mercy, billion-dollar generosity and unselfish love, and bad is just as obvious in such crimes as murder, theft and treason. But a little investigation reveals that there is a lot of so-called 'good' and 'bad' going on in all of us all the time. In fact, any good and bad behaviour always begins and ends with the choices we make in our mind.

The traditional spiritual outlook of the Western world sees life as separated into opposites – good and bad, heaven and hell, God and the Devil. The traditional Eastern world-view sees no separation into opposites, teaching instead that all lives are on one path, with some more progressed than others, depending on their accumulated *karma* or spiritual influences and experiences. We are each positioned in our own way somewhere along the spiritual path in a world that is neither good nor bad except that we make it so: we can turn science either to medicine or to missiles.

We are forever drawn between separation and connection, and in our search for balance between these two momentums we need reference points. Could it be that our spiritual reference points of 'God' and 'Devil' do not define separate beings or entities in their own right, but instead creatively represent the extremes of connection and separation – God represents our momentum towards the good, and the Devil represents our momentum to the bad? Then good 'God' and evil 'Devil' are purely and simply labels for contrary directions of human intention and behaviour. This is not an argument about whether God and the Devil do or don't exist; it merely highlights the fact that, whatever else we may want them to be, God and Devil exist as states of mind. Our sense of God represents the ultimate in constructive connections and therefore the higher good, while our sense of the Devil represents the ultimate in destructive division, disconnection and separation and therefore the bad. From this reality, traditional concepts such as heaven in the West and Shangri-La in the East may well have evolved to explain in a more tangible way the possibilities for personal transformation realized by the truly wise – the enlightened destination of 'breakthrough consciousness' experienced by the initiated.

There is no reason to assume that God is some entity, a separate being distant from us. God represents the original, creative power of instantaneous transformation and transition, the same power pre-existing and underpinning all of us, yet underplayed within each of us. The fact that there was original creation does not automatically mean that there was also a separate creative being, a creat*or*, doing it. We are ourselves each a fragment of the creative impulse that religion calls the divinity and science sees as the accompaniment to the Big Bang. Human creativity is a spark wired into that original energy of creation itself, projecting a universal *energetic** for change and adaptation but in no way confirming any isolated

---

* 'Energetic' is my expression for any field, force or energy that is not accounted for by physics. Its existence can only be inferred by the observation of its influences and effects.

divine entity. If we want to experience the power we call 'God', and if our call to God comes from beyond the limitations of ego and self-absorption, then just by using our creative powers to visualize God *in any image that is meaningful to us* we can create a direct and divine experience. With this powerful connection we reawaken the forces of creativity and genesis that have been part of us since our creation.

Believers of *all* religions honour something greater than themselves; the key to spiritual progress turns by degrees around increasing selflessness. But faith and belief are, of themselves, no guarantee of selflessness and its liberating loss of self-absorption. There is a big difference between self-righteousness and righteousness. A charitable nature and an open heart are not religious acts of faith but personal acts of unselfishness.

Some actively seek connection to God, but while on that path create disconnection and separate themselves from God's masterwork, our environment. Is it acceptable, or even logical, to have God in our hearts without considering how we affect our world in the name of God? We need only look at the state of the environment to see what happens when we allow separation and self-righteousness to dominate our psyche.

Globally, we are in a spiritual crisis just as much as an environmental one. Throughout our evolution, we have survived many crises. Any emergency requires firm decisions delivered along rigid lines of authority. Men in general and armies in particular have traditionally worked this way. This has served the demand of physical survival, and yet our spiritual evolution, which must eventually reach above and beyond the limitations of the physical, has also reflected this bias towards tribal command and control – and been weighed down by it. For example, during the rise of male-dominated power-structures in the Abrahmic religions, God – who first appeared in partnership with the goddess Asherah[61] – was further and further separated from the Goddess until he became single-sided, domineering and incomplete. To put the balance back into religion and make it spiritually creative again, both men and women must be represented and participate equally. The power struggles that exist within and between religions have nothing to do with religion's inherent spiritual drive. These problems arise purely because of the way in which religion is enacted.

The measure of a good religion should be the extent to which it is a crucible for individual spirituality, since the only things that shine in any religion are the works and inspirations of individuals. However, rigid considerations of doctrine, exclusion of others and rituals of faith are not only superfluous to mature spirituality, they eventually become counter-productive, because they keep us firmly grounded in the identity of an exclusive and separate self and an exclusive and separate God. This pre-cludes any possibility of touching the infinite and inclusive divine, a state extending beyond the separate and singular to the boundless whole.

As the most advanced animal species, we are now leading life's evolu-tion beyond the adolescent age. The more globalized of the world's religions already accept and worship one supreme God rather than a conflicted many. Some religions have even gone further, with no clergy or rigid religious hierarchy to block a believer's higher spiritual experience nor create the bottlenecks of power and the flood of 'expert' explanations we find in many religions. For example Baha'u'llah, the founder of Baha'i, saw religion as behaviour only, with each and every belief system poten-tially bestowing equal benefit. He believed that a Christian living a true Christian life, a Muslim living a true Muslim life, a Buddhist living a true Buddhist life, and so on, would all behave the same, because they are looking over the same boundless, spiritual horizon.

Ultimately, the power that is God has *no* religion, having always served us better as personal experience rather than public belief. It is suspi-ciously self-serving, even arrogant, to assume that any religion has an exclusive relationship with God that allows privileged access to the almighty. Setting up both God and heaven at a distance outside of ourselves conveniently reinforces the assumption of our separate existence. When we say, 'I'm only human; it's not my fault; it's in God's hands; God (or the Devil) made me do it; let God decide...' we abandon personal responsi-bility for our spiritual growth.

This approach to God allows us to elevate holy go-betweens as mes-sengers for God while we cruise along as spiritual dependants, keeping God at a safe distance and avoiding the risk of a direct experience. Under these circumstances, anyone who claims direct experience of God is regarded as suspect – when someone says they talk to God we call it prayer, but when they say God answers we call it insanity.

When we pray, are we listening to what God wants *from* us, or merely begging for what God can do *for* us? There is no such thing as miracles on demand. With spiritual maturity we no longer restrict God to the great god-in-the-sky, an entity that is *outside* us, but instead allow ourselves to experience something more personal, direct, internal and immediate – but no less divine.

However we get to heaven – whatever religious vehicle we use to cross the spiritual space to the God experience – we must finally get out of that vehicle and be within the experience face to face. Spiritual deliverance is ultimately our personal responsibility, and while religion can offer structure and support, when we give up our power to any individual or organization, we hand over the keys to life's safe and abdicate our spiritual responsibility. Buying a religious ticket to spiritual happiness is no guarantee you will get there. Spiritual experience is available with or without any religious notion of God. It is not a matter of accepting or rejecting God; godliness is about supreme unity, something we can experience without even *considering* God.

Indeed, references to God may even be superfluous to complete spiritual experience, because in considering a notion of God, the very act of consideration makes God some kind of intellectual property – a possession to be defended, a distraction that prevents us from developing our full spiritual capacity. In other words, the very act of thinking about God is itself counterproductive, since any attempt to think about the infinite immediately grounds us in the confines of the present – the finite – and so pulls us away from the very thing we are trying to reach. As soon as we tie God to a name, God has gone.

The eternal energy we are calling the infinity provides the power behind the notion of God. Today our spiritual evolution is positioning the human psyche for a universal experience without recourse to space and time – an outlook that dissolves all distance, division and separation. Indeed, evidence is beginning to emerge that consciousness surfaces as a functional part of an interconnected whole.[62] 'Health' and 'whole' are synonymous, with healing and holism now the imperatives for our hazardous times. The whole is divine, and to be divine is to be infinitely whole.

Human evolution is in its adolescent phase, wanting the rights but not the responsibilities. Adolescence marks a natural progression from immaturity to maturity, from dependence to independence; yet, ideally, adolescence should be only a passing phase. By reading the signs in the environment around us and learning the appropriate lessons, we will remain part of the solution as our world moves through its long-awaited transition from adolescence to maturity. There are many positive signs, both person- ally and collectively, to show we are evolving towards spiritual maturity and wholeness. There has been a rapid growth in global environmental aware- ness and action, for example, with a worldwide search for solutions to such issues as global warming. There is also an increase in worldwide generosity, with private citizens from all nations donating to relief efforts wherever tragedy strikes, such as the Live Aid concerts and the 2005 Asian tsunami appeal. There is also a growing worldwide interest in 'spiritual' matters, both formal and informal, with a burgeoning number of inter-faith conferences and communications between religions, all indicating a willingness to open our minds to greater possibilities.

Our quest for spiritual maturity and fitness has become a process of personal rediscovery. By *unlearning* separation we begin to rediscover our deeper connections – connections that were never lost, just lost from view. We are spiritually evolved only as far as we have regained connectedness beyond our current psychology of isolation and division.

In this way, true selflessness is a breakthrough that occurs when our point of consciousness no longer emerges from a sense of separate self. Complete selflessness means a kind of 'loss of self' that is more than personal generos- ity and thoughtfulness, though these behaviours are indicative. The essence of selflessness is profoundly spiritual; it represents a shift in our point of aware- ness beyond the limited, separate aspect of self to the infinite, holistic self. This shift, when complete, marks a profound breakthrough in reality-con- sciousness that affects our whole being and our world. This breakthrough experience is the heart of spiritual fitness and maturity.

We are like fledglings, testing our spiritual wings as we learn to fly. If we learn the lessons before us, we will soar to new horizons and see clearly the way ahead. If we are to continue evolving towards complete spiritual freedom and the highest spiritual experience, we must not surrender com- pletely to religious dogma or its agents. No matter how well given, directions are no substitute for the destination: in the words of the Zen masters, we must not mistake the finger pointing at the moon for the moon itself.

For notes and author contact information, please see website on page 385.

FROM SUCCESS TO SIGNIFICANT CONNECTIONS

CHAPTER 6

The surprising purpose
of evolution

Even more people today have the means to
live but no meaning to live for.

Viktor Frankl

hen Abraham Maslow presented his famous 'Hierarchy of
Needs' in 1954,[63] we were shown several broad, successive
steps of personal development, culminating in the highpoint Maslow called 'self-actualization'. He said the process begins with
basic 'deficiency' needs that we *must* have answered to survive – needs
such as air, water, food and sleep. According to Maslow, once we judge
these needs to have been sufficiently met, we then are free to go on and
satisfy our needs for safety, love, recognition and esteem; with these
satisfied, only then are we free to look to fulfilling our personal best –
our self-actualization needs.

However, Maslow's broad design does not sufficiently account for
why, within the same community, some people aspire no further than the
lower survival needs and are even happy to dedicate themselves to greed
as their life's work, while others choose to remain dollar poor without com-
plaint, dedicating themselves to anonymous selflessness and charitable
giving. Conversely, Maslow's model also offers no explanation for why some
of the poor in a community prey on one another while others, equally poor,
refrain from predatory behaviour, or carry a higher sense of morality, social
values and personal ethics. These variations within any community are well

explained if we consider something the human potential movement broadly calls 'spiritual development'. These are tendencies in personal evolution towards other-person-centredness and selflessness, accompanied by levels of consciousness indifferent to wealth, social position or work status. Without this 'breakthrough consciousness', Maslow's model remains ego driven and ultimately absorbed by self.

Complete spiritual development of the human species can be accounted for only by an additional hierarchy within Maslow's model, a spiritual perspective that traces the path of an individual as they move steadily through the limited consciousness of ego, ultimately opening up into a more significant and ego-free, selfless awareness: breakthrough consciousness. In the upper stages of the spiritual hierarchy, this transformational experience engages the complete range of connections and networks that structure life, consciousness, the cosmos and creation.

Life as a whole is evolving increasing complexity. Intelligence and consciousness have emerged and appear to be advancing. Spiritual evolution, like all evolution, is a work in progress. It's already underway; all we have to do is continue steering ourselves in the right direction. Biological life has so far survived several emergencies on its way from the simplest bacteria through to human consciousness and our more recent large-scale, complex societies. Somewhere in this process, the human psyche has evolved from a biological consciousness solely aware of the *external* world to a spiritual consciousness increasingly aware of the *internal*. Now another major transition is underway, involving a spiritual awakening where we connect to a conscious experience *beyond* all the limitations of ego and the brain's early construction of a separate self-identity through which we frame our experience of reality.

This is life's yearning and the direction or 'purpose' of evolution: the early quest for consciousness and the later development of higher consciousness – culminating in the awareness and experience of the infinite whole within which life is a part. This is mature spiritual awareness.

The first step in expanding our personal spiritual capacity is to evaluate what mechanisms will help us achieve our goal, which is the spiritual experience of our highest (or least common) connections. In order to do so, we first need to consider what it is that we are evolving *from*. If evolution is merely a physical survival mechanism, then there is no more purpose to life in any form than just staying alive. Yet many of us feel, whether intuitively or on the basis of our religious or spiritual beliefs, that there is more to life than this. Many wonder whether the mechanical nature of cause and effect – applied in evolutionary theory through processes of natural selection – is sufficient to explain the workings of choice. We will see that there is more to the evolution of co-operation than simply making competition more efficient and the law of the jungle more effective.

What, then, could provide life's extra impetus? What could provide the collective force needed to create our sense of purpose? What could be moving life forward and driving evolution, if in fact life is evolving *into* anything? In this chapter I argue that the process of evolution is only partially understood if we apply and measure it primarily at the species level. Here I will show that life is evolving as one dynamic, interconnected whole; evolution applies to the collective *whole* of life, functioning as one overarching and integrated system, more than it does to any one species or sub-species, and that while all species continue to come and go, life as a whole continues to evolve steadily. Moreover, we can find indications that *the process of evolution itself* is evolving beyond life's initial need for single and competitive 'survival of the fittest'. Within the human species, while each individual comes and goes, our consciousness collectively evolves as ideas and experiences transfer from mind to mind, supported (as we will see) by the dynamic intermingling and exchange of genes across life's entire gene-pool.

The standard view of evolution sees the winding biological progression from simple molecule to complex organism as having little purpose or direction beyond survival, with the development of complex intelligence just one more evolutionary variation upon an ultimately pointless theme: survival simply because you can! Yet something crucial seems to be missing from this standard model of evolution, a lack not answered by faith-fuelled creationism or other popular alternatives. This chapter lays bare the missing links. Darwin's theory (and modern variations such as 'genetic drift', affecting whole species) states that changes within a species are purely opportunistic, never designed or chosen. This is random selection – in effect, selection by default, where particular changes occur because all the other possibilities that also appeared at random worked less well for survival.[64]* Any change in food, environment or predation brings a wild spray of different circumstances to which all members of an affected species must adapt.

Darwin's model of evolution includes the observation that each species adapts and evolves against a background environment that influences changes in that species. What Darwinism misses is that a species and its environment also evolve *together*, that each is changed *by* the other while changing *with* the other. The standard Darwinian model also misses the ability of a species to *contribute directly to its own evolution*, wherein the many changes a species makes to its niche environment 'feed back' over time to dictate evolutionary changes within the species.[65] Some 'foundation' species even make life easier for other species within that particular ecosystem by (unconsciously) creating a supportive environment for all their neighbours living there.[66] This intimate co-connection between a species and its surroundings modifies some of the standard natural selection pressures, making the environmental link a major participant in the whole process of evolution.

What is important here is that life and the environment in which it develops are not separate, as if one was the cause and the other the separate effect. They are in a continuous symbiotic relationship in which each evolves the other, with the environment as much affected by life as life is affected by the environment. For example, according to the findings of Minik Rosing of the Nordic Centre for Earth Evolution at the University of Copenhagen, Denmark, the existence of granite in the environment is best explained by the early involvement of photosynthetic bacteria.[67]** By overlooking this most fundamental symbiotic relationship on the planet – the co-creation of environment and species *through* one another – the

---

* In any discussion of evolution, the use of the word 'selection' in 'natural selection' inadvertently implies choice and intelligence, though apparently Darwin's intention was not to support any process of intelligent selection. Instead he was identifying a process of elimination, where only the strongest and fittest remained rather than were specifically selected. The expression 'survival of the fittest' did not originate from Darwin's work, having appeared in the earlier writing of Herbert Spencer on evolutionary philosophy.

** Even though all the ingredients for granite existed since the Earth's formation, these ingredients only formed into granite once photosynthetic life appeared, implying that life was necessary to effect this transformation.

basic Darwinian model has missed the central importance of this key evolutionary step: the evolution of systems rather than components; the evolution of holism through the evolution of connections, networks and processes.

Biologists in general say that evolution (as natural selection) is a slow-working process primarily operating at the level of genes, from where changes (as mutations) are reflected up through species, rather than at the level of behaviour in groups and populations and reflected down to genes. But groups and behaviour play a crucial role in the success or failure of any gene. It is the behaviour of groups – breeding, herding, and so on – that facilitates the transfer of most emergent genes and genetic mutations. Indeed, genetic mutations are now known to *arise* from individual behaviour, such as where smoking in one generation has been found to lead to obesity in another, and hunger in one grandparent leading to longer life in their grandchildren.[68] Individual behaviour in any population is what allows ongoing genetic transfer and replication to occur, expressly giving genes their velocity of opportunity. For example, the behaviour of ancestors, accumulated in the genes of the progeny, allows many captivity-raised birds to build the nest appropriate to their species without ever having seen an original. Not only do genes 'remember' the behaviour of a group so as to progressively inform behaviour across the species, but genes themselves also cross species *boundaries*. The science of genetics now offers proof positive for evolution's cross-connectedness: for example, in addition to the universal core of about 60 genes shared in common by every living thing, only 1 per cent of human genes are uniquely human. What's more, while we humans share about 98 per cent of our genes with chimpanzees, we are also closely related to mice and have only 30 per cent more genes than a worm and twice as many as a fly! We might think we are special, yet more than 40 per cent of our (approximately) 30,000 genes are shared with a banana. As everyone shares 270 of the 300 uniquely human genes, this leaves only about 30 genes (proteins notwithstanding) that are both uniquely within the human gene pool, yet not shared by everyone (and widespread enough to have been identified). Also, though many biologists believe that species become permanently separated by the gradual accumulation of many small genetic changes, only a few genes are actually needed to keep species apart, *or recombine them*.[69] And as for genetic change being a slow process, studies with mice in British Colombia have shown that a genetic change brought about in just one generation can be made to immediately cross the reproductive line into the next generation.[70] Life is one fully integrated, constantly swirling gene pool.

Whatever links we see woven through evolution as life adapts and changes, not all successful selections are random in design; at least some are influenced by intelligence and choice. For example, dog-breeders and bird-fanciers can 'design' observable changes into different breeds. This is one example of evolution being affected *from within* by an intelligent choice made between viable options.[71] Intelligent choice also affects human evolution; for example, the growing field of gene therapy allows the possibility of curing previously untreatable diseases, completely eradicating them by taking them out of the gene pool. Equally profound would be the choice to selectively steer the evolution of human nature away from our impulse towards selfishness and aggression, and support nature's emerging momentum towards compassion, wisdom and true altruism.

The question being asked here, therefore, is whether evolution is more than just a biological assembly-line, a mindless progression from the amoeba to the astronaut. The odds *against* lifeless chance alone being responsible for arranging the trillions of finely balanced chemical reactions within complex life are of orders of magnitude greater than forensic experts are required to apply to DNA sampling in a court of law. The accelerating complexity of life since evolution began suggests some kind of momentum, some drive, as if life as a whole carries a direction rather than being bounced along by the variables of random selection. As we shall see, there is something missing from the standard evolutionary explanation that would account for this anomaly.

The immediate problem encountered by evolution's standard model is life's capacity for choice. The very existence of this ability makes null and void the mathematics of random chance within evolution. Many modern evolutionists today are looking *beyond* orthodox genetic selection and 'selfish genes'[72] to explain all the inherited characteristics, changes and transferences occurring within our genetic framework. If choice exists anywhere in life, even with genetic or other biological controls, evolution cannot be completely random. Chance cannot emerge from choice. Darwinian insights on the randomness of natural selection are, by themselves, simply too 'mechanistic' to explain the increasingly complex structures, functions and strategies of higher organisms in all their aspects. Already we know that society and culture transfer behavioural patterns through individuals from generation to generation. Significantly, in 2005, US researchers discovered that exposure to two pesticides in one generation affected reproduction across the next four generations;[73] this is the first documented example of inherited effects being caused by something other than random genetic mutation and favoured selection. In this case, the intelligent choice of the first generation to use the pesticide has featured in the unforeseen genetic changes in the later generations.

Beyond the 'intelligent design' alternative to Darwinian evolution put forward by creationists (who say that 'God' did it), there is another option: evolutionary changes driven by intelligence arising from *within* the design. This intelligence shows up as intelligent *choice* – the ability of life to create change rather than change merely being delivered through external (including godly) dictate. Intelligent choice is crucially different from intelligent design, which holds that God or some other singular entity dictated life's forms as fixed templates. There is no evidence offered within evolution that requires a supernatural designer to do the work. Just because there was creation doesn't mean a being did it; the development of complex intelligence is not proof of any godly participation in the process of evolution. Choice indicates intelligence, and if we take a moment to watch, we can easily see examples of intelligent, individual choices being expressed in response to circumstances: from the flourish of a bird taking wing to the grace of a dolphin's dive, choice is everywhere.

And, of course, this observation also serves to remind us that intelligence is not confined to humans – in fact, some other species are even capable of advanced abstract thought. (Intelligence and consciousness are quite common in the gene-pool.[74]) For example, we now know that dolphins and rhesus monkeys are able to register 'unsure' as a correct choice when classifying objects into categories of 'yes', 'no' and 'unsure'. This ability shows them to be not only intelligent but also capable of reflective, considered thinking.[75]

However, as weird as it may seem, there *is* evidence that we live in a universe where intelligence is not only seeded from inside living, individual structures (such as your body), but is also entangled around and *outside* any given structure, as we will see later in this book. Even stranger, intelligent choices may occur way down at the cellular level within species. For example, research on the surface tension of living cells indicates that prior to any predicted event about to occur in a cell, there is a change in what is called the (electrostatic) surface tension of the cell. This change in surface tension precedes any detectable change in cellular activity as the cell registers what can only be described as its 'intention' to change in those moments before any chemistry of change begins. And it follows that if a cell can show intention, it must also have intelligence.

So where is a cell's intelligence stored? How small do we have to go to dig up this thing called intelligence? Our search must go deeper than the cell, because cells – which provide the basic structure of life – are made up of other ingredients, mainly sugars. Yet we know that sugar is not intelligent, so intelligence cannot be contained within sugar. The only other alternative is that intelligence is not contained at all; it is not 'in' anything.

In other words, while affecting and infiltrating all the structures that define life itself, intelligence is not constrained within those structures. Intelligence is not some *thing* that is contained within us, but something that we access. However, this is still not fuel for the creationist argument. Just because intelligence is not located in a physical structure such as a cell or a brain, and just because our increasing intelligence is accompanied by an expanding awareness of the spiritual, does not mean that universal intelligence needs to be personified in a divine being. Creationists say, in effect, that God 'plugged in' the different pieces of each creature, and presumably plugged in a soul and special intelligence to humans while denying these to other creatures. (Presumably this same God also plugged in the worm in West Africa that lives exclusively in the human eye and drives its victims blind.[76]) There is no reason why the intelligence that is intrinsic to all life could not have evolved into complex intelligence as complex life evolved, to eventually create our human consciousness without the assistance of a divine being. However, an intelligent understanding of holism and an experience of it – a sense of what it is we exist within, *as seen from the outside while remaining within it* – might be expected to accompany, organize and maintain complexity.

Incontestable evidence has been found that culture – the public sharing of special skills, behaviours, ideas and beliefs – not only promotes intelligence but, over time, also favours the evolution of greater and greater intelligence within more strongly bonded and more extensively connected populations.* Greater intelligence selects for stronger groups, and stronger connections between groups, which in turn select for even greater intelligence, driving a spiral of evolution that sees more intelligence attracting an ever greater complex of connections. Intelligence makes intelligent connections.

Scientific determinism asserts that while humans have evolved unprecedented intelligence, we are still ultimately moulded by primitive forces of random evolutionary change. These evolutionary forces have strongly influenced the survival of all species during changes to environment, predatory attacks and so on. However, intelligent choice and intelligence *within* design (*not* the creationist's intelligent design) show that while evolution gives us the cards, it is intelligence and choice that ultimately decide how the game of life is played out moment by moment.

When considering the influence of any individual within a species on the process of evolution, it is more helpful to look at choice and self-control than at free will. Earlier I mentioned Benjamin Libet's work showing that any conscious decision we make comes *after* our brain has already begun the process of making the decision (*see* page 44). This means that the conscious self is not the actual creative point at which our decisions begin – a fact that undermines any notion of conscious free will in the individual. Also, we can quickly see that the will *cannot* be completely free and beyond the reach of external affects – every single thing in existence comes about as an accumulation of contributory causes and influences. This means that no choice or decision we make is ever entirely free; we are always confined by the limitations of our mental preconditioning, the restrictions of our physiology and the constraints of our environment. In this sense, there is no such thing as complete freedom and absolutely free will – any expression of choice (in the form of a decision) is immediately limited by the laws of the physical world. And not every act of choice needs

---

* The capacity of intelligence to arrange structures of increasing complexity can also be seen in wild nature today. In the Kluet swamps of Sumatra, orang-utans gather in great numbers to teach each other the arts of tool making, tool use, jumping games, blowing kisses to extended-family members, and a range of other social skills (*Scientific American*, April 2006).

to be made 'consciously'. While the moth chooses either to land and become unintentionally concealed, or to fly on and inadvertently catch the hungry eye of a passing bird, there is no need for the choice of either the moth or the bird to be made 'consciously' in any human-centric use of the word. Other lives may have a 'little' consciousness, but a consciousness it is, and choices that begin in this little consciousness can be identified in many species. The point is that life in general has evolved the collective ability to make intelligent choices, and there is no need to address the impossible question of free will.

And there is one final point to be made regarding the complete explanation of evolution. The traditional and incomplete theory of evolution explains well the mechanisms for how life evolves once life exists, but leaves us none the wiser about how or why life came to exist in the first place, and continues to exist today. Darwinian reasoning explains only a process of interactive change and how we have adapted for survival and growth (by overcoming or distancing from threats and accessing rewards) once life was under way. Darwinism takes no account of how life began – original genesis – or the necessity that at its very beginning, life must have been both *spontaneous* and *instantaneous*, because that's what 'being first' means: something appearing from nowhere, spontaneously, in the first instance. In bypassing the greater issue (the origin of life) to look at the lesser origin (the origin of species) Darwinism concentrates on the mechanics of adaptation while sidelining the origins of intelligence and choice, and the original forces of genesis and creativity. These original forces are still afoot in the world today.

We have evolved from the one and simple cell into the complex, the social and the many; now we are evolving from the complex and the many into the whole.
Author

As life has evolved to become more complex, it has developed from a supremely competitive 'every individual for itself' approach into a strategy that drives an unfathomably complex, cooperative, interconnected system of networks. Not only can this interlinked complexity be seen *within* animal biology across most levels of life, it is also present in life's *external* interactions, from the social networking of ants and bees to the emotional, intellectual and technological complexity that defines human life. Although evolution's early function was apparently to create the strongest individual, we can now see that its overarching focus has always been something more exciting: an impetus towards interlinked systems and, ultimately, conscious, mega-scale, unlimited holistic networks.

At present, evolutionary theory is incomplete, not having fully grasped the implications of this thrust towards holism without end. The meaning of the term 'survival of the fittest' now needs to include survival of the most deeply networked, consciously aware and wholly connected.

Our personal boundaries become blurred when we realize that identical genes and proteins are being shared across many species rather than held exclusively, while some genes are not shared by all members within a species. This is one reason why physical appearance – which provides the most obvious line of separation between species – is becoming less and less important as a way of identifying evolutionary changes and the roots of individual behaviour; the scientific focus has shifted to the microscopic study of proteins *within* genes. We need to break free of our old view of evolution that sees the differentiation of species as all-important. Species die out but genes transfer and live on; life lives as a whole and continues to evolve as a whole. We are each part of a bigger living picture, and can choose to continue with the limited view of ourselves as separate individuals, or expand our viewpoint to one that also sees a fundamentally unified universe in which each of us is an integrated part of the total, living environment around us.

This is also true of our health. Individual life and the contact environment are as inseparable from each other as our lungs are from air; content and context intermingle and merge as intimately as breathing. Our personal health depends on the health of the whole around us; our lungs are only as healthy as the air we breathe, and our personal wellbeing only as secure as the social environment we live in. And remember that the whole around us – which from beginning to end is an energy field – has two aspects: one created and 'physical', the other original and infinitely energetic. If we extend the meaning and definition of health into this whole and go beyond individual or personal health to *'whole-health'* (the health of the whole in which we exist and upon which we depend), we widen the focus of evolution to include these subtler networks of interconnectivity that support the creation of whole-health. To this end, we can view the ongoing process of evolution as progressing to interlink life beyond the *physical* environment, all the way into the unseen environment.

The emerging vehicle for this subtle yet advanced interconnectivity is consciousness, and we humans have evolved a lot of it. It is this holistic 'upshift' now engaging evolution directly in the higher connections that we translate as human spirituality and our mind's search for the meaning of life. The natural beauty that can result from evolution's primary process of random mutation and selective pressures – the miracle of a butterfly's wing, the magic of the human brain or the mystery of the lotus leaf's self-cleaning process – are related and informed through a common theme, if not a common purpose: to create whole-health. Each species evolves to fill a niche within a greater whole so neatly that not only can the removal of a key species cause a collapse of the surrounding environment, but any attempt to reintroduce a vanished species to its previous environment often fails because the 'gap' or niche it once created and filled has disappeared, making its original environment hostile to the reintroduced species. In fact, the 'whole' has evolved and moved on. The imperative of holism to be healthy and complete ultimately determines species diversity; any species survives and evolves only as long as its connections serve the multi-level matrix of holism.

Mere survival requires only adaptation to our immediate contact environment whereas, by definition, holistic health requires integration into the *total* environmental context, including by logical extension the original, unseen, infinite territory. Health is invisible; only disease remains identifiable. People, nature and life are all creative, with health the ultimate creative achievement. Like creative people, nature solves problems creatively (by spontaneously creating mutant genes that are then selected for or against) while also producing a swarm of changes that neither help nor hinder, such as the useless patterns on some deep-dwelling shells that never see the light of day.

As life developed into three domains – archaea, bacteria and eukaryotes (we animals are among the eukaryotes) – communication (information transfer) became more complex than, for example, a simple amoeba's mechanical reflex. Genes began to reflect choices – where we chose to hunt, whom we hunted with and what changing environments we chose to wander into. Along the way much of the original genetic record evaporated from the evolving gene pool, as life's many organisms progressively adapted to new conditions and discarded genetic material that had been superseded.[77] As a result, today's living species are an assortment of intermingled genes from different evolutionary sources and influences. Whatever the power may or may not be that propels life and its evolution, life is an intermingled, interchanging, dynamic and evolving whole. Not only are genes passed down *through* generations, some species such as bacteria can actually pass genes between members of the *same* generation.* Either way, what is attracting the transfer at that cellular level? What is choosing the genetic changeover? What power, field, force or energy is working to bias living existence beyond the purely mechanical and allow the novelty of choice?

Our brain has evolved faster than perhaps any other organ of any animal in history. After taking hundreds of millions of years to create the 400cc brain of our early ancestors, it has taken only the last four million years for the brain almost to quadruple in size. Much of the increase in brain size has happened in the last 600,000 years, indicating that our

---

* Bacteria and other pathogens – the microbes that cause disease – have the ability to share genes 'horizontally' within one generation through the pathosphere. The pathosphere is the growing gene-pool in which pathogens mix and mingle worldwide. This genetic trading-floor blurs the distinction between microbiological species, (*New Scientist*, 8 October 2005). Also, research by Robert Pruitt of Purdue University in Lafayette, Indiana (*New Scientist*, 26 March 2005), shows that genes can jump generations by utilizing 'templates' stored in RNA.

brain has been growing 300 times faster than before. Even though this is also the period when our extended social communications began to develop, there was no corresponding change in evolutionary influences such as predators, food and other environmental factors to drive the change. Yet something has promoted the accelerated size of our brain and its highly interconnected neural networks. There has even been a growth spurt in the number of genes being selected for: more than 2 per cent of the genes in the human genome (about 700 of a total of about 30,000) have been selected for in the last 10,000 years.[78] Our lives are on the move!

As we saw earlier, the Darwinian theory of random natural selection is too simplistic to account for either the physically complex structures of higher organisms in general, or the 'recent' exponential acceleration in the complexity of our brain. Pure chance is just too slow for advanced evolution. And while we have said that we cannot assume a divine being is doing it, something appears to be at work.

All the parts of each form must have a relation to each other and to the whole; and the whole itself must have a relation to the other parts of the universe.
David Hume

Neither of the two conventional reasons given for evolution – survival of the fittest, or favouring relatives ('kin selection') – explains all the behaviour we are now seeing in life's shared gene-pool. The fundamental selfishness of the Me-Me gene, either crude and blatant or cleverly disguised, fails to explain some of what we see. There is new evidence emerging that goes directly to the heart of holism and suggests our traditional view of evolution has been too limited by far.

The traditional view of altruism (the care and regard for the welfare of others, often to the altruist's personal disadvantage) has now been documented in many species, including the great apes, some birds, many fish and almost all insect colonies.[79] Hamilton's rule, which provides the traditional benchmark equation for the study of altruism, concludes that altruism is ultimately self-serving, and of course most successful when passed on genetically amongst blood relatives within a species.[80] A highly evolved example of 'reciprocal' altruism – you scratch my back and I'll scratch yours – is found in the Arabian Babbler. A small bird of unassuming appearance, the Babbler seems to place the highest social status on generosity, with the birds falling over one another to do a good turn for a neighbour, including grooming and feeding each other.[81] But this biological view limits altruism to being self-interested and species-specific; an altruist's behaviour does offer an advantage to the selfish (in that the altruist will look after the selfish individual), making the altruist attractive to the selfish, if only for selfish reasons.

However, the key to the emergence of altruism as a dominant momentum within evolution (rather than merely having a support role) is the discovery that altruists have a strong weapon at their disposal: a sense of justice is evolving in many species, and is big in the animal world (as we will see below). This sense of justice and injustice is observed as specific behaviour in the species involved, and is almost certain to be expressed more by the altruist than the selfish on behalf of other individuals. This group justice is supported by anger – evolution's single most important emotion, and used to force a contribution from the selfish free-loader to the group.[82] Armed with this, an altruist ceases to be a pushover. As the development of our consciousness progresses and we evolve the holistic outlook, we realize that acts of altruism can benefit a whole *group* of individuals while at the same time resulting in incidental disadvantage to one or more individuals within the group.

A sense of justice features as an aspect of whole health, helping to balance survival of the individual with protection of the whole, and several species have been seen responding to perceived injustice and unfairness suffered by others. This is an understandable development in a healthy group, requiring the participation of every member to ensure no one is being unfairly disadvantaged or favoured. In a study at the Northwestern University Medical School in Illinois, for example, a Rhesus monkey was observed *not* taking food so that another monkey would avoid an electric shock.[83] Similarly, rats have been observed *resisting* an action that they knew would cause pain to another rat.[84] In a human study, 62 per cent of participants playing a wealth creation game actually *paid a price themselves* to protect the principle of 'justice and welfare for all' and take away another's wealth if they thought it had been unfairly gained.[85] The study concluded that we will spend our own hard-won money to protect the group from members who behave unfairly, without expecting any of the spoils for ourselves. Choosing to go beyond reciprocity (where good deeds are done, but with the expectation of some gain in return) to incur our own loss while removing another's unjust gain and protecting the larger whole, indicates an advanced spiritual point of view and a step beyond isolated self-interest.

But for altruism to break the bounds of group favouritism it must break the confines of kinship, and that is exactly what seems to be evolving in life's shared gene pool. In an extraordinary study, one group of side-blotched lizards (*Uta Stansburiana*) was found defending another unrelated group against a third group, even when this behaviour gave the first group *no kinship advantage whatsoever*.[86] This was the first of several studies on altruism to break new ground, showing that evolution itself is extending beyond the favouritism seen in kin selection, to embrace new dimensions of collective selection – a state we might call 'super-connectedness'. In particular, the side-blotched lizard study shows how personal advantage and kin relationship are no longer the sole reasons driving evolution across life's genome. Moreover, selfish genes have learned to cooperate within cells and also allow cooperation between cells, with a gene having been found for that.[87] With genes being shared extensively throughout the gene pool, the altruism genie is out of the bottle and advancing across life's landscape.

There are also many cases where altruism has been witnessed in the overt behaviour between different species: elephants attempting to save a baby rhino from death in a muddy quagmire; a gorilla rescuing a little child who had fallen into the gorilla's zoo enclosure; dolphins assisting human swimmers in danger of shark attack; pelicans banding together to protect a heron from attack; and humans caring for any number of unrelated species. Though the evolution of altruism may well have begun as a support to both individual and group survival (by helping the wounded return to health and so re-strengthen the tribe),[88] it has now genetically superseded the boundaries of kin, entered the genepool and used behaviour to cross the species barrier; by this combination of genetic and behavioural modification, and with only a few genes keeping species apart, altruism is evolving to serve the complex whole of life.[89]

Although some naturalists have claimed that there can be no true altruism in nature because the self-sacrificing altruists would eventually die out, this position makes the false assumption that altruism is necessarily and always self-sacrificing. It assumes that there is a choice to be made between self-sacrifice (altruism) and survival, whereas care for the welfare of others does not have to mean self-sacrifice, even though the altruist is willing to pay that price – quite the reverse in fact. In altruism, self-survival is incidental – the altruist may or may not survive, but their survival or otherwise is beside the point.

Rather than being a conscious act of self-sacrifice, the altruistic impulse is a significant moment of transformation for that individual, an instant in which the very distinction between them and the other dissolves, and the altruist's individuality becomes incidental. At that very instant when any sense of individuality disappears, all that is relevant to the altruist is the whole (or group), with their own survival merely an incidental benefit in the process.

Individual acts of altruism have had a cumulative positive influence across our species. At present, every privilege and advance that we enjoy in our world today is built on the back of the anonymous and selfless contributions, gifts and insights of millions of others who came before us. Women, racial minorities and indeed whole populations can work and function today in freedom and equality not only because of the enormous personal sacrifices made by those famous few acknowledged by history, but also because of every individual who, abandoning self in a moment of transcendence, overcame the constrictions of tradition, prejudice and injustice to ensure the welfare of society as a whole. No matter how unpopular or even heretical their ideas might have been, the wiser amongst our ancestors saw how the whole of society is enriched by the participation of all and diminished by the exclusion of any. And the wisest of these insightful minds went even further, seeing that our living connections don't stop on the outskirts of our species – that uninterrupted altruism fortifies life as a unified and balanced whole.

This principle of enlightened altruism applies beyond small groups, particular societies or even individual species, and is involved in the evolution of life as a complex and uninterrupted whole. In the beginning, the bonding of individuals into groups of increasing complexity is ensured by the imperative of survival, since the strength of the group derives from both its size and the durability of the bonds linking its individual members. However, now the imperative has changed. As we have seen above, the momentum now extends beyond the drive for greater inclusivity *within* any particular group or species, to an emphasis on diminished exclusivity *beyond* a group or species. The fewer hostile 'others' that are left outside to pose a threat to the group, the more inclusive and stronger the group becomes, and therefore the better its chance to thrive as an intact unit.

As a result, enlightened altruism is selected for, since its existence ensures more alliances that extend the survival of the group. To paraphrase traditional Buddhism, no one is safe until there is not one single, solitary, unhappy life.

From this it follows that the highpoint of evolution is the creation of holism. Through the 'true' altruism of its individuals, the group's collective or social consciousness will be favoured to evolve beyond its early boundaries, becoming ever more inclusive. Unrestrained, this spirit of inclusion will continue to grow, making any distinction between individuals ever more irrelevant. At this point we are no longer threatened by outsiders, and everything is acknowledged as existing within the whole, even while individual integrity is maintained. This 'generosity' is already found in the fluid world of genetics, where almost all genes are in constant transference and shared across many branches of life. With several altruism genes already identified in life's interlinked gene pool, the survival of any specific individual, group or even species is no longer a sufficient end in itself.

Life is not a mechanism but a phenomenon. While evolution includes the evolution of influence – the transference that occurs between what is called an 'actor' and 'reactor', often involving the transfer of information – evolution also involves the activation of ever more complex connections to allow this transfer of influence. Life is more than the sum of its spectacular formations, more than its component parts. All of life is an irreducible and interconnected whole, undivided by the ephemeral structures of species.

Evolution is now transcending the purely selfish gene – the 'MeMe' gene' – and effectively stepping beyond cooperative-competitive socializing behaviour to enter the dimension of the truly selfless. This selfless aspect – often seen in human behaviour, as well as in other species – displays the existence of some awareness beyond automatic self-survival. Emerging selflessness within our own species shows us that consciousness itself is evolving an appreciation of the whole beyond the short-sightedness of any self-absorbed individual, or the opportunism of any one group.

It is because of life's indivisibile unity that holistic evolution can be witnessed: life has maintained and progressed the link between the individual and the whole – from the cell to the organ, from the organ to the individual animal, from the animal to the social group. The changes we are seeing in evolution show that we need to shift our focus from the function of the separate parts to the integrated workings of the whole. In the four-phase evolutionary process – from simple bacteria, to complex cells, to multicellular organisms, to complex societies – increasing complexity reveals increasing interconnectivity, since something can only grow and become more complex as it makes more connections. Because life is becoming more complex, it follows that interconnectivity (complexity) is being favoured and selected for. And because altruism enhances social complexity, this is another reason that we can reasonably assume that altruism is also being selected for – that life is becoming more complex as part of becoming selfless and holistic. Selflessness exists in evolution as a survival mechanism because in whole-health, *any particular part is healthy only when the whole is healthy.* Altruism does just this; it keeps the whole healthy. Though whole-health is an imperative that exists over and above the survival of any particular individual, altruism selflessly favours the survival of more individuals within any group in the long term, and so of complex society *as a whole.*

When self-interest extended beyond the individual to include the interests of the kinship group, we witnessed the evolution of society. When this became enlightened self-interest and reached beyond the known kinship group to include strangers, we witnessed the development of *civil* society. However, now even this is being transformed and surpassed. We humans are developing the capability of seeing beyond the self-serving reciprocal arrangements of the kinship group and symbiotic relationships where two or more species (such as birds and bees) exist co-dependently. Humanity, more than any other species, is developing a sensitivity to the interests of *all* species. We are active witnesses to the birth of spirituality, the consciousness of holism and the beginning of wisdom.

However, there is nothing to say that spirituality – an individual's search for the experience of the whole that ultimately supports the many – is exclusively human. Spiritual evolution is happening to life as a whole. Humanity may represent spirituality's leading edge, but we should not arrogantly assume that humanity represents its total capacity or momentum. An understanding is growing that all of life is one genetically bonded, mass network, awash with an interchange of shared energy and mutual experience. Empathy and altruism are just two ways of plugging into that linked-up network, of registering a deeper sense of an overarching connectivity running through all levels of life, strong enough to supersede the interests of any individual, group or species.

The conditions and systems supporting life have always been dynamic and complex rather than static and simple. As life has evolved more complex forms, the ecological systems *supporting* complex life have in turn become more complex and finely tuned – everything from pollination cycles to atmospheric gases has to be balanced and constantly maintained. Into this mix has evolved the mystery we call consciousness.

Once life evolved complexities beyond the simple, unconscious, cellular level, consciousness became the missing link to further development and complexity. To create an *internally* complex living organism on evolution's way to creating an *externally* complex organism called a society, the introduction of consciousness became unavoidable. Many species not only have consciousness but, even more importantly, they also have self-awareness, with great apes, dolphins and elephants able to recognize their own reflections.[90] As we saw in Chapter 4, our five senses provide a connection between our internal workings and the outside world, but this connection can only be completed with consciousness present to interpret the impressions from our senses and thus provide an overall sense of external reality. Societies are made up of connections created between the individual and outside, and those external connections can be fine-tuned through the facility of consciousness and conscious influence. With this being an energetic universe rather than a material one, the evolution of influence can be seen as part of the evolution of systems needing to transfer energy through an increasingly complex whole. Consciousness is a clearinghouse through which energy can be responded to, its transference arranged and its influence fine-tuned between actor and reactor.

What's more, if the evolution of consciousness was inevitable, the development of intelligent choice was even more so, as intelligent choice is what allows the conscious to readily recognize changing circumstances in a complex reality, and to design successful and timely responses. Today, different levels of consciousness – from super-consciousness to sub-consciousness and group consciousness – register different levels of energetic reality. If we had none of our senses, reality-consciousness would be travelling blind and must inevitably break down, because our senses provide the bridge between internal and external reality, between what goes on inside our head and what is happening outside it.[91] On the other hand, if we are restricted to *only* our five senses for information, consciousness is limited to the material world of physical concerns. Remember, there is more to reality than meets the eye.

As we have seen, genes – the information library and building blocks of life – are shared across species, and very few genes are exclusive. We all need selfish genes, but evidence is mounting for the existence of a number of *truly unselfish* genes – perhaps compassion genes, altruism genes, creativity genes, spiritual intelligence or 'God-sensitive' genes, and a range of other genes that favour *connectedness*.[92] Genes for altruism have already been found, allowing cells to cooperate and live together.[93] This is what has allowed cells to become complex organisms, and complex organisms such as ours to form communities. If the underlying purpose and meaning of our vision and actions remain singularly selfish, then the potential power available through us is diminished. On the other hand, when our vision draws meaning from beyond our 'self', then we draw from a greater power than we alone can generate. Selflessness creates strength for the unselfish.

Selflessness (and the necessary detachment) begins with the capacity for self-observation and self-awareness. There is a big difference between self-awareness on one hand and selfishness, self-consciousness and self-absorption on the other. Self-absorption reinforces the existence of the separate self, while self-awareness eventually sees beyond the superficial, physical, separate self to a deeper connection with everything in existence.

Just as the leading edge of evolution is becoming sensitive to higher health networks, so too the outer limit of any supposed acts of altruism depends on how far out from our 'self' we set the outer horizon of our sense of separation and distance from 'other' – our spiritual boundary.

And it is our capacity for higher consciousness – the ability to transcend the limitations of the isolated, individual self – that provides the ultimate hope for our continued survival as a species on this planet. If we can bring ourselves to shift our perceptions and change our old, damaging ways of doing things, then we may ultimately preserve both ourselves and the many environments that sustain us. If, on the other hand, we humans fail to rise to our present opportunity as planetary managers, then our uninformed and poorly evolved behaviours will relegate us to geological shale, while the process of evolution elevates another species to the capstone position of spiritual manager in the hierarchy of increasingly complex life. The choice is ours.

We are not human beings having a spiritual experience. We are spiritual beings having a human experience.
Pierre Teilhard de Chardin

The next stage of our evolution is a self-styled spiritual process. Without spiritual evolution, goodness and hope have no meaning. Although spirituality is difficult to define, its impact on our health is beginning to be measured in studies on placebo effects, prayer, meditation and positive thinking, as well as the effects of imagination, expectation, belief and will. Evolution now means going beyond personal health to creating holistic health, embracing the understanding that personal health cannot exist in isolation. Indeed, our physical health is beginning to look like it relies on the conscious activation and interaction of dimly understood networks within our brain and the outside world. These networks are running through our biological processes and the exterior environment in an unbroken continuum, creating a matrix of cascading influences and inter-connected pathways.

Our new, expanded view of evolution includes the evolution of influence. The power of influence is driven by genes and is stored in them. However, influence does not originate within the gene nor end there; it begins and ends with the acts of intelligent choice made across the broad sweep of life's various designs.* With its emerging emphasis on whole-health, evolution is therefore better described as the evolution of balance between the influences of separation and connectedness within the individual, the group and the whole.

This is also the definition of whole-health, which supports individual strength and survival but also means more than that. The survival of any one individual is insufficient to make the group endure, but without the support of the whole the individual can't last long, no matter how healthy they are personally – it's not much use being fit if your environment can't feed and sustain you. Wholeness is therefore our most strategic protector, and in its breakdown we have an early warning indicator that we are no longer healthy. Meanwhile, while physical strength and personal fitness will always be imperative for survival, we are now discovering that both are last-lines-of-defence: bodyguards that protect but do not define the whole.

Once evolutionary processes have filled each niche in a food-chain and a support-environment, a basic stability is reached. This evolutionary attainment of safety and security describes the first level of Maslow's hierarchy of needs. When this has been attained, life can freely evolve to the next level – achieving status and standing within life's pecking order. But life on this planet remains precarious, and a repeat of any one of the cataclysmic events that have caused the five mass extinctions to date – such as an asteroid strike or massive volcanic eruption – would almost certainly plunge life and evolution back to the base level of individual safety and survival.

---

* A sense of beauty is now part of the selection process for health in the gene pool. Females of many bird species choose males with the brightest and most attractive feathers. These colourful males are known to carry other biologically healthy qualities that are transferable to his offspring. Similarly, in the human population, women admire and choose the sweat of the man most compatible with her immune system to produce the healthiest children. We also know that day-old infants prefer to spend more time looking at an 'attractive' face than at an 'ugly' one. Beauty has become an inborn sense, genetically secured, and through beauty and attractiveness, life is advancing towards greater health.

We are on the edge of just such a cataclysm right now. Although the present ecological arrangements have positioned humans at the top of the food-chain, we have not lived up to the position's full potential. Instead of acting with wise restraint in this role, we have exploited it so recklessly that human activity has placed life at a turning point. Without an upgrade in outlook and a corresponding change in collective behaviour, the next two decades will trigger events that quickly lead to an irreversible deterioration in the quality of life for all. Global warming, climate change and other human-caused threats will upset the ecological balance and risk a relapse into the primal state of fear and the ordeal of daily survival. If we allow this to happen it will mean that through a lack of our spiritual maturity, life will have failed to achieve its current potential for higher balance and holism. On the other hand, our species can still opt to consciously engage the esoteric networks and connections that elevate spiritual practice into a fully developed spiritual maturity. There is still time to choose between separation and connection, or what religion broadly calls the devil and the divine.

We need to remember that our position at the top of the evolutionary tree is not genetically assured: what we think of as characteristically human and special qualities are in fact genetically shared across many other species. This means that we have no monopoly on significance. Gene research is showing that humankind has little hold on any claim to be the eternally chosen ones, divinely immune from the consequences of our earthly actions. Even our famous accelerated intelligence (with our accelerated brain size) is not evenly spread across humanity. For instance, it is now known that there are variants of at least two genes that indicate for intelligence, but not everyone has them yet – and, if the track record of gene transfer is anything to go by, they may not even remain exclusively ours. Our assumption of permanent genetic superiority is a delusion.

Within this lies an implicit warning: we are dispensable. Evolution's impetus towards holism needs a linch-pin species, without which the harmony of evolution's whole devolves back into its primal competing parts. If we don't fulfil this role, another species will surpass us. With consciousness, abstract reasoning, altruism and a sense of justice emerging in other species in the collective gene-pool, we might be witnessing a sense of goodness evolving to support the health of the whole. Evolution is indifferent to the survival of any one particular species; humanity can get shuffled off at a moment's notice if our behaviour places the whole at risk. If we remain a source of infection, the wound we cause will close over and eliminate us like just so much harmful bacteria.

The development of human consciousness is evolution's crowning achievement so far. It has allowed evolution's path to become conscious choice; we have emerged as the vehicle that carries evolution forward on its inexorable process towards wholeness. With our special form of intelligence, we are becoming capable of remarkable things, even being able to control life's genetic building blocks and the vital proteins within them. However, as with any knowledge applied in the absence of wisdom, the danger of possessing technological intelligence without spiritual intelligence is that when we don't take the *whole view* into account, we make mistakes, with long-term negative effects outweighing short-term benefits – though the benefits often appear to be many at first. For example, we already eat cold-resistant tomatoes that incorporate anti-freeze genes transferred from fish, and super high-protein mould-resistant grains. Developments in stem-cell therapy, cloning and targeted treatments for specific ailments are producing body spare-parts, human tissue factories and the possibility of designer babies with pre-selected characteristics such as high I.Q. or athletic or artistic talent. However, with our misguided use of the powers of conscious choice – the very thing that put us at the top of the evolutionary tree – we are capable of causing untold damage. Our present outlook neglects to assess the complex surge of downstream effects released by our heightened intelligence, an intelligence that has designed a global economy of increasingly rapacious, even suicidal over-consumption.

It is worth repeating that if we continue causing disruption to the whole, evolution won't tolerate it. If we cannot learn that life requires more of us than just benefiting ourselves, and unless we begin to temper our actions with wisdom, we will just become an unexceptional fossil in the sediment of evolution.

Knowledge alone will not be enough to make this the century of healing, nor will action without wisdom. Down through the ages, most of the myths, legends and ancient texts from all cultures have promoted either heroic leadership or the getting of wisdom. Either approach has intended one lesson above all others: only decisions and actions that serve the population, achieve pre-set targets, and avoid disaster and disappointment while encouraging the highest reach in others will bring lasting happiness and prosperity. Without greater wisdom, mere knowledge cannot heal us or the planet we live on. In our ignorance we are well on the way to deconstructing nature's external environment. Ultimately, no one can solve our issues for us; we must liberate ourselves. Our genetic make-up provides the compass, our upbringing sets the compass bearings, and our choices point us towards our destination. Indeed, wherever we are – right here and now – gives us our best opportunity to not only evaluate where we are going wrong (as we have done earlier in this book), but also to uncover what we are already doing right and *keep doing it*. This present moment is the best time for each of us to influence outcomes for the better. There is no guarantee of success or failure, and the risks we presently face are great, but how we fare in the future depends on how each of us decides to act right now – whether we choose to make the positive changes necessary or continue doing more of the same.

If we do decide we want to consciously accelerate our move forward and evolve a better future, it's reassuring to realize that marginal changes in our personal outlook and circumstances – sometimes just a slight shift of emphasis – can in fact make a massive difference. Even evolution itself is becoming increasingly affected by the private and personal choices of all of us. Understanding this is to uncover the path to significant success, since the power-point of all change is now seen to originate within the individual. Our reality-consciousness is a powerful thing, and recognition of this power is the moment of liberation in which we finally stop trying to manipulate the world around us by either adding to something in it, subtracting from it, blindly holding onto some of it or denying the effects of our influence. Once we recognize this power – the power of our own choices – we awaken the possibility of achieving global influence while never leaving our home base. By taking control of the flight-deck we gain free access to all destinations.

CHAPTER 7

When effort becomes effortless

Loyalty to petrified opinion never yet broke a
chain or freed a human soul.

Mark Twain

So now we are ready to accelerate our drive towards spiritual
maturity, but where do we begin? Perhaps the best place is with our
personal preparation programme, because even the most exciting
voyage can disappoint if the traveller is unfit or packs the wrong equipment. Worst of all is to misread the map and misinterpret the directions.

To be proactive about our personal evolution, we need to start with self-observation. Self-observation begins with us seeing ourselves as we are now, up close and personal, looking at what we are doing and how we are doing it. Only then can we hope to match where we are with where we want to be and take corrective action. Self-observation is the ability to observe our actions, attitudes, ideas and influences as they happen, rather than running on reflex. It is only when we can stand back and objectively evaluate our own behaviour without self-congratulation or self-recrimination that we can positively influence our spiritual direction. Indeed, when we do so we soon realize that many of our behavioural traits have evolved from those good old survival tools, namely habit, fear (the avoidance of pain or loss) and our reliance on the other 'negative' emotions such as anger and guilt that have traditionally kept us out of harm's way.

Survival is a competition for energy in which we manipulate the available resources to extract what we need. However, it is our competition for energy – food, resources and support systems – that now puts us most at risk, as we use survival as an excuse to deplete and distort our living and social environments for personal advantage at the expense of all else.

If we can identify the techniques and tools we use to manipulate our way in the world, and recognize how we use them and why, we can better understand the strengths and weaknesses of our position. One technique we use to tame the world around us is to adopt the functions of evaluator, critic and judge. The *evaluator* decides on strengths, weaknesses, opportunities and threats in any situation; here we assess the obstacle course around us and work out who is friend and foe, and what is to be done. The *critic* in us then fine-tunes our evaluation and allocates the mix of emotional energy we need to succeed at what needs to be done. Finally, after we have taken the action we critically evaluated previously, the *judge* in us assesses the outcome, and this allows us to plan our next move.

These three key functions remain vital for our survival, both personally and collectively. In fact, we have become the dominant species by adopting and mastering them. They have allowed us to compartmentalize and manage the risks and rewards of any situation we encounter. Even today, without these powers of discrimination we would perish. However, their effectiveness is restricted to helping with our lower-order needs that support physical survival in a hostile and competitive world. In such a reality, dominance means success, and after judging and critically assessing a situation, we then need 'tools' to apply our view and successfully manipulate the world around us to our advantage and outlook.

Remember that whatever we apply our attention to is instantaneously affected by our mind – we are both physically and psychologically inseparable from our surroundings, as if also using our attention to access reality from the 'inside' in some way. Yet because of how our usual way of looking at the world has evolved, we are unaware of the existing connection available to us; instead, we see everything from the outside, as if at a distance. As a result, the only way we have learned to influence our surroundings is by evolving a set of purely mechanical connections – by adding to or subtracting from something, denying change, or denying whatever our senses have set upon. Most of us habitually make those closest to us – the ones we have easiest access to – pay dearly for our efforts to influence a misbehaving world. We make lovers responsible for our happiness, seek out friends for favours they reluctantly offer, and blame circumstances for our poor behaviour rather than choosing to take responsibility for ourselves. Moving on quickly from moment to moment without reflection, we have little time or inclination to anticipate all repercussions and adjust for them.

These tools are used whenever we compete for energy and influence, which is in every conscious action we take in every waking moment, in some form or other. We attempt to push and pull the surrounding territory to our will by habitually using the four tools in conjunction with the functions of evaluator, critic and judge. This is all done to establish a protective safety-and-support zone around us, and secure the widest possible influence for ourselves – all this in an attempt to gain maximum advantage in this lifelong competition for energy and resources.

But there is an alternative: we no longer have to be competitive if we are creative. Although force is favoured in a largely aggressive world such as ours, and although energy resources are necessary at all times for our basic survival, unbridled force is counterproductive in a creative world, because it is accompanied by unexpected outcomes which undermine results and diminish them. Most of us habitually manipulate for control over energy and use tactics and manoeuvres to cause a desired effect. On the other hand, in those moments when we are freely creative – and we all have such moments, even if they are fleeting, disorganized and often unnoticed – we see beyond old ideas and ways of doing things, and think up new ideas and valuable solutions seemingly 'out of the blue'.

To move on from our present gridlock down at the level of conflicting causes and competing effects, we must first identify some of our most entrenched habits that keep us there, those repeated patterns that keep us from finding true meaning and fulfillment in our lives. Only then can we give up these habits, and move on.

The chains of habit are too weak to be felt until they are too strong to be broken.

Samuel Johnson

At some time, breaking old habits becomes as important to our spiritual progress as fresh air becomes to a drowning swimmer. Habits bind much of our daily behaviour, making each new day easier but more tied to the one before. Almost all of our daily activity is a repeat of the previous day – same thoughts, same actions, same questions, same people, same feelings. Yet to lead a significant life we often need to break old habits. In order to evaluate our behaviour with objectivity (and so ultimately influence and change it) we first need to be aware of which of our behaviours are negative and most easily avoided – the habit patterns we need to identify and break.

From infancy to old age, we use imitation as a mechanism for learning; much of what we think, do and say began as an imitation that became a habit, then stayed on as our reality. However, the action or idea that we imitate had to originate somewhere; an imitator will never achieve anything significant without adding some originality of their own. Original thoughts come to us all, although we don't always recognize them as such or harness them. However, those of us who do are frequently the ones who make a lasting and significant contribution. This could be you, if you allow it. Human advancement has often come from free-thinking non-professionals enthusiastically following their interests and inclinations. Antony van Leeuwenhoek, for example, sold sewing supplies for a living but gave us the microscope. Lazlo Biro was a sculptor and journalist who invented the ballpoint pen. Bill Gates was a university dropout. Enthusiastic amateurs are often more innovative than the 'experts', and more productive – proof that when you follow your creative passion and the natural direction of your insights and interests, anything can be done.

On the other hand, whole cultures can break down and disintegrate simply as a result of accumulated habits and norms. The Easter Islanders, for example, almost certainly met their demise when their social practices and rituals caused them to systematically degrade their once lush

rainforests, resulting in long-term and unsustainable deforestation.*
Hitler's Germany, Stalin's Russia and Mao's China all relied on getting
certain ideas deeply entrenched by forcing large numbers of people to think
and behave identically. These leaders gave their populations behaviours to
mimic – from marching and callisthenics to official languages and slogans
– whose habitual messages became the norm but began as planned indoc-
trination through early childhood propaganda programmes. In all cases,
this stifling of creativity and independent expression resulted in habits of
compliance that ultimately led to a breakdown of culture and society under
their regimes.

The gravitational pull of our habits and conditioning determines our
reality. These habits come to us as messages and meanings beamed up
through history and absorbed through our experiences with family,
friends, community and culture. Through the filter of our five senses and
the focus of our attention we build our stories, and through these stories
our reality is created. What we think of as the 'truth' is the common
assemblage of stories and ideas we adopt as facts – some positive, some
negative, some good, some bad. But these 'truths' are not absolute: today's
facts often become tomorrow's fallacies, just as today's fictions often
become tomorrow's reality. This mutability of 'the truth' is important to
recognize since, while rigid certainties can reassure us, they can also
desensitize us; belief in one right answer risks the blinkered vision that so
often leads to dogma. As opinionated adults bolstered by our accumulation of certainties, we still don't know what we don't know, and risk
setting for the compliance and conformity inherent in many of society's
lesser storylines.

However, our communities also have a strong influence over our spiritual development. Communities are the expression of cooperative
relationships and connections forming as layers of trust and trustworthiness. There is a strong connection between the level of trust and the
velocity of opportunity generated in any community. A community is only

---

* Even if, as is now suggested, it was Polynesian rats brought by the Easter Islanders
themselves that ate the seeds of the trees, broke the pollination cycle and prevented
forest regeneration, this does not change the final result. Sixteen million trees
disappeared between 1200 and 1500. Whatever the cruel impact of later European
slavery and disease, habitual practices had previously destroyed the island
environment.

as strong and as good as the morals, trust and truths told in the greater stories curated by its elders. Without a transfer of knowledge, meanings and beliefs throughout a population, the community's storyline is broken and the population's common connections are lost. Yet in many Western societies where urban tensions swirl and where work is rapidly becoming the overriding reason for living, there is little time for working on a communal storyline that embraces much more than the shared shopping experience.

We imitate much of what we identify with or admire – culturally, linguistically, professionally, politically and emotionally. As well as helping us successfully copy early survival skills, imitation almost certainly was an early step in our *psycho-social* development, as it meant we were able to develop a point of view outside ourselves, a point of view shared by the person we were imitating. On the flipside, imitation undertaken without discrimination becomes mimicry – blind habit without originality or integrity. History records how slaves and other downtrodden have rebelled, only to mimic the habits and sins of their tormentors and become the new oppressors. If we merely imitate we remain followers. By all means copy success to become successful, but don't try to *be* someone else, because then there will be two of them and none of you.

Blind trust is as dangerous as blind habit. Ultimately, *we* are responsible for what we *do* with whatever happens to us, and we must remember that experts are not infallible: economists have predicted every boom and bust that never happened; medical doctors sometimes harm their patients with the wrong medication or treatment;[94] and media misinformation and other manipulated messages are blindly accepted as fact.

We must recognize that our choices are often forged by the groups we are in. Our reference group influences our dress, our speech, our thoughts and our actions; an original thought is rare. Having our own thoughts is difficult enough when we are alone, but rarely do we know our own mind in public. And for most of us, going with the flow means following the drift of the tide. Drifting will not do it, however; only a dead fish forever follows the flow. Spiritually, the true direction for each of us is neither an accident of birth or culture, nor a matter of guesswork; it is forever and finally a matter of *choice*. So choose your friends wisely: our reference group teaches us what to feel and what to believe, what is real and significant. Our choice of reference group helps shape our self-concept, self-esteem and sense of meaning. Seek out like-minded people capable of swimming against the current in your stream. And if you can't, find another stream.

The French philosopher Foucault described five 'enclosures' through which we move from cradle to grave: education (and religion), work, health, the law (including prison) and family. His view was that these enclosures of knowledge and power are almost invincible, their dictates and constraints unavoidable; we are forced into compliance, desensitization and depersonalization.[95] Within the family 'enclosure', for instance, instead of experiencing the greatest sanctuary, support and acceptance, many people find the severest criticisms, cruellest personal attacks, and harshest judgements. Although many families anticipate Christmas with its gifts and supposed goodwill, the reality is that police attend a record number of family disputes during the festive season.

I cannot stress enough that the people we surround ourselves with are the ones that help shape us and give us our direction. Group psychology is as potent and measurable as personal psychology. Indeed, the connections operating within different cultures and communities are evidenced by the way in which some communities collectively display either more negative or more positive and optimistic characteristics than others. Research by American psychologist and happiness expert Ed Deiner and his team shows that Latinos are the happiest (though Scandinavians, and Swedes in particular, rate highest if income is included in the test). As a group, Latinos tend to look at what may go right rather than go wrong; they have a *positive* attitude and outlook. People of Eastern cultures, on the other hand, tend to have a more *negative* outlook.[96]

Some of our habits are poisonous. We eat, drink and smoke poisons but ignore the health warnings. Practice makes *permanent*, not perfect – practise the wrong thing long enough and it becomes *permanently* wrong. Life is a mind-game. We can't have a positive life with a negative mind. If we want to make a significant difference with our life, first we need to recognize our negative mind-states, then consciously replace them with helpful outcomes we desire, and a positive, agreeable predisposition. Practise this again and again and again and again until you are rewired, retrained and realigned. A different world first requires *us* to be different.

The strongest habits can be broken by a stronger need. Mental and physical addictions can and have been broken – even cold-turkey (and in spite of any genetic predisposition). Liberation from the pull of old habits can empower us with new freedoms, new possibilities. Breaking free and overcoming the gravitational pull of our habits is not easy, but it can be done once we have a big enough reason to shift our reality. A big enough reason is what gets anything done. Spiritual liberation cannot be forced or compelled. It only happens when we are convinced that our old way of doing things no longer works for us.

A free man, having no binding fear, thinks of things greater than death. An unfree man, being bound by fear, gives himself only to things less than death.
Spinoza

Among the worst habits are our fears, and almost all our fears are learned. Another step along the path of our evolutionary progress is to understand and acknowledge the role that fear plays in holding us back from our full spiritual potential. On the edge of fear stands courage, and beyond courage sits fearlessness. To become fearless is to become truly free.

Fear is the anticipation of a future event we wish to avoid – fear of loss, of missing out, of being hurt, of being deprived or left incomplete in some way. Fear and hope are both strong mental forces. Each of them is capable of attracting into our reality whatever we picture in that state of mind. In effect, fear is negative goal-setting, leaving us weakened to the extent of our fear and waiting for the trouble we are expecting. Fear happens when we anticipate something we absolutely don't want, and in matters of health it can stop us taking the first step on a guided journey of personal recovery.

The funny thing about fear and worry is that if there is a solution to a concern we may have, then we have no *need* to be fearful and worried. And if there is no solution, then fear and worry are no use to us.

Fear changes our behaviour. Watch a dog barking fearlessly from the safety of a boundary fence. Take away the security of the fence and the dog will behave differently – lose its courage and run, become rigid and roll over with fear, attack, or come forward with tail wagging. Just as with the barking dog, beyond the security of our mental fence-line many possibilities await.

Today fear remains fashionable, encouraged by today's communications. Our brain is evolved to relate to and communicate with a social circle (tribe, village) of approximately 200 people. Originally, this reference group of 200 'locals' accounted for our range of experience for everything that mattered, from beauty and ugliness to our morality, beliefs, hopes and fears. However, with the aid of modern technology, today's global village now gives us a reference group in excess of six billion. Modern media makes us yearn for unattainable beauty as the standard, just as it makes us believe that horrifying events are the norm, whether or not we are likely ever to experience them personally. Our senses, which once gave us our experience, now give us everyone *else's* experience. Every frightful thing now seems close at hand, imminent, local and personal, helping to make depression the first global mental disease. In this climate of dis-ease, politicians parlay power by emphasizing the risk of transnational, misanthropic events. Thus we all suffer post-traumatic stress disorder, not realizing that the news is almost always better than we are encouraged to imagine. In general, human beings are good-natured and well-intentioned; it is fear (and mostly the fear of loss) that brings out the worst in us.

Fear erases hope, just as hope erases fear. When we give up hope, our fears fill the vacant space. Indeed, although the tension between fear and hope is necessary for our survival, it becomes problematic when fear becomes a fixation: driven by fear, our search for safety immobilizes us and keeps us small. Up to a point, fear is necessary, helping us shield ourselves from risks so that we're never caught off guard, but in living this way we risk missing life. Instead, to begin the process of overcoming fear and dispersing it, concentrate on your most immediate and necessary actions and, while feeling the fear, mentally prepare the very next action to be taken. The fear will diminish and disappear, for it is only by taking action that we can erase fear, every time.

Courage may bring success, but courage is not fearless. Courage comes from acting in spite of our fears, where we have fear but the fear does not have us. However, true fearlessness sees beyond self-protection or self-defence to realize that ultimately there is nothing substantial to protect or defend; real fearlessness comes when we have crossed all spiritual horizons and are fully alive to the one true, interconnecting nature of all things. If we learn to elevate our viewing-point beyond our physical self and beyond our separate existence, only then do we have a chance of becoming fearless. Ultimately, *creativity* – expressed through flashes of insight that accumulate as they happen over and over again – combines to make us fearless by elevating our view of reality and taking our experience beyond our self with its limiting sense of separate existence.

In the meantime, fear emphasizes the exact opposite of creativity – which is *reactivity* – and reinforces our fundamental focus on the self. Without the courage to act on what we know, any wealth of knowledge is worthless. Courage allows us to take action even when we are frightened, but true fearlessness always comes with the liberating loss of self that we call *selflessness*. Many individuals have selflessly given up their lives for a stranger. Only when we spontaneously make ourselves absolutely insignificant and free of ego can we be truly heroic and truly significant. Indeed, it is only when we realize just how completely and absolutely unimportant we are in the larger scheme of things that we have the possibility of being free and fearless. And only with the fearlessness and humility that comes with selflessness can we awaken breakthrough consciousness, unleash our full spiritual potential and have a chance of real liberation.

Major spiritual texts such as the Bible, the Koran, the Bhagavad Gita and Buddhist writings all stress the importance of overcoming fear. Fear is overcome by letting go of the 'twin' separations: the 'external' *dimension* of separation, and the 'internal' *sense* of self as something forever separate and distinct. Self-preservation is a fearful thing, a way of looking at life that arises from fear *of* life. We awaken our breakthrough consciousness into fearlessness as we learn to access freely the spiritual levels of self-observation that take us from self-absorption to selflessness.

Take nothing for yourself, and everything is possible. When Mahatma Gandhi accidentally dropped a sandal out of a moving train, instead of bemoaning his loss, he immediately threw out the other so whoever found them had a pair. Expect nothing for yourself *from* others and expect everything of yourself *for* others. A truly selfless outlook experiences the self as one with the world – one uninterrupted, borderless whole. This spiritual release from all boundaries can last for a fleeting moment, or it can last forever.

We may seek success, but how do we move beyond success to significance? Bookshop shelves are crowded with books full of 'success secrets'. However, life becomes significant only when we move beyond searching out *how* to be successful and fully realize *why* we do the things we do. When seeking success we look at how valuable we are, while significance looks to how we are valuable. We are most valuable when we are beyond fear, because fear keeps us self-centred and forgetful of others. Success needs courage, but true significance needs fearlessness.

Both success and significance are mindsets. But whereas the outlook for success is anchored *within* the self, the outlook for significance begins in the psychological borderland where self and other merge. Significance begins with self-observation – the ability to look back at oneself. The secret to spiritual significance is in the point of view, our viewing-point. To sail the oceans of mind we must learn to look back at the shore from a distance.

Take control of your thoughts. You can do what you will with them.
Plato

Another facet of our psychology that inhibits our evolution towards spiritual maturity is our emotional ignorance – not knowing how to consciously develop our emotions and manage them. Emotional illiteracy is commonplace, where emotions inappropriate to a situation prompt unhelpful responses and negative outcomes. Acquiring emotional literacy is a necessary step on the path of our spiritual maturity.

However, our emotional evolution has favoured the negative. Of the ten universal emotions defined and generally accepted by psychologists, eight are negative: anger, fear, disgust, sadness, guilt, contempt, embarrassment and shame. Surprise is neutral; only joy is positive. We have evolved with a bias towards negative emotions, to the neglect of our positive feelings,* yet research shows that it is the *absence of positive* emotions rather than the *presence of negative* emotions that is more identified with depression and suicide.

If we are emotionally illiterate our communications are limited. While emotional illiteracy and immaturity often drive us to speak with our fists, emotional literacy and maturity use less force yet have a greater reach. Stirring our emotions is easy enough; the difficulty is guiding and elevating them. This ability to select appropriately from an expanded range of emotions is also known as emotional intelligence.[97]**

We accompany every moment of our life – every thinking, breathing, conscious moment – with a corresponding mix of emotions. This complex raft of feelings is created behind the scenes to colour our days, framed by our genetic inheritance and our personal experiences. Our view of the world is set within this emotional matrix; every event, object or experience to which we are exposed is linked to this ocean of emotion. We are spiritually liberated only to the extent that we can control our emotions rather than allowing them to control us or be manipulated by others.

If you want to see emotional honesty and integration, watch a child. Young children are walking, talking examples of how to 'let it all hang out'. They may not be able to control their emotions, but they sure are in touch with them, from tantrums to the sublime. Between 10 and 16 months of age, we begin the fun of developing, selecting and learning to control our range of emotions. It is then that we begin to select our own mix of positive and negative psychology. By adulthood the child in us has been 'socialized' to manipulate and manage life along proven lines of belief and behaviour. As adults, we settle on a mix of emotions and behaviours that

* Most psychologists agree that we have about 50 major combinations of emotions, and over 400 subtle yet discrete emotions. Many of our regular combinations and most of our basic emotional 'clusters' are inclined to the negative. In addition, we have higher 'cognitive' emotions such as love, jealousy and pride. While simple emotions can be instantaneous, moods can linger for days, and emotional traits can be carried throughout our whole life unless we receive training. Regarding love, in this book I concentrate on love as a spiritual state rather than as a simple emotional charge.

** Emotional intelligence highlights the powers of optimism, altruism, empathy and delayed gratification. A high degree of emotional development features what psychologists call an 'internalized point of control', where we no longer make the world 'out there' responsible for how we feel 'in here'.

we come to favour more than others. This becomes hard-wired into the synapses of our brain, and infiltrates our whole physical being – so much so that we become a recognizable personality, expressed through our actions, utterances and outlook. As our access to spiritual intelligence advances, we learn to select and control our emotional state rather than be controlled by it. From there we are free to use our emotional self-management to design a life beyond the basic competition for power, control and manipulation for energy.

Emotions synchronize our responses to what we sense is happening at every instant in the energy field around us. Without emotions our life would grind to a halt. Just as essential oils are blended to create the fragrances of the world, so too our emotions are blended to create our different feelings. Though the exact figure is still hotly debated, about 50 per cent of our temperament – whether happy or sad – is predetermined by genes, and the other 50 per cent by our social and physical environment. Happiness studies show that we may have a genetic inclination for unhealthy addictions and cravings, anxiety, depression or violence, but this predisposition can remain forever dormant unless triggered by our choices and daily experiences.[98]

Emotions are stimulated by thoughts, impressions and experiences, which then go on to produce their own thoughts, impressions and experiences in one continuous cycle. Our outlook, our physical health and our relationship with our environment are all affected by the positive and negative pictures we create in our mind. Our mood influences the way we learn and think about things, imparting lessons and impressions that are retained long after that particular mood has changed. Some tried and true ways of lifting mood include music, exercise, meditation, and any activity at all that simply makes us smile. Ours is a mental world more than a material one, a world where spirit, body and environment intermingle as one single vast network reflected creatively in the observing mind.

Leaving context aside, however, it should be noted that to be whole we need available access to all emotions – *including* the so-called negative emotions – because each emotion has a purpose. For example, although we are taught that happiness is positive and anger is negative, anger also has its place. Swiss research reports how anger, more than any other emotion, binds societies together in co-operation.[99] Love moves us forward,

- Of all the emotions, guilt deserves a special mention if only because it is used so often. Along with shame, guilt is a 'disease' we catch from the climate of our upbringing and hold onto throughout our lives. Many people even feel pangs of guilt without having enjoyed the pleasures of sin first. We must take responsibility for our actions, but this can happen without guilt or shame. Other peoples' judgements are mere opinions, not verdicts. We are natural success machines, and taking on guilt destroys success. Feelings of guilt, shame and failure immobilize us and undermine our health.

- If someone throws guilt at you, just catch it and throw it back. Ask the thrower, 'You're not trying to make me feel guilty/ashamed/not good enough, are you?'

but anger is the primary emotion that protects us and keeps us together as a group. In fact, the areas of the brain activated when we punish someone are the same as when we feel pleasure. In nearly every successful team there is a mechanism for dealing with freeloaders – those who reap the rewards of a group without contributing to it. Freeloading individuals almost always become targets of anger from other group members, done in a bid to drive guilt and force the required contribution from the freeloader. In this way, anger is used to threaten a non-contributing individual or sub-group with personal loss or exclusion. Punishment of individuals can be good for the group. This tactic is perhaps one of evolution's oldest examples of using the threat of isolation (and its loss of connection) in a psychological gamble to maintain and strengthen a group's cohesion.

Once our evolving spirituality has passed beyond both the primary needs of early survival and the adolescent period (where we are filled with self-importance and the increasing awareness of our influence), we reach a spiritual turning point. From here we will either stay with a limited viewpoint and an immature emotional range, or continue on towards spiritual maturity. In the process, spiritual states such as love, altruism, empathy, generosity, kindness and rapport are amplified by higher emotions such as bliss, rapture, ecstasy, thrall, awe and enchantment. These are our lost emotions – our evolving 'spiritual' emotions that accompany higher connections.

At present, in an insecure and unsafe world, the majority of us concentrate on the so-called 'negative' emotions and leave the higher emotions to the misfits and mystics, the evangelists, poets, novelists and the better-behaved recreational drug users. However, this does not make their promise less real and attainable. These elevated or 'exotic' emotions are key to the experience and expression of mature spirituality.

We need emotional education. Just as we have learned to feel emotions such as fear, anger, hate and outrage, we can also learn to feel these lost higher emotions. Like actors alive to their world of images, we too can choose the emotional lens of our day-to-day outlook onto the world. Our emotional climate is part of the atmosphere we create around ourselves.

However, by concentrating on the ongoing emergency of survival, we have mythologized the higher emotional states, even sometimes labelling them as unrealistic. But how has their absence inhibited our health? We now know that negative emotions and negative stress (stress caused by perceived threat or loss of some kind) can cause physical problems in the long term, but psychologists have yet to define the opposite positive effects of bliss, ecstasy, enchantment, rapture and love. We know that humour is very attractive, and laughter is good medicine.[100] We also know that love heals. If we extended our emotional range to reach more and more of these transcendental states, imagine the cumulative effect on our health!

What's more, immune cells, brain-cells and our nervous system constantly chatter with each other via neuropeptides and other hormones, and some of these neuropeptides are multilingual, both communicating with our immune cells *and* influencing our emotional states. This means our emotions are linked to our immunity and our general health. All emotional states – highly evolved or rudimentary – affect us along detectable chemical pathways. By learning to consciously control our emotional states we allow 'intelligent' neuropeptides to communicate these upgraded emotional choices to our immune system; in other words, regulating our emotions also regulates our health.

The connection between emotions and health has already been comprehensively recognized in the traditional medicines of some cultures. The Indian tradition associates emotions with the endocrine system and the seven *chakras*. Traditional Chinese medicine links emotions and health with the *qi* (*ch'i*) meridians. More recently, Joseph Griffin's pioneering work on the origin and purpose of dreams highlights how our mental images and their accompanying emotions connect us with the world at many levels.[101] Every thought is accompanied by an emotion, and every emotion creates an effect in the body: our biology and psychology are inseparable.

If we want to master our emotions and advance our spiritual life, we need to master what we say to ourselves; we need to manage the pictures we make in our head, and even go to the extent of deciding the set of our shoulders, the expression on our face and the way we breathe. When we do, our whole state of being can change for the better. Even though a large part of our emotional make-up is left over from evolution's dark ages, we have the capacity to raise or lower our emotional platform.

As we mature spiritually and move further into states of mind that register higher connections and holistic reality, we can look forward to more highly positive emotional states becoming commonplace. The goal is not to *eliminate* the 'negative' emotions of separation and survival but to *extend* our emotional range to include higher states. Worldwide, the emotions of separation and survival are already yielding to the emotions of connection and higher meaning. We are at the launching place of a psychological and emotional revolution.

The universe is transformation; our life is what our thoughts make it.

Roman emperor Marcus Aurelius

I have said that we, as a collective species, are in a crisis. But the news is not all bad. From crisis can come opportunity – as the German philosopher Nietzsche said, whatever doesn't kill us makes us stronger. What he is describing is 'breakthrough' suffering, where severe endurance can take us to a new level of clarity. Before we make the breakthrough, life often seems complex and our own lives cluttered, with our mind easily distracted and our actions confused. This is the 'long path' outlook. After the breakthrough, life becomes less complex and our own lives less cluttered, with our mind unwaveringly clear and our experiences direct and immediate. This is the transformational outlook of the 'short path', where change is found to work instantaneously, instead of merely bumping and grinding through time and place.

At all times we have a choice. If the stress of suffering becomes so unbearable and pushes us into a pain so deep there is no other way out, then we may choose the path of transformation. At such extremes, we choose either to be driven mad, let ourselves die or break through the suffering and regenerate. While learning to let go is hard for those of us in a culture that doesn't teach us how to die, many terminally ill patients let go of their suffering to enter a state of profound release and acceptance where they find the deepest sense of peace, connection, freedom and unconditional love. Our present environmental crisis offers us *our* chance to let ourselves go beyond suffering and separation, to stop holding on quite so tightly to our ancient survival tools where we obsessively add, subtract, hold or avoid until death overtakes us. With the aid of this book we can quickly and personally evolve to a point of emotional maturity and spiritual fitness where we live beyond any need merely to compete for control as judge, critic and evaluator.

With every breath of air our *environment* becomes *us*; with every change we are changed. Our current environmental crisis should be as riveting to us as anything afflicting our immediate family or a near relative, where not only do we live their loss, but because of close genetic links we may expect to share their fate. We and our planet are sick. Ill health can be a wakeup call – and it is only once we realize not only *that* we are ill but also *why*, that we can finally start to think about how we can make ourselves well again.

For all of us, any personal loss – death of a loved one, divorce or unemployment – is a testing time. Yet after the denial, anger, blame and sadness, there comes a time when we have to accept and move on. Whether we do this successfully or slide into depression and ill health depends on three things, as we have seen: our attitude, our emotional mix, and our spiritual maturity. And sometimes personal development is suddenly forced upon us. We only change our way of doing things when we realize the old ways will no longer work for us. This is why we must break out of our habits: the whole world needs big changes in us, and fast. Anaïs Nin, the feminist writer, said that she became fearless only when the risk of remaining tight in a bud became more painful than the risk it took to blossom. We let go and grow beyond our primal addiction to separation and fragmentation only when we realize how little this addiction is helping us, and how much it is holding us back.

Committing to action for the wrong reasons is a significant problem for many of us. We often feel clear about *what* to do and *how* to do it, but not about *why* we are doing it. Indeed, Nietzsche said a person could bear almost any sized 'what' if they had a big enough 'why'. 'Why' gives us our purpose. 'Why' is the navigator's compass. If we don't know where we are going any road is good enough. Without 'why-vision' we are travelling blind. Nelson Mandela led South Africa to freedom after 27 years in prison – his reason why was bigger than what was done to him and how it was done. Mandela's grand vision from his small jail cell inspired the world and won his freedom.

We also need to know where we are. Look up from this book and point north. Not many people can. My point is that if you don't know where you are, you may not be going where you thought you were.

For many of us, the way we live our life is much the same as being lost in a maze, where we assume the solution lies somewhere out there in front of us. Although mazes can be fun, they can also be a little scary. Just a few paces inside and we are presented with a dilemma: with our line-of-sight suddenly restricted, any path we choose can get us lost or get us through. Yet this difficulty would be quickly overcome if only we could somehow elevate our point of view and look down from above. Imagine finding a large mirror and raising it above the top of the maze. Suddenly all the blind alleys are revealed in the mirror and you see clearly the shortest way out.

In life, this elevated or strategic overview can always see the distant objective as well as the path ahead, and so has no need to risk shortcuts; in fact, the short path *has* no shortcuts. Shortcuts attempt to speed things up by cutting corners, missing out crucial steps and pushing the pace around the sudden twists and uncertain turns in life's maze. This impulse to take a short *cut* on the long path – rather than take the direct path that needs *no* short cuts – sees us lunge for the outcome before we have all the connections in place and have made the necessary preparations. Our impatience of mind is a major cause of accidents and disappointment.

We know we are on the short path when our mind, body, actions and circumstances are all working towards the same outcome. This 'alignment' brings into our lives the resources, connections, opportunities and experiences that allow our hopes, dreams and highest intentions to manifest, as if by magic.

Whichever path we favour gives us a different outlook on reality. The long path viewpoint shows us everything as it appears from the *outside* and as separate. From this mental position, when we see something change we interpret the change as something that arrives, something separate that appears between a cause and its effect. On the other hand, the short path viewpoint shows us everything from the *inside* and lets us see the interconnections that weave the parts together into a seamless, indivisible whole. Here, change is welcome as essential to reality. On the long path, which is where things appear to be assembled, we see change as something we work at controlling or imposing. On the short path we see change differently; here we interpret change as an unending process of transformation that arises within the fluid interrelationships interlinking every part into the whole. On the short path nothing is pushed around and meddled with; as there is less need for control, change can be left alone to create unforced transformations. This is because on the short path we are free to stay in touch with the whole, not just the parts. The long path mentality sees us stumbling along through time and place, blinkered in our outlook and distracted by creation's many separate things. The short path removes the blinkers so we get to recognize the unending, fluid interconnections of parts and their evolving possibilities rather than being limited to seeing mere separation and distance.

Every instant of our life, everything we think and do involves a choice between whether to tread more heavily on the long path or the short path. This means more than a simple choice between personal safety and growth; this is a choice between an ultimately pointless life and a life of endless significance and insight. We walk both the long and short paths simultaneously, always adjusting our weight between the two.

Whenever we set our spiritual outlook more towards the long path, our psyche becomes less creative and more reactive and opinionated. In this state, even when we don't openly express our opinion, the voice that chatters endlessly inside our head about anything that takes our attention still remains active. Take a moment to look at this parade of chatter as it is happening in you right now. This mental commentary may keep you entertained, but it also keeps you distracted and essentially out of touch. By fixating on these mental formations and remaining essentially *reactive*, we fail to focus on the higher connections and power of our psyche, which hold the secret of transformational change in our lives.

The short path mentality or wavelength is our so-called spiritual position, creating an outlook on the world that accesses higher levels of insight and bypasses separation. Just as there are two levels of reality (the created and the original, as we saw earlier) so too there are two levels of mind – the material and the spiritual. Each has its own energy or frequency that 'picks up' and emphasizes one or other reality, depending on whether we are tuned simply to reactivity and survival or something more creative and transformational. At this higher level, whatever we visualize (as opposed to what we react to) is energized into existence. The short path is the personal path to the 'secret' powers of mind.

Consciously accessing both sides of this dual outside-inside view of reality is like gaining a complete view of life's maze from above while remaining down in the hedgerows – a twin view of reality. This elevated or 'altered' view of reality is sometimes called an out-of-body experience and it can be beautiful to some, while puzzling or even terrifying to others. A similar though much greater promise – the promise of elevated spiritual experience – is the motivation driving many mystics and spiritual seekers as well as modern evangelists. At the more elevated levels of reality we are released into higher states such as bliss, rapture, thrall and ecstasy as well as giving expression to extended powers of healing. First coming as momentary flashes of inspiration, these transcendent experiences are often long remembered. As we progress, they stabilize and endure to illuminate our daily life.

Sensing only the surface of reality, life lived on the usual long path is weighted down with surprises, sudden changes, unexpected outcomes, tactical manoeuvres and compromises galore. Here we develop strategies and trade-offs, while we remain stuck in the maze of our judgments and reactions. Within the habits of this long path outlook, we expect most outcomes to happen 'down the track' after a period of time, however brief, and after we overcome obstacles. Most of us live this reactive life of cause and effect, where everything takes time and where sometimes we unleash surprising effects way beyond original plans. On the long path we may begin with the end in mind, but in that very moment of beginning we immediately become distracted.

On the other hand, life tuned in to the undulations of the short path is unhurried yet spontaneous. With this highly evolved mindset we consciously live within the present moment, and the end is always in sight. On the short path, the journey and the destination always consciously coexist. Here we *transform* obstacles rather than try to overcome them, and create possibilities rather than plans – we keep the viewfinder clear and focused and let things unfold naturally. This is the path of creative transformation. Stepping beyond the boundaries of time and place, we enter the instantaneous.

The long path outlook identifies problems (having often caused them), while the short path outlook creates solutions. The long path mind is like a thermometer that records the temperature, whereas a short path mind is like a thermostat that changes and controls the climate. The long path looks only as far as knowledge; the short path looks to insight and wisdom. On the long path we look to overcome disease, while on the short path we regenerate health. On the long path we say, 'I can't', while on the short path we say, 'How can I?' On our way to spiritual maturity we break through causes and their effects to re-access the power of direct, creative transformation.

On the laborious long path we fill our hands with necessities, but on the short path we find ourselves requiring less and less. With empty hands we are free. Realizing that the short path gives us nowhere to go, it seems absurd to try and take anything with us. With the long path mind-set we pursue success by overcoming resistance (with force if need be), while on the short path we find there is significantly less and less to resist.

As our reality-consciousness moves from the long path to the short path, the judge, critic and evaluator in us is transformed into coach, supporter and motivator. We move from perspiration to inspiration. When we try to assemble outcomes and race after results we are on the long path. When we allow our influence to inspire and create possibilities beyond the scope of reasonable expectations we are on the short path.

When we ask 'why' and seek the *context* of something, we are seeking the bigger picture and have begun turning our attention to the short path. Ultimately, the short path puts everything into its context. Little kids are always asking 'why?' They ask it about *everything*! By answering these questions we, as parents, give context to the curiosity and enthusiasm of our children. But now that you are an adult, do you remember when you stopped asking why? After all, the same big questions remain unanswered. Imagine a world where every child's natural curiosity is guided and encouraged rather than thwarted or punished. How different would our world need to be for all children to be raised in such a positive environment? How different would the world be if they were? Our inborn creativity and curiosity would then lead to a more immediate exploration of higher connections and wider spiritual consciousness. Remember, the big picture is still there – we've just lowered our gaze.

Our most enduring search is the search for higher meaning. Notice that whenever we ask the question 'how', we are almost always looking at something from the outside and asking about its workings or contributory causes. But whenever we ask the question 'why', we are almost always asking to illuminate the purpose or context of something. This question 'why' is key to strategic thinking, more so than the operational thinking of other questions such as how, when, where, who, what or which. The voice of leadership asks the question 'why', and answering it is the leader's first task. In the words of the philanthropist and businessman Nido Quebein: 'If you know how to do something you have a job, but if you know why you are doing it you are the boss.' Whenever we ask the question 'why', we awaken the leader within.

Context matters. Facts taken out of context are meaningless and can become lies. Not only does everything in existence have a context, existence is impossible without one. When you think about it, any single thing is the context shared in common by all its collective parts. This collective context appears as the surface surrounding the parts. Without parts nothing exists, and without a context to relate to nothing makes sense. Change the context of anything and that thing itself is changed.

Good leadership is sensitive to context; consideration of context and its influence is a vitally important part of what leadership brings to a situation, and it is what wisdom brings to life. Both leadership and wisdom involve connecting knowledge into a context that better informs our actions in the world. With context so important to the sense we make of our world, it is interesting to discover that Western and Eastern people see the world differently.[102] However, wisdom and its insights ultimately come through reflecting on our actual experiences, not merely through study – we can be taught what someone else knows, yet still be left none the wiser. With wisdom, our knowledge becomes insightful and our activity farsighted.

The immature mind, usually healthy in younger people, gives humanity its risk-takers – firebrands and ideologues who carve out humanity's place in the physical world. These use the long path mentality. The more mature mind produces the peacemakers, judges, spiritual thinkers and great theologians who sense the short path and give voice to higher connections. The younger, immature mind emphasizes content, while the older, more mature mind emphasizes context. However, it is the fully awakened mind, seeing more of the truth behind the facts rather than just the facts alone, that makes waves but no ripples – such a person leaves behind no mess to be cleaned up later, and nothing to be resolved.

The uncluttered mental wavelength attained on the short path cannot be gained by fee or force, nor can it be forced onto others. If we try to force the letting go of our separation mentality, our fixation will only tighten. We can let go only subtly, agreeably. Remember that the long and short paths are not mutually exclusive; we forever remain in touch with both, merely shifting our balance to favour one or the other. In this way, the position we take at any moment can change, while our long-term inclination suggests our degree of spiritual health and maturity.

The art of healing comes from nature and not from the physician. Therefore the physician must start from nature, with an open mind.

Phillip von Hohenheim (Paracelsus)

In large part we choose to be healthy, or not. At one level, the choices we make – from sex to food to politics – are decided by a mix of genetics and upbringing, as if our choices were decided before we got to them. At another level we can see that our power of choice can turn failure into success, ignorance into wisdom, and can even break the strongest of our habits. To make and remake any choice available to us, we need only to be convinced by a big enough reason. Whatever cards we are dealt, in the end we decide how the hand is played. We are given influence over our personal evolution, our own transformation. In the end no agent or teacher can do it for us, though some may help along the way. Ultimately there is no one to blame – no preacher, teacher, leader or boss. In fact, from here on there is no boss; there is no one else to give us final permission.

Often when we are told to do something, we react like a shopping trolley and head in a different direction than instructed. I know from my early days as a professional masseur, telling a client to relax often induced more tension. Even when I gave a more specific instruction like 'Relax your leg muscles', the response was not much better. Then I discovered a curious thing. When I began by saying, 'Yes, that's it, relax your leg muscles/neck/arms…' as if I was simply identifying something they were *already* doing and had *freely chosen* to do, the client immediately relaxed! The power had always been theirs to use, with or without my permission. In the same sense, all healing involves some self-healing. The healing relationship often involves giving someone permission to give *themselves* permission to heal.

In the West we are inclined to think that *any* ache or pain – either physical, psychological or emotional – can be taken to the clinic and fixed there. This is untrue. We remain our own best physician, with levels of psychic health and the energies of self-healing arising naturally within us as we gradually refine our levels of self-observation, balance and aware-ness. Health, like spirituality, is not a thing to be fixed but a state of being

– a state of being in balance, complete. One of the best things we can do for ourselves is practise giving ourselves permission to be healthy, because without this permission we cannot begin self-healing. Giving ourselves permission is a choice we can make at any time, and taking back control from external sources lies at the heart of our personal health and spiritual fitness.

Whether we like it or not, at some point we remain in charge of our choices. There is a widening acceptance, both within scientific disciplines and the broader community, that we directly or indirectly make ourselves sick. This ability of ours to heal or harm reaches beyond us personally and physically, extending to the global and spiritual level. By our presence, by our actions and inactions – themselves driven by the choices we make and fail to make – we contribute directly and indirectly to the condition of the whole. Whatever the meaning of life may be, our answer to the *purpose* of life must not stop at talk. It must also translate, through the choices we make, into action in the world.

The newspaper editor's slogan 'If it bleeds, it leads' illustrates how our media sensationalizes human failure, frailty, foolishness and excess. If our personal life continues this theme, we miss the elevating spiritual power of positive choice that ultimately links us from the personal and the transpersonal to the transformational.

Human history is the history of small choices. All that is great in human history would not have happened without the participation of 'small' people and their personal choices. Rather than being a parade of military victories and defeats, human history is, in truth, the unbroken stream of choices made and stories lived by us, the untold masses – the interconnected experiences of humanity's supporting cast of millions, not the decisions of a few. The deep and unseen networks operating across the whole of humanity and beyond – magnetized by the countless unrecorded acts of courage, cooperation, charity, generosity, selflessness, trust and trustworthiness chosen by us all – cross the boundaries of religion, race, age and knowledge. These are the true spiritual links that light up the phenomenal potential of what truly is humanly possible. Without these networks and choices to accumulate the good, we could not have left the confines of the cave.

CHAPTER 8

Life is one big cross-connected relationship

For Man is joined in spirit and body,
And therefore must serve as spirit and body.
Visible and invisible, two worlds meet in Man.

T.S. Eliot

ave you ever been at a performance when, quite spontaneously, audience and performers really connect, creating a moment when the 'gap' is gone? Have you been to a party when the event suddenly comes to life, in an instant? These are moments when the electro-spiritual network of our awareness becomes attuned to a higher level, creating new-found synchrony out of what had been a much looser collection of parts.

Connections rule! Everything is made up from a collection of parts that came from somewhere else and got connected and so became inter-related. In fact, every single thing ceases to exist without the connection of its smaller, constituent parts and contributory causes. Simultaneously, everything is also connected to something else as part of another progressively bigger entity – an interconnectedness that continues, uninterrupted, all the way to infinity. Everything has a context and is part of a system: every whole is not only a relationship of its parts, but also a part of something else. For example, your heart is a relationship of valves, muscles and blood vessels, *and also a part of your body*. In turn, your body is part of humanity, humanity is part of life's gene-pool, life's gene-pool is part of the created universe, and creation is part of the infinite field of energy in perfect balance...

Similarly, any community is a living network – an interconnected system that constantly assembles, disassembles, disperses, then reconnects and recreates itself every day. Every night, each community around the world almost completely disintegrates as it shuts down to sleep. But morning comes and the relationships within the community are reactivated. We rebuild the life of the city, the town, the village and the community all over again. Every day our private and public lives are created out of relationships, either physical, chemical or spiritual. Each day, we go ahead in trust that other people will return to their stations and create their part in life's tapestry of relationships all over again. In this way, culture and civilization can be pictured as the sum of countless private moments of cooperation where individuals network, interrelate, entrust, make and break connections, and exchange information, ideas and materials. Society is a cooperative work in progress, with each of us a reflective part of its living weave of relationships and unwritten agreements – electro-spiritual connections that seem to appear and disappear in endless undulation.

All of reality is an interconnected, unending relationship of bigger and smaller parts and influences. Life is awash in the fields of electromagnetism in which we rotate, inseparably bound by laws of gravity and influenced by 'strong' and 'weak' forces of radiation common within the cosmos. Matter itself is a collection of clumped 'packets' of energy that have a magnetic attraction – in effect, they have formed a relationship. And just as physical reality relies on interrelationships struck between separate material parts, greater reality (the combination of created reality and original reality) is a relationship that combines the physical with the infinite. We are *all* related and *all* connected. Our intimate connection to the Big Bang runs through every cell in our body – the hydrogen in our bodies has been around since that initial creative starburst. The salt level in our bodies is the same as the oceans', identifying us with our aquatic past; indeed, one of the omega-3 fatty acids originating in oily fish is the main constituent of human brain cell membranes, and is vital to the healthy functioning of our brain. Every drop of water has always and endlessly been recycled. Similarly, everything that circulates within us – our blood, sweat and tears – has connections going all the way back to creation.

Moreover, as we saw in Chapter 6, with the processes of evolution so indifferent to a species' boundaries, none of us has much that is unique to call our 'own'. The genetic matrix in which life is suspended means that every living thing is deeply connected and interrelated. Physically, we are the accumulation of the myriad relationships, formed through living history, that make up our physiology. The influence of our cross-connections has no beginning or end – we exist in a state of unending relationship with everything that comes to us, and our influence continues long after our actions have been forgotten.

Just as any physical existence is impossible without its context, life also is nothing without its connections. Connections, relationships and recognitions underscore the very building blocks of life. Pfizer Inc., the world's largest pharmaceutical manufacturer, earns most of its multibillion dollar income from about 100 molecules, all of which could easily fit on the head of a pin. These molecules are used in medicines to heal the patient's body. However, it is not the mere mechanical presence of the medicine that heals, but the *relationships established by the molecule* at the microscopic level. A pharmaceutical company delivers a likely medicinal molecule 'candidate' to a site either within a cell, or close by. A form of recognition between medicine and cell occurs, and it is this mystifying recognition that provokes a measurable reaction within the cell. If the recognition is negative the patient suffers. If the recognition is positive the patient benefits. Medical history is full of these relationship triumphs and disasters – think of penicillin and thalidomide, for instance. The global rush to medicate and find a panacea-in-a-pill fails to recognize that *relationships* heal; the cure is not in the compound but in the *connections* the compound makes. Heal our relationships and we heal; restore disrupted connections and we are restored.

Health is built not only on relationships established at the cellular level, but also at the molecular – which is why breaking molecular connections undermines health. For example, Vitamin A is proven to be more effective when partnered with antioxidant vitamins C and E. In turn, this combination of vitamins is more effective when consumed *directly* as the original whole food rather than broken down and recombined as a supplement.[103] Whatever is being 'recognized' between the vitamins remains a mystery, but there is some form of recognition and connection at the molecular level. To maintain the best of health, we require more than the benefit of any single nutrient taken in isolation, but the benefit of all the relationship-combinations linking the hundreds of micronutrients and trace elements contained in the whole food. In fact, what we are actually benefiting from is not so much the individual nutrients, but their immeasurably elaborate relationships with one another.[104]

If we don't understand how the whole works, then we cannot identify how the relationships within it work either – which is why, as we saw earlier, doctors have difficulty defining health. Although we don't usually think of health as being a relationship, that's what it is: a relationship, a cell-to-cell recognition, an integration of parts into a working whole. Anything removed from its context or background environment – whether a vitamin, a plant or even an innocent comment – is irrevocably changed, and so the whole is also changed. This is because any single part cannot be extricated without rupturing and rearranging the connections and relationships that inform the structure and nature of the whole. When we heal we are actually witnessing the fundamental healing power of cell-to-cell and molecule-to-molecule relationships as they re-establish themselves.

This impulse towards recreating the healing relationships that underwrite the health of any living whole can be seen not only in humans but also throughout the natural world. Many animals choose certain plant groups known to ward off parasites; for example, Navajo Indians learned of the medicinal power of osha roots from watching how brown bears sought out these roots, chewed them to a pulp and rubbed their fur with it to keep parasites at bay. Similarly, wild monkeys in Venezuela crush a particular millipede and rub it over their bodies to ward off mosquitoes repelled by the millipede's noxious chemicals. Seen in this light, doctors, therapists and nutritionists are only doing what nature intended: seeking out healing relationships that make us whole and therefore healthy.

Relationships make whole, and to make whole is to heal; therefore relationships heal. Repairing connections in our personal relationships now becomes the first logical step towards reactivating connections at all levels – from the microscopic to the personal and transcendental – and so creating what we are calling whole-health. Once we accept that we have an infinite number of connections and influences potentially available to us, making a positive difference in the world begins with something as simple as paying attention to how we interact with everything and everyone around us at every moment. To begin healing the planet, we must first learn to create healing relationships – connections that sustain both ourselves and our personal interactions. Achieve this, and the rest will follow.

Most people are other people. Their thoughts are someone else's opinions, their lives a mimicry, their passions a quotation.

Oscar Wilde

Having now recognized that the health of our relationships *at all levels* is critical, and not only to our internal health but also to our ability to make a positive difference in the outside world, it follows that we need to identify which of our existing skills will help us achieve our goal of healthy *personal* relationships. These are the personal skills we need moment by moment – skills and habits that have not only developed to ensure the survival and success of our species, but will also continue to evolve and help us on our quest for spiritual maturity as the next stage of our evolution.

The first skill through which we rediscover our connections is imitation. From the moment of our birth, imitation helps us make early connections – stick out your tongue to a newborn baby, and the baby will try to mirror you. Imitation, like empathy and altruism, is an effective connector. Humans learn extensively through imitation and teaching; we can copy something minutely and exactly, whereas other species merely mimic. The difference is that a *mimic* (such as a talking bird) operates as an unconscious copycat, while *imitation* requires mimicry plus the ability to make sense of the behaviour – to understand context, intention and their ongoing implications! Our ancestors were accomplished imitators by about 2.5 million years ago, which led to the widespread use of tools.[105] Among other advantages, our personal survival was helped during earlier phases of our evolution by learning to imitate the most successful people in our group – copying the best axe made us a better hunter, and copying the best public behaviour won us more approval, social support and reproductive opportunities.

However, our ability to imitate extends beyond imitating other people. Historically, ritual dances imitated the target of the hunt, the enemy before battle, the gods, the seasons and an array of communal hopes and fears. As well as giving us insight into the target of our imitation, early imitation also gave us a viewpoint outside ourselves, the capacity to observe ourselves from the outside looking in. This has been a most profound historical development. This capacity to self-reflect from the viewpoint of another and outside ourselves (supported through other powers such as altruism, generosity and empathy) is key to our higher spiritual potential and advanced evolution.

Imitation, when practised with precision, connects us to the object of our imitation. The more enlightened we become, the more we look beyond *what* we imitate, and consider *why* we do it. It is only this elevated point of reflection that can make our acts of imitation more personally meaningful, allowing us to mesh with others of a similar mind.

Of course, the capacity for connection is not confined to imitation. Reflective thinking is also essential for us to uncover and expand the range of both our conscious and mystical connections; we can't progress without it. *Reflective* thinking requires a *reflection* – the ability to look back on itself 'from a distance'. Self-observation is therefore an aspect of reflective thinking.

Yet our modern social environment encourages shallow thinking, the loss of mental clarity and originality. Our social intelligence is awash in a toxic fog of information, media clutter, advertising effluent and psychopollution. Violent, erotic or sensual images compete to capture our attention. Today, mediocre exhibitionism is headlined and encouraged, the average exalted, and the ordinary elevated, while the type of vibrant and unrestrained creativity that challenges our limiting assumptions frightens most of us. The worldwide drift towards trivia, fast-food mentality, disposable culture and anti-intellectualism takes us away from realizing our best possibilities for personal improvement. The 'dumbing down' of social discourse has conditioned us into some sort of sluggish disinterest or collective denial about the causes and cure of the looming global crises (environmental, social and spiritual) we are facing. If we don't start prac-tising some joined-up thinking and self-observation soon, more parts will become disconnected, change will become even more chaotic and collec-tive clarity less likely. The whole will get sicker and so will we. This time we are in is the tipping point, the moment between 'Don't worry, she'll be alright' and 'We're sunk'. Whatever we have a mind that needs to be done, needs doing now.

On the other hand, the very existence of shallow thinking gives us hope, because deep thinking is just lots of shallow thoughts strung together. This is how we move from the known to the unknown and vice versa: the act of imaginatively 'painting inside our head' or joining 'dots' of information to create a whole picture. In this way, deep thinking is just shallow thinking that keeps progressing without distraction. Socrates knew the power of this process, which is why jealous authorities had him killed. The more links, clear patterns and logical associations we detect, the more intelligent our worldview. As we join the dots, a deeper understanding begins to crystal-lize and we become rapidly intuitive and insightful. Anyone can do it. Lots of closely related 'shallow' thoughts become a deep thought; lots of deep thoughts become a spontaneous flash of insight; and lots of spontaneous flashes of insight synthesize to become a single burst of creative genesis that can change the world. Einstein, whose work led to the new age of quantum physics, created his groundbreaking equation $E = mc^2$ from lots of older ideas – a synthesis of many smaller, brilliant, mathematical sparks of insight that Einstein gleaned from other scientific minds.

Creative thinkers tend to be malcontents who see beyond the myths of popular beliefs and common practice. This is in part why idleness – a precondition for reflective or critical thinking, and for deep contemplation – is not encouraged: idleness creates the conditions in which social norms can be challenged. As a result, the status quo has imposed the unspoken dictum, 'To work, and therefore not to think too much!' In a system in which we live to work rather than work to live, there is little time to become an informed global citizen – an active participant who develops new views that liberate the community into expanding its outlook and seeing beyond set assumptions and limiting boundaries. In a community challenged by freely expressed creativity, creativity is pushed to the margins, corralled outside the safety and security of established norms. But creativity at the extremities of any whole – whether the margins of society, the tips of a tree-branch in springtime, the edges of ignorance or at the surface-edge of everything in the universe – creates new possibilities that transform reality. Creativity is a force for change that transforms by forging new relationships, connecting the parts at their extremities, and originating a new and healthy whole.

We need training in sustained mental focus and self-awareness. By restricting ourselves to isolated shallow thoughts, we end up with a fragmented mentality and a fragmented, vulnerable life that can be easily manipulated by others. However, activating our own creative capacity for either deep thought or self-reflection (the self-awareness that allows us to see why we are doing what we do) does not come easily. They both require resolve, a good deal of discipline, and practice. However, as far as they help create connections and extend our healthy relationships, the better off we are for developing them.

The way we communicate with others and with ourselves ultimately determines the quality of our lives.
Anthony Robbins

Along with critical and reflective thinking, our language and communication skills are among our most effective tools to rediscover and rebuild better health connections.[106] The 'relate' part of the word 'relationship' is about relating or getting connected, which is an aspect of communication. In order to actually exist, communication requires some kind of mutual recognition or receptivity – some interchange or identification between two or more communicating parties. Without a recognizable transference of information, there is no meaningful connection or interrelationship – just proximity. For example, if I don't know how to read, then the individual letters on this page appear to be just a series of unrelated marks that happen to be next to one another. However, if I can read, I can *recognize their relationship* to one another and how this creates meaning and communication in the form of sentences. In other words, I understand their true *significance* as a relationship. So too, in order to understand our own significance and where we fit with creation and reality as a whole, we also need to be able to 'read' the connections bonding us to everything around us.

Relationship *is* communication, and in this sense, people who are having 'trouble' with their relationships are in fact having trouble communicating. Couples may think they have grown apart, when in fact they are stuck together without any mutual connection. A relationship is the connection between two or more parts, and when two or more parts are connected in this way they become something greater than they were separately, something more substantial. A loving relationship is no less substantial, no less recognizable and energizing than the relationships linking the genes, proteins, sugars and other molecules that give structure to our body and mind. This substantial energy of relationships invests them with a capacity to cross-link the immaterial or energetic world with the physical. Just as our *internal* relationships and biological networks give structure to our body and define our physical appearance, so too our *external* relationships, perceptions and social networks extend our influence and presence in the world. Our internal and external realities interconnect and intermingle, with this bipolar balance being managed through the biochemistry of our mind.*

Succeeding at intimate, loving relationships requires more than a set of skills for free and conscious communication. True connection also means that each person allows the personal boundary of the other – the membrane of their psyche – to remain intact. (Even when the love remains strong, relationships can end because one or both parties have lost their sense of being personally free while remaining connected to and in touch

---

*Neuroscientists have shown us that our consciousness is not some local and confined physical mechanism, but more a far-reaching electro-chemical phenomenon of mind that expresses the relationship between the inside and the outside world. Consciousness is an energy that has the expanded potential to register everything within the material, created reality as well as the immaterial, uncreated reality; in this sense consciousness is the connection between the physical and spiritual dimensions of life. The term 'electro-spiritual consciousness', which is used throughout this book, is therefore intended to express and encourage an awareness of the inextricable role consciousness plays as an energetic in all our interactions. Consciousness is synonymous with our experience of reality.

with the other.) A spiritually immature person may be a skilled communicator, but only at giving-to-get – doing a favour and hoping to be offered something in return. However, intimate, personal relationships develop their structure and durability through creating such things as shared values, attitudes, directions and beliefs (along with complementary life-skills and other capacities). A successful personal relationship is created as a circuitry of communications and connections from the physical, through the emotional and psychological to the holistically spiritual.

One of our greatest needs is the need to be heard, and one of our greatest gifts is the ability to listen. In this way, communication creates connection. Many love relationships are lost through wrong language, while others are healed by each person learning to speak their partner's preferred language of love. In this sense, communication is less what you say and more what they hear. A key to successful communication is 'active listening'. When we are actively listening we are recreating within ourselves what the other person is feeling and seeing in their words. Active listening does not mean simply preparing what we want to say back to them the moment they shut up. Often we don't even wait that long. Distracted by the mental chatter that rarely leaves us, we prevent ourselves hearing their full story and miss the opportunity of creating the other person's picture in our world.* Only when we have recreated their picture accurately and fully in our own mind, in a moment of deep pause, is a meaningful connection made and mutual progress possible. Complete listening becomes a point of empathy and rapport, a profound source of deep connection. Active listening includes listening from emptiness, listening from the deep silence beyond assumptions. Listening from emptiness means letting go of the accompanying fog of dialogue in our head that prevents complete communication.[107]

Remember that the true value of a doorway is the emptiness of the opening.

We too often listen to correct someone, rather than listening to connect with them. Practise listening in silence, because silent listening stops us jumping in as judge, critic and evaluator to make comments or

---

* Present a person with any object, from a cup to a coconut, and ask them to describe what comes to mind. They will begin to report an endless stream of images, ideas, impressions, concerns, hopes and experiences that they associate with the object. Our mind is always chattering at this level.

recommendations, pass judgements and give suggestions on what we've just been told. In this way, we are able to pick up the essence of the communication and check for true meaning. Doing this, we have begun listening with unconditional positive regard. With this level of connection between minds, we avoid the pitfalls of replying to incomplete or misunderstood information. Be a listener who connects, not corrects.

Active listening happens without interruption or amendment. We may not say much ourselves, but nonetheless will be considered a great conversationalist! And remember, effective listening also requires us to act appropriately on the message – it is no use listening, then ignoring. We must listen, be affected, AND act.

As well as listening, successful communication also often involves negotiation. Successful negotiations are able to focus on making connections and reconnections rather than highlighting differences and distances. In any negotiation we have *six* options: we can capitulate and lose everything, we can try coercion in an attempt to win everything, we can cop out by abdicating and refusing to make a decision, we can postpone things until later, or we can compromise – which means neither party is completely satisfied. Then we come to the final and wisest option: *collaboration*. Collaboration creates the possibility of outcomes that satisfy all parties. This is healthy. To do this we have to 'let go' and surrender positions in favour of interests; our separate positions denote *where* we are, but our interests disclose *why* we have taken our position. When we use collaboration, all viewpoints are lifted from their separate positions and connect at the higher point of each other's interests. This is almost always the only way to a durable solution.

Defending our separate positions is exhausting, but securing our mutual interests is liberating, and healthier in the longer term. Whereas most people think surrender means defeat, the collaborative approach is in fact the art of surrendering to win. Indeed, proving your point may cause lingering resentment that may still see you lose. There is a difference between being right and being effective: we may self-righteously defend a position while undermining our interests. Being right point-by-point is not as important as being effective overall.

One example often cited to explain collaboration involves three people fighting over an orange, only to discover that one person wanted the orange peel for cooking, another wanted the fruit for juice and the third wanted the seeds for planting. By surrendering their separate positions and discovering each other's interest, everyone is satisfied. Sometimes it's better to concede a little and gain a lot.

It doesn't take much to create collaboration out of conflict and competition. All it takes is the kind of joined-up thinking that recognizes mutual benefit, a regard for the other person's position, and an ability to see the world through others eyes. Collaboration means connection, creating a bond. The health of this bond then depends on its balance and rapport with the surrounding environment.

There is more hunger for love and appreciation in this world than for bread.
Mother Teresa of Calcutta

Another way in which we forge interpersonal connections to create healing relationships is through building rapport, experiencing empathy and establishing harmony with others.

Empathy is at work whenever we see someone bite deliberately and slowly into a sour lemon, only to find our *own* mouth beginning to salivate as we watch them wince and squirm. Our capacity for empathy and understanding of others is supported by specialized 'mirror' cells in the human brain. These cells, which develop their own brainwaves (called *mu* waves), make a web of connections in the brain that activate either whenever we perform a task or whenever we *imagine* ourselves performing it. Our imagination and real life engage the same parts of the brain, and can excite the same emotions. Most excitingly, mirror cells also activate when we watch *someone else* performing the same task, or even when we *imagine them* performing it. It is as if these cells have stepped beyond the physical boundaries of their human host, taken in influences from whatever and whoever comes before them, and positively 'entangled' everyone and everything in the process.

These mirror cells are more evidence that another sense, a sixth sense – an unrestricted, *empathic* sense – may be evolving in life's genome, a sense capable of registering the greater reality. (At the very least, empathy is not restricted to humans; even laboratory mice respond to a cage-mate's pain more keenly than to the pain of a 'stranger' mouse.[108]) Mirror cells have certainly helped us develop integrated, complex societies, since it is mirror cells that provide a mechanism for us to imitate someone's behaviour, empathize with them, and anticipate what might happen around us by 'reading' into someone's behaviour. These comparatively recent developments are highly evolved skills, needed in activities such as advanced tool use, architecture, mathematics and art. We only fully developed 'mirroring' skills in about the last 40,000 years – which is also when we began to utilize our 'God-spot' (despite our brain being full-sized 200,000 years earlier), suggesting that the development of empathy is an evolutionary progression, part of the biological momentum towards heightened spiritual intelligence and wholeness.

Empathy also allows compassion, which begins with us putting ourselves in someone else's shoes, and imagining what they are feeling – we get impressions rather than give opinions. When we experience empathy, we are seeing how the world works through someone else's eyes – we understand their position as if we were experiencing it ourselves. When we feel compassion for another life, we are acting on our empathy, in their best interests.

Empathy creates a powerful connection that can heal. While it may be helpful to see ourselves as others see us, the healing power of empathy is learning to see others *as they see themselves*. Ever noticed that when we try to energize others forcefully (our children, parents, boss or employees) and get them to do something, they often resist? This is because everyone hates being pushed around against their will. Anyone who has been pushed around and forcefully dealt with, rather than worked around and *shared with*, knows how much resentment we can direct towards our controller. On the other hand, when we feel invited and allowed free choice we are much more sympathetic and agreeable.

We can never win a fight against someone's convictions, yet how often do we really know what's on the other person's wish-list rather than the list *we* wish for them? With most of us well and truly set in our ways, it is wiser to wait for an invitation to give help or advice than to offer them prematurely, before help or advice will be accepted. Don't worry about not being asked, because when we have set a good example in whatever we can do, invitations will come for us to repeat what we have done well elsewhere. Achieving this balance in our upward spiritual momentum is the art of influence by invitation. Don't advertise, act; the invitations will come.

Often the world seems to misbehave and disobey. But remember, before we can influence something to the good, we must fully connect to it. When we fail to approach another person with empathy or rapport, we risk treating them as an object that needs to be *managed*. We manage objects but we *lead* lives. By learning to live in a state of empathic connection, we go beyond the mechanics of management and step up to the true spirit of leadership, which is the ability to connect where we are to where we are going, and bring others with us. Leadership that heals connects *what* we are doing to *why* we are doing it. If we want to lead someone to a new position, we first have to *connect* with them where they are. Rapport and empathy are places in the mind, giving us points of view beyond ourselves. These are spiritually healthy vantage-points.

Rapport is part of effective communication. High levels of rapport also feature in love relationships that are unconditional. This is because rapport requires us not only to maintain our own self-esteem, but also to acknowledge and enhance the self-esteem of the other. Rapport favours us finding common ground before we enter into areas of difference. Rapport inspires us to focus on how close we are rather than how far apart. Rapport has us share a common viewing-point, harmonize attitudes and align outlooks. When we tune in with empathy and respond with rapport it is almost impossible not to reach a new and mutually beneficial position (though rapport and empathy are wasted on us if we don't have altruistic intentions).

Empathy and rapport are not confined to human-to-human contact; we also have the capacity to enter a state of rapport with our environment, and empathize with all living things. Empathy and rapport are about 'tuning in' to where we are and being 'in touch' with what's around us. This is why South American Indians have developed over 100 words for potato, and the Inuit have almost as many words for snow. Who would have guessed there was so much to say about potatoes and snowflakes? Like the Amerindians and Inuit, the more we pay attention to something and discover its features, the more we know about it and the more we develop ways of describing it. This process may take years and span generations – creating expertise by placing us in almost constant contact with the material of a subject, immersed in it and absorbed by it. This creates the environmental conditions for a state of deep connectedness.

These states give us part of our capacity for connectedness that began as imitation for survival, evolved into seeing the world through someone else's eyes, and now has the possibility of passing through compassion for all of life, to culminate in an unbroken experience of the whole. With the capacity to take us beyond all attachment, our sense of an exclusive self, boundaries and limitations, empathy, rapport and compassion can overcome our survivalist instinct for separation and open us up to the possibility of a more significant life – a truly spiritual life.

The early existence of imitation, along with the rise of empathy and the emergence of rapport and compassion, give us a hint of a transformative energy that has the power ultimately to encompass everything. Simultaneously, this power of transformation has released humanity on a search for meaning that, when unrestrained, can reach out to include the whole of creation. When we have this outlook activated within us, we are able to see clearly the uniqueness in everything and every situation.

The ability to see the specialness in someone is particularly valuable in helping to build healthy relationships. When we honour someone we are acknowledging their special value, their worth. Any criticism, on the other hand, risks causing depletion by dishonour. This depletion affects us instantaneously, as does the uplifting and enriching energy of honour. Honour is a state of mind, an attitude, an energetic. We have all been party to conversations that are case studies in dishonour, veiled in shades of censure, disrespect and cautionary distance. When we honour someone, we turn on wholesome circuits in our mind, in our psyche, in the very core of our being – circuits that heal, connect, uplift and restore. In fact, honour, respect and reverence fine-tune all minds to the higher path, while dishonour and disrespect are the mindset of distance, disconnection and defeat. Who have you forgotten to honour today? Who have you dishonoured? Giving honour (as opposed to flattery, which is merely a mask to hide unflattering intentions) is one of our highest virtues, and key to higher connections.

On one occasion I took a group of students to the beach. The kids ran, laughed and swam. But one young boy stuck fairly close to me, and so we chatted as the day mooched along. At one point he picked up a rock and, smiling at me, threw it against the large boulders behind us where it smashed into little pieces. He picked up a broken shard of rock, examined it briefly and held it out to me. 'See that?' he said. I nodded, not quite sure what I was supposed to be seeing. 'No one's ever seen that before. When the volcanoes stopped, what's inside that rock got locked away, and you and I are the first people ever in the whole world to see it. Pretty cool, eh?'

I looked at the cracked surface of the rock, and at that very moment everything else receded. I gazed at the child with amazement and respect as I realized what he had done. This little boy had 'tuned in' to something unique and special, something from within the rock's hidden surfaces but also something profound from within himself. We all have his capacity to see something common in an uncommon way.

Traditional communities lived and died on their sense of honour – Native Americans, for example, honoured the prey before and after the hunt. On the other hand, modern man uses technological efficiency to largely ignore honour and conveniently overlook the catastrophic global impact that such insensitive disregard is having on the environment. Ordinary people who live up to the good and the specialness they see in every encounter are giving honour by their actions, and often achieve extraordinary things.

Whenever we recognize the specialness in something or someone, we are tuning in and turning on. We are seeing them through loving eyes – seeing their excellence, free of faults and imperfections, whether real or imagined. Moreover, the other person recognizes these special qualities *in themselves* every time we smile, hug, maintain gentle eye contact, give praise, admire or encourage them. It is finding the points of special worth in little things that can activate our deeper connections and energize the circuitry of healing relationships across our lives.

It takes a very long time to become young.
Pablo Picasso

In some respects, spiritual development, which is the art of activating the highest connections and healing relationships available to us, is like returning to aspects of the child within us – the uncluttered innocence, spontaneity, creativity, openness and sparkling insight. This was illustrated clearly during the Cold War, when groups from the US and the USSR were asked what they would say to those in the 'enemy country'. Adults from both countries mostly uttered the standard litany of criticisms, instructions and hostile suggestions, while the children almost without exception suggested one word: 'Hello'. There is no better single word in the English language to register open recognition and instantaneous connection.

As we saw earlier, whereas children arrive in the world fully creative but impulsive, by adulthood we have largely unlearned and suppressed our inborn creativity. What adults *have* replaced it with are skills important for basic survival, as well as complex social communications, work skills and other activities required in the real world. Once they are learned, we adults access most of these skills spontaneously. Spontaneity is impulsiveness combined with skills that have been accumulated through practice. A child's annoying impulsiveness is simply their creativity left unguided until, for most children, it is then largely suppressed within the design of our conditioning process. Part of successful parenting is therefore to guide children into their most creative moments while helping them to overcome distraction and learn to stay the distance that is needed to move from impulsiveness into a skill-set and mental framework that supports informed spontaneity.

On the other hand, children say some of the wisest things. For adults to rediscover the kind of insights that children experience, we have to work at it. Life's first emergency – the daily struggle for survival – remains a constant, but in the process of succeeding at this struggle we have suppressed our ability for spontaneous insight in favour of improving our survival and social skills. However, if we are to live a significant life, we will need to rediscover both our missing connections and our creativity. This is why impulsiveness can happen anytime, but informed spontaneity takes practice.

Adults can learn a lot from the very young. As children, we have the advantage of few preconceptions and little self-doubt – unless it is taught to us. To observe this, we need only to watch children connect with computer games, or program the household entertainment centre with an effortlessness that leaves the adults dumbfounded. Because children *expect* things to work, they simply go ahead and enthusiastically try it, while we adults are hampered by self-doubt as we go looking for problems, which then upset us when we find them.

Watch children at play and you might suddenly realize that they are not just frivolously wasting time or mucking about. Child's play is deep learning: a self-directed state of deep connectedness and personal engagement. It is also an enthusiastic and absorbing state of relaxed attention – healthy qualities often missing from adult life. Play is a creative learning exchange linking mind, body and circumstance into one integrated and healthy whole. Awash with symbols and mental imagery, children at play are learning in a way that can be wildly creative, insightful and visionary. Similarly, some of the most effective psychological therapies and counselling techniques ever developed incorporate the client's symbolism and creative imagery specifically as a way of freeing the client to hear and recognize their *own* words of innate wisdom (rather than the counsellor's), and unlock healing solutions *within themselves*. In the hands of an adult, the symbolism, creative imagery and imaginative role-playing of play can help put the Humpty Dumpty pieces of a fragmented life and psyche back together again.

Research shows that the more animals play, the bigger their brains grow. Moreover, brain-imaging techniques show that social play seems to rewire our brain, increasing the activity of connections between our brain-cells.[109] Play also helps develop our logical reasoning, our ability to learn and our behavioural flexibility. Many successful, wise and significant adults put time aside to play. Indeed, an attitude of agreeable playfulness is often uppermost in the public and private persona of spiritually advanced adults.

So let's not underrate the importance of play to adults as well as children. With play, life becomes thrilling again, joyous, engaging and freely creative. When we invest too much time in the tactics of *getting* somewhere and regrettably forget our childhood experience of already *being* there in play, we often miss life's spontaneous capacity for transformation and magic. The healing power within play's sense of wonder, improvization and curiosity are available to all of us. With these powers, we come closer to the freedom that can effectively turn impossible situations into manageable and happy ones. What would it be like to be more childlike in our quest for our goals and life's purpose? How would we feel having no sense of failure, and being so actively engaged within a sense of wonder that there was no room for doubt?

Play is also how we all learn best at any age – active participation, total immersion and relaxed attention. The good *do* die young – young at heart whatever their age, unburdened, enthusiastic, eager, open to transformation, with life in their years rather than years in their life. When we are light on our mental feet like the child we once were, our spontaneity and creativity combine to re-emerge as part of mature spirituality.

They are not truly husband and wife,
Whose bodies merely come together;
Only they are truly wedded,
When two bodies have one soul.
Guru Amar Das, *Guru Granth Sahib*

Another way in which we rediscover our connections is through the healing power of touch. Building healthy relationships is about being in touch physically, emotionally and spiritually – in fact, emotional connections, physical touch and health are all interlinked. Caring connections heal. For example, in a 1950s study of the effects of touch on babies, all groups of premature babies were treated in the same cold and impersonal manner normal for those times, but one group was touched and stimulated three times a day. Touching a baby three times a day doesn't sound like much by today's standards, but these babies gained almost 50 per cent more weight every day than the others, were more alert, and left hospital on average a week sooner than the other group.[110] Moreover, we now know that babies massaged for 15 minutes prior to sleep fall asleep in half the time they did before, are more alert during waking time, suffer less colic, and have more efficient immune systems.[111] Loving touch heals.

Touch changes our physiology. If a young brain is deprived of the emotional inputs that come from physical touch, the structure of the brain and personality is negatively affected.[112] Intimacy and interaction are vital to our healthy development: prolonged separation and isolation become destructive, while love and acceptance are always curative.

Both sexual and non-sexual touch can heal. Our power of touch is so finely tuned that the *way* we touch someone transmits our feelings and intentions as powerfully as the readout on an earthquake Richter scale. For example, studies show that the hormones released during sexual activity (particularly oxytocin) are linked to cancer prevention, weight loss, cardiovascular health, boosted immune function and a measurable lowering of anxiety and depression. Falling in love happens in a primitive region of our brain developed about 100 million years ago – way back in the survival era of evolution. To ensure our species' survival we are programmed to pass on our genes, and when we actually engage in sexual activity we are rewarded with a massive blast of dopamine; according to Mary Sharpe at the University of Cambridge, full sex is actually addictive.[113] Instead of an addiction to orgasm, however, we connect better through sensual massage and cuddling, which favour the hormones oxytocin and vasopressin over the more overwhelming dopamine. By slightly changing our behaviour and tweaking the way we make love – by including lots of kissing, cuddling and hand-holding – we enhance our ability to produce oxytocin and vasopressin (and their receptors), the chemicals we need when we want to fall in love and stay in love.[114]

Unfortunately, one of the greatest areas of imbalance and general misunderstanding between the sexes surrounds sexual touch, particularly the difference between sensuality, sex and love. This difference often confuses us – in fact, the personal experience of many people is that closeness and sex are mutually exclusive. Rape is an extreme form of sexual disconnection, with the act merely a violent vehicle for power and control. However, sex itself is neither good nor bad, it's what we *do* with it that makes it so. The sexual connection can transport us so profoundly that we abandon our absolutely separate sense of self to momentarily enter a state of boundlessness, even transcendence, enough for the French to call the experience *la petite mort*, 'the little death'. Sex practised as part of tantra (the name given to esoteric forms of Hinduism and Buddhism) originated as a process of harmonious balance and communion that took the emphasis away from orgasm. Tantric sexual highs are built on a delicate base of contemplation, psychological fine-tuning and emotional refinement that are missed by many tantra-technique junkies. The ancient Chinese also knew about this higher connection, as did the ancient Christians. It is even found in the Sufi tradition and written into the Jewish Kabala, that when men and women use their sexual energy in a very relaxed way without a fixation on orgasm, they can realize all the benefits and the harmony of love without the destructive forces that often accompany lust.

Part of the misunderstanding about how sensuality, sex and love differ is undoubtedly due to the fact that the touch sensations of men and women are fundamentally different. Men have approximately 50 per cent less touch-sensitivity on their skin than women, and even their response to pain is different.[115] This is a fact both sexes need to be aware of, as it has an impact on how effective we are at taking touch beyond 'he' and 'she' to become 'we'. Stimulating the skin releases a mass of chemicals that boost the immune system, making physical touch vital to the health of both men and women, whatever our sexual differences.

Most of us live in a world where we are 'touch-deprived', even 'touch-damaged', a world where kisses become contracts and touch is greeted with caution. Touch does not always lead to better connection with one another, and although touch is possible at many levels, many of us never experience the higher levels of touch that come free of 'baggage', free of any intention or expectation. Touch that is free of selfish motives or personal agendas is almost a forgotten art, which is such a pity because unforced touch develops its own rhythm and pace, during which spiritual circuitry is activated and higher connections made. As a health professional, I have experienced being so 'in touch' with the other person that the physical connection itself is transcended. In those situations, the connection was transformed into what is best described as a psychic ability; I was able to accurately read the client's health trends beyond expected professional insight, and describe specific events unfolding in their life. Physical touch has such power to form higher connections that if every person were massaged regularly, we would see less depression, less violence and a better, happier world.

However, if we concentrate too much on the physical sensations of any form of touch, we hold ourselves back from the real connection, the actual energetic of *being in touch*. In this state of physical preoccupation, we concentrate on what we are getting rather than experiencing the joys of giving. This process allows our hormones to control us rather than us controlling our hormones, elevating their status to that of primeval gods and devils – the lustful-but-addictive Dopamine, loving Oxytocin, stressful Cortisol, aggressive Testosterone, happy Seratonin, enough-is-enough Prolactin, and many others. Indeed, biochemistry is often cited as an excuse for inappropriate behaviour. But these hormones don't *make* us touch, and don't *make* us seek or avoid closeness and connection; in these instances body chemistry doesn't decide or excuse our behaviour, but merely informs and facilitates what we do. Biochemistry can be demanding, sometimes dictatorial, but in many situations – including many addictions and their compulsions – mind can overcome matter and change our biochemistry. Mind and matter intermingle and, like love, sometimes make it hard to tell who's on top. We can never assume that biochemistry is boss; just because hormones *accompany* behaviour does not mean that they are the ultimate cause of it.

There are many other factors at play that influence outcomes; for example, some people become depressed when serotonin is low while others remain depression-free, indicating that chemistry alone cannot be the cause of depression. In other words, our choices and behaviour are not reflexes simply based on biochemistry. We already know from Libet's work that choice begins somewhere beyond our familiar consciousness (see page 44), and we also know that every aspect of our individuality – both biological and psychological – is formed at a convergence of external influences that becomes our self. These facts regarding consciousness and contributory causes make it clear that our power of choice must also be driven, at least partly, by influences originating beyond our self. Either way, blaming our behaviour on our hormones is a cop-out that abdicates responsibility for any self-control and relegates our choices to a chemical-driven reflex, putting us on no higher intellectual and moral level than an amoeba. We can do significantly better than that.

Putting too much emphasis on stimulating our hormones and enjoying the ride prevents us guiding love to awaken connections that heal beyond the limitations of the physical. When two people cannot bring love into their sexuality, their relationship may be stuck at an immature level of self-absorption that misses sexuality's higher connections. Love is a state of mind, not mere gymnastics for the body. Love emphasizes what we are giving, while sex emphasizes what we are getting. Women seem wired to emphasize the internal *chemistry* of relationships, while men seem predisposed to the external *physics* of relationships. Sex is as much about communication as procreation, as much to do with connections as with kids, and maybe more so – which is why the average human has sex thousands of times in their life yet only produces two or three children.

Understanding the energetic of being deeply 'in touch' – an energetic that has connected us as a species throughout the ages – might also inform how we can strengthen and extend our connections from this point on. Part of what holds us back from being truly in touch with this intimate power is our adherence to the traditional, masculine way of doing things.

In the early days of our evolution as a species, we needed dominant male energy that formed tight, exclusive groups in order for us to compete and survive. Overcoming life's first survival emergency favoured an ongoing command-and-control style of leadership, best suited to separating us from potential danger at a moment's notice. But now a new emergency has been created by these selfsame attitudes that once protected humanity. Men themselves seem stuck in transition, divided between the old and the new, with adolescent males four times more likely to commit suicide, twice as likely to be learning disabled, and nine times more likely to be delinquent than adolescent females.[116] Obviously, the traditional domineering male behaviour has become self-defeating, with our current crisis now calling for a wiser and more inclusive solution to humankind's global excesses.

Many of us are presently fortunate to be enjoying a time of civilized abundance – plentiful food and relative security. This has meant that we are no longer driven to bully one another in competition for food, clothing and shelter, or to rely on cruelty and aggression to ensure our daily survival. However, just because we are not engaging these destructive instincts at present, we ought not to assume that we won't revert to them when threatened if we don't find a better alternative in the meantime. This passing moment of plenty is therefore an opportunity for pause and reflection, to consider how force and dominance can be tempered by decision-making options other than command-and-control. As we have seen, there are three other options to choose from – consultation, collaboration and consensus – all of which are known to come more easily to women than men. These options make for better negotiations and rewarding outcomes, as new-generation business has already seen: companies with the most female executives have more than a 33 per cent higher return on investment. This is attributed to the fact that women are less inclined towards 'groupthink' – those dominant patterns of thought and behaviour that are often accepted as truth within a 'masculinized' group and are resistant to change or improvement.[117]

However, the tribal male continues to deny these implications, so causing immense havoc by doggedly holding onto his command-and-control attitude and using his historical position of power to dominate the global scene. The emerging holistic age requires us to expand our horizons beyond our reliance on conquest, calculated advantage and competition. Individually and collectively we are evolving towards a greater unity: closeness, consensus and connection to others, arising as it does from a position of personal responsibility for our spiritual maturity.

The day will come when, after harnessing the winds, the tides and gravitation, we shall harness for God the energies of love. And on that day, for the second time in the history of the world, man will have discovered fire.
Teilhard de Chardin

There are more levels to connection and being in touch than touch alone. Our ultimate and greatest power for connection is, of course, through love; in any search for higher connections, love must lead. We need to think carefully about the connections offered through love and not be mistaken, because just as we may touch and still not be *in touch*, we may also mistake possessiveness for love, and we may speak of love yet still not make a loving connection. Love is not so much a *separate* force or form as it is a *powerfully energized connection* affecting us physically, hormonally and spiritually.

Love is first brought into life with the mother-child bond, which is the original, creative connection. The parent-child relationship, and particularly the mother-child relationship, is primal and the hardest to break or ignore. For the mother, gestation and incubation create a uniquely close bond not available to men. However, being without access to the mother's original relationship with the child, men attempt to recreate the same intensity of loving connection in other, more external ways, such as in architecture and works of art, or through great exploration and adventure. Women engage and connect more intimately with the social environment, while men are more adept at engaging with the physical environment. Each complements the other. By giving birth, a woman nurtures love's original bond and brings it to life, while man proves more adept at building shelter and providing this new life with physical defences and protective boundaries.

Love is vital to health. A study conducted at Yale University, for example, found that the *quality* of love in a relationship was more important for predicting the severity of coronary artery blockages than the *number* of relationships a person had.[118] Feelings of being loved and emotionally supported by a husband, wife or partner reduce the risk of angina even in the presence of high risk factors such as smoking, cholesterol, family history and other risks.

Of all the things we can lose, loss of love is the most depressing; even the mere risk of rejection can be enough for us to become clinically depressed.[119] Loss of love is a psychic amputation. Loneliness and lack of love – feeling unwanted – is the worst poverty, and can break the strongest will. The psychological pain of personal rejection and exclusion is now scientifically linked to the same location in the brain that registers *physical* pain. When we say we are suffering a 'broken heart' or that someone we love has 'hurt' us, we are speaking more than poetic metaphor.

Loneliness and isolation – separation – create a dispirited and depleted life-force in which opportunistic microbes and viruses can grow. A Swiss HIV/Aids study found that people living within a stable, loving relationship had better-functioning immune systems, better response to treatment and longer lives than single patients, in whom the virus progressed much more quickly.[120] Feeling loved, nurtured, cared for, supported and intimately connected makes us physically happier and healthier. When we feel appreciated by others within a network of mutual obligations and shared experiences, our risk of disease diminishes and our health improves. Interestingly, psychologist John Gottman (who has studied long-term relationships for several decades) has found that it takes a ratio of five positive statements to one negative in a conflict situation for a relationship to have the best chance of lasting.[121] Anything that promotes feelings of love and intimacy seems to heal us. Love relationships protect us by strengthening our immune system and increasing our resistance to disease.

Loving connections are healthy connections; if we stay connected in this way, we live longer. With a direct link proven between our close social network and our health, the fact that women are better at interpersonal connections (having evolved a greater network of contacts who then provide support and encouragement in their later years) may go some way to explain the longer life expectancy of women than men. Studies of older people have shown that older adults who stay in touch with family, friends, church and society stay in better shape physically, mentally and emotionally.[122] However, there is a need for balance. Love does not bestow ownership. If we sacrifice too much of our autonomy in the hope of maintaining loving connections, we dis-empower *our* part of the loving partnership and lose the integrity of the spiritual bond. To avoid creating this breakage, one thing many successful couples create is a psychological breezeway between them – a gentle and refreshing 'distance' or 'space' where a balance between personal freedom and connectedness is maintained. In this way, love relationships work much like a spark-plug – if the points are too far apart there is no spark, if the points are too close you have a short-circuit, but with the right gap the spark is strong and illuminating.

In a world created around levels of separation, connection and complex networks, all personal and social relationships are affected by how much free choice and autonomy we have, within supportive and healthy structures. Many relationships break down, not because of some insurmountable incompatibility, but because we rebel against losing our freedom and substituting our 'sense of self' for that of our partner. We all need to express our creativity, and if a relationship represses or inhibits the need for individual self-expression, the creative connection that is the relationship's lifeblood will also suffer. When a relationship is under this sort of pressure, we end up sweating the small stuff and arguing over the smallest points of resistance rather than focusing on what we may need to do to maintain the health of the relationship as a whole.

At this point a brief look at happiness and pleasure would help us. While they are often considered one and the same, happiness is more our emotional state, while pleasure is our sensual experience. Broadly, there are three 'levels' of happiness – sensual happiness (pleasure), interpersonal (social) happiness, and spiritual happiness – and the words 'love' and 'devotion' are regularly associated with all three. As the name suggests, *sensual happiness* comes directly and only from the five senses such as when we experience good music, wine, fine food, touch, dancing, perfume, physical beauty and so on; this is the happiness of the hedonist. Sensory pleasure and pain – sensuality – have both figured closely in our survival and evolution by encouraging us to repeat things that were good for us and felt good, and avoid things that were bad for us and felt bad. Next, *interpersonal* or *social happiness* comes from helping others and being accepted and appreciated by others; it may also involve a sense of living a meaningful life and includes evolved emotional states such as empathy and altruism. Finally, *spiritual happiness* is more esoteric and ephemeral, involving a sense of the mystical, the unworldly, the selfless and the infinitely divine. While sensuality excites us, and intimacy connects us to another person, it is often within silence and solitude that we connect to our own spiritual side.

While the word 'love' is used freely and widely, its characteristics are less well understood. The main features of true love are worth identifying.

Love is more a journey than a destination, more a process than a project. Love looks to the good. In loving relationships, we are intent on catching the other person doing things right, not doing things wrong. Our attention shifts from 'Here I am' to include 'There you are'. Love unseats us from our small self-enclosure and isolation. Some people find it impossible to extend the spotlight beyond themselves, to really understand a partner's needs and find pleasure in satisfying those needs.

Love can only be kind; without kindness there is no love. Acts of kindness are more powerful than words and more deeply felt; any act of kindness is an act of applied love. If you want to make a difference in the world, begin this very second. Begin right now with an act of kindness, big or small, to something or someone. Don't read on until you have done it.

Love can only be fearless. Where there is fear there is no love, because fear is about self. True fearlessness comes as we loosen up and release our grip on the two separations – the external 'surface' separation outlining and defining all things, and our fixated sense of an ultimately separate self. When we reach fearlessness we have reached selflessness, and when we have reached selflessness we release ourselves into the power and freedom of unconditional love.

It's a proven fact that romantic love heals.* When we speak of the person-to-person *chemistry* of love we are referring to our feelings – our hormones and our emotions. Unfortunately, when the first heady hormone charge has passed, we often feel let down (if we haven't evolved spiritually enough to create loving connections that are deep and enduring). This is the moment in the development of a relationship when we reach *volitional* love – the moment when we choose to drive our emotions instead of being driven by them. This moment is spoken of by the great sages and teachers as a personal turning point, an instant when we consciously choose either to stay 'tuned in' and in touch with our partner or turn away and disconnect. Our decision in this moment reflects how far we have evolved spiritually. In that sense, love is not something we get from another or give to another, but something we choose to *build with* another – something created or emerging between people. Remember that divorce doesn't necessarily mean our next relationship will be any better; until we stop blaming our unhappiness on others and learn what blemishes we bring to a relationship, we will carry on making the same ignorant mistakes for the rest of our life.

Beyond the chemistry of love is the spiritual outlook of love: part of our selfless, original nature whose essence predates separation and survival. A truly loving outlook, steeped as it is in selflessness, is the living expression of our original connections that extend unbroken from the infinity, through everything, to the core of our being. By activating love's spiritual connection within ourselves, we no longer seek it in others; we

---

* A study at University College London scanned the brains of volunteers who described themselves as 'truly and madly' in love. Among other positive effects, gazing at pictures of their lover deactivated areas of the brain known to be involved with feelings of depression and suicide. *New Scientist* 8 July 2000.

no longer make others responsible for a level of happiness that only we can really provide.

Love can only *be unconditional*; if love is conditional it is not love. Love that is conditional is self-serving and therefore unhealthy and defeated before it starts, because it is calculated to keep the focus on you the lover and not on the person who is loved and the connection. If our self-talk is more about what we are receiving from our love than what we are giving, then we are not in a state of unconditional love and so there is no love. A search for personal happiness through a calculated love that focuses only on oneself is not love, because love is not about self. True love – unconditional love – is selfless, effortless, inspirational and healthy.

The power of unconditional love is in the giving rather than the receiving. Love can only be selfless; when selfishness stops masquerading as love, love is free to come truly alive. At this point of truly selfless love, the words, 'I'm in love with you' no longer mean, 'You excite a state of love in me that isn't usually there, so now I am dependent on you for my happiness, and you are responsible for keeping me happy.' Instead, the words now mean, 'I'm already happy and live in a state of love all the time. Now that we have met, you are embraced and included in my happiness and love, and as such are completely free to come and go without the love-bond being diminished.'

However, most of us don't love ourselves enough to give love. We remain self-absorbed and withdrawn, and feel severely hurt when we think even a slight blow has been struck against us.

The best gift we can give ourselves is to develop a place in the heart where love may enter, no matter for what reason, what person or what time. The most important words of love we will ever hear are those we say to ourselves, and the most important voice we will ever know is the one true voice deep inside us. Many of us haven't realized that we are the soul-mate we look for. The first place to look for love is in the mirror. The lingering sense of loneliness many people feel often comes from not being in communication with themselves. Only when you can calmly, sincerely and without any sense of vanity or foolishness, say, 'I love myself', will you be anywhere near ready to love someone else. No other love exists except unconditional love, and we can only give unconditional love to others to the extent we give it to ourselves.

Love means deep, subtle yet profound connection, perhaps the strongest and most reliable link in a disconnected and uncertain world. How far apart can friends be before that connection breaks, the circuit is cut and there is no friendship? How close must two forms be before they are truly in touch? Is an elderly war-widow standing forever faithful at the grave of her long-dead hero and quietly grieving across the years, any less connected to her man than she once was as the young woman with her lover? We can be committed in love and connected as a bond without being physically in touch. Dependency or closeness without the right connections remains mere proximity. Though we communicate and connect through imitation, reflection, empathy, rapport, touch and play, it is through love that our relationships are transformed. True love is forever a bond, never a bind, a quantum connection of the softest kind. True love transcends time to become eternal. Eternity is not a long time or some distant place, but a quantum dimension that bears no relationship to created time and space. True love – unconditional love – is the glue of higher networks.

CHAPTER 9

There's more to health than popping pills

The same stream of life that runs through my
veins night and day runs through the world
and dances in rhythmic measures.
  It is the same life that shoots in joy
through the dust of the earth in numberless
blades of grass and breaks into tumultuous
waves of leaves and flowers.

Rabindrath Tagore

I n Wisconsin, soon after sunset, certain species of firefly start their evening
light-show by flashing randomly, then spontaneously change their display to a rhythmical, massed synchrony. This switchover occurs for
no apparent reason, and much too suddenly for any chemical 'communication' to be its trigger. Nor is the *suddenness* of this group behaviour explained
by individuals gradually copying each other one by one across the whole
swarm, because each firefly can see and be immediately influenced by only
a cluster of five or so other individuals nearby. On the contrary, what is
happening is that each individual in each cluster intermeshes with a different adjoining cluster in their immediate range to create an invisible matrix
that spontaneously engages to become a single, unbroken network. It is
through this formless network – this super-unity – that order has emerged,

as if from nowhere, without mechanism or structure.*

Fireflies are not the only creatures to exhibit such behaviour. Most clusters of living things can be observed at some time behaving in a similar way – exhibiting identifiable, and sometimes spontaneous, group behaviour, or even adopting common physical characteristics. Even bacteria do it.[123] Again, such behaviours can now be predicted, emerging as they do from the many simple and random interactions among the individuals. However, while the predictability of such swarm intelligence is one thing, identifying a mechanism for its transfer is another. Whether it be a shoal of fish navigating steep obstacles not seen by any single fish, or a chaotic clutter of grasshoppers spontaneously organizing into an unstoppable wing, all individuals benefit yet no single individual is in control.

These behaviours illustrate a dazzling truth: that every single thing we can identify *also* forms part of another greater whole, and every thing ultimately interconnects and cross-links with everything else at some level. This mystifying synchrony where compatible parts become a new whole is also one reason behind why your income will almost always be about the average of the incomes of your five closest friends:'birds of a feather flock together'. The reason personal exercise is more successful as a group or team activity is because of the support offered by other people. Even the often dubious art of social climbing is driven by the desire to network at a higher level – a level at which the perceived support, benefits, characteristics and behaviours are assumed to be an improvement.

In 1967 Harvard social psychologist Stanley Milgram ran tests that found we are all linked to one another through a short chain of shared acquaintances – the now-famous 'six degrees of separation'.[124] More recent studies have advanced our understanding of networks, with successful predictions regarding the movement of money, the spread of disease, political fortunes and the impact of mass marketing all validating the mathematics of networks.

The word 'network' implies entity and structure, such as a computer network or electrical circuit. However, many networks have no identifiable

---

* Though mathematical models anticipate such occurrences and even predict their probability and frequency, maths cannot predict their timing with any precision or their incidence with absolute certainty because maths cannot measure a formless structure such as this.

point at which all the parts join up to give the network structure – think of gravity and love, for example. In these cases, the influence or 'network effect' occurs over the whole entity rather than at any single identifiable point of contact or entry. It is this formless nature of some networks that can make them appear insubstantial and 'unreal', when in fact they are merely *intangible*.

This unstructured appearance of some networks even operates at an intergalactic level, with macro-scale astronomical maps revealing thousands of galaxies mysteriously aligned, as if supported and interlinked along a stream of dark matter or energy. For example, most smaller galaxies around the Andromeda galaxy inexplicably line up in one plane that intersects Andromeda. With none of the available forces of physics able to explain this phenomenon, we are left to rely on the existence of extra dimensions as an explanation for this and other mysterious cosmic alignments. (Extra dimensions are foreshadowed by Einstein's general theory of relativity, with black holes offering the best evidence of their existence.) And if other dimensions exist, then it becomes possible for networks to extend indefinitely.[125]

The communities we live in are effectively networks of human relationships – clusters of connections that exist as a shared experience. Though some relationships seem stronger than others – for instance, the biochemical forces or 'fields' holding the parts of our body together seem stronger than the forces holding the particles of water together in a cloud – everything in creation is a relationship of parts networking as a greater whole.

In all networks – from galaxy spirals to the cells of our bodies – there is a point at which order emerges from chaos. In all dynamic systems there is a 'tipping point' or phase transition where new order emerges, a critical mass of fresh interconnections is created, and synchronicity is renewed. Instantaneously, a new 'whole' emerges from the many parts, such as the pulsing flash of the fireflies or the spontaneous navigations of a shoal of fish.

We know that the 'glue' holding some biological networks together is bioelectrical. Studies in bioelectrics reveal that every cell in our body is surrounded by a naturally occurring electrical field in the order of 40 millivolts. Indeed, our whole body is completely built around bioelectrical networks. Electrical fields and currents attract new and healthy cells to damaged areas in our body.[126] Break down these networks and our health breaks down; these charged networks keep us alive. When healthy, we are a harmonized orchestration of electrical fields. We have a mass of electrochemical membranes throughout our bodies binding us together. Many of these (including the skin, which is both our largest membrane *and* our largest organ) serve as gatekeepers, escorting ions (charged particles) and other matter into and out of our cells – sometimes at the rate of a million ions per second (the significance of which will become apparent in Chapter 17, when we discuss the implications of our relationship with the electrical universe). It is as if ions know no boundaries, and our structure is made to support their movement; we certainly can't live without them. Physical aging occurs as our membranes fail to prevent a multitude of micro-assaults, including electrical changes and chemical imbalances. In effect, getting old involves a disintegration of our membranes. Aging is partly an electrical imbalance or disconnection, a breaking down of the positive and negative electrical pathways that swarm our body through its cloud of membranes. These short-circuits are brought on by a variety of influences, including unhealthy diet, poor lifestyle, misuse or neglect, physical injury, and the harmful electrical potential of our negative attitudes.[127]

Similarly, our *social* fabric is held in place by membranes no less vulnerable to disease and premature aging than those of our bodies. These social membranes act as invisible lines of defence that protect our communities from harmful 'outside' influences. For example, well-regulated customs posts block the free flow of dangerous imports, and national quarantine regulations prevent the spread of disease. So too, laws and regulations are designed to inhibit corporate corruption that would corrode the economic fabric of society and even cause the body politic to fail. Indeed, as we saw in Chapter 3, one of the major problems with current corporate practice is the fact that businesses forget they are part of a larger whole and behave as if they exist merely in a market rather than in a community. (This failure to recognize the greater whole as integral to the business can be seen when companies 'downsize', unaware of the priceless networks of internal and external contacts being lost as employees leave; or when offshore trade arrangements are made that do comparatively little for the communities involved and everything for the corporation.)

Another form of powerful yet vulnerable network on which we rely is communication technology, where the failure of just one seemingly insignificant electronic component can trigger a network malfunction that can wreck a nation's infrastructure, crippling transport and allowing entire power grids to shut down and short-circuit. This was seen in August 2003 when a massive, cascading failure of the electrical grid across the northeastern US and Canada blacked out more than 240,000 square km (93,000 square miles), and in November 2006 when a power supply problem in Germany left 10 million people in darkness across Europe.

In our increasingly unstable times, all supply lines can be similarly affected – such as health services, training and education, law and order, and food supply. This is because our modern lives depend on interlinked chains of networks. For example, the average pound of food in America travels through many processes across 1,900 km (1,200 miles) before it reaches the kitchen table. The ingredients in a pot of German yoghurt travel in total a distance of over 1,000 km (600 miles).[128] There are untold numbers of workers interlinked into these food-mile journeys. This chain of unseen communication is organized around a fabric of sole traders, small businesses and large corporations. Break any link in this fragile sequence of unseen communications from farm to table and the population it feeds is at risk. According to the book *Food Wars*, in the US just four companies control the price-points, participation and product flow of 81 per cent of beef packaging and a similar per centage of maize and soybean crushing, while another four companies control approximately 50 per cent of pork, chicken and turkey production.[129] In some monopolistic networks, bigger is better for business but bad for the security of the community as a whole, not the least risk being that highly centralized food production allows the rapid spread of food-poisoning pathogens throughout the network.

Now that we have seen how networks appear in various forms, we need to ask what could it be that holds them together, and does the same energized dynamic apply to human society? How is the internal information that is passed along a network transferred throughout? Can a network of parts hold together without some form of internal interconnecting, organizational force, some form of guidance or leadership? Vision and leadership certainly work well to hold human networks together: without a communicated sense of purpose, groups and bodies disperse. However, as with fireflies, while any network needs a point of shared commonality, it does not always need a single leader. Shared vision and purpose can be developed by the parts, then maintained and evolved in common. The strategic point of view, regularly seen in the form of individualized leadership that gives context and direction to a group, is just as often atomized and taken up by *all* members of the group.[130]

However, sharing leadership does not mean that *hierarchies* can be necessarily dispensed with. Just because we have learned to spread leadership across a range of positions does not mean that we all share it equally or all of the time; some people have more extensive connections than others (or are momentarily positioned to exert a decisive influence) and can achieve greater results on behalf of the group than others – whether those connections are civic (such as a prime minister), corporate (the CEO), creative (an Einstein or van Gogh) or accidental (such as the lone Chinese citizen filmed confronting the army tanks in Tiananmen square).

In this more evolved way of looking at the enlightened leadership of a network or group, the shift is not just one of structure but one of emphasis and outlook: those who are in positions of power are recognized to be working for and on behalf of *the group,* not the other way round. Everyone in the group is the boss, and everyone, no matter what their position in the hierarchy, is supporting everyone else and working for them. In this situation, the emergency-based command-and-control leader still exists, but has been surpassed by the host-facilitator who understands the higher leadership arts of collaboration and consensus. Only then, win or lose, will the staff, the electorate and the rank-and-file, cry out: 'We did it ourselves! We are responsible!' This reaction is the sign of effective, enlightened leadership, empowering each individual to act directly within the wider scheme of things.

In these circumstances, human leadership has progressed to where the leadership role ultimately operates as a 'funnel' for decisions *needed across the whole group.* Enlightened leadership consciously achieves this by empowering and motivating the different parts of the group in a way that energizes it into a whole. In effect, organization throughout any living network – the human body, a beehive or a corporation – requires the development of some form of leadership, though not necessarily a leader.

Effective leadership creates an integrated and healthy whole by creating internal group cohesion while also integrating this now-whole group into its context seamlessly and sustainably.

From this view of the evolution of leadership, every part of the group also works to support the overall health and durability of the organic and dynamic whole.

In human groups, delegating levels of decision-making *up* to leaders (whether political, religious, legal, scientific or educational) is a wise move, because it frees the remaining individuals in the group to concentrate on decisions and choices that satisfy more personal needs closer to home. With this healthy development, leadership has evolved as a working part of the collective consciousness – operating as much from the bottom up as the top down. While we assume that leaders recruit followers, we now see that in any healthy whole, followers also recruit leaders. To this end, the most savvy chief executives know that many of the best of any new business ideas come into the business from outside, brought in through connections with the marketplace, industry, environment and the wider community, to then be communicated up and passed on through internal networks.[131]

Just as human leaders organize activities that support the harmonious workings of the group, so too our brain stimulates the separate workings of our body into a coordinated and cooperative whole. By integrating both the internal workings of the body, *and* the body with the external world, our healing brain leads us in the maintenance of a holistic network that creates a healthy harmony between inside and outside. In our search for significance, it is imperative that we recognize the conscious three-way connection between our outlook *into* the world, our influence *on* the world and the world's influence *on* us. This conscious interaction reflects the ability we all have to influence the world around us every day, simply through the power of our minds. If we approach the world with hostility and criticism on the inside, then our *exterior* climate becomes overcast and hostile and our negative outlook is confirmed. But when we approach the world with acceptance and tolerance, this is also mirrored more and more, both within our health and around us.

So if improving our lives is merely a matter of using our minds differently and creating more connections appropriate to our greater need, why aren't we doing it already? As we have already seen, the answer lies in our entrenched habits and fears: our habit of seeing ourselves, both mentally and physically, as a thing apart, and our habitual fear of personal loss in any form. The fact is, if we don't aspire to higher connections, we are left trying to satisfy ourselves with the short-lived gratifications of the material world. By maintaining a fixation on our separate selves and the possessions we amass, we remain imbalanced and incomplete. We continue a blinkered, unhealthy and divided view of the world, where we see ourselves and everything that belongs specifically to us as more valuable than anyone or anything else. This predisposition of ours is well documented. For example, in loss-aversion studies, participants were asked to guess an item's 'true' purchase value, while others were asked to guess its 'true' sales value. Participants invariably downgraded the object's worth when required to buy, as if the object was not yet theirs. However, they upgraded its worth if they were put in the position of being a hypothetical owner required to sell (and therefore lose) it. In other words, we value most highly whatever we consider to be ours, and diminish the value of what we do not own and therefore have no fear of losing[132] – which is also why we place more value on 'self' than on 'other'.[133]

Placing more value on self and on the objects we own, allows us to successfully protect our existence and secure our circumstances, but also confines us to a limited mindset of separation and distance. Such behaviour is similar to that of a hermit crab, briefly coming out of the safety of its shell and grabbing what is needed, only to withdraw back into the shell again, minimizing contact with the unsafe 'outside' world. While this behaviour may protect us from some dangers, the cumbersome shell of our suspicious, self-protective outlook weighs us down and holds us back. Not only does it make us unable to see or escape from other dangers when they come, it also blinds us to the wonderful possibilities beyond our safe enclosure.

While locked in the grip of possessiveness, it is easy to be trapped by the fear of personal loss – a psychological trap that is sometimes used in the wild to catch monkeys. Some monkey hunters will confine a banana behind bamboo bars then quietly leave the area. A passing monkey sees the banana and extends its hand through the tight bars to grab it, but cannot then pull the fist that is now closed around the fruit back out through the narrow gap. Instead of letting go, the frightened monkey clenches the banana even tighter and maintains its terrified grip until the hunter returns. Like the monkey, if we get too attached to some things – whether material possessions, ideas, personal relationshipsorreligious beliefs – we can lose more than we bargained for. The power of attachment and the fear of loss are often greater than the appeal of letting go; they will keep us in the grip of a separation-from-risk mentality that catches the monkey in us every time.

Not only do fear and loss stop us from letting go of old habits and assumptions, fear often stops us reaching out and connecting in the first place. Few of us know how to completely let go of fear and live beyond the self-limiting psychology of loss-avoidance. This mental zone of separation keeps us small and contracted, cocooned and out of harmony with the whole. In this state, where we are diminished by a constant undercurrent of self-protective fear, we become deaf to the resonance of higher influences. These influences – subtle and unseen – are the organizing principles that give networks their potency. These are the influences that synchronize the workings of many parts into a dynamic and unified whole – cells into a body, fireflies into a swarm, and planets into a single, swirling cosmos.

The science of networks is promising to be one of the greatest discoveries of our century, allowing us to identify patterns of influence that have previously been seen only through the veil of religious metaphor. The emerging insights into the drive behind these patterns offer new possibilities for understanding our significance in the world. They allow us a more enlightened way of seeing life and our place in it – a new awareness of the power and influence we unknowingly exert, at every moment from wherever we are.

Life has its own hidden forces, which you can only discover by living.

Søren Kierkegaard

In 1972, the mathematician and meteorologist Edward Lorenz presented a talk that famously described how the flap of a butterfly's wing in Brazil could, in the right circumstances, theoretically amplify and extend through fractal effects to set off a tornado in Texas.[134]* Lorenz's 'butterfly effect', as it came to be known, was a graphic attempt to illustrate the tremendous power of networks in our everyday, physical surroundings. These effects arise from the exponential growth of self-similar patterns called fractals – irregular repetitive geometric patterns that reflect greater and greater complexity however much they are enlarged. Fractal effects give force and form to the science of networks.

Fractals often arise when physical systems are changing phase and new order is emerging (this is called 'phase transition',[135] a phenomenon we may be witnessing in the wildly undulating weather patterns world-wide). These patterns can be repeatedly subdivided into parts, each of which is more or less a smaller copy of the original. These limitless, interlocking effects show how things unfold through an endless cascade of influences, which in turn go on to form further parts of endless outcomes. Within fractals, fractal effects and the fractal dimension of relationships, we can trace how networks network.[136] Fractals help us see the forms and forces of nature in a new light. Fractal systems represent exponential effects, the capacity of the smallest events to gain momentum and snowball within a swirl of endless, intermingling influences and energy dynamics.[137] Our physical world has many formations that display the telltale repetition of fractal patterns or systems, including clouds, mountains, wind and ocean turbulence, and coastlines. Even the exponential acceleration in the evolution of complex life in recent millennia (described in Chapter 6) can be seen as the accumulation of (intelligent) fractal effects within biology.

---

* Lorenz was attempting to illustrate how unpredictable, minute, inaccessible influences within any particular system work as interdependent variables to make chaotic systems unpredictable and unstable. This leaves chaotic systems open only to probability analysis and uncertainty, not certainty.

A fractal effect is an organizing principle that can radiate so far into the future as to make distant outcomes and events appear random. Indeed, the entire material universe can be considered as one huge fractal pattern, a chaotic yet mathematically predictable system – only we don't have the maths yet. Every cell of our body is a network of fractal influences. Our body is awash with fractal networks and fractal effects. For example, our heart-rate is always adjusting up and down, varying ever so slightly from beat to beat, fluctuating in answer to the body's constantly changing needs and signals passing through interlocking networks of cells and sinews.

From very small to very large, the scale of fractal influences knows no limits, with many of the planets in our solar system, including Earth, orbiting the sun unpredictably, buffeted by the extrastellar force of fractal effects.

The science of fractals and the discovery of fractal effects remind us that everything affects everything else all the time. Fractal networks ultimately interconnect every single thing with everything everywhere. Understanding this, the best of the world's share traders know never to trade US steel shares without also knowing what is happening with rubber prices in Malaysia (because any change in rubber prices affects the price of tyres and therefore the cost of cars, which will have unforseeable exponential effects on a whole range of industries). The effect of fractals means that everything you do – or everything you *fail* to do – profoundly affects the things around you in some way or another. Global warming is the most compelling example of this, with rising sea levels and shifting pollination cycles only just the beginning of its chaotic fractal effects looming over all of us. Everything in the world and in the physical universe has only come about as the result of its contributory causes. Even your body and the level of health you enjoy have been built up around many, many contributory causes and effects – culture, family, climate, seasons, exercise, diet and life's experiences. In this way everything ultimately interconnects with everything else in a never-ending stream awash with unpredictable outcomes; there are no beginnings or endings, just the majesty of continuous change.

One alarming revelation that arises from the study of fractals is that the disruption of the Earth's systems – which we are already experiencing

– will, with the compounding effects of fractals, almost certainly accelerate an already dangerous and unpredictable environmental situation.[138] The
effects of what began as the industrial revolution 300 years ago, and
became our love affair with fossil fuels in the last 150 years, are culminating in global warming, and this is already producing inundated coastlines,
displaced communities,[139] species extinctions, and economic and political dislocation. Fractal effects are skewing even further these environmental
changes – changes that have largely originated from human interference
based on our presumption of divine authority, the belief that the world was
ours to manhandle, and the assumption that if we screwed it up God would
clean up after us.

However, it should be remembered that fractal effects do not necessarily have only negative outcomes; they can also release accumulative *positive*
effects, such as when an inspired leader makes a speech at Gettysburg and
moves his nation for generations, or when the invention of a wheel rolls
out a whole new world. Some people, places and events function as hubs
or 'super-spreaders' – focal points through which fractal effects allow a step
up to the next level of synchrony and organization. These hubs of inter-
connection – and the people who occupy or create them – stand as radial
points of immense power and influence.

Fractal patterns running through us and around us drive the principle of unexpected consequences, and amplify the effects of the accidental
outcome – the 'oops!' factor. This means that the forces that diminish may
also increase: any insignificant action or incident can become enormously
significant, while any effort can multiply, divide or disappear. Therefore,
once we grasp their significance, we begin to realize that fractal effects also
imply the possibility that all efforts – no matter how small, by whom they
are made or for what reason – can directly affect the greater good. While
untold acts of private courage may pass without immediate recognition,
their long-term effects radiate exponentially and live on. The power of
fractal effects means that everyone everywhere can have personal access
and influence anywhere, at any time we choose.

However, simply because we have recognized the power of fractal patterns does not mean that we can absolutely define and control future events.
Fractals are the great equalizer; the efforts of both the mighty and the miniscule are soon brought into balance by the cross-flow of an infinite number

of intersecting influences. Fractal patterns allow us to make a mountain out of a molehill and a molehill out of a mountain. Absolute certainty is a vanity fuelled by a mixture of arrogance and fear – our human assumption of superiority and the fear of what we cannot control. Yet, like the hermit crab, the more rigidly certain we are, the more constraints and less freedom we also have. Our egocentric paranoia overlooks the fact that while fractal networks skew all certainty, they also allow infinite possibilities.

And it is this uncertainty in our world that makes us free.

I had the sense that ... reality was endless interaction... I had no desire to state or define or analyse this interaction, I simply wished to constitute it – not even wished to – I constituted it. I was volitionless. There was no meaning. Only being.
Nicholas Urfe (John Fowles' character in *The Magus*)

In a world of influences *ad infinitum*, where do we each begin and end? If everything is a system of networks and relationships within larger systems and networks and relationships, what are the points of connection that link us into those larger systems, and where is the starting point for us – the point where we become 'ourselves'?

Brain-mapping by neuroscientists has shown there is no central place in our brain where information is sorted and decisions made, or where our actions and reactions are issued. There is no special and separate little spot we can call 'us'. Even the consciousness within our brain itself, absorbing and reflecting and building upon samples of whatever it encounters around it as well as from within, is scarcely something we can call our own – original and independent. We don't even know where our consciousness begins or ends.[140] The brain itself provides a massive processing system, endlessly dealing with the wash of information criss-crossing from several internal locations simultaneously throughout our life, awake or asleep. With our life hanging from a bundle of mental states, very few of our decisions reach our conscious mind; the decisions are made without us becoming aware of them.

Not only do we not have a centre point, we are also missing any clear outer limit, making transferences between us common (as we saw in Chapter 6). Bone marrow donors can pass on immune system 'memories' such as allergies and other acquired immunities to the recipient (via immune B memory cells). Organ donors have also been known to pass on their quirks and tastes to the recipient, with some recipients reporting changes in diet and musical tastes exactly in line with the donor.[141] Many of us carry the body cells of two or more individuals, akin to the Chimera of Greek legend, a fabulous hybrid of lion, serpent and goat.[142] We are effectively beings without borders; at some level, we are unlimited.

Our deepest connections are unaffected by distance, which is only to be expected when no one can pinpoint where connectedness begins and separation ends. In the book *The Secret Life of Plants*,[143] we read about well-designed tests in which lie-detector recordings of a person's responses to a series of questions were compared to the changes occurring at the same time in live cells previously taken from that person's mouth and held in another room. The readings were identical – the responses in both rooms were exactly the same. But how could the removed cells show any connection to the donor when they were rooms apart? The mechanism for this phenomenon remains unknown.

Many of the influences on natural behaviour remain unidentified and apparently inexplicable. For instance, Professor Frank Brown, Jr, of Northwestern University, Illinois, discovered that live oysters sent across country from the US East Coast continued to open and close their valves in time with the ocean tide of their old location. After two weeks they began shifting their timing and finally stabilized their rhythm in synchrony with the lunar cycle of their new location.[144]

Sometimes the bonds established between previously 'disconnected' and unrelated parts can become particularly strong, even life-giving. Evolution itself has produced some unlikely connections that blur the boundary between one organism and another. For example, we could not live without mitochondria – small energy 'organs' that exist within every cell of our body to supply the cells with energy. Yet DNA studies show that more than one billion years ago, mitochondria (our energy cells, without which we die) were bacteria that made an intelligent pact with our cells to supply them with energy in return for food and shelter. This again goes to show that we cannot and do not keep ourselves separate from our environment – our living planet is one integrated system within an integrated cosmos within an infinity of energy in perfect balance.

Such examples blur any assumptions about set boundaries, genetic or otherwise. It is our discriminating mind (supported by our five senses) that creates the separation of phenomena into banks of opposites – light and dark, hot and cold, good and bad, heaven and hell. But all boundaries eventually blur. Even the separation between space and matter is uncertain. Science tells us there is no such thing as 'empty' space – space is real and can be pushed and pulled, existing in a dimension beyond matter. Einstein was the first to demonstrate that space shows matter where to move, and matter shows space where to bend (much like how a person's weight distorts the flat surface of a trampoline). Space and matter intermingle; each provides the natural context or background for the other. Without one, the other cannot exist. Similarly, without a background not one thing can exist, as everything needs a context to give it borderline or definition. Existence and context are inseparable. *I have context therefore I exist.*

Beginnings and endings are also hard to track and separate. We assume that when we walk, each step is clearly separate from the one before. Yet just as each foot going forward is connected through the body to the other foot going back, so each foot going behind is part of the next step forward. There is no real boundary, no separation. Walking cannot be divided into separate steps: while the whole of anything is more than the sum of its parts, it is also inseparable from them.

Even something as beautiful as a rainbow shows how boundaries blur. While we can broadly identify its separate colours, any two colours of the rainbow merge – red into orange, orange into yellow, yellow into green, and so on – with a greater number of shades across the visible spectrum than the human eye can differentiate. It's the same for any object and its environment – the edge of one is the shared, affixed and *identical* edge of the other, making separation impossible. As there is no separation 'out there', the perception of separation can only be coming from within us and our outlook of separation.

Think of a cloud. It is made up almost exclusively of particles of water. If the particles are densely crowded the cloud appears dark. If they are lightly packed the cloud is white. Yet in either case there is still plenty of moisture beyond (what appear to be) the outer edges of the clouds, except that the water outside the cloud is a bit more dispersed and so invisible to the eye. This means that the sky, even when it seems clear and blue, is full of stretched-out cloud stuff. The illusion of separation between sky and cloud is created by us. Similarly, the sky and ocean blend and merge, with the sky often being wet enough for rain to fall, and the ocean having enough oxygen for fish to breathe. And who can pin down the point of separation between wet sand and sweeping wave to definitely divide ocean from beach? There is no *actual* separation between sky, sea and sand; any separation between them occurs in our mind.

Similarly, we see the sun and the moon as quite separate from the ocean and the tide, and we say that the sun and the moon *cause* the ocean tides. Yet what we mean by 'cause and effect' needs to be re-examined. The idea that causes and their effects are each separate, distinguishable, sequential operations is a perception we create in our mind from our limited view of what we think we see going on in our surroundings. Yet it is only when we observe cause and effect from a higher level of understanding that we realize that sun, moon and tides are in fact connected and inseparable – they are in a *relationship*, an association that forms one dynamic whole where isolated causes and singular effects disappear. When we select a mere *section* of the whole we see cause and effect, one after the other; but when we select the whole, we see endless continuity.

In general, we have committed ourselves to a restricted outlook that identifies separate causes and simple effects without us seeing the whole. Yet we have also become so locked in behind our assumptions about personal space and separation that we don't identify the extent of the downstream effects we personally cause. This is because we fail to see that 'out there' is the same as 'in here'. If we saw this connection, we would never release poisons into our environment the way we do – after all, we would never consider putting the same rubbish on our dinner plate. It is only when we recognize how everything is connected – whether or not we can physically see those connections – that we can act effectively to keep both ourselves and our supporting environment healthy and whole.

**I went to the woods because I wished... to front only
the essential facts of life, and see if I could not
learn what it had to teach, and not, when I came to
die, discover that I had not lived.**
Henry David Thoreau

I t is one thing to know of this endless continuity and believe in it, but
quite another to see it and experience it. By looking at the world with
fresher eyes, children are often the ones to let themselves see beyond
everything.

Several years ago a group of students and I went on a trip. The outing
began as a hike in the forest, then evolved into something unexpected,
something profound and unforgettable. We started off in high spirits,
laughing and joking. After some time we reached the edge of the forest and
headed down one of many walking trails. The ferns were breathtakingly
beautiful, and the forest's deep silence was broken only by the occasional
shrill screech of birds. Dappled light shone through the canopy of trees,
and the children stared in wonder at the enormous ferns.

One particularly beautiful specimen took their attention. It had a
short trunk with a huge, green umbrella-spray of fronds. The children
gathered around it. The sprinkle of sunshine gave gentle highlight to the
repeat of fractal patterns that contoured each leaf, giving such ferns their
famous symmetry. Unfurling from the fern's centre were the coiled-up
beginnings of next season's new growth. At this point I suggested we play
a game – a mind game. I asked the students to gaze at this beautiful old
fern and then, without shifting their eyes, widen their attention until
they could focus on the whole of the fern at once. They were meant to fix
their eyes on one point while also paying attention to the whole fern. In
silence they practised doing this.

With their gaze still gently fixed on one point, I invited them to do
something more. I asked them to narrow their attention down 'into' the
fern and, without moving their eyes, become aware of one of the many
green fronds making up the whole fern. During this switchover their eyes
were not to move, only their attention. In fact, they were being asked to

shift their inner point-of-view, moving their attention between the one (the whole fern) and the many (the separate fronds).

At first, some of the students found it difficult to shift their point-of-view without moving their eyes, but soon almost everybody was able to do it. And so we stood there quietly switching our attention back and forth, eyes unmoving and unblinking, alternating our inner eye between the 'one' fern and its 'many' identical parts. Then, quite spontaneously, the children began using this technique on trees, moss-covered rocks and other objects on the forest floor. Some even paired off and tried it on one another. After a while, they found they could quite easily switch from seeing the whole thing to seeing all its separate parts, and then switch spontaneously back again.

One boy had moved from the group and was sitting by himself on a rock with his eyes closed. When he opened them I asked what he was doing. He replied that he was doing the exercise but instead of doing it with whatever was around him, he was doing it with the 'stuff' in his head! When the others heard this, one of the kids suggested we try the whole planet.

'What do you mean?' asked one of her friends. The girl then explained that we could try picturing a mind's-eye view of the whole world.

With all our eyes closed and standing in an easy silence, this young student guided the group with her description of the world while we created a mind's-eye view. Then she described us 'shifting' this global awareness from the picture we had created in our head to an awareness of the real world we knew was in front of us and around us – an awareness of the surrounding world we were standing in, all the while keeping our eyes gently closed. We repeated this process back and forth a number of times, moving our attention between the global picture in our head and what we knew was the actual world surrounding us. Then together we all quite naturally went one step further, and stood there, arms relaxed, breathing slowly and easily, everything quiet, eyes now open, but with our attention no longer fixed on anything in particular. This gentle, receptive state of relaxed, open-minded stillness continued for some minutes. Then one child, not more than ten years of age, began to silently sob, with tears streaming and shoulders shaking. Concerned, I leant down and quietly asked what was happening for him. He replied he was crying with happiness because he could see 'beyond everything'.

When we have seen beyond boundaries and separation we have entered 'God's house', and begun to answer the primal call for home.

Where is the life we have lost in living?
Where is the wisdom we have lost in knowledge?
Where is the knowledge we have lost in information?
T.S. Eliot

Health and wholeness are one and the same; if we lose one, the other is gone. Recognizing and understanding the networks that govern our daily lives is vital to our wellbeing, because networks have such a tremendous impact on both our spiritual and physical health. Indeed, 'new age' healthcare professionals of all persuasions who have recognized this fact describe themselves as holistic practitioners. There are over 200 alternative therapies practised in the US alone, and 80 per cent of the world's population uses non-Western methods of treatment. According to a survey by David Eisenberg of Harvard University, 40 per cent of people in the US already use complementary and alternative therapies.[145] Alternatives to mainstream medicine have become phenomenally attractive in the West because in general they give the patient a substantial role in the healing process, promoting the return of power and primary responsibility for health to where it has always been – with the patient.

An equally important benefit is the fact that alternative therapies see health as something holistic, generated wherever the sum of our interconnected parts are in perfect balance. This is quite unlike Western medicine, which has divided our parts into separate medical specialties. Contrary to the underlying assumption of Western (allopathic) medicine, a patient is a whole living being, rather than an incidental life-support system carrying some specialized, localized pathology. Like humanity in general, Western medicine suffers the collective insanity of 'fragmentitis' – division and segmentation to the detriment of the whole. Future evolutionary psychologists will consider our present psychological outlook to be primitive, as indicated by its prehistoric fixation on separation to the exclusion of holistic connections.

The holistic, fully integrated approach to health is supported by the knowledge that 95 per cent of disease is triggered by a combination of environment, diet and lifestyle. Genes may predispose us to illness, but more often than not it is the combination of these three that activate the unhealthy predisposition. Environment, diet and lifestyle are all factors we can personally manage.

Our deep relationship and co-evolution with the natural environment is highlighted by the fact that 60 per cent of modern medicinal molecules originate in nature, and many of these are still directly extracted from natural sources. However, the burning of the world's forests is obliterating an irreplaceable library and storehouse of healing molecules; in Brazil, for example, the combined extinction of native communities and the destruction of the Amazon rainforest is killing off traditional healing knowledge and sinking the entire world 'into a kind of amnesia'.[146] Moreover, we only know an estimated 10 per cent of land-based life and 5 per cent of the organisms living in the world's oceans – in fact, every drop of sea water contains unknown species and unknown genes.[147] This means that, because relatively few life forms on Earth have been identified and their inter-relationships understood, we are almost certainly missing out on an untold number of medicinal molecules in life forms that are entirely unknown. This ignorance about the wealth of our external environment is paralleled by our ignorance of our complex internal workings. For instance, our intestines contain nine times more viruses and bacteria than the total number of cells in our body, yet many of these remain unstudied (some refusing to grow in the laboratory) so their overall relationship to our health is unknown. When viewed against this background, there is much still to be learned about the connections between life, the universe and our whole-health.

But 'holism' is not just a physical health issue. Mental health, and indeed our very appreciation of reality, both depend on how clearly we grasp the true extent of holism. The holistic mind is the healing mind; holism and health are one and the same. As we saw in Chapter 7, with our mind attached to the long path we see ourselves somewhere in the world, but it takes the holistic short path with its limitless viewing-point to see the world within ourselves.

Imagine that you are a leaf on the tree of life. Decide at what time in your life you want to fully realize and experience all that you are part of. Is it when you are still connected to the tree, alive and full of bloom, or falling to the ground in autumn and looking back, too late for you to make a significant difference? You choose. It is easy enough for us to observe a whole from the outside; we do it all the time – every object we see is an example of observing wholeness from the *outside*. Spiritual insight is the capacity to see the whole from the *inside* – beginning as empathy when we enter into the viewpoint of another being, or culminating as deep meditation where we directly experience the full extent of all that we are *within*, and sense the larger whole of which we are part.

Part of our mind is always sympathetic to this infinite vantage point of original reality, and capable of making observations from there. It's just that to see holistically we are called on to sense something not seen by our normal senses, and often we don't have time, don't believe, or don't know how. Our common five senses allow us to create shape and size, colour and form, dimension and boundary – the appearance of what we call objective reality – but this is not enough. This 'worldly' capacity allows us enough perception to observe anything from its *outside* but not enough to see the whole we are all part of from the *inside*. Our spiritual intelligence grows in proportion to our ability to tap into and directly experience these infinite energy networks and exchanges within the integrated *whole*, and not merely those holding together some of the *parts*.

Because of the advances being made in the science and technology of healthcare, and also because we are now at the stage of being able to recognize our broader impact on our environment, we have the opportunity to make this the healing century. This is our big chance, our point of significant choice. To this end, our personal transition towards whole-health ultimately depends on how far we develop our point of view into holistic

Here is a quick test of your functional holistic attitude: When you are caught in traffic, do you complain about the traffic in front, but ignore the fact that you are simultaneously part of the same traffic problem?

networks. This gives 'holiness' a completely new meaning. No longer a rare and distant spiritual state, holiness is now available as a personal and immediate state of mind and a realistic, healthy experience.

Our whole Earth has a measurable metabolism, a measurable rate of energy moving through it just like any other living organism. Measuring this energy flow indicates how fast organisms grow, how quickly nutrients such as nitrogen and carbon will move up and down the living systems, and is helping predict events such as the effects of global warming. Earth is one vast interconnected and dynamic system, from its molten core, through its living biomass, out to the outermost reaches of the atmosphere, and on into deep space – in one unending continuum.

Without a sense of the infinite whole, we have no spiritual compass-bearing or divine reference point. The secret to expanding our spiritual capacity is to find the ultimate holistic viewing-point – the outlook that dwells in the one while dealing with the many. The holistic view allows us a way of knowing where we are going while seeing what we are becoming, forever.

It suddenly struck me that that tiny pea, pretty and blue, was the Earth. I put up my thumb and shut one eye, and my thumb blotted out the planet Earth. I didn't feel like a giant. I felt very, very small.

Neil Armstrong, Apollo 11

Our first overview of Earth, when we saw our beautiful, blue planet cast alone against the timeless sweep of deep space, came from images taken aboard the Russian Sputnik on 4 October 1957. Since then, many astronauts have reported that looking back at Earth from outer space was the most significant spiritual experience of their entire life. Like the astronauts, we too can expand our horizons and elevate our outlook until we have evolved an angel's eye view of everything.

Yet the big *spiritual* picture takes in more than the intergalactic vastness, though that vastness is an inspiring beginning. Complete spiritual freedom transcends space and time, entering a state not confined to created reality. While astronauts experience the cosmic big picture from the outside, we can do better – we can discover more profound and wonderful horizons from within ourselves wherever we are, right here on Earth.

Society has almost only ever been advanced by individuals whose outlook expressed a more highly connected consciousness. Today's civilized society is the collected expression of numberless personal insights accumulated down the ages. In earlier times, city-states existed behind high fortress walls. Trust and cooperation between separate warring states was low. However, even enemies need points of contact, and so philosopher-sages such as Confucius (Kong Fuzi) were free to move between opposing warlords and rival city-states, maintaining durable connections against the warring forces of separation. Similarly, early European monasteries housed monks who were accepted into the confidence of rival kings. These early civilizers bridged the gap between the less civilized, enclosed minds of the day. In pre-European Australia the same collective consciousness existed, with wandering Aborigines welcomed across another tribe's land to trade, travel or visit the shared sacred sites of their ancestral dreaming. More recently we have developed the United Nations, an international body that includes all nation-states in an expression of our emerging global consciousness. These are examples of where minds already evolved and insightful enough to transcend the confines of ego and self-interest have translated this higher experience into a civilizing influence – helping to transform humanity as each of them transformed themselves. Able to turn any difficult situation into a positive one, they carried within themselves the simple capacity *to see connections that others missed*. Yet this capacity is not restricted to the enlightened few. We are each capable of – and responsible for – elevating our own conscious point of contact with endlessly wider reality. Knowing that there is no central place within us to call 'us' makes it easier to surrender the limitations of self-interest and engage the ultimate experience of true spiritual integration and elevation.

Now is forever – the past exists only as memories, and the future only as dreams. The present moment is the one possible time we have in all of eternity in which to make a difference, to uncover our significance within our simplicity, and experience the everyday power of our ordinariness. By loosening our own grip on fear and loss as we develop higher perception and awaken to breakthrough consciousness, each of us can transform our outlook on reality and grasp the full significance of our day-to-day existence.

If we get this right – if we make the break with ego and the separate self – we then become free to experience the fully integrated, networked and healthy whole that we are part of. If there ever was a magic pill, one supreme 'cure-all', this is it. Welcome to infinity's timeless creation: the essential spirit of integrity interlinking us with all things.

For notes and author contact information, please see website on page 385.

ACHIEVING SPIRITUAL MATURITY AND HEALTH

CHAPTER 10

The three stages of complete spiritual integration

If you have built castles in the air, your work need not be lost; that is where they should be. Now put the foundations under them.

Henry David Thoreau

When a holistic system is working perfectly, there is no negative stress, no excess of push and pull, no blockage, no disintegration or disease. There is balance. There is *integrity*.

Integrity, in this fullest sense of the word, involves more than ethics or honesty; it is also about full integration and wholeness. Health and happiness do not come from what we have, but from what we have *become*. We are all afflicted by the fall from wholeness and the loss of its embrace; we all suffer under the pain of disintegration, since disintegration allows disease; while integration prevents it. Most of us can identify our visible means of support; now we must also explore our *invisible* means of support. Having discovered why we need to reawaken our dormant connections, this is the point at which we start thinking about how we go about it. Now we begin to find the structure and links needed to become fully integrated and fully empowered, connecting us into the mysterious, infinitely divine whole.

If we are to attract anything good into our life, some form of integration or alignment is always needed at the most fundamental level. When what we think, do and say are in tune, and there is no deep doubt or distraction lingering unconsciously in the background to spoil the focus, then our actions are in energetic harmony with our intentions. Until we are in this integrated state we are unable to generate truly positive and lasting outcomes, solve intractable problems or overcome everyday obstacles. Then, once we have achieved this energizing alignment within ourselves – and also discovered the secret of how to extend this harmony into the surrounding context so that our mind, body and environment are in symphony – our momentum becomes unstoppable. In that moment, the miracle of creative manifestation begins to emerge in our lives; by becoming attuned to the resources needed, we have entered a state of affinity that attracts miracles into our lives.

It is timely to introduce the natural law of attraction. This is a powerful law, and because of the way it works in our lives we need to understand it. The law has four aspects or parts to it. The power of attraction is at its strongest when all four of its parts are working together in alignment rather than in opposition. The first part is our psychological attitude – often called the power of positive or negative thinking. This aspect of attraction says that whatever you think about and wish for, you are more likely to attract into your life – because what your mind sees on the inside it actively works to produce on the outside (as we saw in Chapter 4 with mental rehearsal and visualization). The remaining three parts to the law of attraction are the most misunderstood and the most powerful. They are the three fundamentals of integration we are about to discover in this section of the book. Without having these three fundamentals integrated and in alignment, all attempts to release the secret law of attraction into your life will fail. However, once we master these three fundamentals of integration, we awaken to the highest levels of spiritual consciousness – breakthrough consciousness – and along the way the law of attraction brings an abundance of all the best that we might want and need into our lives.

However, the secret law of attraction cannot work if it breaks the fundamental law of integration. The law of integration says that any disruption to one or more of the three fundamentals – our mind-body connection, our connections to society and the natural environment, and the less obvious connections between our psyche and the infinity of original reality – causes a break to our energetic relationships with the whole of reality, and we suffer.

Another reason we need complete integrity at all levels is for good health; we all know how important physical and mental health are. Yet these alone are not enough to guarantee our complete and lasting wellbeing: no matter how healthy we are personally and individually, if our surrounding environment is sick then we too will be sick. This applies not only to the physical environment, but also to our social environment – the societies we live in and the structures we set up within them to support us. Even then, achieving a perfect balance between ourselves and our immediate environments is still not enough to guarantee our complete wellbeing. Whole-health can be realized only by integrating all elements of ourselves and our material world with the greater background environment that holds *all* of these physical parts together – what science calls infinite energy in perfect balance, and spirituality calls divinity or eternity.

This then is our spiritual task: to balance our mind and body with the three environments: the *physical*, the *social* and the spiritual or *infinite*.

Have you ever warmly greeted a visitor or smiled at a customer you secretly wished to avoid? Ever taken your body to work while your mind went on holiday? Ever forgotten to exercise because you were 'too busy', then wondered after years of neglect why your get up and go has got up and gone? We are full of paradoxes and self-contradiction. Many of us want things to be different in our lives yet we don't want to *do* anything differently. Many of us want to go to heaven, but few want to die. We love the new and yet resist change, forgetting that change is *necessary* for renewal. Seventy-five per cent of us in the West are in favour of organ donation, but only 25 per cent of us carry organ donor cards. These are all examples of mind and body in different places: a state of *dis*-integration.

We suffer this disintegration because of what we have done to become the masters of self-preservation. We retract to preserve ourselves and keep ourselves intact. But by withdrawing into our personal safety zone at any sign of threat or risk, we have come to rely instinctively on separation as the key to solving *all* our problems at every level. Unfortunately, the downstream effects of excessive separation and dis-integration are what we are witnessing today: the dismantling of nature's web and the breakdown of the integrity connecting our minds, bodies and environment. We have mastered separation and retraction too well, and in so doing have disconnected our spiritual circuitry from its source.

Personal integration in the form of individual integrity and honesty are our entry points to begin accessing the spiritual energy flow (remembering that all of reality is energy in some form). By maintaining personal honesty and integrity we activate our spiritual circuitry, with the possibility of then increasing our spiritual capacity while engaging directly with the creative power behind all health and healing.

However, total integrity involves more than personal moral issues such as honesty, consistency and truth. Spiritual integrity is better seen as the 'spirit' of integration, of being whole. It is this spirit of integration that affects our health both personally and collectively. We don't disintegrate and become decrepit because of old age; we age and become decrepit because we disintegrate.

Spiritual integrity includes the integration of mind and body with our physical and social environments, and then, ultimately, integration with the whole of creation and the infinity itself. These elements may be thought of as the three fundamentals of spiritual integration, each of which will be discussed in more detail in the next chapters. The *first* of these is the mind-body fundamental, where we discover the powerful internal fusion between mind and body. The *second* is the connection of mind and body to our environment, where we discover our inseparability from the physical and social environments, and our personal dependence on them. Zen Buddhists recognize this in their saying, 'When thirsty, drink. When tired, sleep. When sad, cry. When happy, laugh.' These are statements of pure mind-body integration. The *third* and final fundamental is created by the renewal of our ultimate connection – the connection with the spiritual or infinite environment. This is expressed in us as the indefinite point at which mind, body and environment merge into the infinity, and through which we experience the fullest extent of our boundless capacity for connection – the so-called psychic and spiritual dimensions.

If any one of these three fundamentals of integrity is underdeveloped, the structure upon which our spiritual integration rests is weakened, and so our relationship to the 'whole' is at risk. Suffer a break or disconnection with any of these three fundamentals of integrity and we literally begin to 'disintegrate' emotionally, physically and spiritually, leading to personal and, as we are seeing, global discord.

Although our spiritual position is advanced more by positive thoughts than by negative ones, positive states of mind by themselves are not sufficient. Although success needs positive thinking and a 'can do' attitude – and a lot of modern training in motivation promotes this – we will not win any heavyweight title just by saying, 'I am a champion' and believing the fantasy. Merely saying positive things without taking appropriate action in harmony with our positive target and its environment, can be as useless as striking matches underwater and expecting to start a fire. In this, something is out of place to keep our thoughts and actions from creating the new reality, and that something is the necessary integration of the three fundamentals.

When we *visualize* anything, we begin the creative process; when we *energize* ourselves we begin action; but it is only when we *harmonize* both our mind and our body with the total environment that we complete the cycle. Without such harmony we are almost guaranteed to remain forever held back by our mindset of separation, with little chance of moving from the reactive mindset and wishful thinking of the long path to the creative connections and transformative mentality of the short path. Without first establishing within ourselves the three fundamentals of integration, we will be forever ambushed by unexpected outcomes and repeatedly disappointed, however positive our thinking.

At every stage of our life we can be completely spiritually integrated. Spiritual integrity is a state *beyond* our years; age has little to do with it. A fully integrated person can appear in any shape and size, and they almost certainly will be respectful, caring, sometimes forceful (but not pushy); they will honour others, be insightful and astute, know the value of silence but be capable of boisterous enthusiasm; be bright but not overbearing, self-contained but not aloof; and be interested and interesting in equal share. They are quietly helpful to others, happy, independent and engaging. They are capable of true intimacy (unity with another). They will have a full and complete emotional range available to them, and play no favourites. Being balanced and integrated they live harmoniously, experiencing love, kindness and compassion as second nature. Anyone in this highly evolved state can reach beyond their insulated and self-serving outlook to meet strangers easily, as if the stranger was already known and well regarded.

The way we treat strangers is a practical indication of our personal spiritual development and social evolution. The 'tribal' mind as a rule presumes the stranger a threat to be excluded until the stranger proves otherwise, whereas a 'civilized' mind happily includes the stranger as a brother until the stranger proves otherwise. This socio-spiritual progress is already evolving across humanity, as shown by our progress towards a less violent society. Most forms of physical cruelty towards one another – including torture, murder and execution – are becoming less common, despite what we may think.* Through our emerging understanding of connections, we now have the tools to continue this altruistic momentum to the living world around us.

Key to the full development of spiritual integrity are our electro-spiritual networks within our bodies and around us. At one extreme, neuroscientists study electro-spiritual networks as biological structures within the circuitry of the brain, while, at the other extreme, centuries of poetic insights and musings by sages and mystics address the less tangible aspects of this super-circuitry. Without an appreciation of these extended psycho-spiritual networks, our physical health and spiritual fitness will remain mutually exclusive and problematic. Although the clinical study of them is somewhat new to western science, their existence has long been appreciated by health practitioners elsewhere. For example, the system of acupuncture – practised for centuries in China, Korea, Japan and India[148] – is based on a network of 400 acupuncture points and twenty electro-spiritual 'meridians' or energy 'highways' along which flows *pran* or *qi* (*ch'i*) energy – the energy of life and the universe, a vitality that can be blocked but never broken. These meridians running through us are not regarded as beginning and ending within our bodies, but are seen as part of the energy fields and dimensions extended into the unseen or spiritual environment around us. Similarly, the Vedic tradition of India produced the

---

* While approximately 30 per cent of males in hunter-gatherer societies died violently, today the figure has plummeted to one per cent – and that includes wars, genocide and atom bombs. In spite of media sensationalism, most forms of cruelty to fellow human beings – including human sacrifice, genocide, torture, homicide and execution – are becoming less and less common. (J. Payne, *A History of Force*, Lytton Publishing, 2004.)

system of seven major energy centres (*chakras*) and 42 minor ones in the body, through which vital energy enters, moves and leaves us, all related to the spine and the seven most important endocrine glands.

As Western medicine becomes more open-minded, and more accepting of influences beyond the physical at work within health and wellness, holistic alternatives such as meditation, massage, herbalism and acupuncture are now becoming increasingly accepted. These alternatives all have a common interest in energetics, the bio-electrical networks on which our body is built and kept functional. An appreciation of energetics and bioelectrical networks is essential in any modern health practice because not only are we a mass of energized atoms, but behind our physical appearance we exist as a complex of electrical circuitry. In fact we are *alive* with measurable electrical oscillations; our brain cannot function without the integrated rhythms of energy that wash through and across it. In addition to the 'God-spot' mentioned earlier, there is a range of other micro-currents and voltages involved in our brain and helping to regulate our health.* What's more, a change in the electromagnetic fields of our brain can have a measurable effect on our memory: magnets strategically positioned on our head have been shown to alter our memory and other creative functions.[149] It's almost as if to be a good doctor you should also be an electrical engineer.

To be alive is to function at many interconnected levels that embrace both the material and the energetic. While at first sight life appears as a purely physical event, down at some indefinite point everything physical – the animate and the inanimate – becomes electrical, built on atoms that are themselves electrical circuits. Our own bodies are integrated with our electromagnetic environment right down to the cellular level, since the water molecules within all cells have a minute electrical charge that creates 'attractive forces' between cells that hold them together. It therefore follows that any interruption to this electrostatic balance – such as happens through the known effects of mobile phone emissions on these attractive forces[150] – could be expected to undermine our health. As we are in reality one big fully integrated bioelectrical circuit, the possible implications for our health are many.[151]

* For example, alpha and theta waves are associated with our creative states, and 40-Hz gamma waves undulate across different regions of the brain.

When we remain spiritually underdeveloped we act from a 'disintegrated' position where many of the things we do – either consciously or other-than-consciously – ignore or break our electro-spiritual connections. The result for us is further *dis*-integration and *dis*-ease in body, mind and spirit. Whole-health comes with the integration of the physiological, psychological and electro-spiritual connections – a truly holy communion with the whole of creation. Though we often look for the hidden 'angle' in life, there are no angles in a full circle, and no disconnections within infinity. Creation then is the supreme zero-sum game wherein everything ultimately forms an integrated whole within the infinite energy in perfect balance. And when we sense this, we see what Buddhism calls our true face – our true nature or essence beyond the physical.

When our three spiritual fundamentals are in balance, only then are we fully in balance and spiritually integrated. However, remove any one of these foundations of spiritual integration, and the whole person is diminished – we are healthy and whole only to the degree to which we develop in *all three*. Indeed, our only chance for full health is to rebalance our lives by overcoming the bias that favours endless separation into the many at the expense of the one. We are made up of three regions, not merely the physical, and it is only as we expand our spiritual intelligence and allow our own spiritual integration that we give ourselves the chance to become whole again.

CHAPTER 11

Keeping your mind on the matter
Stage one: our mind-body connection

Treat people as if they were what they ought to be and you help them become what they are capable of becoming.

Johann Wolfgang von Goethe

Any system is healthy and whole only when it is functioning without interruption – when its parts are fully integrated, balanced and working in harmony with one another. In fact, at some point the words 'whole', 'balanced' and 'one' become interchangeable. Therefore, any search for health and wholeness must also include a search for balance and integration.

Before we can heal our physical and spiritual worlds and make them whole, we first have to heal ourselves. To do our best work, we have to be in the best of health ourselves. Moreover, to achieve personal health we also have to recognize that physical and mental fitness are not separate things; they are inextricably linked, each affecting the other. Even within the system of our personal health, all parts must be working in perfect relationship with one another: damage one and the rest is damaged. This is why our mind-body connection is so important.

The need for mind-body balance has long been widely recognized across many cultures. In parts of the Indonesian archipelago some tribal groups still practise a tradition where each morning every person dances their dreams of the previous night to the assembled villagers. In this way, the dream-dancers harmonize their mind with their body, and begin their day more balanced and integrated. Dissolving the separation between mind and body, these communities also record a lower incidence of hostility and stress. Indeed, while almost any form of dance – whether religious and shamanic, traditional and tribal, or the modern rave – can help balance our mind and body, some dance can open us up to a sense of heightened reality, where we feel released into something beyond or bigger than ourselves.

Sportsmen and women win and lose depending on their mind-body connection. Much elite training is about strengthening this connection with the same discipline athletes use to train their body. Any athlete whose positive self-talk and visualization propels them across the winning line even before the race is run, is that much closer to the top spot on the podium. By tasting, smelling, seeing, hearing, feeling and knowing success *before* it happens, we align the body with the mind to create success – whether out on the sports field or anywhere else in our life.

The first step in healing our mind-body connection is to uncover how we damage this relationship and make it unhealthy in the first place. Paradoxically, although we know relationships are vital to our survival, the relationship we have with ourselves is the one we most neglect. Our relationship to employment is a good example of what happens when we fail to allow our mind and body to communicate and work in harmony with one another. If workers were musicians, then most of us are playing instruments we would rather not play. Almost 90 per cent of us admit we would rather be working at something else, and only about 5 per cent of us are absolutely and completely happy with what we are doing. That means almost all of us spend our working lives doing something we don't want to do, at a place we would rather not be![152] Though we work to earn an income and survive, the *way* we work throws us into a state of denial that is exhausting and unhealthy. While we may act responsibly and professionally on the job, we are often just suppressing the fact that we would prefer to be somewhere else. This split between where we are and where we want to be is a split in the mind-body connection – a break in the first fundamental of integrity. This is why we eventually need a holiday – to rebalance our mind with our body and recharge ourselves. The brain loves leisure time for the same reason; by giving ourselves permission to relax, hang out and do whatever we want to do, we get our mind and body closer to the same place. The more closely we integrate mind and body, the more we lower our negative stress levels and improve our whole-health.[153] Similarly, we promote our own mental health when we learn to enjoy our work. Many people have discovered that achieving a work-life balance is not as hard as it seems.[154] Finding work we love to do makes work a pleasure – and a sense of pleasure indicates we are aligning our mind and body. It is this integration of mind and body – two fundamental aspects of ourselves – that promotes the health of both.[155]

Stress in small bursts saves us from dangerous situations, but when our stress response remains turned up to 'high' over a long period, it can injure us.[156] This is why abused or traumatized children often suffer measurable shrinkage to key areas of their brain.[157] Importantly, our whole lifestyle – where we live, our control over our work and living conditions, sleep patterns, diet, exercise, social networks and so on – affects our accumulated negative stress, our 'allostatic load'. Elevated levels of stress hormones, such as appear with sleep deprivation, reduce the production of new brain cells.[158] Treating stress and depression with pharmaceuticals is merely a band-aid solution; the long-term fix must be holistic. This is why any segregation of ourselves from our surroundings is problematic: even when we try to restrict our concerns merely to the health of our own mind and body alone, we still cannot ignore the influence of our environment. Only when our social systems permit a day-to-day lifestyle that minimizes tension between mind and body can we find durable happiness and decrease our allostatic load. This rebalance leads to a greater number of healthy individuals in a society, and so enhances the health of the *whole* community.[159] A healthy society needs strong, well-balanced individuals just as much as well-balanced individuals need the support of a healthy society that they help to create.

None are so old as those who have outlived enthusiasm.

Henry David Thoreau

There are many ways to rebalance and repair our broken connections, whether it be exercise, medicine or the power of the mind. One simple and traditional way that we humans have developed for repairing the connection between mind and body is the contemplation of stillness that we call prayer or meditation. While some people use meditation for relaxation and to release stress and tension, others take it further, using meditation as a spiritual discipline to transcend the 'self' and develop an advanced understanding of life's deeper meaning and value. Meditation can be relaxing, but it can also go further and be enlightening.* Spiritually, meditation brings more benefits than mere relaxation.[160] This is why true religious leaders spend many hours a day in states of attentive meditation, quite apart from their more common religious rituals of supplication and devotion. It is also why many hospitals and workplaces provide meditation spaces such as chapels and gardens designed for quiet contemplation. We have a hunger for integration, and meditation is high on the integration menu.

Because our mind tells our body what to do, anything that influences our mind also influences the mind-body connection and needs to be acknowledged in our search for whole-health. So watch what you feed your mind; too often our unchecked response to external influences allows our fears to rage out of control. The psychological effect of a bomb exploding, for example, can reach much further than the bomb's actual impact – if we allow it. (A bomb will strike fear, and sometimes terror, into the vast majority who are not actually at physical risk.)** It is therefore vital that

* Meditation is far from mere relaxation, its many states ranging between the extremes of exaltation and human hibernation. Advanced meditators have markedly different brainwave patterns than non-practitioners – they have resculpted their brain (see endnote 196).

** Modern culture now recognizes that post-traumatic stress is commonplace, and that grief and trauma affect people deeply. As a result, counselling is now part of any strategic response to public disaster and corporate misadventure. Counselling is too often neglected, used only as a last resort – when the pain of not changing has we become aware of the pressure our circumstances can place on the health of our mind, and therefore on the health of our body.

In addition to monitoring our influences and practising meditation, physical exercise is also integral to the health of the mind-body connection. With exercise we keep both our heart and mind healthy.[161] With exercise we sculpt our minds. Animals that exercise freely (running on a wheel) make twice as many new brain cells as a sedentary animal; exercise also helps overcome depression, promising new possibilities of thought and behaviour.[162] When we exert ourselves through exercise – the heart pumping, muscles stretching, and lungs re-oxygenating the bloodstream – we breathe new life into the body at the cellular level by allowing the unseen currents connecting mind and body to regenerate. With this in mind, the process of ageing could be described as the body slowly forgetting itself bit by bit, as the energy of the mind disconnects from the bioelectrical energy of the body.[163]

Exercise is known to stimulate overall brain function, and the ageing brain is known to be just as powerful and capable of learning as a younger brain. In fact, the actual structure of the brain is not completely developed and its wiring fully integrated and cross-referenced until mid-life; adult brain function is proving much more supple and dynamic than we realized. Brain plasticity – where we can voluntarily and with training rewire changes to such features as personality and long-term disposition – is now an accepted neurological fact. Mental and physical exercise is proven to boost the immune system in elderly patients and increase life expectancy, whereas with three weeks of completely inactive 'bed rest', the actual size of our heart shrinks by 11 per cent.[164] So try practising yoga – stretch, strengthen, meditate, and boost your health and wellbeing. Discipline yourself; make yourself do it. Or, next time you see the slow-mo dance of the 'wrinklies' harmonizing body and mind with tai chi in the park, join them.[165] Find your dance, whether it is judo, athletics, swimming or any other. Without this first fundamental of spiritual integration working for you – without creating, activating and maintaining the connection between the mind and the body – your development is hampered.

(cont.) become too great, with the patterns of stress and pain so entrenched, and our mind-body connection so split that we need outside help to find our way back to spiritual integrity.

The mind has an extremely powerful influence over the body and its health, as professional hypnotists have long shown. With the right suggestion, many hypnotized subjects can change their heart rate at will, develop blisters where no burn has occurred, and prevent blistering in certain situations where a burn *has* occurred![166] The power of mind is now also being recognized in the Western scientific and medical communities. For example, neuro-feedback trials – where people watch their own specific brainwave patterns displayed on a screen and attempt to change them – are helping uncover the extent to which our mind-body connection can be consciously controlled to improve our health. Conditions such as epilepsy, depression and stroke – and even the physical experience of pain – can be influenced when we are able to visualize our own brain activity.[167] We also now know that even our immune system can be taught to turn itself on and off – it is intelligent and can be trained.[168]

Further compelling evidence for the power that our mind exerts over our body is the proven existence of 'the placebo effect': the measurable or felt improvement in health that cannot be attributed to treatment or the passage of time, relying instead on the mind-body pathways.[169] A placebo (an inert substance believed by the patient to produce genuine health benefits, hence the placebo *effect*) is a trigger for self-healing, and its effect is so strong that the United States Food and Drug Authority will not approve any drug unless it is tested against a placebo, because this 'background' effect can have such a profound impact on the patient's response.[170] Examples of the placebo effect are numerous and well documented. They include doctors eliminating warts with inert dye and promises about its effectiveness; asthmatics in remission after being falsely told that they were inhaling medication; and the pain of post-operative dentistry being significantly diminished when the patient *and* the dentist thought the ultrasound machine treating the pain was functioning.

In one notable experiment, an inert saline (salt) solution was substituted as a placebo pain reliever, taking the place of morphine (which had been working up until that point). The patient, who was not informed of the change, continued to feel no pain. Then a morphine blocker was added to the saline placebo. This blocker should have had no effect, as morphine was no longer minutely detectable, yet, within moments, the patient's pain returned (a similar saline effect has been found to reduce

- Jeanne Achterberg, author of *Imagery in Healing*, says that 'all healing is magic'. In every healing tradition, the patient and the healer 'must both believe in the magic or it doesn't work. Western doctors make secret markings on paper and instruct the patient to give it to the oracle in the drug store, make an offering in return for which they will receive a magic potion.' Achterberg lists several factors that inspire trust in healers of all types, including the actual 'pilgrimage' to visit the healer (distance is also important); the impressiveness, both exterior and interior, of the building or other site; the healer's demeanour; the healer's training credentials; and the pervasive air of power and mystery, even fear.

Jeanne Achterberg, *Imagery in Healing – Shamanism and Modern Medicine*, Shambhala, Boston, 1985.

tremors and muscle stiffness in sufferers of Parkinson's disease).[171] This shows that the placebo effect works beyond our present presumptions about the limitations of mind: it seems our cells themselves have an intelligence and memory that can be tricked.

Dr Helen Mayberg, Professor of Psychiatry and Neurology at Emory University, Atlanta, has discovered that pharmaceuticals, placebos and psychotherapeutic 'talking cures' (counselling) all work by activating the brain in some way. Although these three therapies begin by stimulating different regions of the brain, the effect of each therapy is ultimately delivered to the rest of the body along the *same* pathway.[172] This means that of these three distinct ways *into* healing, each of which creates healthy physical changes, two are via the power of mind! In other words, placebos are *not* about dealing with imaginary problems in the suggestible patient.[173]* Rather, placebos actually inspire us to trigger detectable chemical responses

* Dr Herbert Benson, of Harvard's Mind Body Medical Institute, explains that the power of the placebo might be better understood as 'remembered wellness'. The mind is a powerful instrument that, with training, is capable of consciously controlling blood pressure and heart-rate. Believing in a placebo is not a sign of weakness, but a sign of the tremendous healing power of the mind-body connection.

within our bodies that heal real medical conditions. Moreover, psychology and psychiatry can initiate the same structural and metabolic changes in the brain as external medication, such as a prescribed drug.[174] Our healing brain is a marvel of possibilities, allowing us to produce our own opiate-like painkillers merely by 'deciding' to, and affecting our health by harnessing the power of belief and optimistic expectation. Mind and body each operate as an extension of the other.[175]

According to studies by Professor Hans Eysenck of London, for example, between 30 per cent and 70 per cent of all medical effectiveness (including surgery) is due to the placebo effect.[176] *This means that no less than 30 per cent of the power of any medication or medical procedure is due to the patient's mind and willingness to heal.* These and other studies confirm that for the placebo to be effective, the patient must first have a strong expectation and a positive anticipation that the healing process will work. There is a direct relationship between expectation and therapeutic outcome. Next, the patient must trust both the healer and the healer's method. Finally, the patient must undergo a process of reinforcement where they are reminded of the positive outcomes they expect. All of these elements vary in detail depending on the particular healer's technique and cultural background, but the effect is the same – the patient is enrolled to cooperate at a deeply personal and psychological level.

In this way there is little difference between the effectiveness of a Filipino faith healer's hands, a shaman's magic potions or a conventional doctor's prescription pad – all can evoke a biochemical change in the brain allowing healing to occur in the body. We are the ones who create the negative or positive expectation of the outcome, not the medicine or healer. One of the most popular and mistaken beliefs of modern times is that doctors will make us well. But although a doctor can close a wound, it is in fact the body that heals it. Doctors may offer the best conditions, but finally it is some resource within the patient that causes the healing to occur in a mysterious and as yet unmeasured way. Researchers are now finding that the best work any healer can do, besides mastering their usual method (conventional Western or traditional), is to help the patient believe in and visualize positive healing outcomes for themselves. In other words, whether we use modern medicine or mediums and mystics, we won't be healed if we don't also give ourselves permission to heal deep down at the biomolecular level.

The opposite of the placebo effect is the 'nocebo' effect – the capacity to self-injure through the power of the mind. The Australian Aborigines traditionally 'point the bone' at cultural transgressors, signifying permanent condemnation and tribal rejection. This symbolic act of extreme exclusion – acted out merely by pointing a ceremonial bone and performing other rituals – throws the luckless outcast into such deep despair that they often die without coming under any physical attack. Similarly, with our own minds we also can literally worry ourselves sick: when we become elderly, levels of the stress hormone cortisol rise as we feel increasingly vulnerable. Some badly injured patients are kept heavily sedated because the less pain they consciously feel, and the less they believe they are injured, the faster their wounds heal.

Both the placebo and nocebo effects offer us a window into the powers of the mind and how our beliefs construct our reality. We now have the evidence that healing cannot be analyzed and understood on a purely scientific, physical level; healing includes the profoundly psychological, even spiritual. The power of healing can be found in myriad unquantifiable factors, from a doctor's bedside manner to a person's will to live, with wellness and willingness almost synonomous.

The mind-body connection is the internal support we need to develop personal control, whole-health and a holistic outlook. We have the choice – the power of mind – to harm or heal ourselves.

Whether you think you can or think you can't – you are right.
Henry Ford

By now we can see that positive thinking not only feels good, it also has the power to heal. Now that we understand the powerful influence that our mind has over our body, the first step in ensuring a healthy mind-body connection is to recognize the vital necessity of maintaining a positive attitude towards ourselves. In almost anything of importance we undertake, success and a positive state of mind go hand-in-hand.* Studies in psychology show that the person most likely to succeed will be someone who is agreeable (while not appearing indecisive), enthusiastic, conscientious, and open to new ideas; and unlikely to be neurotic. The reason we are attracted to people who are positive and agreeable (making us more inclined to imitate them, or at least get near enough to collect their autograph) may be the fact that their attitude stimulates the same health-giving chemical changes in us that come with being more successful and effective. Positive and agreeable equates with success and effectiveness. Sounds too easy, but the research is in! A positive attitude precedes success and has multiple benefits for the individual and the community.[177]

In addition to a positive attitude (which often matters more in life than schoolroom intelligence), a person has a healthy personality to the exact degree to which they are inclined to look for the *good* in every situation. We have nothing to gain and much to lose by causing anyone to feel bad about themselves. When we wish someone ill or push them into action against their will, at least two things happen to hurt us also: our own negative state of mind causes imbalances in our chemistry (for example, toxic cortisol is released); and we cause resentment in the other person. Someone who is forced against their will still holds their original opinion, only now it is concealed and primed, lying in wait on our path like a psychological landmine.

Studies on attitude and self-concept show that most of us think of ourselves as more positive and optimistic than we really are. Psychologists have

---

* While it may seem contradictory to be discussing worldly success when I have earlier said that the aim is to strive for spiritual significance rather than mere worldly achievement, it should be remembered that success in this sense is somewhat more than the worldly accumulation of riches or glory, which often involves success at someone else's expense. The success that we seek here is that of personal achievement and the satisfaction that comes from the fulfilment of our personal potential, whether or not it brings with it financial wealth and the esteem of others, or disregards these measures entirely. In this broader sense, success allows us to become less fearful and ultimately, therefore, better able to contribute to the greater social good. The removal of fear while gaining the benefits of personal achievement allows us to become both productive and effective, and in the best position to help those around us rather than merely remaining dependent and helpless. As a result, this form of individual success supports the wellbeing of the whole by creating increased success for everyone. In this way, success skills become social skills that are also early spiritual skills.

discovered that most of us are deluded about ourselves. On a five-point scale ('extremely optimistic', 'mildly optimistic', 'neutral', 'mildly pessimistic', 'extremely pessimistic') most people are mildly pessimistic in attitude and outlook – even though most of us like to think of ourselves as realistic *and* optimistic. But the truth becomes apparent when we are asked to dream optimistically of an ideal world; we usually say that this is childish and unrealistic. So why do we assume that pessimism is more realistic than optimism? After all, the real world is neither pessimistic nor optimistic, the real world just 'is'; it's our viewpoint that makes it appear good or bad. The single most empowering life-skill is a positive mindset, an attitude that promotes healing connections between the mind and the body. A positive, free and active state of mind has also been shown to promote brain cell growth and health at any age. So choose to think positively. This is the first step towards making ourselves whole and healthy, while simultaneously opening up the possibility for us to begin healing the world around us.

Happiness is vital to our mental health and physical wellbeing. Happiness is healthy – happy people develop 50 per cent more antibodies than the average person in response to flu vaccines.[178] Happiness also affects the way we see and respond to the world. Psychologists have tested people in good and bad moods on their ability to view a picture and then recreate it from memory. These studies found that happy people process information differently from sad people. Happy people concentrate on the general effect and the big picture, while sad people miss the big picture and go for the detail. In a good mood we tend to think globally and more broadly, while in a bad mood we stumble over the details and sweat the small stuff.

Yet the majority of us spend a lot of time *making* ourselves unhappy; depression is the largest single health cost in the world today, and the World Health Organization has predicted that depression will be the world's leading cause of disability in adults by 2020.[179] As witness to a severe breakdown in the mind-body connection, depression is more than a mood-altering mental disorder; it damages the whole body, and the brain in particular. Stress or abuse can trigger poisonous chemicals that force structural changes to our body while destroying existing brain cells, preventing new ones forming, and increasing the risk of heart disease and stroke.[180]

The Mayo Clinic in Minnesota has studied the relationship between a person's state of mind and how long they live. A positive self-concept is known to create internal changes that make us less likely to succumb to stress disorders and cancer. A group of almost 850 people were first interviewed in the early 1960s and graded according to their degree of optimism or pessimism. Re-interviewed 30 years later, it was found that the pessimists had 19 per cent higher likelihood of early death than the optimists.[181] Similarly, psychiatrists in Norway have found that people with a negative view of life (brought on by such threatening factors as poverty, housing stress, grief, loss or other shortage) are 25 per cent more likely to develop cancer.[182] *Attitude matters.*

If only for selfish reasons then, knowing that depression and negativity kill brain cells and corrode our whole body, it would seem insane ever to let ourselves have even *one* negative thought! Pay attention to your attention. Let a smile begin on your face – you never know where it will end up.[183] Today's global epidemic of depression is an early warning to humanity – similar to the early warnings of ecological damage sent out by our physical environment more than 50 years ago[184] – that our mental environment is trying to tell us something. Along with the epidemic of obesity sweeping the world, we are also participating in the psycho-spiritual breakdown of many nations and their populations.

Spiritual health is a state of mind. We can be our own worst critic, with low self-esteem the result of our self-inflicted intimidation. On the other hand, positive emotions free us up to think faster and more creatively. People with the happiest, brightest outlook display the most creative thinking and work more efficiently.[185] Optimism also helps make us healthy. For example, Professor Stewart Dunn at the University of Sydney, Australia, has found that optimism and a sense of personal control are consistently associated with a longer survival rate in melanoma and breast cancer patients.[186] We won't go without breakfast, coffee, our morning jog or the daily news, so why do many of us think a program of daily positive energizing and visualizing is optional, when the benefits are unsurpassed and the power of mind so strong?

We live the life that our mental outlook allows us, and therefore a small shift in attitude is the first step in overcoming almost any problem. The best problem-solvers don't worry about the problem once they have clarified what it is; instead, their energy is directed towards applying the best solution. On the other hand, those of us who turn away from finding a workable solution have actually allowed ourselves to be put off by what we perceive is the scale of the problem. It is as if we see the bulging freight container and think that all of it needs to be unloaded in one almighty back-breaking lift, and have therefore given up without even trying, not realizing just how easily the individual boxes can be moved if tackled one by one.

In fact, small changes are almost always the key to turning around big problems. There are *never* any huge solutions, only lots of small ones linked up. Similarly, the creation of huge problems can be avoided by small, preventive actions: a ship can avoid a huge iceberg just by the slightest movements of the helmsman's fingertips at the wheel. Tiny changes, huge outcomes. This brings us to a powerful realization: the ability to create the small but consistent changes required to solve problems, satisfy needs, and fulfill goals and dreams is not a talent restricted to the elevated few. It operates easily and always in all of us, providing a momentum behind everything we do – whether changing a light bulb or changing a life. This is why we should always find reason to be optimistic about our own competence: whatever else we might think we are doing, all any of us is *actually* doing is creating change, every moment of every day.

Rather than just applying ourselves to self-limiting activities and mundane goals, why not exceed them and explore new territory? After all, the champion athlete is focused *beyond* the finishing line; only the runners-up are fixated on the winning post.

The only way of finding the limits of the possible is by going beyond them into the impossible.
Arthur C. Clarke

Imagination and visualization are powerful components of our mind-body connection. The power of our positive thoughts is underwritten by the power of our imagination. Imagination and visualization effectively bring into our lives most of what happens to us. Therefore, in order to develop a healthy attitude towards ourselves, and so enhance our mind-body connection, it is important to recognize the power of our mental imagery.

You're mistaken if you think you can't visualize; in fact, to think is to make images. You visualize every time you remember where you parked your car or left your keys. Each of our five senses collects fragments of data that we assemble into working images and store in our mental filing system. These sensual impressions and visualizations are matched against our beliefs, expectations and previous experiences, then accepted, rejected and prioritized accordingly. In effect, our inner and outer realities merge in our mind's eye. When we change our expectations and beliefs, we also reallocate our attention and reshape our impressions – we create new images and possibilities as we adjust our emotional emphasis and redesign our worldview.

Our long-term intentions and immediate actions are not separate from one another; they energetically coexist in our mind, simultaneously. For example, when we walk, not only are we calculating a track ahead through *immediate* obstacles, we simultaneously picture the vehicle we will be driving in a few *minutes* somewhere in the car park. Then, if someone asks us where we were headed with the car, we could answer, 'To the airport for an *extended holiday*'. These three quite different levels of personal management, operating simultaneously within our physical body, also correspond to the three general levels of management that operate within business: staff do the foot-slogging track work; supervisor-managers keep things on target and maintain direction; while the chief executive embodies the larger purpose and overall vision of where the company will eventually end up. These levels also embody the *how, what, and why* of any form of life. All living things display the same three-tiered structure of organization as an evolving part of their survival strategy: their day-to-day activities (*how* they do whatever they do); the guidance given to these activities by information gathered from the surrounding environment (*what* they do); and the long-term strategy or intention (*why* they do what they do).* From this we can see that the way different levels of management work in a business is not original – it is borrowed from nature and is part of life.

* In business, every key performance indicator (a point where we measure how well we do what we do) also happens to be a reason 'why' the business does what it does up to that particular point.

While we may consciously visualize desired outcomes, something other than the conscious mind frames our beliefs and, more importantly, our expectations. Expectations are the deepest and strongest of our visualizations, but often pass beyond our conscious radar. The difference between whether you live or merely exist depends on your deepest meaning and your highest expectations. Expectations lead outcomes that create reality. Most highly effective teachers share one outstanding characteristic: their consistent application of high expectations, especially in the face of negative behaviours and results. Expectations set the boundaries of our achievements, and so for greater achievements, we need greater expectations. This aspect of mind-body balance is crucial knowledge for parents, teachers, managers, leaders and healers: expectations are a force; they have the power to harm or heal, to help or hinder.

What are your most intense expectations? Perhaps personal peace and happiness, wealth and financial security, or a long and healthy life? You may want these things, but do you really *expect* them? One of the secrets of manifestation is having deeply aligned expectations firmly established in your mind. What vision of the future do you carry for yourself and your children? It's important to ask ourselves these questions because, no matter what career we have, what job we do or life we lead, our main toil is on the inside of us. Remember, we are the gatekeepers of our own perceptions: our 'inner' work is to constantly select and control our visualizations, and be careful of the thoughts we allow to arise.

Visualizations – whether positive or negative – gain full power when they match expectations, and the combination can be very powerful. For example, given the right expectations and training, people can learn to manipulate their heartbeat up or down. Similarly, negative emotional pressure can suppress growth hormones in children, while laughter is known to speed recovery and support general health after major surgery. The power of our expectations can be set high or low, with dramatic downstream results either way. However, without consistently high expectations, perseverance and harmonious integration, most visualizations downgrade to fantasy and fade away as wishful thinking. The secret to effective visualization is the willingness and capacity to take appropriate action, and keep taking it – all the while maintaining balance and harmony between what we think and what we do, thus allowing the integration of mind and body to emerge within the interconnected whole of reality.

This is the powerful secret of spiritual alignment. If our dreams are not in harmony and alignment with the overall health of the whole, then sooner or later the law of attraction will work against us to draw the unexpected and the unhelpful into our lives. On the other hand, when we integrate mind and body with our deepest expectations, we activate the second part of the law of attraction to better bring the outcomes that we want into our lives.

The medical profession once considered running a mile in four minutes impossible – they didn't expect the human body to withstand the stress. They said muscles would tear, hearts would explode, we would stain our shorts and embarrass our mother. But in May 1954 a 25-year-old British medical student named Roger Bannister ran a mile in under four minutes. Then, in quick succession, several other runners also broke the four-minute barrier. They could all have done it before then, but it took Bannister's example for them to believe in the possibility, expect it, and get their bodies to do it.

Dream the impossible. Impossible today is achievable tomorrow. As we have seen, many champion athletes use mental visualization as part of a winning strategy; it is part of their daily discipline. Likewise, many hospital patients are achieving profound results after being taught conscious mental visualization as part of a healing strategy. The implications of this linkage between mind and matter place health science and healing at the leading edge of research into mind over matter and other psychic phenomena.

Perfection is not considered possible but it is worth striving for – visualizations and visions are, after all, pictures of perfection. Knowing that optimism is healthier than pessimism, let us spend a moment to create a mental picture of a perfect world. Allow yourself to imagine the impossibly good – however different from 'reality' it may seem – and allow it to exist for a moment in your imagination. As hopeful or as positive as we might like to see ourselves, most of us will conclude with, 'Great in theory but not very likely' or, 'Stop dreaming; that's not realistic' or, 'I'm ready, but nobody else is'. Yet we know that our imagination can be the beginning of creative miracles. Why should we stop living in a dream-world when our world is *driven* by dreams? Imagination has given rise to some of our most farsighted inventions, innovations and ideas: Arthur C. Clarke pictured satellites in geostationary orbits;[187] Jules Verne imagined air travel and a global communications network;[188] and Leonardo da Vinci was designing helicopters 500 years ago.

Just for fun, right now, start thinking the impossible. By doing this, we begin the pleasure of breaking old habits of mind and opening up to new possibilities. Imagine how our relationships would be if we only tried to catch our partner doing things right, and resisted catching them doing things wrong (or pouncing when they behaved in ways we disapproved of). Think of what would happen if society gave the highest status and recognition to artists, thinkers, teachers and research scientists instead of the rich, the fleetingly famous, the merely athletic, the charismatic or the scandalous. Picture a world where celebrity status was also given to the people of inspiration, kindness and creative insight.

Imagination – the ability to think of something that is not immediately present – is more than a self-indulgent luxury. It is a necessity, central to living consciously – a key to survival moment-by-moment, and crucial to extending our horizons beyond today's frontiers. Wherever we are in space and time, reality and imagination are inseparable; creative imagination is our preview of tomorrow, allowing a vision of the future that can be brought into being by positive expectations and perseverance. It is in this way, through the powerful interaction of a positively aligned mind and what we now know as the influence of networks, that what seems unbelievable today becomes tomorrow's truth.

Nothing in the world can take the place of persistence. Talent will not; nothing is more common that unsuccessful men with talent. Genius will not; unrewarded genius is almost a proverb. Education will not; the world is full of educated derelicts. Persistence and determination alone are omnipotent. The slogan 'Press On' has solved and always will solve the problems of the human race.
US President Calvin Coolidge

It is one thing to imagine and visualize possibilities, another to bring them to fruition. Visualization, expectation and creative imagination all come to nothing without persistence. Without persistence, why bother? Almost all great athletes, artists, musicians, leaders and career professionals achieve mastery in their field only after sustained effort. To do anything well takes dedication and discipline, and to be able to spontaneously perform our part 'at call' can take a lifetime of practice. Part of any practice is to bring mind and body to one point for focused action. There is no shortage of talented people, just a shortage of people who have practised long enough to upgrade their talent to a skill. This is why, when we witness a moment of victory on the sports field, our cheering is not merely a display of simple, distracted boisterousness; we are also loudly proclaiming our joy at witnessing a moment of true excellence, an instant of artistry, a glimpse of spontaneous transformation, a flash of the creative power within our own lives remembering itself.

One big difference between those who limit themselves to unimaginative or trivial lives and those who overcome disadvantage to achieve personal excellence is the ability to maintain one eye on the compass and the other on the course – starting with the end in mind and keeping it there. For us to see any of the benefits of the law of attraction in our lives we must also apply ourselves persistently to its practice. Through focused persistence, thoughts eventually become things. We now know that personal greatness is within the grasp of almost every one of us. Greatness and genius are not inborn; they are learned and can be encouraged or discouraged. While some minds are brighter and perhaps find the going a little easier than others, they can still fail if they lack the necessary application. On the other hand, outstanding achievement in any field – whether it be Einstein in science or Tiger Woods in sport – does not necessarily require more than average intelligence or talent. What *is* always required is about *five times* as much time and effort as an accomplished amateur is willing to dedicate.[189] Again, what they are working on is the integration of mind and body, and the research shows us that with the right mentors, the right core enthusiasm and the deepest personal application, we too can achieve our impossible dreams.

Management theorist and author Stephen Covey advocates beginning with the end in mind – mind-body integration – whenever we start anything.[190] But if we think about this advice for a moment, we realize that it is impossible to do anything else; we cannot consciously begin anything *without* having the end in mind, otherwise what's being begun? We may be instantly distracted and lose the plot, but without an ending in mind at the outset, there is nothing for us to begin! In this sense, beginnings and endings are inseparable; remove either and everything stops.

Beginning with the end in mind may seem a bit daunting – not only because of what we see as the scale of the problem, as we saw earlier, but also because of how frustratingly far away in the future the desired result seems to be. Yet even thinking of how long we will have to wait to achieve a result is itself a distraction. This causes resistance, making the task ever more daunting and giving us an even bigger deterrent from starting at all. We all know that our sense of time is *very* flexible, speeding up or slowing down depending on how much we are 'into' what we are doing. So to avoid this self-defeating spiral, all we need to do is trust that once we begin and relax into the momentum of the task, this momentum alone will carry us along. And with the right outlook – which needs our mind and body to be aligned and in harmony – even the simplest act can become an act of creation in which time is wondrously suspended. Artists call this the creative state, or their muse. Modern athletes and others call it 'the zone' – an experience of the perfect alignment of mind and body, where the action and the outcome are one and the same. When we're in this frame of mind, the next thing to do is all we are doing, and the arrival is a foregone conclusion.

However, the real skill lies not only in beginning with the end in mind but *continuing* with the end in mind. The easy part is having the vision that gives us the end in mind and gets us started; the hard part is *maintaining* that first spark of applied vision and continuing to see things through to the end without distraction.[191] In our daily lives we are surrounded by distractions that compete for our attention at every moment. To survive this stream of distractions we must be like dancers pirouetting at speed without falling over. Dancers achieve this impressive feat by fixing their eyes on one particular point and turning their heads quickly back to that same point at every rotation. Like them, we must keep our eye on our target, and when *anything* comes along to divert us, we must straighten our gaze, turn the other cheek, and continue. Intention without action is wishful thinking, and action without intention is mere impulse. Mind and body must come together. The ability to simultaneously see where we want to be as well as where we are, *and maintain both positions*, depends on being able to let go of distraction without letting go of intention.

The secret to achieving the end we have in mind lies in the art of 'time-bending'. This is the ability to bend or project a point of our attention forward to where we want to end up and, without distraction, allowing our body and world to eventually join it. The instant we picture a future event, we actually begin to physically enter that future by creating an actual particle of that quantum future in the cells of our brain (we also bend time backwards with our memory in the same way). In this sense, the most successful salespeople know that the initial contact with the client is not the first phone call; it is instead when they first see the client in their mind's eye and feel the client's presence. While many of us operate on fairly short timeframes (and addicts only to their next 'fix'), strategic planners bend time to position themselves years ahead, and spiritual masters bend time into eternity. All champions – athletes or otherwise – are masters of long timeframes. The less easily we are distracted, the further out in front of us we are able to bend time and achieve long-term goals. In this way – with mind, body and action kept in complete alignment – the possible becomes the actual. This is the secret to making achievement effortless.

However, once we have projected some of our mental energy into the future and begun with the end in mind, we must also continue to live and act in the present, because this is where real life energizes and activates the

- Central to being able to stay focused and continue with the end in mind is the ability to delay gratification. We use delayed gratification to our benefit in everyday situations, such as when we cook our food rather than buy take-away, forego stealing for earning, and save for the future rather than spend everything now. Indeed, an early ability to delay gratification apparently predicts a successful adult. In his book *Emotional Intelligence,* Daniel Goleman describes a social experiment where children were given two sweets. They were told that they could choose to eat both straight away, but that if they only ate one now and kept the second until the adult returned some time later, the child would be rewarded with a whole bag of sweets. In follow-up studies, those kids who were able to sit calmly and wait for the bigger prize were the ones who did better in school and in later life.[192]
- Delaying gratification is an essential part of any success strategy. The prehistoric hunter who resisted the desire to rush in impulsively (and scatter the prey) was more likely to bring food home for the tribe. In this way, any inborn talent for delayed gratification was passed on through the gene pool after bestowing more status, social desirability and increased breeding opportunities on the successful hunter. Similarly, successful professionals gain their skills through years of study rather than yielding to more immediate distractions. If you are inclined to 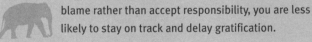 blame rather than accept responsibility, you are less likely to stay on track and delay gratification.

future, bit by bit all around us. But even as we act in the present, if we *attach* ourselves to whatever is unfolding immediately, we risk distracting ourselves with a roller-coaster of reactions and emotions that disengage us from the end in mind. On the other hand, if we manage our mind well and take a dispassionate view of whatever we find in every moment – understanding our perceptions to be no more than a feedback system to guide us towards our ultimate goal – then our mind and body remain fully aligned, with our present actions synchronized to our future outcomes.

Hardly anyone gets things right the first time; it's just that when successful people are blindsided and lose momentum they are brave enough to take a new course of action and not give up. This is the self-discipline of persistence – the capacity to do what needs to be done over and over and over again until the goal is reached.

Creating success can look like it is *off* target most of the time. So-called failure is just the name we give to the information and experience we need to help us correct our position, stay on track and reach our target. This is how most radar works; the radar only detects the aircraft for brief moments in the antenna's rotation cycle, but it is constantly checking the rest of the sky (the aircraft's context) to confirm the correctness of the plane's position. In any single day we make countless decisions that then need to be corrected and adjusted. In this sense, so-called failure is actually fundamental to success. If something is worth doing, it is worth doing badly long enough for us to learn how to do it well.

If there was one single feature we could call failure, it would be the failure to maintain momentum. Not all dreams will succeed – the flood of intervening influences that intersect our lives and are driven by the forces of change will see to that – but all dreams can be maintained. Sadly, when we fear so-called failure, we often give up in the hope of avoiding it, which becomes failure's guarantee. Keep leaning towards the goal. Mistakes by themselves are not the problem; the problem is our failure to fix them. Giving up without correction leads to wasteful duplication of mistake after mistake.

In 2002 Steven Fossett became the first solo balloonist to circumnavigate the world non-stop. It was his sixth attempt. Someone with a defeatist attitude, after trying once or twice, might have mistaken the pattern of going up then coming down too early as failure, and accepted it without further attempt. After five failures, some of Fossett's wellwishers had lost faith in the project, yet he found a way to break the pattern. Fossett will always be remembered not for his five losses, but for his record-breaking triumph.

Nobody can give you wiser guidance and leadership than yourself.

Cicero

Our experiences are our only teachers, and what we do with our experiences shows how much we have learned. All training is mind training, and the state of our mind is ultimately a responsibility we must each shoulder for ourselves. Just as an employee trains for job skills, or a health-conscious person trains for *physical* fitness, we need to be trained in *mental* fitness to reinvigorate our mind-body connection. Unless we push ourselves, we can never know how fit we can become, and this applies to mind training as much as to physical training.

Certainly the brain is capable of astonishing achievements. At the age of 30, Dominic O'Brien could memorize no more than about five or six playing cards, yet after only six years of practice became World Memory Champion. Like many memory experts, he had quickly developed the ability to memorize the card sequence of several entire packs of playing cards in just a few minutes.[193] O'Brien likened our need for brain training to having our car regularly tuned. Whatever we are capable of becoming is powered by the engine of our mind.

The mind-body link is so strong that to change one is to change the other. Philosophers from Aristotle to modern brain theorists would support findings made at the Chinese University of Hong Kong, that music lessons act like fitness training for the brain, significantly increasing our spoken vocabulary and verbal memory.[194] Brain scans of children being trained in music show that their brain-processing systems work faster than those of untrained children, with a general memory advantage and cognitive boost after only four months.[195] Brain training – of which there are many types on offer – creates lasting changes. Negative emotions can be seen to fade as positive emotions are made more durable. Children trained from primary school in communication and negotiation, basic philosophy and higher values become happier, more balanced adults. As we saw earlier, we can sculpt our brain and shape our mind at any time throughout our life; age is no limitation. Richard Davidson, Research Professor of Psychology and Psychiatry at the University of Wisconsin-

Madison, has even linked brain training to the immune system, and shown that significant positive changes in both our brain and immune system can be produced by only a short few months of meditation training and practice.[196]

In other words, science is confirming what has been accepted wisdom through history – that the brain can be trained to promote our health and happiness. In the same way that physical exercise changes the shape of our muscles and body, so too mental exercise helps us independently manage the wiring of our own brain. Our mind is fluid, not fixed, and it needs to be trained.

At critical moments we may need help to keep our lives on track. The right help can never guarantee to move us, but it can inspire us to move ourselves; the decision and responsibility always remain ours. A teacher can offer us their information, perspiration, inspiration and motivation, but ultimately we have to go it alone. And while many purported spiritual coaches and teachers do a good job of guiding our attention away from the many distractions, while at the same time illuminating the path directly in front of us, some do not. Beware the teacher who seems to be inspirational while also encouraging the student's dependence. Not only does this display an arrogance of spirit or attachment to the status and possessions of the position, it can equally indicate the teacher's own dependence on the dogma of their beliefs. All of these caveats and enclosures interfere with spiritual integration and personal development. Direct spiritual experience lies beyond both the teacher and the teaching.

Eventually, all mastery must become self-mastery. This calls for personal responsibility, mutual respect, freedom and informed choice. We control the doorways of our own perception – whether of God or anything else – and we are the only ones who can ultimately decide to step through that doorway onto the short path, or turn away. Until we realize and accept that everything and everyone around us exists as a point of energy inhabiting our sensational mind, our expectations of the world around us always risk being disappointed, and in the end this misbehaving world will leave us dissatisfied.

One of the main ways in which we exhibit self-mastery – the control of mind over body and action – is in the way we use our power of choice. Choice helps us navigate our environment and stay alive. Life as a complex whole would at some point be impossible to maintain without the power of choice. Change may be constant and inevitable, but choice stops change being random. Choice is how we navigate change. The present moment is not a moment of time, but a moment of choice, endlessly unfolding between past and future. We add to or subtract from life with each and every choice we make. The human story has developed around pivotal moments of choice, when an instant in an individual life became a hub of transformation. Our personal power is enhanced when we recognize these moments in our own lives and decide to take action rather than hesitate and watch the opportunity pass and fade.

We don't evolve unless we also evolve our way of looking at things. Though change is one of life's constants, we are motivated to change only when we become convinced that our usual method of operating no longer works, or that another outlook or course of action will be better for us. This conviction may come to us slowly or suddenly, arising either from increased frustration and desperation or as revelation through inspiration. However, we often do just enough to stay alive but not enough to flourish and thrive. Every decision we make involves deciding which way we move – towards the safe and familiar, or towards growth and the new. Every moment revolves around the choice either of living the re-runs of all our old stories, or moving on, informed by the past yet unencumbered by it.

Victims of abuse are a case in point. I have run counselling workshops where we talk about terrible acts of personal abuse. I give my clients complete permission to acknowledge the crimes against them, and support their idea that they were indeed victimized – no excuses, no denials; the fact is they were victimized and the other person was wrong to do it. Once that is established, we then move on to a new idea: that from this moment, the choice is theirs to continue carrying this aspect of their past as a storyline into their future – or not. The moment this insight takes hold is often the exact moment when their personal power kicks in, a moment in which I have seen miraculous breakthroughs begin in health and outlook. For them, this becomes an instant when the mind and body have aligned to liberate and transform.

Ultimately, no one can liberate us; we must liberate ourselves. We are the only ones who can give ourselves permission to change, heal and move on. When we heal ourselves we begin to heal the world, because personal healing is part of planetary healing. In fact, in our interconnected world, without personal healing there can be no planetary healing. This enlightened course of action is our duty, our privilege and our birthright. By tuning in the mind-body connection and experiencing the first stage of true, holistic unity, we stand shoulder-to-shoulder with the very best – the very best people that have ever lived, the very best outcomes, and the very best possibilities that life can offer.

CHAPTER 12

You are your environment, and your environment is you
Stage two: our mind-body environment connection

Happiness is when what you think, what you
say and what you do are in harmony.

Mahatma Gandhi

Just as the first fundamental of integrity, the mind-body connection – our internal environment – is gaining medical recognition and creating general interest worldwide, so too is the link between ourselves and the external environment. Welcome to the second fundamental of integrity: the mind-body-environment connection.

With the first fundamental of spiritual integration we saw how the brain regulates our *interior* environment. With the second fundamental we make sense of our *external* surroundings – the physical and social environments. The physical environment includes man-made structures along with the 'natural', while the social environment includes our network of relationships as well as our political and economic situation. How we relate to both branches of our external environment – the physical (natural) ecology and the social ecology – is a matter of life and death for us; our interaction with them is a proving-ground for our spiritual development, or lack of it.

In the long term, our life stays healthy only to the extent to which we recognize the greater whole of which we are part, and act on it. Get this wrong and there are far-reaching repercussions, both personally and globally. As we have seen earlier, there are clear links between a healthy social environment, a healthy physical environment and healthy humans. This applies not only to our physical health but also to our psychological wellbeing. When our mind-body disconnects from our environment, so can our sanity. If deprived of any reference to the outside world, imaginings and visualizations risk becoming hallucinations. Delusions are simply mental visualizations, but with one big difference: they are no longer anchored to our five-sense reality.[197] In fact, hallucinations *replace* the view of our senses, leaving a deluded person tragically unhinged. For this reason, our mind-body-environment connection is as important to our mental health as it is to our physical health – without it we become completely disoriented, disengaged and helpless.

We are equally entwined within both the physical and social environments. Within the physical environment is something we call 'nature', from which many of our medications originate. We make the false assumption that we can 'go' to nature, as if nature were some wild or distant thing. But nature is not something separate from us; we are within nature and nature is within us. Equally, from birth we are intimately bound up in our social environment; almost all the improvement in our health and wellbeing across the last 150 years has come from environmental factors such as better diet and nutrition, better sanitation and hygiene, better social services and justice systems, and improved working conditions. Moreover, separation from the ecology of our social environment is known to undermine our health. In a study of more than 138,000 people in Denmark, living alone was one of the strongest predictors for heart disease and other health difficulties.[198] Most of what we identify as being 'us' – our looks, expressions, personality, nationality, language, ideas, values, beliefs, ethics, feelings, aspirations, hopes and fears – are almost completely an accumulation picked up from our social environment and the cultural context in which we live. Society's influence – frequently backed up by religious beliefs and spiritual practices – lies behind some of our most powerful feelings and motivations. These are often the most difficult to shift.

The second fundamental of integrity also gives us the ideas, information, experiences and social communications necessary to build and maintain our network of social connections and support. However, this socializing influence is not without cost, which we can see in the power of group psychology or 'group-think', and how this collective consciousness can impact each of us personally. For example, society's belief in the effectiveness of pharmaceutical medicine is known to be as important to the patient's recovery as what the manufacturer says about any particular drug.[199] In the US and the developed world generally, the use of prescription drugs is doubling every 15 years. In this case, our willingness to accept the popular idea of a pop-a-pill cure rather than face the difficulties of managing an across-the-board personal lifestyle change – and all the long-term benefits flowing from that – highlights the impact of social influences on personal choices. In any situation, most of us find it hard to swim against the tide of group-think.

Our mind plays a major role in connecting us to our social environment in particular and the outside world in general. A large part of this

- An early way in which we are conditioned by our social environment is through the effect of language upon us, beginning at birth. A child is not born with a particular self-image; our self-concept begins forming early in life, and parents and guardians play a crucial role in this development. Parents who criticize the child rather than the child's behaviour create self-concepts of pessimism in the child, who then says privately, 'I'm always losing/breaking/forgetting/spoiling things. Nothing I do ever works out. I can't do anything right.' On the other hand, a parent who criticizes only the unwelcome *behaviour* while supporting the child, creates a self-concept in the child that says, 'I am good! Worthwhile! OK!' This child grows into an adult with a higher sense of self-worth, someone resilient who, when faced with adversity, can say, 'Some things are bound to go wrong occasionally – like this, for instance – but I'm a good person, and certainly good enough to get this right given half a chance. Next time, I know I'll do better.'

multi-level connection is activated by language and vocabulary. We are closely affected by negative and positive words and ideas at all ages. For example, in one experiment, a group of elderly people was exposed to positive words regarding age and illness, while a second group of seniors was exposed to negative words. They were then asked the hypothetical and unrelated question, 'Would you request and consent to an expensive but potentially life-saving medical treatment without which you would die within one month?' Most of the group exposed to positive words and stereotypes chose the life-saving treatment, while the other group mostly turned the treatment down! Just hearing such words as 'senile', 'forgetful' and 'diseased' diminished the drive for life, while words such as 'wise', 'astute' and 'accomplished' turned decisions in favour of health and hopefulness.[200]

Our language thus helps shape our view of the world and our view of ourselves – our self-image. Vocabulary helps form our sense of reality – our mental pictures and the emotions and moods that accompany them. This is why our self-talk is crucial to our evolving state of mind. The person we talk to most is ourselves. If communication matters, then the conversations we have with ourselves are the most important, as we talk to ourselves incessantly at almost 1,000 words per minute. Self-talk is not only what we say about ourselves on the *inside*, it is also reflected in what we say about the world we see on the *outside*. We have the ability to be our worst critic or our greatest fan. We choose what we tell ourselves, and these instructions decide how we walk in the world.

We declare war on drugs, war on cancer, war on terrorism and war on poverty. Our language helps shape our world, so we need a new and less aggressive metaphor for progress, one that takes into account the shared nature of life and creation. An aggressive mind drives an outlook of separation and disintegration. If we think by the sword we live by the sword, and if we live by the sword we die by it. An aggressive and manipulative mind is a dishonourable mind. Civilization helped create a safer *social* environment and helped us organize the dominant position we occupy over all other species in the *physical* environment today. If we choose words to conceal our intentions and what we want with the world – if our intention is not on our tongue, if we have a hidden agenda or are playing one-upmanship, if we are lacking in moral courage or are just plain scared – then the mismatch between what we communicate on the outside and what we incubate on the inside cuts our spiritual capacity and creates a disconnection in the world of our personal relationships. This disintegration devalues our social environment by distorting our connections with it. We strengthen the community by honouring the individuals in it, and we achieve honour by integrating our intentions with our words and our aspirations with our actions. Whatever happens in our world through us is a direct measure of our spiritual integration at this second fundamental, expressed in the relationships between our self and others.

Indeed, our personal relationships are an integral part of our social environment. It's interesting to note that many high-achieving, workaholic executives admit to having low-achieving intimate relationships, resulting in high rates of separation, divorce and dysfunctional relationships with their children. This represents a breakdown within the social environment of the second fundamental. When confronted with the grief and loss caused by the breakdown in personal relationships, workaholics frequently lack the self-awareness and personal development needed to deal with the crisis. Ill health often follows. As the British psychiatrist Henry Maudsley (1835–1918) said, 'The sorrow that has no vent in tears then makes other organs weep.'

Also pivotal to our evolving spiritual integration is the way we treat strangers. It may be easy to say that strangers are friends we haven't yet met, but this flies in the face of our deeply entrenched and self-protective bias against strangers. Our fear of strangers is part of the highly evolved risk-management strategy that has made us so successful as a species to date. But the paradox is that though our early evolution biases us *against* strangers, we also favour altruism, compassion, kindness, connection and cooperation as the impetus for our spiritual evolution. If we are to continue with our evolutionary progress towards integration and holism, we need to find a way to balance these two apparently opposing impulses.

Physical risk aside, the psychological distance implied in society's 'stranger' story is a self-limiting fiction we have authored. Ironically, more assaults and murders are committed by someone *known* to the victim than not. If our outlook always attaches to our early separation-bias, we will never get beyond an assumption of stranger-danger. I'm not advocating gullibility and vulnerability, just suggesting we each immediately choose an initial shift of emphasis from negative to positive and from hostile stranger to possible ally. To advance our spiritual evolution, we need to choose an outlook towards strangers that sees beyond our deeply entrenched survival mechanisms that are presently working against us. We need to let go of social anxiety and learn one another's stories. When we know someone else's story, the misunderstandings diminish and we find fewer strangers. This applies to nations as much as it does to individuals. To choose such an outlook and so contribute to a truly significant global spirituality, we need first to master and then integrate the three spiritual fundamentals set out in this section of the book. Until we create the spirit of complete integration within ourselves wherever we are, our present societies are as good as we are going to get.[201]

Integration and healing, both personally and collectively, can only be brought about through the actions we take in the world. Telling others what is going on for us and letting them know how we feel (our inner reality) is often a good first step of action to engage us with the external world, an initial way to connect our internal environment with the outside one. Even something as simple as writing a 'to do' list is more than just a memory jogger. It is an example of that first externalized point of contact through which we begin to exert our influence in the world, the trigger for releasing an unbroken sequence of actions that will eventually bring about our desired outcomes.

This fundamental is also where we most often break the law of attraction in a big way. We may have successfully integrated mind and body (our *internal* reality) but fail to extend the spirit of integration into the twin environments that are equally a part of us (our *external* reality). In missing this fundamental step of spiritual integration, we break the law of attraction by failing to engage and align with our external, extended connections. On the other hand, with this second fundamental well integrated, we satisfy the third part of attraction's law – aligning our inner reality with the outer environment – to position ourselves just one step away from unleashing the full power of attraction into our life.

However, as we begin to connect with our social and physical environments and adventure into the outside world, we must heed a warning. It is dangerous to believe that our enthusiastic intentions and actions alone are enough to guarantee exclusively positive effects in the long term; we

- A historical example of mind-body-environment disintegration occurred during China's Boxer Rebellion (1900). The 'boxers' were anti-foreign Chinese rebels whose pre-battle tai chi exercises were mistaken by British soldiers for shadow boxing. The rebels truly believed their ritualistic exercises made them both invisible and immune to rifle bullets. When thousands of them fell before the rapid-fire, self-loading English rifle, those who survived accused their dead comrades of poor training and preparation. The lesson from this is that if we do not harmonize with the environment, we risk having our beliefs and expectations fail; we risk ending up in a state of wishful thinking and hallucination. Lack of a reality check has spelt the death of many great ideas.

must also understand the interconnected nature of the environment in all its forms. Without this understanding, we are liable to keep demolishing the natural environment while we enthusiastically lunge for our successful outcomes. With this misaligned flourish into the world, any newfound impetus we add to the previously integrated mind-body connection will itself have unexpected consequences. To be effective, we also need a corresponding respect for the whole of the physical environment, including nature, and a deep recognition of our integral relationship within it. With this, we are positioned to accelerate the fundamental process of complete spiritual alignment that is the fulfillment of our reason for living.

It is as necessary to have air, water, plants, insects, birds, fish and mammals as it is to have brains, hearts, lungs and stomachs. The former are our external organs, in the same way the latter are our internal organs.
Alan Watts

As we saw earlier, climate change and its effects, the worldwide destruction of the Earth's lungs (our forests), and the chemicals polluting our food are the emergency red line on nature's warning gauge. We have a red alert that the attitudes and actions of each one of us need to be reintegrated with our living environment *now*! By re-engaging with the natural environment, we soundly support and protect both our own health and the inheritance of future generations.

Continuous as we are with our surroundings, our outermost 'boundary' is to be found somewhere beyond our skin and yet, as we saw earlier, many of us are out of touch with most of what lies beyond our immediate self. Emotionally we are distanced by being touch-deprived and love-starved. Physically we are insulated from the electrical Earth by our footwear; our clothing warms and protects us while it also shrouds and desensitizes our skin; and in cities we feel more inconvenience from than affinity with the natural elements of sky, air and sun. (African elephants, on the other hand, are profoundly in touch with their surrounding environment, being able to pick up the vibration of a thunderstorm through their immensely sensitive feet pads from a distance of over 40 kilometers (25 miles) and then migrate towards the thirst-quenching downpour.[202]) Yet all of life is so connected to its environment that even a small change to one feature of the physical environment, for even a short period of time, can change a species forever. To give an example, between two recorded seasons of drought in the Galapagos Islands, the type of emergency food available for one particular species of bird meant that only birds with a severely small bill could reach the food and avoid starvation. The subsequent young of that species, born exclusively from this 'runt' gene-pool, began a whole new sub-species of small-billed birds.[203] Even more striking in today's climate, changing levels of oxygen haave almost certainly allowed we mammals to thrive, while consigning dinosaurs to extinction. [204]

Counting down any number of species to extinction is no accurate indicator of the real catastrophe facing us. We may save the whales, dolphins and wedge-tailed eagle, but the breakdown of connections and relationships interconnecting the countless component parts of the biosystems along the complex food chain and within the living ecology as a whole is the greater loss – and one that mostly passes unseen. And nature is more than just unimproved land or a bunch of plants and animals; nature also includes the living systems below land and sea as well as above. On land, every kilogram of harvest reaped from the surface is supported by five kilograms of life working below ground. Yet our disconnection and disregard for the global ecology extinguishes the complex interaction of climates in the tiny places, the essential pollination cycles, the moisture and temperature changes, the nutrients, the seeds, and the minute nooks, crannies and breeding places.

Even the ecosystems of the blackest deep-ocean abyss are connected to the sunlit world miles above, where changes in surface conditions transmit to the seabed within a few weeks.[205] The whole of life is a network, intelligent and interconnected, and we tamper with it at our peril. In this interconnected system of which we are part, pollution of our rivers is akin to blood poisoning. Unfortunately, since the Industrial Revolution, economic development has been fuelled by a relentless and overriding arrogance towards the natural environment.

In the past, ecological issues were regional; today they are global. In earlier times, the collapse of one society (whether due to deforestation or other forms of ecological suicide) did not impact noticeably upon another region. The Easter Islanders, the Pueblo Indians, the Mycenaean Greeks and the Greenland Norse were all separated by time and place. Now the complexity of our global networks means that what happens in one place – Somalia, Afghanistan, Minnesota or Melbourne – affects us all in large measure sooner or later, and sometimes instantly.

Nature is not primitive, nor is it wild and in some way distant; it is alive and with us. With each breath we take, our natural environment is confirmed as inseparable from us at a most fundamental level. Our digestive tract connects us through the food we eat, and our skin absorbs and secretes in constant contact with our surroundings. It is not a matter of us destroying conditions for life on the planet, but a matter of destroying conditions for *our* life on the planet. If we miss our collective chance for planetary stewardship, nature will simply pick up the cards where we have let them spill, reshuffle the deck and play on without us.

There is always something we can do to diminish the awful sum of human misery.
Bertrand Russell

We have an urgent need to re-engage – with our environment, with one another, and with ourselves. Looming around us are the local and global repercussions of messing up the fundamental physical and social ecologies of our 'external' world.

In the mid 1970s there were three million refugees worldwide. Today there are almost nine million (with almost twenty-five million uprooted and displaced persons)![206] That means seven times more people are dislocated and separated from their background, looking for sanctuary and seeking to connect with a place called home. Domestic violence, social dislocation, regional and international conflict, the global epidemic of refugees and displaced persons all point to fractures in the twin environments of this second fundamental.

Economists predict that by 2100 the world as a whole will be more than five times richer than in the year 2000, having already multiplied its wealth 500 per cent in the 20th century. Yet 100 million more people were living in poverty at the start of the 21st century than ten years earlier.[207] It is time that we questioned this disparity between wealth and poverty, and asked ourselves what use this wealth can be to the wealthy in an unsafe world separated into rich and poor. How can such prosperity be enjoyed for long in a depleted physical environment and a strife-torn social climate? By disenfranchizing so many people through poverty and ethnicity we are fragmenting ourselves. This is a fundamental disintegration of the spirit.

In the twin environments in which we all live, our social ecology (and our sense of freedom within it) is just as important to our physical health and wellbeing as our relationship with the physical ecology. Poverty is more than just not having enough income: it can be spiritual, mental, physical, circumstantial or environmental. Poverty is not just a *material* lack – it also damages self-esteem, dissolves dreams and enforces low expectations of life. In this way, poverty kills hope. As a result, it can only be truly overcome with information, communication, action, accessible options and the material freedom to choose them.

As we develop more fundamental spiritual integration, we see the personal need to reconnect with one another. Progress is being made. Global consciousness is rising. More people are heeding the call to personal action. Conservation is becoming more attractive and corporations more active in this. Top-down political leadership is failing us in the present crisis, a case of too little too late. While the oceans are rising, the tide of global consciousness is turning: ethical businesses are flourishing, and global certification programs confirming that a company's products are made without sweatshop labour, do not use 'old growth' forest timbers, or do not otherwise damage the environment, are becoming increasingly popular.[208]

Unfortunately, government structures are not geared to produce enlightened responses. Whatever we consider – whether it be failure to establish sustainable fishing quotas for North Sea cod, failure to control nuclear proliferation, failure to agree on environmental regulations or resolve inequities within global free trade – global politics are divided by sectional national interests. Global corporations often operate above the law, where they seek to privatize the benefits of doing business while socializing the costs. In this light, we should have no false expectations of our leaders, and not demand false promises from them. The solution begins with integrated, enlightened individuals, privately and within organizations. We are each the start and finish of any solution. We each can create spiritual integration within ourselves wherever we are, and within the world, by connecting the three fundamentals.

However, the biggest challenge to global awareness, and limiting a truly global point of view, is cynicism – the belief that nothing can or will ever change, and therefore all effort is pointless. But achieving complete balance in this second fundamental of spiritual integration renders such cynicism redundant. In an interconnected world like ours, establishing personal harmony between inside and outside means that a personal shift in us is automatically reflected out into the widest global environment to subtly connect and engage everyone. There are many opportunities to do more to reconnect with each other, whether through community programmes, personal political involvement (knowing that the personal is political), charity work or any random act of kindness.

A leader now is absolutely anyone who can truly help. With personal spiritual integration, every problem is found to have a solution, and every solution comes within our personal range.

A flower falls, even though we love it; and a weed grows, even though we do not love it.
Dogen

The reason why we must commit to going further with our own spiritual programme is that we are suffering by spending too much time walking the long path. (We covered the short and long paths in Chapter 7). On the long path, too much happens beyond our control. Things get thrown off course because a cloud of unexpected, interweaving influences moves in between where we are now and where we want to be. I call this the 'Oops' factor, where every one of our actions begins an endless chain of interlinking outcomes, many of which we are unaware of. When something around us goes unexpectedly wrong we often say 'Oops!' No one in the world anticipated the nuclear fallout from bomb tests in the atmosphere, but the effects on our health are still being calculated. Oops!

Most disappointment comes from something unexpected happening that ambushes our best plans. Avoiding the 'Oops!' factor is what makes the nuclear waste disposal problem such an important example – radioactive consequences can take thousands of years to reveal themselves. The 'Oops!' factor is also the root of worldwide concerns that gene technology and genetic modification (especially of food) will release a horror of unexpected outcomes. As we have learnt by bitter experience, there will always be something we cannot plan for. Not much is predictable; indeed, we can't even forecast much of what will affect us tomorrow. Revolutions, wars, political changes, commodity prices, epidemics, scientific discoveries, technological breakthroughs and other advances – most of these spring as surprises easily predicted *after* the event.

To minimize the effects of the 'Oops' factor, we need to lengthen our spiritual line-of-sight through alignment and harmony with this second fundamental and its twin environments. Then our prior intentions, already focused through mind and body, find least actual resistance, fewer distractions, and create fewer disappointments. Whenever we allow distractions to divert our view and subvert our intentions, they do this by dominating and eventually becoming all that we sense of this second fundamental. Then we are like a hunter who sees a bird on a branch and looks away to pick up his bow and arrow. In that instant, the bird moves to another branch. The hunter looks back to re-aim … no bird. In this gap of space and time that separates all things and cuts through our attention, every unexpected thing happens. Across this dimension of separation – the gap between our aim and target, equally as big as the distances we create between us and everything else – our day-to-day life gets ambushed and sidetracked onto the long path. Only when the aim and target remain in alignment across this second fundamental is there any real hope of hitting the target.

However, unseen influences and consequences remain. Throw a stone into a stream. Plop! The stone settles quickly to the bottom. The surface ripples radiate outwards, and we watch as the flowing water soon bends and carries the ripples downstream. The ripples' excursion exceeds the stone's. However, the stone changes forever the contour of the riverbed, while the ripples continue to radiate outwards to erode the banks of the stream and sparkle across the water, attracting or disturbing small creatures nearby. So too flows the stream of life, where effects unfold and continue unseen, long after the ripples have passed.

If we hope to bring about real change in our lives and our world, and do it without causing an accident or raising the likelihood of error, then it is time to discover the art of seeing into the unseen. This requires the ability to transform ourselves and also dissolve the obstacles and distractions before us – to take the short path. It is only when we have a better view of the whole of reality that we cease to make mistakes or leave things to chance, because it is only then that we can be in the future right where we are now and foresee the consequences of our actions. To experience this state beyond limitations, we must install the final fundamental of integrity on our way to breakthrough consciousness and spiritual maturity. The fundamental connection we are about to delve into is the big mystery to some, the big secret – the connection that interlinks ourselves, the social and natural environments, and the unending 'background' environment that is the infinity.

CHAPTER 13

Sensing the whole in holism
Stage three: our connection to the infinity

If the doors of perception were cleansed,
every thing would appear to man as it is,
infinite.

William Blake

We now take up the third and final fundamental of spiritual integration, and here we explore our connections to the third aspect of the word 'environment'. In general, 'environment' refers to the background or context of something. In the previous fundamental we dealt with the physical and social context in which we live, now we look into the infinite background. When this notion of background is extended to its ultimate reach, our total environment includes everything seen and unseen – the physical, the immaterial and the energetic state of the infinity itself. Welcome to the emerging world of the mind-body-infinite connection.

When we recognize the existence of this third and ultimate environment, we have begun consciously exploring the third fundamental that finally establishes our experience of the infinite and undivided whole. This is the fundamental that empowers all hope while also fulfilling it. This is where our personal access fully opens to the short path and engages us in the experience of instantaneous and enduring transformation. This is the fundamental of ultimate self-mastery, and the last frontier of our transition to wholeness and whole-health. Whereas our common senses put us in touch with the many parts, now our uncommon senses put us in touch with the whole.

Here we link our mind, body and external environment to the immaterial and infinite environment – the background without end – as we move from sensing created reality to also sensing the original reality. Here is where the eternity referred to by faith-based religions finds shared expression with the original infinity of energy referred to by science. Beyond a mere understanding, the actual experience of the whole emerges in every awareness fully awakened, fully connected, fully released, and fully engaged. While earlier chapters reveal some of the many parts that make up the reality of our life's experience, this chapter establishes the fundamental that ultimate allows the many parts to integrate as one.

This third fundamental is also the final part in the four-part law of attraction. After beginning with the powers of attitude, perseverance and positive thinking, then aligning our mind and body with the social and physical environments, we now complete our spiritual circuitry by connecting with our mystical environment – the infinite field of energy in perfect balance. With all aspects of our spiritual consciousness synchronized and in harmony with the infinite whole of reality, here we are moved beyond all resistance, all blockage, all intrusions and distractions. Fully integrated and aligned with the original powers of transformation, our full compliance with the law of attraction is confirmed. Now we witness the mystery of manifestation, and experience the wonder of abundance working in our life.

At this point we need to take another quick glance at what is potentially the most unfathomable part of reality: infinity. Infinity exists not only as a conversational concept but also as something 'real'– an infinite field of energy in perfect balance, nothing less. Infinity, while not created, is the ultimate context and background for everyone and everything in the created universe. The infinite field of energy exists almost as another dimension simultaneously outside and inside everywhere and everything. Having given rise to everything, everything is essentially part of it, just as it also remains an essential part of everything.

This is the mystical fundamental, the secret key to the miraculous and transformational, the fundamental where greater networks connect with the infinite unseen. Its prolonged misalignment in our lives and absence from our mental outlook remains the deep source of almost all unhappiness and personal disintegration. This fundamental is where we at last supersede the isolation of separate religious systems, to truly reintegrate and reactivate the circuitry of our highest spiritual connections. But more than that, this is the fundamental through which all networks – including all of the created universe right down to the electrochemical and electro-spiritual networks of our own bodies – ultimately come into harmony and balance as the whole of reality, the created and uncreated. Here we find the super-unity of which we are part.

The meanings of the words 'individual' and 'whole' have something in common. 'Individual' is anything undivided within, indivisible. The word 'whole' also means to have nothing left out or divided into parts. Yet something is missing from both definitions, and that something is *background*. You see, every single independent and whole thing is also an inseparable part of its context or background; neither the whole nor the individual can be divided, either within or *without*, meaning they cannot be separated from their background. This sense of *extended or continuous* reality is essentially the spirit of holism – a continuous, all-embracing, energized singularity. In any interconnected and balanced whole everything has its place and function, and can be clearly found there within its context; in the complete whole there can be no random events. There are no blind corners in a complete circle. In this sense there are no surprises, just events that arise as the whole dynamically rebalances itself from within. This energized wholeness is the ultimate spiritual experience, strong enough to be given names like God, heaven, enlightenment, etc. We have this experience when we master this third fundamental.

Of the three fundamentals of integrity, this infinite, universal connection is the most promising but also the most neglected, maligned and misunderstood – partly because it involves unseen dimensions that include our creative consciousness as well as our 'psychic' circuitry, the so-called sixth senses. We are evolving to have two sets of senses, one geared towards created reality and the other geared towards original reality. We could look at it this way: our common senses feed us contrasts and differences (in light and sound, for example) from the created territory around us, while our psychic senses are tuned to holistic connections already existing with the uncreated (infinite) territory around us. Our success at surviving in the world has so far relied on our common senses, evolved to register the physical and social environments of our created reality. Just as a tennis player can have up to 40 per cent more bone mass in their serving arm, so too we have developed a bias in favour of our dominant five senses and let any higher senses drift, unattended. But, as we saw in Chapter 6, we have already evolved the capacity for empathy and discovered at least one gene for altruism – and these certainly allow a greater sense of connection than do our ordinary senses. Our psychic development is evolving a balance between our dominant common senses and our underdeveloped and immature psychic senses.

Sadly, discussions of psychic ability are almost invariably surrounded by cynicism. However, such bias is often misplaced, because it tends to be based on the assumption that the sixth sense is somehow unnatural (or 'supernatural'). As we shall see, this assumption misses the point: the emergence of such 'psychic' abilities is a natural progression in the healthy process of holistic evolution and integration, a process supported by the accelerated development of our rapidly evolving brain.

For those who believe, no words are necessary; for those who do not believe, no words are possible.
St Ignatius of Loyola

No study of an integrated life would be complete without a brief look at our brilliant, integrating brain.

The brain, a healing organ that has thinking as one of its healing functions, is constantly producing a spray of new neurons. For example, in the olfactory (smell) region in the front of the brain where we interpret odours, we make about 10,000 new neurons every day.[209] The neurons that are selected to survive do so by helping us adapt to changes in our external environment. The major function of the brain is to maintain our health – internally through our immune system, externally through our social relationships as well as our interactions with the physical environment, and spiritually through our deeper connections to the unseen networks. Though our healing brain organizes our intelligence and consciousness (which in turn help us adapt to the changes swirling through the infinite territory around us and the environment within us), consciousness is only a small part of brain function. Our brain regulates our personal physical health by embedding us and integrating us into the energy field flowing around us. This balancing act keeps us healthy, whole and integrated, and to do this our brain needs to bridge all dimensions, including ultimately the seen and the unseen. This becomes the complete state of full spiritual integration and deep personal integrity.

Kilo for kilo, our brain uses ten times more energy than the rest of our body, consuming 20 per cent of our total energy. (Most other mammalian brains typically use only about 3 per cent of total energy.) The human brain is an electro-spiritual powerhouse. With training, our brilliant brain can be induced to re-route new connections around damaged areas within it – it takes just three 13-minute sessions for volunteers to learn how to adjust various brain activity levels and develop more control over pain. London black-cab drivers, who undergo two years of intensive training to memorize thousands of routes and addresses around the city, have been found to develop a larger hippocampus (memory region of the brain) than the general population. What's more, the overall differences in the relative size of the hippocampus among the cabbies themselves reflected the number of years each had spent at the wheel. Our amazing brain can lay down new patterns and connections well into old age.[210]

As we saw earlier, the human brain has undergone an explosion in size in the comparatively recent past. While the increase in size has allowed the creation of more neuron-to-neuron connections, all the necessary functions to maintain our existence were already well handled by the smaller brain, and no species or other environmental factor was challenging our superiority. So, without any obvious need, and with environmental factors discounted, why the accelerated change in brain size?

Professor Robyn Dunbar equates the increase in brain size to the historical rise in our religious enthusiasm – our search for higher meaning and purpose along with our capacity to express it.[211] Our search for higher meaning has coincided not only with the development of brain size, but also with the development of religious ritual and direct personal spiritual experience. Nature doesn't waste energy evolving any feel-good factor – from sex to psychic sensations – in a species without a reason. Evolution fills niches, selects means for ends; nothing actively evolves as superfluous distraction. The intensity of our spiritual attention has developed in stride with the development of the human brain. As we have evolved up from a multitude of superstitions, through the architecture of religious ritual and now on to the capacity for direct spiritual experience, our brain's godly circuit of cells – our 'God-spot' – has developed apace. This offers us more circumstantial evidence of a transcendental faculty evolving in life's gene pool and emerging through us as more than superfluous distraction, a faculty wired between the whole network of living creation and the super-singularity of reality.[212]

In the physical world around us – where we compete for resources and establish collective domination – we humans were handling everything very well with the smaller brain long before its growth spurt. This means that the only significant place left to look for the influence that has stimulated brain growth must lie *outside* or *beyond* the dimensions of the created environment – and that points directly to the field of infinite energy in perfect balance, our mystical and unformed original environment.

The difference between the formed and the unformed environments – the created state and the eternal – is momentous. To illustrate this, picture the miraculous moment of conception. This precise moment marks a creative cross-over of realities, a dimensional leap no less creative than the Big Bang. Like creation's Big Bang, something traceably different instantaneously begins to emerge at conception, and continues to emerge, that is unlike any of its original component parts. Yet what emerges is reflected as those parts forever, an orderly yet endlessly changing complexity of cells. This original point of fusion, the actual energetic of our conception, can never be isolated or identified separately from any of the cells it creates.

In Chapter 2 we were introduced to the twin realities, one original, the other created. We are born into both, and to know our true origins is to know them both equally. Our mind stands as a doorway between the finite and the infinite, with our consciousness the ever-searching point of contact between our physical selves and the endless (yet intimate) backdrop of the infinity. Our brain is evolving to extend our conscious reach beyond created reality, parts of which we have dominated and now abuse, into the infinity from which we arose. Today, life is preparing us mentally to move beyond the confines of religious dogma and ritual to a direct, *personal* experience of spiritual holism and super-reality.

The stages our human brain goes through during development offer an example of how we can expect life's collective consciousness to progress. Two months after conception the brain suddenly begins a burst of development, and in just five weeks the number of its neurons goes from zero to about one hundred billion – a gigantic population explosion, not unlike the human population explosion in recent centuries. Then the emphasis changes and we suddenly develop massive interconnectivity *between* the new brain cells; from week 13 the brain's emphasis of development turns from neuron production to linking up the separate neurons of the brain into an interwoven, interconnected whole.

Let us imagine for a moment that humanity's collective consciousness has reached the equivalent of the 13th week of brain development, and is now set to embark on that massive burst of interconnectivity. Just such holistic consciousness – supported genetically by the development of altruism and empathy, and buoyed by our higher conscious states such as rapture, bliss, ecstasy, compassion and kindness – is already accellerating-ing humanity's potential to access the transformational directly, as our higher neural networks continue to evolve and become fully connected with everything around us. In this way, we may think of evolution as not only changing individual expression within the genes of any one species, but also as transforming all of life *as a living whole*, spearheaded by one species: humanity.

How deep and wide can our connections go if we encourage them? Though often dismissed, reports of psychic experiences are commonplace, as if a sixth sense is creeping into a five-sense world. Indeed, just to be conscious is to be psychic. Every time our thoughts move our lips, we stand as a living example of mind affecting matter. The only question is how far can this effect reach? Psychic abilities such as prophecy, clairvoyance, telepathy and healing may be hard to define and prove, but it's a bit like love – when we experience it, we know it.

Psychic powers seem improbable to many people because they challenge our fundamental sense of reality – our sense of real distance and time passing, and our sense of separation from one another in time and place.

Yet we are all visionaries and time-benders – we all create images in our head of what we want, and then bend and turn our circumstances towards those images. In fact, all conscious influence is in some respect an expression of psychic power, because with every decision we make, some cell in our brain begins to inhabit and create that next place or time. We all have original reality's creative powers of transformation, manifestation and regeneration working within us constantly. What we often neglect is to keep our visualizations and intentions in harmony and aligned with the whole. This is fundamental to the law of attraction: an intention can come to fruition only to the extent that it aligns, integrates and balances with the complete whole.

While the idea of some sixth sense may seem irrational, it must be remembered that just because something appears irrational does not prove it to be non-existent. The apparently miraculous doesn't contradict 'normality', it just contradicts our *concept* of what is normal. There are no miracles or magic at work, just laws and principles we don't yet fully comprehend. The universe of mysteries is merely waiting for our circuitry to power up and our consciousness to become more finely tuned and fully receptive.

Because many of us are still locked into an outlook of separation and the defensive attitudes it fosters, the presence of psychic powers seems abnormal. Those of us who have had psychic or ESP flashes may well discount the event. We fear being judged by a society that for the most part says, 'it doesn't exist'. Successful business people, often cynical about so-called 'spirit' and psychic ability, usually have a highly developed sixth sense – an intuition – which allows them to play the right hunch at the right time, even when all the available facts say 'NO!'

Mind-over-matter and mind-to-mind (thought transference) are the two broad areas of psychic function, and there have been more than 40 studies of them using the Ganzfeld ('whole field' in German) sensory isolation technique. The original Ganzfeld studies – considered to be some of the most scientifically credible tests of psychic sensitivity – were conducted with high-voltage, elaborate copper shielding around the site to rule out electromagnetic interference. The eyes and ears of the receiver were effectively neutralized with eyecups and headphones, the sender and receiver positioned in different locations. The sender was then asked to visualize randomly selected images and transmit them to the receiver. The overall hit rate was more than 33 per cent, even when subsequent targets were on the other side of the world (in another Ganzfeld cage) or when subjects sat their test several days after or even several days *before* the recording sessions.* The mathematical probability of this result happening by accident is a million billion to one.[213]

Two friends, miles apart, begin thinking of each other at almost the same time. One reaches for the phone and calls. 'That's amazing! I was just thinking of you too!' says the other. Events such as these are often revealed to be nothing more than the sharing of subliminal cues such as mutual knowledge of the significance of that day's date, or other shared subliminal information. Or sometimes these experiences are merely examples of coincidence and probability – 23 people in a room gives a 50 per cent probability that two of them share the same birthday. Yet some examples defy such logical explanation. From our new knowledge of connectedness and wholeness, we have learned that intelligence also passes beyond structure, via dimensions of deeper energetic connection that interweave the apparent world of form, separation and isolation.

If we want to see the power of mind to move matter, we need simply consider the process of thought. Thoughts trigger complex chemical reactions in our brain cells and these in turn cause a cascade of reactions throughout our whole being; with every thought, our mind changes the chemistry of our body. Even the person who says they don't believe in ESP is also experiencing these chemical reactions. Our intentions and thoughts directly affect molecules and matter in our brain. Mind and matter are entangled. To be alive and conscious is to be psychic.

The truth is that we are all mediums. Throughout our brief and fragile lives we all channel energy, only some of us limit our achievements to competition for energy, food and survival while others gain access to higher potencies. Health is our life's business, and part of this is mind training.

---

* Arguments over the Ganzfeld results have not been enough to deter scientific interest in this field. Other approaches to studying psychic ability (including studies at the institute of Transpersonal Psychology at Palo Alto California) show that the mother-child bond exhibits more psychic potential than other relationships. In addition, experiments are being conducted to identify which parts of the brain are involved in ESP; and the link between psychic ability and creativity is also being investigated.

The two go hand in hand. Psychic healing – the power to heal using the mind – is a potent power in all of us. We are healing ourselves all the time, every moment of the day, and we also have the psycho-spiritual power to contribute consciously and directly to the healing of others. No one needs to be saintly to be a healer or psychic, though our ego often creates a pattern of interference in all psychic matters, including prayer. Unfortunately, our sense of separateness emerges to either contemptuously dismiss the

- Many people claim psychic powers, and some of these are undoubtedly charlatans. However, others exhibit unusual and inexplicable capacities that in some cases allow them to heal. The renowned Brazilian healer, Joao Teixeira da Faria, a trance medium, is purported to channel 33 different spirits who were surgeons, doctors and psychologists. On occasions he has treated 3,000 patients in one day. I have seen him treat hundreds in an hour. When he performs surgery, he never uses anaesthetic or antibiotics, and there is negligible bleeding and no post-operative infection. Visitors are free to photograph or film the operations, and visiting doctors trained in Western medicine are freely invited to stand nearby and observe the surgery. This humble and gentle man has been doing this work of focusing a healing presence for more than 40 years and is one of the most powerful trance healers of recent times.[214]
- Many alternative healers say they can feel the energy and health of a person when they touch. I have personally witnessed this many times, both in my own work and in the company of other therapists worldwide. In skilled hands, psychic touch is an important diagnostic tool. Jesus himself reported feeling the movement of energy. And another Brazilian faith healer, Arigo, famously practised surgery with a rusty knife – the wounds were real and, as with Joao da Faria, no anaesthetic or antiseptic was used. What little bleeding occurred was stopped with a wave of the hand, and not one case of post-operative infection was ever reported or detected.

healing connection before investigation, or interrupt the connection with judgement and evaluation during the actual process of transference. Remember that the absence of evidence is not evidence of absence, and while scepticism is a healthy protection against gullibility, cynicism is never a healthy option in any situation.

As we have already seen, our normal senses are laughably unreliable because they are capable of perceiving mere fragments of energy from only a minute sample of reality. Only when we recognize the limitations of our perceptions can we challenge our assumptions and consider what other aspects of reality we might be missing. Locked as we are into our present framework, how many additional dimensions are we prepared to tolerate, and how different can we expect our future to be?

Time present and time past
Are both perhaps present in time future,
And time future contained in time past.
T.S. Eliot

To better understand this third fundamental, we need to see time differently. If we want to fully appreciate how our expansive mind and fragile body are connected to our total environment at all levels, it is important to understand the influence of time, because our sense of time affects our experiences. If we change our *view* of time and how we relate to it, we change the priorities of what we turn our attention to, which as we know changes our actual experience of the world. However, if we want to make significant spiritual progress we may also need to access dimensions beyond time. This missing link in time is, paradoxically, the timeless: the dimension of the eternal present, allowing us to consciously uncover the experience of the instantaneous and the transformational.

The first thing to note is that time is simply a scale by which we humans measure change. Neither the rate at which things change nor the speed of time across the universe is preset and constant. Science confirms that if we accelerate one, the other speeds up; slow one down and the other slows down. If nothing changes at all anywhere, then time stands still.

Similarly, our sense of time, and time passing, is not fixed. Even within the Western take on time, each one of us varies our time horizon from moment to moment, depending on what we need to get done. We have developed different time-frames for our personal use. While dreaming or under hypnosis, for example, we are capable of vividly experiencing in only a few seconds memories and events that actually span enormous periods of time and distance.[215] Some belief-systems see time as cyclical, where world history and personal lives repeat over and over; various interpretations of karma and rebirth incorporate this cyclical view of time. In China, the Mandarin language pictures time in terms of up and down, rising and falling as if spouting like water from a fountain.[216] The Piraha people of the Brazilian Amazon have no creation story. They disregard beginnings and endings, and actively discourage discussion of anything beyond the reach of personal experience. Having no abstract sense of time at all, their attention reaches only to whatever falls within their immediate experience. For them, even the most mundane of daily occurrences is suffused with a sense of wonder, and any sense of past and present is virtually non-existent.[217] The Western outlook, on the other hand, is linear and horizontal, seeing time as unfolding in a straight line from past through present and into future, with no reverse gear. Animals and insects offer other alternatives, with a fly evolved to see reality and time in what we would think of as slow motion, which allows the fly to react very 'quickly' in our terms.[218]

Time involves much more than rolling out reality in one unvaried line from past into future. In fact, the future and the past are interactive, inseparably conjoined. Indeed, the parts of the brain that think about past and future are almost identical, as if all times are the same in the brain, allowing us to create memories of the future.[219] Today is simultaneously yesterday's future and tomorrow's past; in the ever-present now, the past and the future merge; the past and the future become aspects of the present. In that sense, old or young, wrinkly or smooth, we are all the same age; we are merely different accumulations of memories, future projections and physical changes experienced in the present.

Like a navigator watching the stars and peering across the oceans to distant horizons, we set a time horizon at the start of every action we take, and then navigate towards it. Sometimes we end up where we planned, sometimes we don't. There is no limit on the span of time we can bend, though 'eternity' and 'infinity' offer attractive options that have emerged within common language. *The collective future is alive now, seeded within each of us.* Our ability to bend time and begin creating outcomes ahead of now is one of the secrets to manifesting desirable outcomes in our lives. Think of yourself as a point of creative transformation and attraction, a point of conscious power using mental constructs of time to influence reality. We can only do things and create influence from where we are; there is nowhere else. Our awareness is our entry point to reality, and we instantaneously begin to physically inhabit each future space and distant situation the moment we become aware of it. In turn, we are also affected by each space and situation that we are aware of.

This is not just a philosophical nicety: it is actually happening in our brain every time we picture a future event. Every time we picture an event yet to happen, some of the molecules of our brain enter that future the instant we think of it. In fact, without these molecules there can be nothing we call 'future', because future is just a product of the way the molecules of our brain interpret the relationship between the present and intention.

In other words, past, present and future are tools created by the brain to help us function in the physical world, just as our senses do. Yet, as we have seen (in Chapter 4), these tools prove inadequate to grasp the spiritual breadth and depth of life and reality. To support our unreliable senses with their almost non-existent hold on reality, something else is needed – another sense, a 'super-sense'. Before we baulk at this possibility, we should note that the existence of a sixth sense has already been established – an extra capacity for sensory perception is already seen in animals in the form of the magnetic sensibility many species have (as we will see below). Therefore it is not such a leap to consider that there might be other senses developing in us. For example, Richard Heath, a psychologist at Sunderland University, UK, discovered that some people have a special gift for predicting the twists and turns of chaotic systems and sequences such as the weather and even the financial markets.[220] (Unlike randomness, which is absolutely unpredictable, chaos is highly disordered but it is measurable and predictable.) These sequences are so difficult to calculate mathematically that banks of computers are needed; yet Heath found that

25 per cent of people could make accurate predictions when shown chaotic sequences. Similarly, George Soros, one of the world's richest men and an internationally renowned fund manager, has even gone on record to say that his back tells him when to sell by causing him acute pain.

While all this may sound weird to us today, let us not forget that much of today's common knowledge also once seemed ludicrously far-fetched, even heretical, to our ancestors – a round Earth revolving around the sun, the existence of bacteria invisible to the eye ... let alone the possibility of a man walking on the moon! Similarly, when New Guinea highlanders first witnessed the art of writing, they thought it was as impossible as we might consider ESP today – that a person could simply make some random marks onto a piece of bark or wood, whisper the same message to an incredulous highlander, then instruct him to carry the bark to someone else who would stare at the marks and be able to repeat the original message the highlander himself had heard. To the highlander, the piece of bark was possessed of magical powers. Similarly, the secret of psychic power is concealed within circuits and processes we are only just beginning to understand.

An extra capacity for sensory perception is not only showing early signs in humans, but also exists in animals as well. For example, in one early (and heartless) experiment, baby rabbits were killed suddenly at random times. Though the deaths occurred by design miles from the mother, the mother's brainwave pattern was monitored and shown to change at precisely the moment each of her babies was killed.[221] Furthermore, we know that a variety of creatures – termites, homing-pigeons, bats, sea-turtles and some bacteria, for example – detect magnetism and use the Earth's magnetic field as a navigational aid through some form of 'sixth' sense.[222] We know that the Earth's magnetic field variously affects the movements of butterflies, oysters, whales, salmon and honey-bees. Some creatures actually use this magnetic sense to hunt others: sharks detect the electrical fields transmitted by other creatures, and use these sensations for hunting, as does the Australian platypus. This is substantial evidence that life's gene pool has already evolved senses beyond our familiar five – but how many? Any psychic sense, even the more bewildering, could well access similarly uncommon electromagnetic pathways. The main question is, how much of everything are we potentially in touch with this very moment, but just not tuned into? Our emerging sixth sense – the unifying sense, the time-bending sense, the psychic sense – operates *beyond* time and place to complement our usual five senses operating *within* time and place.

Our five senses allow us to register only the separate parts of our wonderfully varied world, and then to manipulate them.[223] However, merely manoeuvring the parts of any system randomly is not enough to create a healthy whole: what is required is a plan, an overview, *a holistic view*. Without developing an overall sense of how the various parts of our world fit together and interact with one another, we are only ever treating the symptoms, not the disease – only ever seeing the problems without hope of finding lasting solutions. This is why life is driven to evolve a more insightful set of senses: to complement our classical senses as they concentrate on the contrasts and distinctions that shape created reality, and give us a sense of the other levels that make reality whole. (However, at this point it's worth keeping in mind that whatever we feel inspired to do from here with our new-found power and purpose, what matters when we are gone is not how much we owned or how psychic we proved we were, but how, in our wisdom, we affected the minds of the children in our care, how we lifted the lives of everyone we made contact with, and how small a footprint we left on the environment in which we lived. This will be our legacy.)

Experience is only half the experience.
Goethe

The metaphors used within religion to tell us about the extraordinary aspects of reality have long hinted at what is now being discovered in the science of networks: that everything in the universe is ultimately connected to everything else by series upon series of networks and interrelationships. Everything affects everything. Networks of all descriptions interlink with others to make up further, larger networks, in an unfolding series of ever-expanding clusters and links that ultimately interconnect one with the other. These links continue exponentially, until *everything* is ultimately joined together as a single, open and infinite network. This ultimately refined and harmonious whole is what religion calls the divine, spirituality calls the infinite reality or source, and science calls the infinite field of energy in perfect balance.

Because of the fundamental interconnectivity of all things, it is imperative that we understand the power of the small to affect the large. As we saw in Chapter 9, one way this power manifests is through fractal effects – powerful influences that give each and every thing the inherent ability to affect every other thing, beginning at any moment. In order to survive the next stage of our evolution as a species while developing personal significance in our own lives, we must grasp this central truth: *the energy behind every thought we have, and every action we take, affects matter, becomes matter, and is directly transmitted and influential everywhere.* Mind and matter are each an insepable part of the other.

The power of accumulated effects gives us the capacity to turn a little input into a massive output, but only if we align our energy and maintain focus without distraction. Anyone given to a monastic or contemplative lifestyle, therefore, may not be idly wasting time, but may be harnessing their contemplative practices to focus on the free-flowing power of fractal effects from a highly developed point of view. Carmelite Christian nuns who devote their life to peaceful prayer, or Hindu devotees who dedicate a lifetime to chanting one holy name, may be operating from levels of consciousness that have an impact on the physical we cannot easily recognize. Not only are these 'hermits' attempting a life free of negative repercussions, they are also allowing impersonal and potent healing outcomes to flow freely into the world through levels of connections and networks that most of us overlook. Though we still need to develop the right techniques to reliably probe the properties of true prayer (recent problematic challenges notwithstanding), the rise in globally co-ordinated, multi-faith prayer sessions testifies to the growing awareness of what our personal power of observation can do, especially when connected in concert and focused through quiet faith.

Since fractal effects are so open-ended that we cannot effectively resist or control all outcomes, any attempt to do so is a pointless waste of energy by us, and a distraction from the only thing we *can* control: our own outlook and actions during each and every moment. In a holographic world of endless uncertainty and constant surprise, the most effective way for us to live is where we adopt the outlook of the engaged but disinterested witness. This is not to be confused with an attitude of resignation or defeat, because now we have stepped *beyond* defeat, and have nothing to give up or resign from. Here we renew and maintain our expectations ceaselessly, while at the same time pre-empting any sense of disappointment by letting go of outcome. Faced with the laws of chaos and the effect of fractals, the best we can do is guide the content of our mind into harmonious, aligned and focused action – and let go beyond that. Take action *now*, immediately and to the very best of your ability; set events in motion, then let go of all attempts at control, simply letting nature and wider influences take their course. This is the short path to miraculous transformation and manifestation, and inner peace. By guiding our mind and not distracting ourselves into manipulating the outcome (which we do by adding to, subtracting from, holding onto or avoiding anything around us), we thrive beyond criticism and approval. Simply change the things we can, and let go of the things we can't. Whatever we begin continues, so start something good then release it and let it go.

Trying to control outcomes all the way along distracts us from the present, and we stumble. On the other hand, having no end in mind, our life becomes pointless and so we drift. The moment we let go is the moment when spiritual alignment and integration begin; then our actions become effortless, and in the face of whatever happens, our vision, faith and hope gain more and more power to transform. To let go in this way is to release ourselves from fears of a future over which we have no ultimate control. This can be a liberating moment. Consider that life is part of a process that may have no beginning or end. Remember that when we are gone we still live on in the hearts of those we have reached and touched, those whom we have moved. Recognize that everything is a whole, seamlessly connected to the timeless. Fractal patterns and chaos are the great equalizers: kings and paupers, the wise and the foolish, all are dead for the same duration. Unseen fractal effects level the playing field, with no person or country immune from the problems of any other, no matter how remote. At some point, everything in the world is shared in common.

Understanding fractal theory confirms that spiritual development and creative transformation on a global scale are possible from our own back yard. Even something as simple and personal as prayer has the power to create transformation. Prayer is one formula developed to align the mind with the infinite and directly engage the creative power of transformation. We already have evidence that this works. For example, well-controlled studies have shown that patients being prayed for in hospital recover more quickly than those not being prayed for, even when both patient groups were unaware of the study *or* their participation in it.[224]* As we saw earlier, quantum physicists know that the mere *act of observation* is enough to cause minute particles at the subatomic level to change, which means there must be an influential connection that disregards the distance between observer and observed. In other words, science has shown that focused intelligence can change reality – which is one way of describing the observed power of prayer. Reality's total interconnectedness, when viewed in the light of the power of fractals to amplify outcomes, allows for seemingly miraculous possibilities. Having read earlier that our imagination and 'real' life engage the same parts of the brain, and knowing now that everything is interlinked and entangled as an indivisible whole, we can see how one act of effective prayer can radiate fields of influence that leap the walls of logic and reason.

When the legendary apple hit Newton on the head, his study of mechanics had prepared him for his historical insight into gravity. So too we must prepare for our own breakthroughs. What do you do when opportunity knocks? Do you lock the door and hide behind the curtains hoping it will go away, or open the door and embrace it? There is no such thing as luck, only preparation meeting opportunity – a moment of convergence where fields and forces combine. Influences accumulate to roll on from generation to generation, through families, communities and whole societies, entering the psychology of individual members for better or worse, where they are repeated, reworked, reframed and re-energized. Personal reality, outlook, attitude, self-concept and spiritual position are developed, inherited and then developed some more in accordance with the momentum and subtext of fractal effects and other influences in our

---

* Many vouch for the power of prayer, although the largest study conducted to date has recently found against prayer having a healing effect. While other well-designed but smaller studies still support the claim, the large critical study was poorly designed, failing to adjust for the sabotaging effects of performance anxiety and ego intrusion in the subjects. These negative effects on the power of prayer and meditation will be discussed in more detail in Chapter 19.

lives. Fractal patterns of influence and energy converge in moments of serendipity to put us 'on a roll'; these are the times when we seemingly can do no wrong.

With reality revealed as impermanent and our future not predetermined, we each have the power to create our own reality every moment. As reality is only accessible through the mind, and with the observing mind able to change reality, it follows that together we are always co-creating our world of possibilities as the output of our collective consciousness. At this third fundamental of spiritual integration we now understand that everything we do enters a stream of change that flows into an ocean of creative possibilities. The fractal effect makes it impossible for any one of us *not* to make a difference. The sort of difference we make depends upon the quality of our spiritual integration.

Experience is not what happens to a man; it is what a man does with what happens to him
Aldous Huxley

One feature of spiritual integration is our capacity to get beyond the self and ego. To transcend self in a healthy way and become selfless we need to progress through levels of self-observation. For a brief experience of self-observation, take notice of this page; observe the paper and printing for a moment. Now become aware of yourself observing it. When you can observe yourself observing, you have just become conscious of being conscious. This is the first level of self-observation, an entry-level ability sometimes called 'observing the observer'. This gives us the capacity for self-awareness.

The practice of self-observation (where one level of our mind observes another) is central to spiritual progress and deep healing; it is the beginning of our ability to reach around the edge of our reactive mind and operate beyond the limits of cause-and-effect. By developing the power of self-observation, some schizophrenics have even learned to ignore the voices in their head and refuse to accommodate schizophrenia's more bizarre behaviours![225] Likewise, we can all use self-observation to control our own worldly hallucinations and projections, and thereby attain greater spiritual integration.

As we will see later in this book (when we discover some of the power of meditation, in Chapter 18), we can make observations from different elevations, and these are key to evolving any real spiritual capacity. Remember that the best view is always found at the top of the mountain, and the freshest water at the head of the stream. Advanced spiritual practice involves more than adhering to belief, dogma and rigid thinking. Though many of us live accelerated lives, racing headlong, driven by reflex and reaction, without a moment free for pause and self-reflection, self-observation and self-reflection are key to spiritual progress and fitness. From now on we have the choice: stay with an outlook that favours defensiveness and reactions after the fact, or upgrade to an outlook of proactive anticipation and stealthy transformation. The gentle practice of simple forms of self-observation begins the process.

Self-observation is different from egocentric self-absorption or self-centredness. While self-absorption operates from a retracted viewpoint *within* us, self-observation operates from an elevated vantage point of attention *beyond* ourselves. It is as if there are two broad levels of mind available – one physical, the other spiritual. Psychologists agree that a capacity for self-observation benefits mental health while advancing our emotional intelligence (astuteness in managing our own feelings and dealing with others), personal effectiveness and overall happiness.

Our individual ego and self-absorption are only a small part of mind overall; just a bubble of consciousness in an ocean of mind. Our individual free will is not so completely free. As we have seen, we only become conscious of decisions we have made some time *after* the brain fires up, which means many of our decisions are being made in our brain other-than-consciously, without consulting us. Meanwhile, we bumble and stumble along spiritually unaware, assuming we are consciously making decisions yet never quite getting where we want to go.

Through this third fundamental of spiritual integration we see beyond our previous self-absorption and now consciously integrate with the *total* field of energy around us and through us. We have engaged uncommon senses associated with this third fundamental. We are consciously awake to all dimensions within the infinite field of energy in perfect balance, a field from which we are ceaselessly emerging, within which we are forever existing, and to which we are inevitably returning.

There is a story I am telling you [in my paintings] – special, sacred, important – the land is not empty. The land is full of knowledge, full of story, full of goodness, full of energy, full of power. Earth is our mother. The land is not empty.
Wandjk Marika (Australian Aboriginal artist and elder)

Spiritual integration is not the monopoly of any one religion, race or time. The Australian Aborigines are said to be the descendants of the oldest culture on Earth. During the last two centuries of the old millennium they suffered the large-scale dislocation and destruction of their culture and way of life, and the murder and displacement of many people. I knew Jimmy,* an Aboriginal elder of the Gurindji tribe in Central Australia, in the late 1970s. Jimmy was an inspiring example of someone steeped in his ancient culture who was fully integrated and connected.

In recent years Jimmy's tribe has gained some political clout and achieved a degree of independence, but life in the semi-desert remains bleak. Not that Jimmy minded; in fact nothing seemed to phase him. He knew all the tribal legends. He knew when the different flowers of the desert would bloom – not just the season or the month but often the actual day – and he regularly demonstrated this fine-tuning as we went about occasionally looking out for traditional healing plants.

Even though Jimmy had seen massacres as a young boy, as an adult he bore no grudges. He said men anywhere do crazy things. What I remember most about Jimmy is the way he sat. Not only the way he sat but for how long! When he sat, he became so completely still that he looked to me as if he had become an extension of the ground around him. Jimmy told me he could sit this way because his father had taught him how to listen to the earth, and the ground had taught him how to sit.

* In the Aboriginal tradition, full names of the dead are not spoken.

This generous, humble and splendid man had remained connected and in touch with his spiritual roots, evolved through word of mouth across thousands of years. To do this he'd had to let go of things that would disturb lesser minds. But the younger men of his tribe were angry and many of them confused, pulled between the semi-desert life and Western ways. They scorned the rituals of the tribe and were ambivalent about their role in continuing the tribal traditions.

In contrast, Jimmy had let go of hate and resentment and anger; Jimmy had none of these feelings. He knew that hatred extinguishes higher human values, and he opted instead for laughter, spontaneity and an eye keenly set to find the unique 'specialness' in any experience in that harsh environment. All the time I knew him, Jimmy was the enthusiastic personification of harmony, equanimity, forgiveness and grace.

Late one afternoon, having just planted a mango tree at a secret men's place, Jimmy and I were walking near the tribal waterhole when I asked what would happen to the spiritual history of his people (Aborigines call this the 'dreaming' or 'dreamtime') when his generation of elders had passed on. Jimmy immediately sat down, sat right down there on the bare earth, instantly relaxed, deeply still, motionless, watchful and alert but with no distraction important enough for his attention. I saw his chest gently and slowly rising with each considered breath.

After some time – a long time, perhaps thirty minutes, long enough to feel the pulse in the desert silence – Jimmy answered: 'Gurindji drimmin' [dreaming], him bin finish up, him bin finish up [for] good!' In other words, Jimmy saw the passing of 40,000 years of accumulated and profoundly deep awareness, of a people living consciously in touch with the earth, the surrounding sky and themselves, all as one whole; a people dreaming tribal transmissions that embraced the deep, deep stillness of the desert. Jimmy knew that with the passing of the elders and the cultural dislocation of the young, the tribal dreaming would also pass. And with that passing, the ancient tribal techniques that allowed the direct experience of reality's fundamental unity would be lost forever.

In his wisdom, Jimmy knew intuitively what quantum science is now observing – that mind and matter are intermingled and inseparable, each contributing to the existence of the other. He knew that at some point, mind and matter are one and the same; that a people's spiritual history cannot exist without its context, because everything is connected. Without connection to context, we are lost. Jimmy knew that the dreaming *was this connection*, transmitted through the land to the people as part of a larger, infinite whole. He knew that at some level every place becomes the same place, that there is nowhere else to be except here, now, living as the actively engaged witness, beyond distraction. Jimmy ultimately *lived* within the liberating experience of this profound and timeless understanding.

For notes and author contact information, please see website on page 385.

SETTING YOUR SPIRITUAL LINE OF SIGHT

CHAPTER 14

Assessing your spiritual maturity

If a man has no thought about what is
distant, he will find sorrow near at hand.

Confucius

I n Charles Dickens' *A Christmas Carol*, the character of Scrooge is one
of the most bitter and withdrawn figures in English literature. Yet the
story tells how the ghosts of Christmas past, present and future are able
to invoke profound revelations in Scrooge by taking him on a journey
across time. After a series of devastating self-realizations where Scrooge recognizes how low he has sunk as a human being, he is spiritually awakened
and ends the story as a redeemed character.

Like Scrooge, we are all capable of intense episodes of insight that spontaneously propel us to higher ground. Indeed, as we continue on the
road towards full spiritual integration, integrity and maturity, we may think
of our spiritual development as a series of evolutionary stages, each one
bringing us closer to enlightenment and absolute connection. By observing these stages in ourselves and in those around us, we can better plan our
personal path towards spiritual integration and complete spiritual maturity.

To picture how these stages unfold, and knowing that spiritual development also involves mental development, imagine yourself in an external
glass elevator on the side of a tall building. As the elevator takes you
higher, your view and perspective improve at each level to include more
of your surroundings. Your view to the horizon becomes increasingly wide

until, finally, it becomes clear to you that what you thought was a solid, fixed line separating the earth and the sky is no such thing at all. The horizon apparently keeps moving away the higher up you go, until eventually everything comes within your elevated line of sight.

There is no fixed horizon: you see that what you thought of as marking the extremity of your world view – a boundary beyond which you have no access, placing everything there outside your reach – is actually a progressively diminishing limitation created within your own mind. The horizon line you are seeing at any moment is an interpretation of the world you construct around you, limited by the abilities of your five senses and your position in the world – a boundary that says more about you, and the limitations of your vision, than it does about whatever you are looking at.

In this sense, 'horizon' can be used as a metaphor for the level of conscious spiritual awakening we have reached. As our spiritual awareness expands and more of our spiritual circuitry activates within us, the dynamic horizon-line of separation becomes more and more distant, and we get to see and connect further and further. Just as in the elevator – where the horizon appears to remain a solid line that moves away as we go higher – so too we can observe how far someone (and ourselves) has developed spiritually by being aware of how much they still curtail their outlook and embrace limiting boundaries. The elevated spiritual vantage-points we progressively reach allow us an ever more extended appreciation of whatever lies before us in our lives, until the barrier of the spiritual horizon itself ultimately disappears.

This is the sense we will use in these pages – the higher we rise the less spiritual separation and disconnection we experience; the more we take in and connect with. This navigational metaphor describes our progression through eight expanding spiritual 'horizons' of consciousness, from an initial outlook of inherent separation to one that recovers the experience of highest connections and interrelationships. In this way, we may think of the view from each distinct level or vantage point as representing a new horizon, where the line of difference between what we can and cannot see is highlighted.

But the public elevator only ascends so far. After the fifth level, if we are to advance any further, we must step out of the elevator and take the stairs, alone, to reach the final three horizons. Progressing in this way, we eventually come to fully realize that the shifting horizon-line of our outer spiritual limits is an illusion, a figment of our imagination, a structure outlining our spiritual progress. Our view has continued to become clearer the higher we climb until finally, when we reach the top floor, we transcend the building completely. At this point there are no longer any separating horizon lines at all, no limit to what we can perceive and experience.

Each horizon therefore marks a paradigm shift into a new level of consciousness that attracts its own corresponding events and experiences. At the lower horizons life can be harsh; at the higher horizons life is increasingly liberating. As our life evolves, we up-shift our event horizon and become open to higher experiences. These final horizons are where karma and consciousness meet quantum science.

While all eight horizons indicate higher or lower levels of spiritual development,* the progression through them can be likened to a process of maturation – an evolution from birth through adolescence, then adulthood and on to spiritual maturity. However, chronological age doesn't define maturity – either physical or spiritual. Our development in the first five spiritual horizons is a highly *socialized* process, one through which we access the lower level of networks. Such connections are usually activated via good parenting and effective socializing. This is where we develop *social* intelligence. However, it is not until the final three horizons that we fully develop *spiritual* intelligence, where we activate the range of connections that directly awaken creative transformation and breakthrough consciousness. Progress in the final three horizons shifts emphasis from the certain to the amorphous and problematic, from the highly socialized to the highly spiritualized, creative, inspirational and esoteric. Broadly speaking, the development of our consciousness begins with self-consciousness and self-image; then our mind expands into social

---

* All consciousness can be considered to be a spiritual capacity or energy that is first anchored close-up and focused on the world around us but expands as we evolve to allow more spiritual perceptions as we progress through the horizons. Using the word 'spiritual' before consciousness helps to remind us that spiritual progress involves an ever-widening conscious awareness. The horizons represent our expanded or elevated consciousness, where the available view at each level is the extent of our spiritual reach, and outside or beyond the horizon represents the level of perception still to be accessed. The horizon itself represents the line of separation between where we are and where we want to be at any time.

awareness; and, finally, our emerging spiritual awakening takes us through to spiritual maturity. It is only with a fully-developed spiritual conscious-ness that we supersede our acquired sense of self as a separate ego – like a butterfly leaving its cocoon – to directly experience the infinite divine: the unified experience within everything.

What begins for each of us as a process of infant reflex and survival, evolves through a system of socialization and personal development up past the limitations of tribalization to civilization.* If we keep progressing, the quest then surpasses the highest socialization to become highly personal-ized spiritualization that ultimately culminates in complete spiritual integration and transformation.

Love is a useful starting-point to illustrate the changes that come with our spiritual progression through the lower and onto the higher horizons. Whenever love is expressed at the lower horizons it is tainted by self-absorbed expectations, blind loyalty, self-interest or possessiveness. Here, even though empathy develops and altruism appears, the label of 'love' is carelessly attached to behaviours we use as weapons in the com-petition for power and control over people, energy and resources. In the lower horizons, love is lost in the game of giving to get.

In the final three horizons, love is no longer entangled by self-serving behaviours nor limited by restrictions and boundaries; it is uncondi-tional. The higher we elevate ourselves, the greater our ability to see far and give (and receive) unconditional love. In the higher spiritual states we accept our loved ones as they are, not how we want them to be. This is why many of our typical choices and behaviours change when the love 'bug' bites and we fall in love. It is our *boundaries* that fall from us when we 'fall' in love, and for love's duration it feels unlimited. In love, our point of focus shifts from self to other, and we revel in the heady joy of an original state of connectedness. As the spirit of love develops we realize that something

* The word 'tribe' can be used to refer to a traditional people or ethnic group, or to a 'first nation' or aboriginal tribe; and there is ample evidence throughout history of increasing openness and wisdom bringing different tribes together for communal benefit. However, in general, tribes have traditionally operated at a lower, more violent and cruel horizon than civil societies. Therefore, in this section of the book, references to tribalism are meant to evoke the less pleasing attributes that identify with tribes and tribal thinking: exclusivity; hostility to 'outsiders'; antipathy to new ideas; autocratic power (generally); and self-limiting superstitions.

If you're still wondering about the benefits of developing your spiritual freedom as measured through the eight horizons, consider whether it's worthwhile being:

- self-assured, less self-centred
- independent, less needy and co-dependent
- interested in others and impressed by them, less needing to impress or be interesting
- understanding of others, less seeking to be understood
- conscientious and engaged with others, less distracted
- able to listen, less needing to be heard
- giving, less taking
- forgiving, less judgmental
- powerful and assertive, less power-hungry and aggressive
- easygoing and enthusiastic, less forceful or controlling
- passionate, inquisitive and open to new ideas, less cynical or bored
- creative and spontaneous, less affected or mundane
- peaceable, less tormented

other than ourselves is important and real. When the spirit of love fully matures we realize we have been one and the same all along.

Our state of mind gives rise to our style of life, and each of the eight horizons of consciousness is important to our spiritual progress in the world. Each of the horizons indicates a personal level of spiritual fitness or capacity. As our spiritual fitness increases, our awareness – like a muscle – expands and grows with our progress through the horizons. Crossing over the outdated boundaries of nation, race, religion and location, these horizons serve to make each of us more accountable.

The foundation of every horizon is already established within every one of us. As each new horizon is crossed, we link into an ever-increasing network of interconnectivity. With each new level, our sense of psychic separation is weakened, breaking with its previous 'threshold' and expanding the accessible range of interconnections. Degrees of freedom are heightened. We activate advanced networks and intimate connections that we hadn't realized existed. In this way, the 'horizons' are as much about spiritual *momentum* as they are about defining any specific horizon with which we might identify.

Recognizing that our spiritual position is not fixed, it is normal to find ourselves moving back and forth between the horizons, swayed by every choice we make and every new experience. The capacity to return and engage at the lower horizons remains necessary for survival – we never permanently lose access to them, just develop a preference for selflessly helping others and being independently happy. Our spiritual age is not decided by our birthday – infants have powers of insight that dazzle their parents, while young children can be kinder, and more charitable and forgiving, than their elders.

For many of us, the free and full development of spirit remains a fiction, and never becomes our driving intention; any breakthrough consciousness capable of registering and activating the total range of connections and higher networks remains something of which we are highly sceptical. Most of us will only allow ourselves access into higher horizons when we have realized (usually through intense emotional pain) that our present outlook has stopped working for us and is causing too much suffering and too many complications. Even then we can be quickly attracted back to a lower horizon when we feel threatened or sense some advantage there. In this way we are continually expanding and contracting our horizons.

Avoiding pain and seeking pleasure, we live our spiritual horizons on a constantly sliding scale; in 1911 Adolf Hitler was painting watercolours, yet by 1939 he had become a genocidal dictator. Our spiritual fitness is not decided by status or position, nor is it guaranteed by faith alone; blind belief is exactly that – blind. There are no guarantees against backsliding, and most of us operate well below our spiritual potential. There is no guarantee that uncivilized minds will not act to send society backwards in spiritual time to a darker age.

With our spiritual progress fluctuating back and forth as if by accident, we can only gain occasional glimpses of the higher awareness identifying each successive horizon. These higher experiences are reflected in changes to our emotional 'mix' of personality and behaviour; these personal developments are accompanied by progressive 'shifts' in our attitudes and ideas, as well as by occasional flashes of insight, intuition and other altered states. However, by moving to and fro between the horizons in a more-or-less undisciplined and unfocused way, our ability to grasp and retain these altered states is fleeting and unstable. In the lower horizons, we might ignore the significance of any such personal experience we have, or cynically dismiss another's reported encounter because these realities lie beyond the horizon-line of our present spiritual position.

Transfixed as we are by reality's time-worn dimension of separation and fragmentation, the journey across each successive horizon is hard-won and marks the threshold of our emerging spiritual freedom, our progress from duality to super-unity. The further we develop, the less we spend our days competing for survival amongst the shadows and echoes we pass off as reality. Seeing and experiencing more of the interconnected whole, the more we include and connect, and the less we are distracted by material trivialities. The more we develop, the more long-forgotten connections re-emerge into our conscious experience. We stop allowing our habitual attitude of separation to distort our spiritual viewfinder.

Across each horizon we are presented with hard times and stumbling-blocks – challenges to our attachments, perceptions, behaviours, attitudes and pride. In the lower horizons, early temptations often show up as physical fixations, biases and possessive greed; as we progress higher we risk wallowing in the temptations of pride, self-righteousness and spiritual superiority.

There are lessons at every level, and the lesson is repeated over and over until the penny drops for us. Each horizon brings its healing – the healing power of higher connections energized by our developing sense of the infinite divine. Without spiritual healing, health professionals (orthodox or alternative) cannot help us. Our whole being, from mind to molecule, must first recognize and re-activate the health networks in the higher levels. Sometimes this recognition is conscious, at other times other-than-conscious. This rebalancing may or may not manifest in physical healing, however, as there are so many interconnecting influences at work, and what we want for ourselves may not harmonize with the whole.

Like colours in the rainbow, the boundaries between horizons merge. In this way, distinctions blur. Similarly, as each horizon develops within us, we are still able to revisit all our earlier behaviours and attitudes, or try out new ones. By understanding the nature of each horizon, and being able to almost instantaneously mix and match, we build a preferred spiritual profile.

Being able to recognize the horizon that we normally settle for is also important, because this tells us how we generally respond to life. It is also important to recognize the actual horizon at which others are operating, since it is possible for someone to masquerade at any level they desire, simply by appearing to do and say the right things – even if for the wrong reasons. This is why we have politicians who seek office for the power rather than the population, teachers in class for the position rather than the pupils, priests in the pulpit for the cloth rather than the congregation, parents who act for the good of themselves rather than the good of their children, and business executives who speak of human resources but treat their employees as liabilities.

Cultures, civilizations and communities develop preferred horizons just as individuals do. The policies and laws of any government (and a population's willing compliance with those laws) are a reflection of any society's spiritual maturity – its infancy, adolescence or adulthood. Different societies have different levels of spiritual consciousness just as their inhabitants do – a preferred way for its citizens to look at the world; to behave and think; to treat strangers and deal with any difference; to preach war or peace; to favour selfishness or kindness; to trivialize and criticize the unusual and esoteric or encourage them; and to manipulate or liberate the divine. Any civilization rises and falls in step with this changing collective consciousness. For example, though women in China's ancient Tang dynasty could operate with a degree of independence (and one woman, Empress Wu, even ruled the empire), later generations of Chinese women were virtually domestic slaves with crippled, bound feet. The European Dark Ages came after the Roman Empire's successful 500-year unification of Western Europe, while two world wars followed the Renaissance and religious reforms of the Middle Ages. Each culture and community has a favoured spiritual horizon, the effects of which can carry across generations.[226]

However, our species does have a moral compass, and though there are relapses, humanity's momentum to the good is presently finding public expression through modern civilization. To see this, we only need look at the political systems of the nations of the world: of the almost 200 countries in the world today, only 14 absolute dictatorships remain, while there are already 140 countries holding regular multi-party elections (half of these achieving this in the last quarter-century).[227] We are moving towards a better world: the best of civilization is progressing, the worst of tribalism is receding, and humanity is evolving to the good, the just, and the wholly free. We saw also, in Chapter 6, how a sense of justice is alive in life's gene-pool (along with altruism and empathy). By coupling this evolving inborn nature with our capacity for abstract thinking and our ability to plan for the future, we have evolved an intrinsic moral sense that empowers us to value the good and work for it. It is these higher values – such as the spirit of equality, freedom, compassion and justice – that have been hard won. They must be protected and built upon.

Some societies are more corrupt and less civilized than others. Bribery, nepotism and white-collar crime are all self-serving, low-horizon behaviours that can develop into institutionalized corruption powerful enough to rock the foundations of an otherwise just and civil society. When corruption in any community becomes systemic, individuals within that society are more at risk, and the fabric of the community weakened. Civilization suffers. The extent of civilized behaviour in a community marks the horizon that a society is working at, and the simplest indicator of civilization is the extent to which corruption is replaced by care for strangers. While tribalization is more inclined to exclude a stranger until the stranger proves themselves valuable or trustworthy, civilization easily includes the stranger until the stranger disproves their worth or trustworthiness.

Any community gets the leaders it allows; moral and spiritual leadership is a collective responsibility as well as a personal choice. A kind-hearted leader is maintained by a civilized society populated by citizens who are not misled by charisma and charm, whereas a cruel-hearted leader makes uncivilized demands of people compelled or willing to obey.

As we have seen earlier, the global community is witness to the beginning of an era of famines, droughts and disruptions to ocean circulations resulting from global warming. These reflect the present depleted level of our collective spirit and the inadequacies of our preferred horizon. If we don't see today's risks for what they are – nothing less than the disintegration of our social and physical environments (our second spiritual fundamental) – then our ill-prepared response to the effects of such geopolitical issues as pollution, global health concerns, the refugee crisis, economic disparities and ecological dysfunctions may contribute to spiritual backsliding on a grand scale, with intensified civil unrest. In the choice between whether or not to create heaven or hell, we risk a regression towards yet another age of hellish warfare in competition for increasingly scarce resources. The path ahead is an intensely personal one, though the downstream effects of our private spiritual position have a global reach.

Embarking on a personal program of spiritual fitness has flow-on benefits for those around us. It is encouraging to realize that even the slightest improvement in our personal spiritual capacity or fitness (with the accompanying shift in our own attitudes and actions), heals divisions and creates momentums that lift other beings within our sphere of influence. In this way, as our personal spiritual capacity grows and has greater effect on our attitude and actions in the world, the fractal effects and unseen forces that drive life's interwoven networks combine to give our spirit wings. Even small adjustments in our perceptions and personal behaviours can generate profound and far-reaching changes.

On an interconnected earth, by changing how we operate in the world we also change the world.

CHAPTER 15

From dress-ups to grown-ups

It is the pang of separation that spreads
throughout the world and gives birth to
shapes innumerable in the infinite sky.

Rabindranath Tagore

I n the 4th century BC a group of Greek thinkers called the Cynics used
scandalous behaviour to challenge the assumptions of law and the con-
ventions and taboos of the day. Diogenes caused outrage by
masturbating openly in the market place. If sex is natural and essential, he
said, why is it shameful? While he may have been taking artistic licence a
bit too far, he demonstrated how letting go of old positions for new ones
has never come easily, either to a community or the individuals within it.

While we can progress without creating scandal, it is time for us, too,
to re-evaluate our habits and assumptions, and ultimately let go of old positions. To do so, we must work to persistently elevate our attitude and
expand our outlook to encompass each of the eight spiritual horizons until
we reach the ultimate viewpoint.

As you read the behaviours and other features that identify each
horizon, you might recognize yourself or other people you know. It will
be helpful for you to work out the preferred horizon of your friends, family,
workmates, neighbours, political leaders and others. We are often not aware
of our own preferred spiritual horizon. Recognizing where we tend to get
stuck and where our usual behaviour lies within the full range of horizons

will help us see where we are going wrong. We get to see for ourselves some of the old positions we need to let go of.

In this chapter we begin our account of the process by looking across the five nearest or lowest horizons, and for good reason. Spiritual development is not isolated from the way we live – spirituality would be pointless if it was. Spiritual intelligence begins with the development of social intelligence, and it is this social aspect of our spiritual connections that we develop here. These early horizons are where we establish the worldly level of our spiritual connections, refine our sense of self – our ego – and redefine our boundaries. These first five horizons position us in the external world, while the last three horizons take us beyond externals and complete our 'internal' life.

The first horizon: Creation

This horizon is the 'source' horizon, the point of original transformation where infinite energy in perfect balance gives rise to finite reality. Here we are not describing a level of human behaviour or consciousness, but rather marking the *first* flashpoint of creativity, the original genesis of creation, and the beginning of all background. With the first pulse of creation that accompanied the Big Bang and created our entire universe billions of years ago, everything we know today set out on its way, spiralling across this space-time horizon into its present form.

Importantly, this horizon provides the outer edge to every separate thing we see today, an edge that originally formed around the Big Bang when it was very small and had first begun expanding. This first horizon not only exists as the extreme outer edge of distant space, an extremity we know is still expanding and accelerating. It also remains much closer to us, being the surface edge of every form and shape – every surface, angle, idea and outlook within creation – and provides any gap (which we call distance) that appears to separate any two or more forms in existence. This horizon marks the beginning of the reality of separation that divides our experience of reality into its four common dimensions of space and time. It is from this original separation that the seven remaining horizons of spiritual separation arise. Here is where the reality of our universe began, the created dimensions where causes are seen to generate effects. Because every created thing has an adjoining background – a context of time and space –

everything has crossed this first horizon.

From here, the only possible direction for spiritual evolution and integration is onwards and upwards through the higher horizons.

The second horizon: Newborn

At the times you operate from this horizon, you:

- *see only your own needs, which are all-consuming*

- *have not developed any workable sense of self or other, yet are entirely self-absorbed**

- *require constant care and attention from others.*

While the first flashpoint of creativity gave rise to the Big Bang, this horizon marks the *second* flashpoint of creativity, with each new life bearing witness to creativity's limitless power for genesis and spontaneous transformation. Life is creation's 'second coming'.

This is the horizon at which original separation takes a personal turn, making separate existence and survival every individual's lifelong fixation. By the time of our actual birth, the seed of our spiritual urge to see *beyond* separation has already begun to germinate in us. However, at this second horizon we have little or no real awareness of ourselves or others, being completely absorbed within our own basic needs for nurturing and survival. Here, every action is almost completely reflexive or unconscious, and love is represented by an instinctive attachment automatically focussed on the 'parent-carer' as a basic survival instinct.

Our early innocent encounters at our mother's breast – where we could first be seen reaching out, grasping, then, when momentarily satisfied, pushing away – begins a lifetime obsession for reducing distances or creating them. This is a drive born out of a primal need for self-preservation. (As we saw earlier, we instinctively withdraw to preserve ourselves and keep ourselves intact, and just as easily reach out to explore new possibilities.) This infant reflex for influencing and exploring into our environment across

---

* Note that there are big differences between the progressive, developmental self-absorption of the young child, the neurotic self-absorption of many poorly developed adults, and the enlightened self-reflection we read about in later horizons.

the 'zone' of separation, then withdrawing, becomes a habitual state of mind where we unconsciously strive to grasp everything as best we can, examine it, then decide to either retain it or push it away. We could call this basic instinct the spirit of self-contraction.

Even adults can re-enter this reflexive horizon, and some never grow out of it. Whenever we are challenged, threatened or upset, our survival instincts instantly prepare our return to this horizon – like when we suddenly hear the screech of tyres close by and have already jumped before we consciously realize what we have done. The point is that these and other unconscious 'flight or fight' responses attempt to preserve *a survival zone of separation* around us to protect us against risk or perceived threat. However, if we stall at this horizon, we also risk staying too long in the newborn's phase of total dependency and extreme vulnerability.

Adults at this horizon typically remain totally self-absorbed and without any real self-control; they are vulnerable, defensive, disempowered and often completely dependent on the goodwill of others. At every imagined provocation they may either sound slighted, indignant, miffed or outraged, react agressively or retreat into impotent silence. Often resorting to tantrums or tears when challenged, they expect others to obey and provide for their every need, and are bewildered when the world won't comply. This almost mindless self-absorption may be acceptable for newborns, but it becomes harmful to us in any later phase, preventing us from developing meaningful, honest relationships.

The third horizon: Infant

At the times you operate from this horizon, you:

- *have a strong sense of self-righteousness*
- *are quick to rise to your own defence, placing self ahead of ethics*
- *establish relationships that are extremely self-serving*
- *have an emerging but immature sense of 'we' and 'us' and life beyond self*
- *have a minimal and unreliable sense of empathy*
- *divide the world into contrasting opposites*

- *form strong, primal attachments to your inner circle of family and friends*

- *collect fixations, and may be superstitious*

- *have little or no comprehension of the consequences of your actions*

- *are very judgemental.*

At this stage in our spiritual evolution, we have fully engaged with the dimension of separation and duality and are developing our personal outlook around it. At around 18 months our first glimmering sense of our 'self' as an individual signals the advent of this horizon, and our self-concept continues to flourish throughout the period of our lives spent here. This early phase of spiritual development is best described as narcissism. However, it is at this point that we also begin making early connections, reaching out across the dimension of separation and testing it ever so slightly – although our networks of workable connections still extend only to an elite inner-circle of family and friends. At this third horizon we are still a long way from the point of view that sees strangers as potential friends and allies. Our own survival is still paramount and our self-absorption almost total.

We are beginning to set up an existence in a largely compartmental-ized world. We see life in terms of heroes and villains, of 'us' and 'them'. We start to emblazon our self-concept with our own tastes, an early personal style and a sense of belonging. Yet though we still consider our-selves the centre of the universe, we begin to learn that things are not exclusively ours, and that we must share. We discover subtle differences among things we hear and see – for example, we come to know that the moon in the sky is different from the toy version hanging above our bed.

With no real sense of life beyond our own, we operate at this short-sighted horizon with limited appreciation of the consequences of our actions. We also have no need for ethical concerns such as justice, as we are still predominantly concerned with 'just us'. This is the me! me! me! horizon with its severely limited outlook. We are quick to protest whenever we think we have been personally slighted, while ignoring our transgressions against others. This is the instinct that motivates a child to pour two drinks, then offer their friend the smaller serving rather than the more generous. Possessiveness and greed may be childish and counter-productive survival traits, but we've all seen childish adults who perpetuate these third horizon habits.

The instinct for self-enclosure, contraction and a sense of ownership – where we grasp and pull what we want towards us – is still dominant here. However, we also begin to realize that we can personally influence what happens in the circumstances of our immediate environment. As we become conscious of competition, risk and control, we quickly become enthusiastic players in the world of cause and effect. We become increasingly familiar with the use of force to compel favourable outcomes, largely ignorant of the conesquences; here grow the roots of agression in society – a transitional phase in the overall spiritual development of the young, but too often retained and carried over into adulthood and the wider community.[228]

One skill we are helped with from a young age is person-to-person communication, and early on this involves learning the meaning of the word 'because'. As soon as we realize its power, we commit to being a 'cause' of desired effects, and to avoiding undesirable ones. However, our ability to effectively design and control outcomes by using skills such as diplomacy, negotiation and collaboration is at best rudimentary and fumbling. Here, an outlook that sees only causes and their effects leads instead to the blame game, the avoidance of responsibility and a victim mentality: 'Something made me do it; it's not my fault; I couldn't help it.'

This horizon is where we begin learning to call on other people, in a variety of ways, for help. Studies show that children at this horizon value help and helpfulness highly; only later, as independence grows, do they begin to actively resist and even begrudge assistance. A key to our future success is how well we learn to enrol others for our own benefit, and we begin this here. At this third horizon, we have gradually become aware of the relationship between ourselves and others in our family circle – or, if we are adults stuck at this horizon, in the wider world around us – but we still assume that these people exist merely to satisfy our every need, as they did in the second horizon.

As we start to test the boundaries of a resistant world (including the patience of our parents), we learn the degree to which we are in control, and when we are being controlled. Children are naturally unreasonable and selfish, and test out many anti-social behaviours on their parents and siblings. However, most of these early behaviours are found not to work and are quickly and methodically discarded.

When we operate at this third horizon, any person displaying any sign of authority to which we feel beholden – whether it be a uniform, a stethoscope, a famous face or a confident, loud voice – can quickly persuade us to comply with even their most outrageous requests. (Watch how many people slow down, reluctant to pass a police car, even when the police are travelling *below* the speed limit.) This is most likely hard-wired into our evolution by life-threatening emergencies that have occurred throughout human history, where decisive command-and-control decisions and strong leadership meant the difference between life and death.

Ironically, adults who settle for an outlook at this spiritually immature horizon often seek positions of institutional authority, such as in jails, classrooms, religion, politics, the police or the military. This is not to say that all such people are limited in their spiritual outlook, but this is the horizon where, as adults, the fanatics, the bullies, the zealots and the self-righteous congregate. Children might bully (or learn to resist bullying) as they transition this horizon, but some adults remain stuck here. For these adults, small-group culture can be so strong that they will allow the greater good to be overridden and put aside; for instance, dedicated police officers who take a strong anti-corruption stance within their force are often looked down upon by fellow officers as disloyal. Unfortunately, this narrow sense of loyalty operating here is widespread in most communities, which means that whistleblowers everywhere are almost always made to suffer.

Lying and deception are two more features of incomplete spiritual development found at this horizon. The more blatant the lie or deception, the greater is the ego and push for self-protection – and the lower the horizon. Although lies may help us avoid detection or responsibility, they also risk creating unwanted separation and distance. Lying, of itself, is not immoral, though its use may mask immoral acts. Even when lying is used to lubricate the smooth running of our society and is born of a desire to be tactful or considerate – such as the times we say someone is looking fabulous when we really think the opposite – lying is essentially an act of manipulation and deceit, combining the energies of disregard and dismissal with the instinct for self-preservation and self-promotion. On the other hand, truth means more than factual accuracy, though that is a beginning. Truth ultimately breathes health into our minds and our lives, allowing things to heal and be whole.

If we are to make any progress into the higher horizons, a fundamental requirement during early development is the love and trust of our immediate family. Trust is identifiable in all relationships, including the personal, public, business and political. When any individual within a group breaks trust, the matrix of connections is interrupted and that group's circuits are diminished. As a result, in a just and fair society, missing this spiritual step towards trust and trustworthiness leaves the social fabric diminished and its spirit poorer.*

Our initial carers and contacts teach us our early patterns for staying alive and getting ahead, and we learn to imitate the ideas and behaviour of others, including trust and trustworthiness.** If the people we witness and imitate have spiritually developed into the higher horizons – if they have a sense of care for others and community, a sense of belonging and constructive integration, and a personal identity that includes trust and honesty built on mutual respect – we advance. If not, we are held back and may need to find new mentors if we are to make spiritual progress.

Without a foundation of trust being established at this horizon we may never fully trust – and certainly not trust intimacy. Then, as adults, we risk living the damaged life of a wounded child. Hurt people hurt other people, and few of us know how to love like we have never been hurt. At this horizon, no matter what age we are, the shattering of trust by someone we love hurts infinitely more than the betrayal of a stranger. Therefore, the trust and support of our close ones is at the core of our early psycho-spiritual development.

* When both trust and trustworthiness within any community fall below 30 per cent, countries risk falling into a permanent economic poverty trap of communal suspicion and mistrust. Finland remains the least corrupt country in the world, Haiti the most corrupt (Corruption Perceptions Index, Transparency International. Berlin, 2006).

** Trust is different from trustworthiness. At this horizon a child has not learned the importance of trustworthiness, while the adult stuck at this horizon does not care. A modern paradox is that while most of us consider ourselves trustworthy, we seldom trust others in our wider community nearly as much as we trust ourselves.

As a result of this fundamental dependency, we also learn at this third horizon to fear losing the help, love and approval of our closest family members. The manipulation of this fear can make us vulnerable to some of the worst childhood abuses, although in small doses it has proved a useful parental tool for positive influence, discipline and development. Throughout our later lives we often relive some of these early success-and-survival strategies designed around flight-or-fight, fear, control and calls to obedience. Unfortunately, while this early process of socialization constitutes the first positive steps of our spiritual development, along the way much of our young curiosity and creativity is stifled in the name of learning the basic lessons necessary for survival.

As we are being taught to separate ourselves from potential risks and threats to our survival, we increasingly divide our world into a world of opposites – good and bad, light and dark, 'insiders' and 'outsiders' – and continue with this in everyday situations even when we are merely inconvenienced rather than actually threatened. Here we learn to recruit people to defend us against outsiders or 'the enemy' – and this is where the learned ability to delegate and build teams first comes into play. At this horizon, if we want someone to join our team and they're not willing to fall in with our group and its ways, we may even learn how to bully them into submission, or exclude and punish them further. In this way, we ensure that members of our team more or less function within the boundaries of our preset values, beliefs and customs. This is where the tyrant and the terrorist both operate, seeking absolute power by relying on some grand struggle against such 'enemies' as foreigners, communists, corporations, religious unbelievers, or 'anybody who is not like us'.

While organized religions urge the worshipper to contemplate greater things, they have also literally made an art-form out of this kind of 'team separation' that divides 'believers' from 'nonbelievers'. Too many believers dismiss any religious thought different from theirs as at best misguided, at worst heretical.* The compulsive tendency for the human race to add prejudiced value judgements to the more natural and necessary ability of

* Even the private act of prayer is beset by the limitations of spiritual separation. One thing essential to true prayer is selflessness, yet at this horizon, prayer is essentially self-serving. Without a liberating 'loss of self' and the complete absence of ego during prayer and afterwards, prayer becomes little more than wishful thinking.

our senses to observe contrast (shades of light and sound) in the world, is a habit to which religion, historically, has too often attached itself. When our tribal need to belong to a group and defend it is subverted in this way, religion can divide people, support social conflict and refuse to allow an enduring peace and true universal brotherhood to develop. Ironically, these are precisely the divisions that the core of all religion repudiates. Why is it that fundamentalists almost universally oppose music, dance, poetry and most forms of artistic expression? It's because the creative arts promote freedom and enquiry – a process of growth that eventually denies the fundamentalists their inalienable right of ownership over the truth. This assumption of superiority is wielded as both weapon and defence against all difference, change and challenge. Religious wars are not about religion; they are about bullies who use force and fixity of ideas to mask their own fear of challenge and change. Violence is bad enough, but violence in the name of the sacred is the ultimate hypocrisy.

Perceptions of racial difference and class divisions within society become systemic at this third horizon. The citizens of many so-called 'integrated', 'multiracial' and 'multicultural' societies actually share little more than a shopping experience. The usual politics of identity – including racial history, ethnic origin, language, fashion-cum-identity, secret greetings, special street-wise handshakes and brand-name attitude – are concerned with *separate* identity and little else. Product tags and branding – whether cultural, corporate, or on clothing and other consumables – identify us with that particular tagged group. Creed and race are two such tags used worldwide to identify and elevate – as well as to separate and intimidate.

Like people, communities have an immune system that can be compromised. Any country whose collective psyche is no longer healthy, wholesome and quick of reflex loses its balance of internal process, its healing immunity and integrity. This gives opportunity to underdeveloped minds – the bullying, the corrupt, the self-righteous and superstitious – to creep towards the top and commandeer the decline, taking the community to a new low. Such blinkered leaders – and history allows us all to name a few – are recruited from this polarized third horizon.

This horizon is a valid transitional stage of spiritual development in childhood, but many adults don't develop far beyond this. Habits of exclusion and inclusion learned here can reinforce an exclusive sense of self that blossoms into arrogance and sow the seeds of aggressive self-righteousness. Merely settling for survival and self-protection risks a life transfixed by the attitudes of separation – an outlook that misses the higher connections awaiting us in later horizons.

The fourth horizon: Teenager

At the times you operate from this horizon, you:

- *set the boundaries between 'us' and 'them' less rigidly: the buffer-zone of separation begins to disintegrate*

- *have a well developed sense of 'other' beyond self*

- *are friendly towards the people you meet personally, though remain suspicious of most people and situations beyond your direct experience*

- *are capable of strong opinions, and can fight to be right while still failing to be effective*

- *still have flexible ethics, and assume that the ends justify the means*

- *are readily able to express empathy and behave altruistically towards people known to you*

- *are capable of caring seriously about another person's wellbeing, even a stranger's – but only after having met them personally*

- *care a little about some of the direct consequences of your actions, but take little interest in the much wider implications of your actions and attitudes.*

The fourth horizon breaks down some of the barriers we have previously set up between 'insiders' and 'outsiders'. Here we start to extend our intimate connections, friendship and care *beyond* our elite inner circle … as long as they don't clash too severely with our existing allegiances to family, tribe or 'homeboy' gang. We experiment socially and may even enter controversial friendships (friendships outside the previous boundaries of acceptability or familiarity). Though cross-cultural or cross-religious contacts may develop, life still easily divides into black and white, good and bad, and 'us' against 'them' scenarios. However, instead of seeing things in terms of 'who wins' and 'who loses', at this fourth horizon we now refine our communications and learn to collaborate and negotiate, discovering that both parties can successfully have their different needs met. To do this, trust must replace the fear of loss. At this horizon we begin setting up expanded networks of trusting relationships beyond our earlier, limited loyalties. We learn to trust more widely, and in turn learn to be trustworthy ourselves. At the fourth horizon we get a clear sense of how a lack of trust interrupts our relationships and limits cooperation. This insight marks the dawning of ethics. The elements of mutual trust begun here continue to develop at the next horizon.

With today's extreme sports such as bungy jumping, sky surfing and white-water rafting, along with other high risk activities such as 'binge' drinking and dangerous driving, we test the boundaries of self-preservation by purposely putting our safety and survival at risk. We do this to face down the mother of all fears: the loss of self. In the cultures in which initiation is still practised, the traditional tribal rites of passage – knocking out of a tooth, the drawing of blood, incision, circumcision or other rituals of risk and endurance – feature here at this horizon to signal a youth's spiritual coming-of-age. Though women fare somewhat better, many Western men today, living in comparative comfort but having no such rite of passage into manhood, live as adults stuck with a child's problems and perspectives, devoid of an integrated spiritual life.

It is only by forming successful relationships, both at work and privately, that we can recruit and enjoy the benefits of other people's care, skills and attributes. After all, the greater number of people we can cooperate with and work with, the more security and control we have over our lives. At this horizon our understanding develops far enough to be called successful, but not far enough to be truly significant. We design ways to do things right, even though we might still not be doing the right things. To put it another way, even though we might successfully join up a few of life's dots, we still cannot see enough of the big picture.

At this horizon we have entrenched the features of co-dependency and refined our skills of manipulation – 'you are responsible for making me happy-sad-rich-poor' – but we are also beginning to develop our capacity for empathy, self-observation and self-control. It is only when we are capable of active listening – listening so that we really 'get' the other person's picture without any distortion or editing, and without merely waiting for our turn to speak – that we may really have a chance at lasting intimacy. When we truly hear and understand someone else's story, hate and anger diminish. Marriages can and often do survive even when one partner remains stuck at this horizon, but rarely endure when both partners operate from this spiritual outlook. A marriage partnership has the possibility of developing its full spiritual potency only when *both* partners have evolved beyond this horizon.

This is the horizon of the 'open' tribe where we live within an expanding sphere of contacts and connections. By the time we reach the fourth horizon we have recognized others as individuals having an existence completely separate from our own. We continue to model their behaviour while becoming more calculating about our own. However, we are also sensing the similarity between people, and we start to gain insight into others while learning to extend our capacity for empathy and rapport.

That's not to say that at the fourth horizon we won't still blame the negative on external factors, while claiming all credit for the positive. Here is where we first crave independence without responsibility as students, we assume our problems are the teacher's responsibility and, as adults, that our spiritual life is in God's hands. We expect the government (as proxy parents) to fix things and sometimes even provide for us, without us taking charge ourselves. Yet at the same time we crave freedom and personal control. We are also quick to find safety in numbers, hiding behind such statements as, 'It's not my fault. Everybody else did it too.' Our peer-group and position in society give us a feeling of strength, identity and belonging.

While remaining unaware of all the repercussions of our actions, we mask our many uncertainties and insecurities with a self-absorbed façade of bravado. For example, when a group of younger drivers was asked what they thought about while driving, they listed going faster, freedom, independence, personal pleasure and being out with friends. Nothing about watching out for other drivers and other road users; these considerations are left for higher horizons.[229] The potential of our inner life to affect our outer life is scarcely considered here at the fourth horizon. That's because our psychological tool kit – our emotional range, as well as our capacity for empathy, altruism, delayed-gratification and spiritual insight – isn't developed enough to overcome our more primitive habits of self-obsession, ego and separation, along with our need for recognition and a sense of invincibility. Some of the excellent work being done in the juvenile justice system of various jurisdictions, such as in the UK, the US and Australia, is an example of how young offenders can be lifted to higher spiritual ground. Instead of merely relying on punishment (such as imprisonment) as a deterrent against further offence, these programs also require young offenders to meet the victims of their crimes. By bringing the offender face to face with the consequences of their actions and forcing them towards thinking of others outside their elite-inner-circle or gang, the court extends the offender's spiritual horizon through their capacity for empathy.

There has always been something more extraordinary than individuality and survival going on in the world, and in this horizon we begin to see the long-term benefits of not always putting ourselves ahead of everything else. In addition to a strengthening of empathy here, community service in the form of volunteering receives increasingly strong support as we identify with a wider horizon. Philanthropy – the desire to improve the welfare of humanity through charitable deeds – also begins here at the fourth horizon, although it is still accompanied by a strong desire for recognition and approval.

At this horizon, surrender still feels like defeat. In addition, our tools of mimicry and manipulation are sufficiently developed that compassion and empathy can be faked here by someone wanting to appear more in touch with others and spiritually developed than they really are. Remember that spiritual progress and spiritual capacity do not conform to age, gender or social position. At any moment we can surge towards mystical heights of spiritual significance or ebb towards the insular and selfish.

The fifth horizon: Adult

At the times you operate from this horizon, you:

- *have an optimistic and forgiving world-view*

- *care seriously about another person's wellbeing, even when you don't know them personally*

- *have evolved compassion – the spiritual capacity to feel* with *someone rather than simply feel* for *them*

- *have some sense of 'the whole of humanity' and an emerging sense of holism*

- *see and act on possibilities that are truly other-person centred, though your outlook still remains fundamentally self-conscious*

- *are slow to anger but quick to stand in defence of injustice, the higher ground and the greater good*

- *are often a great communicator, facilitator and champion of the underdog*

- *undertake charitable works*

- *are unselfish but not yet selfless.*

This fifth horizon is the first of the adult horizons, though full spiritual maturity is yet to develop. At the previous horizons, an adult position was not possible, and in the case of children, wasn't expected. Now, at this horizon, we come to realize that a bigger picture exists in which we are no longer the star attraction. We realize we are personally incidental. This is the horizon where we no longer need any *direct* reference to self or public acknowledgement of good works. However, while all our utterances and actions here seem reasoned and unselfish, our deepest psychological reference-point remains the self. Though we are no longer completely self-centred, we remain self-conscious. This is the horizon of enlightened self-interest, where our reality-consciousness is expanded but not yet fully elevated. We have reached the outer limits of separation while remaining essentially attached to it, and our interests remain worldly and humanitarian rather than creative, esoteric, 'mystical', or transformational.

Here we display the ability to look beyond the constricted 'self' and consider the unknown stranger living somewhere far removed from our everyday lives. Controversial friendships are allowed to develop on their merits without a moment's pause. This fifth horizon is the realm of ethics and broad social conscience; many of the world's most philanthropic and civic-minded people reside here spiritually. Philanthropy is anonymous at this level, no longer accompanied by a desire for public recognition and approval. Charitable works and volunteering are now at their strongest, extended beyond the local or regional level to become 'internationalized'. The brotherhood of humanity is now fully appreciated and acknowledged, as demonstrated in our attitude and actions.

Here we not only do things right but also consciously try to do the right thing. In organizations, this horizon marks a move from a management mentality towards an outlook of leadership. As an emerging leader, a person at this horizon recognizes that everything has far-reaching effects and repercussions, some desirable and others well worth avoiding. Leadership inspires management with the bigger picture and its less-obvious connections. Managers create structure, while leaders create strategy. In this sense, spiritual evolution includes a progression from management to leadership, from being confined within structure to gaining a more strategic outlook. At this horizon we are able to anticipate the needs of individual members and balance these with the needs of the whole group or organization and its greater purpose. As leaders at this horizon, we operate beyond the mere functionality of friendship and reciprocal arrangements, and bring more to leadership and authority than the mask of charisma. Here, truth becomes more important than the tribe, and principles more important than patriotism. Loyalty is no longer confined to the local.

We also now have a wider emotional range and are equipped with a more global viewpoint. We are becoming more agreeable in the little things, and no longer agitate over the small stuff. Random acts of kindness are common at this horizon, as individuals begin to see beyond the immediate boundaries of family, tribe or ethnic group, and identify themselves within the wider population and community (an extension of connection that takes courage in some cultures and communities, because many ethnocentric groups consider such wider identity akin to betrayal rather than a demonstration of civilized behaviour, and punish accordingly). Our spiritual fitness has now developed far enough for us to consider more universal issues; our capacity for empathy allows us to look beyond the immediate 'self' and embrace people, events and circumstances outside our usual orbit. At the fifth horizon, altruism is now particularly strong, setting the spiritual stage for the later emergence of completely selfless, egoless behaviour. This reach is not just individual but also global at this horizon – as we saw after the disastrous Asian tsunami of December 2004, which inspired a worldwide wave of generosity. However, while we empathize widely with others and are much less self-absorbed, our sense of 'self' as a *separate* being still underpins our approach to life.

The beginnings of enlightened or unconditional love that began surfacing in the previous horizon gain wing here, and more of our happiness comes from unselfishly doing for another rather than just for ourselves. In this horizon, we recognize that seeing to our partner's pleasure and happiness simultaneously helps ours. Yet even though we pay attention to what our partner does right rather than wrong, our strong move towards unconditional positive regard is still vulnerable to our need to be judge, critic and evaluator, however well-intentioned.

As we learn to delay gratification in favour of more distant outcomes and long-term plans, we fully understand that personal wealth, position and material standard of living do not guarantee safety and happiness, nor do they guarantee a sense of meaning, justice or any lasting quality of life. Consequently, we become less driven by desire and greed.

At this horizon we are also less fearful of social criticism and more committed to social action. Here society is built on trust and trustworthiness, populated with individuals who are willing to defend a community's position beyond smaller group, family and sectional loyalties. The civilized world grows much stronger when those who witness injustice take action against it. An example of a whole society operating at this horizon occurred during the Nazi occupation of Denmark during the Second World War, when the deep-seated humanity of the Danish population combined to protect the Jewish residents, resulting in only a very small proportion of the Jewish community being sent to concentration camps.[230] In less developed societies, fear allows oppression to increase, since the oppressor relies on fear to suppress dissent and so weaken society's immune system – an immune system no less organic and alive than the immune system of our own body. Historically, despots and dictators have always relied on instilling fear (which includes killing off the best minds of a country) in order to maintain their rule – bullies aim to crush what they can't control or convert. The first freedom is therefore freedom from fear: a community operating at this horizon bestows on its citizens both the right to tell bad news and the responsibility to hear it. Otherwise, if we are too afraid to hear the truth and act on it, the bullies will win.

Maintaining the spiritual reach of our higher horizons and the active connections they recognize is the challenge of our time. When enough of us reach the fifth horizon, a civil society flourishes. It is at this point that a public attitude of mutual respect and positive regard between strangers and diverse groups is assumed in unspoken agreement. In private, the strength of our personal contract to others and with society almost always surpasses our more selfish instincts. Business and political leaders operating from this fifth horizon appreciate that a group's mutual needs and higher aspirations can be satisfied only when built on a foundation of informed trust and cooperation. While trust is the basis for cooperation, cooperation is the building block of civilization.

This is the horizon of lasting democracy and political freedom. Much of our civilized life is anchored here. At this fifth spiritual horizon, civic leaders deeply understand that *quality of life* is no less important than *standard of living*. They realize that commerce must be promoted for the credit and benefit of the community, rather than at its expense. At this horizon, rule of man is replaced by rule of law; the ideals of democracy replace the interests of tribalism, absolute monarchy, fascism, communism and theocracy. Fewer wars are fought between democracies than any other social formulation.* However, any democracy needs a voting population spiritually developed to this fifth horizon, or higher, if it is to endure. Otherwise narrow self-interest becomes persuasive, then dominant and all-pervading. Justice is easy amongst equals, while inequality breeds injustice; it takes this spiritual horizon, at least, before spiritual reach is able to offer justice and mercy to the underdog.

There are many ways for a community's connections to be undone, or strengthened. Every culture is the living expression of its entire population past and present, built on the accumulated wisdom and work of those who

---

*However, it should be noted that not all so-called democracies are identifiable by the free and equal participation or representation of all citizens in government and the decision-making process. In today's world, 'democracy' in some countries can be skewed to meet the interests of authorities or the international dictates of mega-democracies. Manipulation of a population's fear risks usurping democracy and becoming the new tool of political command and control.

Where are the Simpsons in the eight horizons?

- To use a contemporary, pop culture analogy, let's tune in to TV's favourite dysfunctional family, the Simpsons, and see where each member is in relation to the spiritual horizons model.

- Sucking her dummy, baby *Maggie* is clearly at the second horizon, that of the infant. While developing a strong little will of her own, her survival needs are paramount – her vulnerability causes her to be completely dependent on her family.

- *Homer* is the star of the show that has been tagged 'the glorification of the moron'. Stalled in a state of arrested spiritual development, he is ludicrously self-absorbed and incapable of taking responsibility for his actions or their repercussions. Homer, the big baby, spends most of his waking hours at the second horizon, occasionally masquerading beyond this level into the third horizon, usually for some self-serving reason such as manipulating his wife Marge.

- The wily and delinquent *Bart* at the third horizon is very much his father's son. Comically resisting all attempts to instil manners, education and compassion for others outside his inner circle, Bart is frequently seduced by the self-serving mentality of the gang, which is typical third horizon behaviour.

- Sensitive, compassionate and intelligent, *Marge* is a solidly family-orientated and community-minded woman at the fourth horizon. Frustrated by the antics of the men in her household, she constantly struggles to lift them to higher horizons.

- *Lisa* is by far the coolest, most talented and spiritually evolved of all the Simpsons. Not afraid to keep her own council or to be academically high-achieving, Lisa is a mean sax player, environmentalist and champion of social justice. She may only be a young girl, but with her spiritual line of sight firmly set at the fifth and sixth (creative) horizons, she definitely has the potential to go higher. Go Lisa!

have long gone. If we elect corrupt politicians and leaders who have no cornerstone of advanced spiritual integration, we will bequeath ourselves a social fabric no longer whole – a torn, corrupted community. Any systemic corruption, which appears wherever officials operate below this fifth horizon, causes communal suicide by a thousand cuts – moments of decision at which trust is broken, the hand is in the till, the blinkered eye looks only to its near support, and the unkind voice no longer gives a damn. On the other hand, whether in the aftermath of a natural or man-made disaster, if we manage to maintain the delicate matrix of public trust and positive regard through spiritually evolved leadership, the lurch towards the morass of disintegration and de-civilization is avoided.

Recreational development is a job not of building roads into lovely country but of building receptivity into the still unlovely human mind. All history consists of successive excursions from a single starting point to which man returns again and again to organize yet another search for a durable scale of values.
Aldo Leopold

U p to this point in our quest across the spiritual horizons, the most compelling drivers of human behaviour are our values, beliefs and ethics. These give us our sense of right and wrong – a sense that orders society and prevents a community de-civilizing and reverting to a savage, frightened brute pack. The fifth horizon marks the outermost reach, the very extremity of the spirit of humanism that drives the best of our values, beliefs and ethics. However, on September 11th 2001, many global corporations had their head offices obliterated by suicide pilots propelled by their distorted values, beliefs and ethics. It is only the evolution of our *inner* vision that will ultimately allow us to distinguish right and good from such misguided self-righteousness. If we choose to go beyond this horizon, we begin to look deeply within ourselves rather than merely around us.

This horizon marks the full development of our social intelligence. Yet for all its good, this horizon of liberal humanism is limited by its assumption that that this is the best that life can offer, seeing itself as the outer limit of human potential. Humanism fails to recognize that, although we have evolved personal and political freedom at this level – along with the attributes of empathy, altruism, generosity and a global sense of the brotherhood of humankind – we still remain separated from any real experience of higher connections. Although the works of great thinkers have given us priceless insights, we are still without the intimate connections that allow us the full and free experience of the creative, the transformational, the timeless, the boundless and the eternal.

At the first four horizons we began to establish order in our lives, and an ethical sense of self. At this fifth horizon, though unselfishness has begun to appear, it remains conditional, and letting go is done stoically and heroically, as if still equated with personal loss. True selflessness, with its liberating 'loss of self', will emerge in the next horizons.

This is the last horizon at which the beat of raw power, however muted and honourably 'humanized', can be used to drive compliance and force an outcome. Beyond this horizon, physical force becomes inadequate to the task. From here spiritual evolution is no longer measured in social terms. From here our measures and indicators move from the tangible to the intangible, and the war drums that have set the recorded rhythm of human history at last fall silent.

CHAPTER 16

An angel's-eye view of reality

Your work is to discover your world, and then with all of your heart give yourself to it.

The Buddha

The path that has taken us to this point has been long and strenuous. However, to arrive at the ultimate point of effortlessness we will need to elevate our outlook through three more horizons. At any stage of our climb we have a choice – take the long path behind us back into the lower horizons of separation and fragmentation, into a world of cause and effect, or continue towards the short path that takes us up and out through the final three horizons to breakthrough consciousness. Up until now we worked closely with the power of compulsion. Now our spiritual intelligence awakens the power of insight and inspiration. Where our outlook previously sought boundaries and created them, from here on we are uncovering the reality that is unbounded, without circumference. We have already moved from small-minded to open-minded; now we become completely single-minded.

By climbing this far and reaching a view of the fifth horizon and fullest possible extent of our social intelligence, we have already conquered our attachment to physical (external) separation. Ahead of us lies the most important phase of our journey – overcoming psychological (internal) separation as we ascend to the horizons that will take us beyond ego, beyond our attachment to individuality, and beyond our death-grip on this 'separate' self. Earlier, as we saw across each of the lower horizons, we became more integrated and stronger as our spiritual links strengthened and our horizons broadened. But by adopting separation's defensive attitude and manipulative outlook, the lower horizons have bedevilled us. Now the higher horizons promise us complete and clear connection to the source of all transformation and spontaneous good.

At this point in the adventure we begin to realize that the task of climbing to the pinnacle of the building, which we first set ourselves, was merely an external reflection of an inner journey – a path that was never anywhere else but *within us*. At this point, to attain an unimpeded view of the final three horizons, there is no mechanism to assist us: we have to get out of the elevator and make the final ascent on our own, by our own means. In this way, progress to higher ground means we once again get the opportunity to tap directly into our innate creative powers of insight – powers that have long been suppressed and diverted into helping us learn those important, early survival skills. We now enter the dimensions of advanced insight and transcendence in which spiritual wisdom finally matures – the third flashpoint of creativity and genesis that is transformational consciousness.

Here our outlook on the world begins to change radically. Whereas in the lower horizons we instinctively saw most things from the outside (and never seriously considered another possibility), now we evolve a vantage point inside everything looking out. Our earlier development of empathy and rapport (where we saw someone as if we were like them but still clearly apart and separate from them) transforms in these three horizons to become our spiritual capacity to see and interpret everything from any position, including from everywhere and looking from within. An outlook that allows us to see and connect with absolutely everything from within is the fully developed holistic viewpoint.

With each of the eight horizons, we access progressively higher connections. While our development in the lower five has been a highly socialized process, progress in the final three horizons will be more intimate and internalized. The first, second and third horizons were where our self-concept was formed. During that time our initial mind-to-body connections developed while we learned to manipulate the surrounding physical environment. At the fourth and fifth horizons our concept of others was refined as we expanded our social environment and began refining our perceptions of the broader world. Once we reached the fifth horizon, our developing spiritual capacity successfully completed its first major transition, passing through decreasing levels of separation and increasing levels of connection so that we were able to supersede all difference and division except the ultimate separation: the energies of the ego and the sense of an absolutely separate self.

This ascent from the physical to the metaphysical and beyond self gives us direct experience of the divinely infinite whole of which we are part. These final three horizons are the healing horizons, where the powers of integration and reintegration defy all the king's horses and all the king's men by rediscovering the whole and putting Humpty Dumpty back together again.

The sixth horizon: Artist-creative

At the times you operate from this horizon, you:

- *are entering the psycho-spiritual realm of the healing powers where reintegration of mind, body, spirit and environment take hold*

- *are an independent, original thinker capable of creative problem-solving, who often operates outside the accepted norms of society*

- *offer profound insights that are far-reaching enough to change lives*

- *are mentally 'playful', being more integrated mind-with-body*

- *may be talented in the arts*

- *may pay little attention to appearances, or dress to express rather than to impress*

- *are simultaneously inquisitive and introspective*

- *may be obsessive and sometimes seek exile and isolation*

- *can seem moody and aloof, though may equally appear intense, distracted, unfocused or even eccentric.*

Here, at the first of the higher horizons, the spiritual emphasis begins to shift from our 'outer' to our 'inner' life. Breakthrough consciousness is beginning to germinate and open onto new ground. This horizon is the beginning of creativity's *third* flashpoint, where the stirrings of original creativity enter our conscious mind and start to emerge in an obvious way in our attitudes and outlook. We now discover that we can transcend boundaries and their limitations through our creative power. However, at this early advanced stage we are still attached to the physical and so drape this burgeoning experience in forms of art, invention, innovation, or performance such as sport. Here, with the beginning of elevated consciousness, the neglected original reality begins to re-emerge, gradually rebalancing our physical, material life with our spiritual experience. With this unfolding process, personal transformation becomes increasingly possible.

The power of creativity – repressed and diverted while we learned those important, early life skills – has always been available to take us outside ourselves, it's just that we didn't know it. Although we are all abundantly creative, many of us may find it hard to remember when we last felt fully inspired by the power of our own creativity. However, most of us already place some value on the artistry of creativity and insight, whether in sport, gardening, science, business, architecture, music, nature or any other personal pursuit. Indeed, creativity and its effects can be found almost everywhere around us. Our communities actually exist as creative 'installations'; artworks of interconnected component parts threaded into the social web of life, with doctors, cleaners, lawyers, parents, teachers, preachers, employees, employers, leaders and led – all woven into the living tapestry that is the artwork of culture and community.

In one sense, we cannot be alive without being creative, not the least reason being that our senses help us create our view of our world; without a world-view we would be living blindly. Whatever we want, we also instantaneously become part of its creation. Happiness, success, friendship, love, a better world – almost everything we look towards, we help create.

Creativity and originality are embedded in every innovative approach, attitude or idea that inspires us and influences our behaviour. Creativity as innovation and adaptation appears where change emerges, at its leading edge. Surgeons invent the tools they need in the operating theatre, sports men and women create the clothing and equipment they need to gain a performance 'edge' in their sport, and computer technologists design the next high-tech trend in their industry. In any business the front line is the bottom line where the money is made and lost.

Creativity emerges through thinking and acting at the edge, the extreme, then synthesizing these thoughts and experiences into spontaneous insights. While intelligence is necessary for creativity, intelligence alone is no guarantee of someone being creative in a celebrated, artistic sense. Creativity may be best described as *uncoverability* – an ability to uncover patterns, links and connections that already exist, merely waiting to be accessed by the insightful. At this level the universe contains nothing new, only old parts in new arrangements and fresh forms.

Creativity as art foreshadows life. Creativity moves within our spirit as it is revealed within the world. There is even a certain clairvoyance within art – the power of prediction and uncanny connection. A work of art is anything that elevates our outlook, even for an instant, beyond the limited boundaries of self. In this sense the creative experience could be defined as any experience through which our outlook draws from both the spiritual and physical dimensions.

Art can be objectively defined as a collection of beautiful or thought-provoking forms and is usually considered a creation of human endeavour. However, beauty itself is highly subjective, and we also see beautiful forms in nature. The visual and performing arts, along with literature and poetry, are the formalized and controlled expression of creative energy as it takes form. Indeed, the more celebrated artists so capture this process of creative transformation within their art that it allows something of a transference of spiritual energy, connecting the artist and observer across time and space.

Yet creativity, with its synthesis of creative insights, is not confined to high art, and could be defined broadly as an ability to solve problems, a sensitivity to deficiencies and gaps in information, and the ability to see different ways of doing things. Creativity is also the ability to make educated guesses and formulate hypotheses, to evaluate and communicate, and to think of new ideas.[231] Human creativity, in whatever discipline – science, 'traditional' arts, spirituality, or daily problem-solving, for example – is not so much one flash of brilliance but more a series of small, spontaneous insights and actions that join together across time to form what might appear to be that single, great flash. All creative output shares a background of sustained focus and, often, hard work.

Tests have shown that a creative person's thinking process is peppered with many lateral, divergent and 'open' or unrelated thoughts. But we all have these to some extent every day. Studies of creativity and brainwave patterns have shown that creativity has two stages, *inspiration* and *elaboration*, each stage producing quite different states of mind. Using a general front-to-back communication between brain regions, the creative process switches across these two states of mind to excite a large number of regions of the brain simultaneously.[232] These facts serve to show that creativity is not a 'thing' that happens in one place in us, a place that some have got and some haven't. Creativity is an 'energetic', available to almost anyone in their daily lives.

Creativity is where our twin minds – one on the long path, the other on the short path – conjoin. As we begin our emergence from the last of the lower horizons, this first of the 'spiritual' horizons straddles both realities – the *created* world of separation and the *creative* world of transformation – while drawing from each of them. This artistic-creative horizon marks the rite of passage between the earthly and the infinite divine. Here we begin to become conscious of a greater, all-embracing reality.

In the artist, creativity often comes as an upwelling of feeling that seeks an urgent and irresistible expression. However, rather than being a liberating experience, this need for personal expression can be thwarted, distorted, and even become self-destructive. This is because at this horizon, where we begin to sense the emergence of a greater reality, we can still be distracted by our links with material concerns and our hold on the material world. These are the tensions that lie behind the infamous 'artistic temperament', which, if unresolved through spiritual practice, have been known to lead as far as madness or suicide.

Although the metaphor of the artist has been chosen as the guide for our ascent to the sixth horizon, we all know that creativity is not restricted to artists. Though it may be more conventionally recognized in the musician, singer, writer and painter, each of us can infuse our days with creative mastery by weaving the pursuit of excellence into everything we do. The spirit of creativity and insight moves within us all, and can ultimately move us to personal spiritual mastery. This state of mind has the capacity to take

As a young boy living in Queensland, Australia, I often visited the ramshackle studio of Ian Fairweather, an Australian painter originally from Scotland whose paintings are exhibited around the world. Ian thought nothing of using one of his newly finished masterworks to plug any inconvenient hole appearing in a fragile wall of his island hut. Ian was genuinely operating at this sixth horizon, above the attachment to material possessions and any need for self-identity. This diminished attachment to a separate self is why some artists are completely uninterested in their finished works once the creative moment has passed. An artistic masterpiece is little more than the beautiful but incidental record of a transformational moment that saw the artist poised between the substantial world and the infinite.

us beyond mundane expressions of creativity-as-entertainment to nothing less than an extraordinary personal experience of the mystical.

All creativity remains the art of originality. The Big Bang stands as the very first act of creation, the original creative artwork emerging from the infinity. As we saw in Chapter 2, this background of infinite reality suffuses and informs every aspect of created reality today, so that whenever we are truly creative we briefly touch the same infinite divine. In science as in art, there is not one big creative flash so much as an accumulation of smaller creative insights. Archimedes famously cried 'Eureka!', 'I have it!', jumped from his bath and ran down the street naked after suddenly being struck by the solution to a long-standing and difficult scientific question – but not before he had learned a great deal about the subject beforehand. Similarly, Einstein selected from the many disparate equations created by his predecessors before synthesizing them into his theory of relativity – a creative breakthrough that revolutionized the way we now see reality. From the beginning of time, the power of creativity has been the ability to make a new single entity where there were previously many parts. This is the ability of the holistic mind. Like Einstein, it is only by learning as much as possible of the accumulated knowledge in our chosen area that we can creatively and productively build on what has gone before.

While creativity is inborn and repressed, it needs to still be liberated and developed within us. Research by Allan Snyder at the University of Sydney shows that we all have profound suppressed creative and artistic abilities. Professor Snyder's work used specially designed magnets strategically positioned to change the electromagnetic profile of the brain, resulting in significant increases in artistic ability.[233] Other research shows that children who study the creative arts improve overall intelligence and performance in a variety of subjects,[234] and the re-introduction of philosophy studies in some schools is showing significant results in terms of improved behaviour and self-esteem, with children displaying a natural interest in life's big questions. Indeed, in all my high school teaching years I never found any child, even the most disruptive or antagonistic, who couldn't be reached with one or two well-designed 'big' questions about life, the universe and their place in it.

However, the shortcoming of the sixth horizon is that it is still referenced in the world of time and place – perhaps as a performance, exhibition, literary work, solution or innovative idea. This strong material reference restricts our reach across the spiritual horizons because the creative 'impulse' is not coming through us freely, in that it is still aimed specifically at the world of surfaces, edges and boundaries. At this sixth horizon our reality-consciousness is elevated enough to be 'toying' with the transformational, but not yet fully awakened to the transcendental.

We are each a proven, creative masterpiece. From the moment of our conception we display a wondrous creative ability, the capacity to transform the material resources supplied by the womb into the complex being that we have become. This is no less stupendous than the creative moment of the Big Bang – indeed, it is a seed from the same creative source. As babies, our brain is fully wired with an almost limitless range of possibilities; in the foetus there are masses of neural connections, many of which go unused.[235] We are born with a brain active and alight – sparkling in blooming, buzzing confusion. Our active brain profile is first sculpted by a selected blend of these inborn connections, and complemented by new ones created through our experiences. Our childhood conditioning gets our spiritual development started by preparing us for a successful life in the lower horizons. While our earlier spiritual preparation in the lower horizons effectively suppressed our wildly buzzing creativity in favour of more basic survival skills, our evolving psyche was also shaping our brain to entrench its new reality, its experiences and responses.

When we dwell in the lower horizons, much of our brain's capacity remains dormant. As we lose our fears or learn to rise above them, overcome our familiar attachments and expand our mental boundaries, then the neural pathways of our brain create new networks amongst themselves and reconfigure the many harmonic electrical oscillations that are known to swirl within our head. New ways of looking at the world and the wider reality require new neural patterns and mental conditions. (In this way, by introducing new ideas and new concepts of living, applied art enriches as it educates a society.) From there we extend our spiritual connections to include the more esoteric dimensions, cross normal boundaries of perception and expand our outer limits as we tap deeper into the power of creative transformation.

It is within the creative capabilities of any of us to stop what we've been doing and the way we've been doing it, and tune our spiritual antenna to a higher frequency.

We have art in order not to die of life.
Albert Camus

Art and creativity are healthy. In 2003, Susan Loppert presented findings of a research program at the Chelsea and Westminster Hospital in London that tested whether art contributed any clinical benefits to health. The result showed a reduction in blood pressure levels in the 'art' groups. Both painting and music also lowered depression by about 30 per cent. Labour time during childbirth was reduced.[236] Creative activity integrates our mind and body; it releases healing powers by engaging and integrating the neural networks. The experience of listening, playing and dancing to music has the power to move us beyond our rational thinking and into our 'spiritual' channel. Creative frequencies such as alpha and theta waves are also associated with the meditative states of mind that are known to decrease stress, lower blood pressure and rebalance hormone levels.[237]

Creativity is implicated in health because, as we have seen, creativity transforms disparate parts into a whole, and only an unbroken whole can be absolutely healthy. With the whole of life evolving to be completely healthy, we would expect to see creativity expressed in species other than human – and so we do. Common examples of non-human creativity are nest-building and improvisational tool-use amongst animals and birds, behaviours which display the creative ability of problem-solving. Creativity can be seen to be involved in driving the evolution of species; for example, innovative species of birds have been shown to evolve more rapidly than others.[238] With creativity being seen across species, we can suspect evolution and creativity of collaborating to realize the ultimate healthy whole.

In addition to its effects on the health of the individual, creativity is also of key importance to the wellbeing of society because of the particular leadership qualities inspired by this creative horizon. Genuine creative leadership has mass appeal. At this horizon, leadership begins turning truly selfless and egoless, seeking to facilitate any wishes directly expressed to it by society. Creatively holistic leadership has a history; it can work. For example, during the Tang Dynasty in ancient China, leaders sent emissaries, disguised in the costumes and manners of the region, to eavesdrop on the local folksongs that voiced the concerns of the day. Public works were then undertaken in answer to the population's needs. With similar intent, today's creative leader is focused on responding by invitation only. A creative economy and society allows the free up-welling of innovative ideas in an atmosphere of trust, security, respect, support and positive regard.

Creative leadership in the spirit of this horizon is not confined by the dogma of party politics, nor by the power of an exalted individual. Instead, it focuses on creating solutions based on 'what needs to be done', from the selfless super-position of benefits for all. Creative leaders lift up by listening down. If business management adopted this approach of creative leadership, more attention would be paid to feedback from the staff at the front line. Smarter employers would facilitate employees to think together creatively, and give time for them to develop new views of the world and new solutions at the front line. Such employers know that the frontline is the 'living' interface where business is in touch with the concerns of customers, suppliers and other stakeholders.

Leadership aside, when did you have your most recent creative thought or experience, that last personal flash of originality? Did you act on it, or did the rest of the day immediately get in the way?

The seventh horizon: Psychic-spiritual elder

At the times you operate from this horizon, you:

- *experience the power of direct and spontaneous manifestation that disregards time and place*

- *experience reality as multi-levelled, and can sense dimensions that defy easy definition or description*

- *are an original thinker, though sometimes seem to talk in riddles*

- *have clear personal ethics*

- *have an increased (yet quiet) sense of responsibility and duty to others*

- *can be fiercely independent*

- *seek out and enjoy quiet times alone for spiritual contemplation, meditation, reflection or true prayer, not fixed on the specifics of ritual and form*

- *are not materialistic, and dress for ease rather than to please*

- *have developed a strong psychic intuition or sixth sense*

- *have developed novel, sometimes unusual and exotic healing powers*

- *may appear unreliable, even impulsive*

- *can seem to alternate between being childlike and innocent, businesslike and direct, aloof and vague*

- *are humble about your beliefs and inclined to serve rather than be served.*

As our spiritual needs are more satisfied and our spiritual capacity extended, our material needs are minimized. At this horizon, our creative powers rise to seek links and references no longer within form, time or place. This is the realm of the mystic, where the experience is unstructured and undefined, but not unfocused. By harnessing our innate creative power beyond all structure, we begin to experience psychic flashes and heightened spiritual intuition. For most people these experiences are infrequent and fleeting. But even so, the memory of these transcendental moments can have profound and far-reaching effects upon our understanding of life, health and the universe. This is the spiritual horizon of the advanced spiritual elder – whatever age we happen to be.

Like the artist-creative experience, this heightened state is still intermittent. However, even a momentary flash of insight at this level can spontaneously move us enough to open up our spiritual boundaries. This is what happened to St Paul on the road to Damascus, who in an instant redirected his whole way of life. The higher electro-spiritual networks are now activated and engaged beyond personal boundaries and beyond any artistic or creative framework. Here our experience of the creative power is no longer enclosed. Here, the creative genie pops right out of the bottle to be expressed more holistically and permanently across our daily lives. Rather than becoming aloof, detached or distant, we become highly and creatively engaged. These are moments when created consciousness re-engages the power of original reality, which is the infinite field of energy in perfect balance.

This horizon is the realm of the mysterious healers and the psychic persuaders, the horizon at which the healing power of mind-over-matter is activated. Here, enlightened guidance, persuasion and influence take precedence over the mentality of command and control. 'Psychic surgeons', along with spiritual healers of many varieties and faiths, engage the harmonizing dynamics of this horizon, allowing the creation of the same electro-spiritual balance that penetrates barriers and transforms matter. These healers activate intimate yet far-reaching connections. This is the horizon of the newly miraculous.

Breakthrough consciousness, germinating in the previous horizon, emerges and buds here, though full flowering must wait. As we increasingly detach from the lower horizons, we open wider our own doorways to spiritual perceptions and connections, allowing ourselves to directly embrace these breakthroughs in our spiritual capacity. This is where our creative power starts to gain insights into the boundless state of infinite reality persisting before or outside time and matter – usually via dreams, psychic episodes and flashes of deep wisdom and intuition.

Here meditation methods upgrade from relaxing to enlightening, and the possibility of surpassing all separation emerges. Enlightenment is a state of mind; effective and deep meditation is what gets us there.

Indeed, at this horizon we are more spiritual than religious. While this is where the intention of religion is aimed, religion as a public ritual unfortunately often opposes spirituality as a personal experience and settles for a much lower spiritual outlook and experience. Similarly, while at the lower horizons prayer is blemished by ego and performance anxiety, at this horizon we enjoy increasingly long periods of time where we let go of ego, allowing ourselves the freedom to experience extended moments of selflessness and transcendent openness. Good prayer – always focused on what we need to give and let go of rather than what we get – does more than warm the hands that pray. Since mind and matter are intermingled, in the advanced practitioner the meditative arts can create the power of direct influence over both.

The more time spent at this horizon, the more our transcendent experiences and insights become an integral part of our emotional landscape, our attitudes and outlook. This boundless capacity for high communion, which we all have, is now even greater than the compassion and altruism of lower horizons. Here we have the capacity to love entirely without judgement, and certainly without any reference to our own personal needs. Ironically, many acts of selfless kindness at this spiritual level are often witnessed on the battlefield, frequently between enemies, as if the mad catastrophe of war releases, in some, the angels of love. This direct connection is implicit wherever selfless charity exists, wherever heroism embraces its enemy as kin on common ground, and wherever cruelty is replaced by forgiveness, kindness and mercy. These aspects of unconditional love are now fully developed in this seventh horizon.

As quickly as these transcendent and profoundly selfless experiences may arrive, they can leave us. This can cause our stability of mind to be called into question by ourselves or others, and for this reason denial of the experience is common. Indeed, psychic experiences can sound uncomfortably like psychotic delusions and hallucinations. Altered states don't always signal derangement, though deranged delusions can be deceptively similar to the experiences of fully integrated consciousness, allowing sceptics to use this shallow similarity to maintain their disbelief. But far from mental disintegration, visionaries such as St Patrick, the Sufi mystics of Islam, and the many shamans, seers, mediums and spiritualists of all the faiths have hovered between this seventh horizon and the ultimate state. An untold number of ordinary people have dwelt here without gaining any public recognition or historical standing.

This state can be entered equally by the young and the old, the educated and the ignorant, the publicly recognized and the anonymous. It is home to anyone excited by the rendezvous between their own mind and the experience of boundless reality.

The brain's God-spot produces mystical, supernatural and transcendental experiences when stimulated. Any single one of these flashes of insight is capable of changing our life. However, until we achieve such insight, our need for external leadership is so strong that we form religions around some of those who have dwelt at this horizon. We excitedly elevate a significant few (who themselves teach that we must ultimately find the supreme experience within our *own* hearts and not through someone else) while ignoring or treating with suspicion the ordinary spiritual traveller who is singularly able to navigate their personal pathway to this infinite, divine experience. The prophets sought sanctuary that would allow deep thinking, silence and quiet contemplation, and so must we if we want to consciously activate the insights and experiences that come with reaching this horizon.

The danger is that these mystical flashes can be so profound and intoxicating that we constantly strive to repeat, share and prove them to other people. This desire for control, though understandable, can corrupt any further experiences. Many of the psychic healers I worked with in the Philippines and elsewhere severely diminished their early powers because of the distractions of celebrity. At that point, some of them even resorted to devices and deception to masquerade their way past this power-failure. Scientific replication of psychic phenomena is extremely difficult for the same reason: the existence of desire – the desire to measure, define and repeat – sets up a framework of expectations and mental distance that disintegrates our spiritual outlook and dissipates our spiritual position back into separation and fragmentation.

At this horizon our conscious state is still in touch with the 'realities' around us, but our awareness, which previously attached itself to target points *within* our reality-consciousness, has given up its deep attachments and distractedness. In this state the view is wide, the infinity is near, and the strings attaching us to our mundane thinking are falling away. We are entering a state of divine paradox, the awareness of pure emptiness, and the experience of transformational peace and inspiration. The scientists and the yogis agree that the brainwaves in this 'theta' state of mind are key to relaxation, concentration, improved memory and higher states of consciousness.[239] Spiritual fitness is a state of mind, and spiritual capacity a matter of perception.

Do nothing and then nothing is left to be undone.

Laozi

This is the horizon of action without effort – which is not a call to laziness, because laziness leaves the work undone. That would be a call to do *nothing*. No, what Laozi meant was for us to *do* everything from a state of mind that understood the secret of effortless action. Effortless action means an end to fixation, not the end of intention. Be active but stay present to this eternally unfolding moment. All effort is the result of distractedness; distractedness leads to disintegration; and disintegration leads to hard work and disappointment as we try to hold things together and put the pieces back in place. Master yourself and then you will make no mistakes. To achieve this, prepare your mind, take harmonious action, and maintain the vision. 'Let go' of outcome while maintaining focus and letting events unfold. This is part of the secret to the law of attraction and manifestation. You see, manifestation is not due to some miraculous sudden jolt. There is a pace to the universal unfolding, requiring us to practise the art of letting go rather than resorting to manipulation, force and demand; the art of effortless release and surrender; the inner peace that allows things to unfold and manifest in harmony with the universal whole rather than distort to our own selfish timing.

In shifting our attention and influence from the material to the immaterial, we sensitize to the power-effects of fractals. We saw in Chapter 13 how fractals are the great equalizer. Fractals are also the great liberator, allowing us to give up the cry for power, the lunge for possessions and the desire for ever more glory. When we understand the meaning of transformational consciousness and experience the power of its possibilities, we see the value of fearlessly 'letting go' of what we cannot control and allowing things to unfold. This is spiritual surrender; the ultimate freedom.

Some artists at the sixth horizon anticipate this seventh, expressing in their art the more advanced level of perception and experience of this horizon. Significant artists of every type tell us that on their 'best days' they reach beyond technique to actually let go completely, becoming submerged entirely in their art, totally forgetting themselves. Musicians know it, painters know it, acrobats know it, lovers know it, the best managers know it and good parents know it. After all the talking, training, practice and preparation one more thing awaits – abandoning ourselves within the experience. This is the letting go that creates room for things to align, unfold and happen in their own time. What we are letting go of is our attachment to the material, and our desire to effect outcomes by manipulating them. This unencumbered state of mind marks the end of doing and the start of being. Now we are rising to our true potential – after all, we are human *beings*, not human *doings* or human *havings*. While taking action do nothing and take nothing – you will accomplish a lot.

By completely letting go of separation anxiety and its limited behaviour, we are free to visualize and be absorbed within the big picture while still taking care of the minutiae and moving forward one step at a time. All of us are capable of this, but may have grown mentally sluggish, constrained by habit. However, as we saw earlier, these habits can be broken at any time we choose. Even age is no limitation: neuroscience confirms that at all ages the brain can be rewired, generate new cells, break old patterns and learn new skills. We know that the more connected we are to the higher networks, the healthier we are. One of the stepping-stones to whole-health is forgiveness. Once we learn to let go, learning to forgive is easy. Forgiveness becomes effortless. When we let go of our unhelpful stories we stop the trajectory of these stories targeting our future. Some of us need to acknowledge our hurt and fear, reclaim our personal power, and release the chains of pain.

At this seventh horizon, the psycho-spiritual zone of separation has receded and we detach ourselves from old injuries. In this instant of release we let go, stop diverting energy that is spent carrying the unforgiven and enter the present more fully. We let go, forgive and move on. Forgiveness is letting go of hate and revenge. By giving up hope for a better past we reclaim our energy for the future. To forgive we need to be heard, felt, understood and acknowledged, yet we must also remember that these rarely come from the perpetrator. Forgiveness is more about freeing *yourself* than about letting some other person off the hook, scot-free. Lack of forgiveness diverts us, and once we realize this, the act of forgiveness becomes completely liberating.

The healthiest time to forgive is immediately after the offence. This is because the instant we feel offended by some word or action, our 'energy' begins to drain down towards the lower horizons where personal offences register. To prevent this backslide and preserve our higher connections, practise instant forgiveness and detachment. The next instant someone offends you, make statements like, 'You may be right' or 'That's an interesting opinion' instead of going on the immediate attack or self-defence. In this way your personal power isn't wasted on the negativity of being unforgiving, destructive and angry.

Buddhism says that one of the most important things we can do with our lives is prepare for the moment of our death by first learning to deal with small and unexpected daily changes and outcomes. In this way we are practising and preparing for our greatest change, which is letting go of our body in death; to prepare for rain, buy your umbrella on a sunny day. So practise letting go of little things now; start with practising forgiveness. Letting go is an attitude, so live in the present and take responsibility for the way you are *at this very moment*. Live up to the expectations you have of others. Forgive now! Make the call, write the letter, say the right prayer, reclaim your future. There is never a bad time to let go of distractions; it is time now to experience the power of forgiveness. Find that person and forgive them, not their actions. The South African Truth and Reconciliation Commission dealt with a cruel and unjust past by abandoning the usual political show trials, in favour of open hearings of testimony from both the oppressors and the victims of apartheid. In many cases the Commission granted full amnesty to perpetrators of politically-motivated acts of violence. Many countries in denial of their past also carry a deep wound in their identity, while others find the spirit to resolve, reconcile and move on.

At any of the much lower horizons, life can seem to be a never-ending series of unexpected situations and unforeseen outcomes. However, here we know that the best way to avoid being caught up in unexpected outcomes is to master the art of working effortlessly. Do everything this way; do nothing without it, because then there are no unexpected outcomes and no accidents to be remedied and undone. In this way our work is always done, wherever we are, leaving us to stand in the pathway of good fortune. This is the art of letting go of one moment to allow the unfolding of the next moment in which to participate. All the power we allow through us is being expressed through us here in this moment; don't miss it. Simply *being there* and remaining open-minded is wisdom's first position. The second position is taking action while remaining still and not adding, subtracting, holding or avoiding.

At this horizon, letting go comes easily, and our bodies exist, operate, and stay alive *precisely* on this principle of effortless action. The heart pumps an enormous volume of blood with impressive force, but down in the capillary bed, where lifeblood is actually connected to every cell, there is little movement, just a soft flow, a gentle diffusion of nutrients from capillary to cell, an unhurried effortlessness of being. We are all connected and capable of active influence with this same amount of effortlessness. Push and pull too hard and the connection is lost. Let the pressure off and the harmony within integration gently resonates. By joining into the effortless flow of fractal effects with their endlessly unfolding emergence and convergence, we are free to stabilize and align our personal energies; in this way, we transform our own lives creatively, and reflect that transformation into the world. Whether we are peasants or kings, at this horizon we are all equal players in the spiritual game, restricted only by the boundaries of what we construct in the lower horizons of our development. Letting go allows the fractal effects to freely flow around us and through us.

At this seventh horizon we understand the healthy need to let things unfold in their own time. Only a foolish gardener blames the plant for poor growth. Shaking, agitating and pulling the plant won't help. Instead, the gardener provides the fertilizer, water, soil and sunlight – then gets out of the way and lets the plant evolve as nature does its thing. Like any organism, nature is self-healing and when left alone will become whole again, until we once again push too far. There is ample evidence to show that things regularly and almost miraculously fix themselves when we get out of the way.[240] Like a doctor with a patient, we don't 'fix' the environment; we can only provide the conditions to let life heal itself. Without us pushing life-support systems so far that we break their natural equilibrium, the Earth tends to restore itself, containing the rampant with a predator, resolving toxins with a cure, and returning the whole to balance. All that we are required to do is practise something we find most difficult – understand the whole, and move nothing blindly. As we saw in Chapter 3, much damage is being done by invasive species above and below ground that have been introduced and allowed to upset the natural whole of the ecology. This is because originally we failed to understand the nature of harmony and integration; we failed to keep our hands off, practise the art of intentional but effortless action, and *do* nothing! As a consequence there is much that needs to be undone.

As we consciously shift our point of view we begin seeking ways of getting out of our heads without getting off our faces or going out of our minds. When we let go of self and so become selfless and without ego, our actions leave no unexpected repercussions. Mind-altering substances can seem to be fun, even illuminating, but are only ever temporary. Meditation techniques (detailed in Chapter 18) propel us through the energetics behind the fundamentals of integration and help us rise through the eight horizons. This personally managed approach to the most profound Zen skill – the paradoxical 'letting go of letting go of letting go' (see page 298) – allows the transformational experiences and psychic breakthroughs we have been discussing to arise effortlessly into our immediate present.

Now we can get high on reality at any time and in any place, now and forever. When engaging the art of 'letting go', what we actually let go of, deep within ourselves, is our compulsion for separation. This is the addiction to fragmentation and isolation that gives rise to both the separate self as well as to the attitudes and outlook of separation that give us our sense of reality. This letting go is easy for some and difficult for others – but ultimately it is the only way forward.

Think of an Elephant

There are three steps to letting go. These are the three mental levels to detachment. Before we get started, allow your eyes to move out of focus while you think of an elephant. Then:

> **Step 1:** Try to *let go* of thinking of it; *try to not think* of the elephant. You can't, but that's the whole point for now: whenever you are aware of *trying* to do something, you can't have succeeded at doing it.

> **Step 2:** Keep trying, but only now add one more thing – try to *let go of trying to let go* of thinking of the elephant. Now you've got an elephant you are trying not to think about, and you're also trying not to think about trying not to think. Sounds wacky but stay with me here. Once we can do these first two steps – once we can let go and also let go of letting go – there is one more simple yet profound step.

> **Step 3:** Let go of those first two steps, meaning that we finally *let go of letting go of letting go* of the elephant. Sit with these three levels of mind and observe them. Let your feelings come and go.

> If we can get to the experience behind this absurd-sounding riddle – sometimes described as almost a physical sensation of increasing expansion – we enter the original silence existing behind creation. We can remain still when life is moving fast. This is letting go of separation and becoming conscious of original connection.

Letting go includes letting go of mental resistance and reactivity. This doesn't mean we become gullible and wishy-washy or are easily led. By letting go of our habitual resistance we make room for new possibilities. Programmed by our deep-rooted habits of mind to be reactive, when we make our mental outlook less reactive, we allow the possibility of also making our actions less reactive. This leads to shorter distances to travel to any destination and fewer troubles along the way. A mind that stays alert while being less reactive is necessarily a mind more open to those spontaneous moments of insight that lead to full-blown creativity.

During an extended stay in Hong Kong I had the honour of several long conversations with Lu K'uan Yu (Charles Luk), a Buddhist master and venerable translator of Chinese Chan and early Zen Buddhist texts. On each of our visits we would be left alone to drink Chinese tea and talk together. These conversations would almost always weave their way to a pinnacle, usually in the form of a question that I formulated and put to Charles for his wise reply. Invariably, at each of these peak moments, just when I felt that the question-and-answer exchange would be the high point of student-teacher transference, Charles would pause, ponder, turn slowly to the teapot, look at it, look at me, smile quietly, then offer, by way of what I took as a deflection, "Paul, would you like another cup of tea?" As my question slid off the boil the next interminable minute or so was taken up with Charles methodically pouring tea, wiping the spout and ... sitting in silence.

With Charles' unspoken response, those particular 'pinnacle' questions of mine seemed always left unanswered, leaving me frustrated. And it was only years later that it quite suddenly dawned on me what he was really doing. Charles was not ignoring my questions, but by pouring the tea he was creating the space needed for the actual answer to arise as if from within the question itself. He was offering the scope for me to find the answer myself, outside the teacher. All I needed to do was let go and see beyond the teapot and realize that what I was asking was unanswerable, because putting it into words would make it impossible to have the experience – words would have locked me into the finite present.

Thank you, Charles, for inviting me to let go of the questions and let the answer absorb me (rather than me absorb the answer) in the serenity of the direct experience.
May the transmission of mind outside the
teaching continue ...

At this advanced horizon we understand that 'letting go' does not involve pushing away: pushing away creates a psychological gap and more psychic separation. When we push something away it still has us and controls us; we have not let it go *effortlessly*. Letting go is a state of surrender without defeat, a process of giving up without losing. To attain knowledge, add something every day. To attain wisdom, remove something every day. As Emerson said, 'Surrender and find affinity with all things.' In this way, letting go unleashes the forces of attraction and supersedes entropy and separation.

At this seventh horizon, we find ourselves developing a type of sixth sense that frames the world differently, enabling us to be in the world in a way we might previously have thought absurd. One of the fundamental characteristics of this sixth sense is its capacity for 'deep-remembering' – in effect, picking up the imprint of those impacts and impressions that pre-date our own lives and even the accumulations of genetic history. Now we are entering the conscious experience of forever. When the constructs of this world fall away and we access cosmic or super consciousness, we experience the heightened spiritual states denied us during our sojourn at the lower horizons. At this horizon we begin to feel the liberating power of being able to spontaneously control our otherwise volatile emotional mix, and are far less likely to be lured into reactive cause and effect situations. We've heard about bliss, awe, rapture and ecstasy. At this horizon we begin to experience them.

By the way, what was your most recent psychic experience? (The answer is at the bottom of this page.)*

---

* Answer: Your most recent psychic experience, believe it or not, was when you leapt to find the answer down here at the bottom of the page. This was a psychic event. Let me explain. Most gold unearthed on almost any hand-worked goldfield was discarded by the miners working there. The relatively few nuggets these miners found, though big in themselves, were minute compared to the gold dust shovelled out of the mineshafts by the naive miners. Likewise, we expect psychic experience to be overwhelming. However, the simple act of conscious thought is an act of mind over matter – thoughts moving molecules in your brain. Even the smallest event can have profound implications.

The eighth horizon: Transformational super-wakefulness

At the times you operate from this horizon, you:

- *exist in a state of complete spiritual wakefulness*

- *no longer identify yourself with form, and emerge beyond ego*

- *have gone beyond distinctions of time and place to dwell in the infinity, the divine*

- *see beyond friend and foe; create no enemies; cause no waves; arrive effortlessly*

- *let go of beginnings and endings, and awaken from suffering*

- *know your own true face as the true face of creation*

- *live truly free, yet with every other horizon remaining accessible*

- *are transformational and inspirational rather than forceful and manipulative*

- *by your actions alone, encourage all life to develop towards the highest horizon*

- *see beyond the higher emotions such as ecstasy, awe and rapture, to enter a state of quiet release*

- *have evolved compassion to the highest degree where it applies not just to* someone *but to* everyone *and all life*

- *know that for every heart healed a universal network of connections is saved*

- *understand that when one species is lost, all of life is diminished.*

The facts of quantum science tell us that, ultimately, there is no separation in reality – every place is connected everywhere, and all matter subtly influences all other matter all the time. There is reality external to us, just not absolutely disconnected from us. Ultimately, there is no 'local' reality; at some point, all of creation remains connected at source.

This highest of the event horizons recreates original connection as a personal and ongoing experience. At this horizon we attain and maintain breakthrough consciousness, a sense of super-wakefulness where we are simultaneously in touch with the entire range of normal and paranormal networks. It marks the culmination of creativity's third flashpoint: first creation, then conception, and now the experience of super-consciousness. Within this, one seamless whole is created from three forces: the infinity, our created reality, and conscious awareness. Here our potential to surpass all separation is fully realized and experienced. We have now conquered the second separation, the separate self.

Selflessness is not weakness but strength. Gandhi told his supporters, 'Become nothing, become empty. Then we become invincible because nothing can find us and attack us.' This horizon places intention beyond any angle of attack, beyond any trajectory of time or control. Having favoured self-consciousness for so long, we are now being recreated forever in total spiritual balance.

To be beyond separation and reach the eighth horizon we need to understand and practise the spiritual state of silent surrender. The state of deep inner peace and silence is common to many cultures and religions. This is the state in which enlightenment meets paradise. Japanese Zen calls it *satori*. Hindus call it *jannat*. Christians call it *heaven*. Muslims call it *jannah*. Jews call it *shamayim* or *haskalah*. Hopi Indians call it *tuwanasaapi*. Chinese call it *tiantang*…

Breakthrough consciousness, having germinated in the sixth and reached bud in the seventh, now reaches full flower. This is the boundless horizon, the unfathomable deep, the stillness that runs beyond all appearances. While remaining active and concerned in the world, here we experience the power and freedom of being whole, with the energy of infinity arising consciously and selflessly through us. Surpassing all dysfunctional behaviour, life at this horizon is highly effective. At this horizon we are fully awake. Our light is on. Our face shows itself energized, radiant, with an inner vision that 'sees' beyond any background. Egoless, our attention arises from beyond 'self'. We are fully integrated, and the infinity is now a personal experience. The intelligence inherent in all of creation is now openly linked through us to its source – the infinite energy-field of original reality in perfect balance.

Just as the segments of an orange can be mechanically described, but the inner sweetness of the orange is only available to experience, it is also experience alone that can reach this highest state of freedom – the full-blown experience of infinite consciousness. Anyone who is no good at anything is unable to make an impression on the people good at many things; anyone good at many things is unable to make an impression on the people excellent at a few things; and anyone excellent at a few things is unable to make an impression on a person *perfect at one*. This is the horizon of mystical balance of the many within the one.

Now empty, our levels of observation have transcended 'self' to become selfless. Our creative power of spontaneous transformation is fully engaged. We are able to live passionately and radiantly without agitation. Having profoundly 'let go' of all fixations, everything matters, yet nothing concerns us. Here we experience no beginnings or endings, and have completely let go of life's two separations – the external zone of separation and the internal, separate self. Life has become a full circle.

> The head abbot in a Zen monastery set a poetry test to decide who would be his successor after his departure. The favourite monk impressed with his poem: 'The cleanest mirror gives the clearest reflection.' However, one of the least impressive monks won the leadership succession. His poem: 'No mirror; no dust; nothing.' Reflect on this.

Having found nothing, we are in touch with everything. We give up chasing across any horizon, and let go into the eternal, boundless present. This has nothing to do with time or space. This is the mysterious 'horizon without a horizon', the dimension that surpasses all boundaries. Here we see that the short path is actually *no* path; nothing. We have realized that 'nothing' refers to more than a conceptual void or emptiness. Now we see that, in a spiritual sense, wanting nothing is not the same as not wanting anything; we in fact want the state of *nothingness* (immateriality) that is beyond every single thing. This is part of the divine paradox.

Vision has become more than planning for the future; now vision is the outlook onto the endless infinity that is becoming the present fully interconnected, singular whole. The old attachments to status, money, power and authority no longer confine us. We are productive and creative, having transcended ego. We have outgrown time and place. We have outgrown self. Being fully and deeply released and in touch, we no longer need quiet sanctuaries and sacred places. The tranquillity we once found only in those places, along with the insight and focus gained there, is now effortlessly and spontaneously available to us everywhere.

At this eighth horizon, creation's intelligence completes its cycle and returns to the source. As we have seen, creativity first appeared as the flashpoint that gave rise to the Big Bang and our classical reality with its familiar dimensions of separation. Then it appeared as life's creative pulse, giving rise to our individual existence. Now creativity completes its third flash, becoming a fully transcendental and transformational, conscious experience. Here, every discovered and undiscovered network supporting our multi-dimensional universe is actively channelled through us. Our thinking becomes subtle and finely tuned and we experience a deep, mystical remembering.

As we searched for meaning, and prior to reaching this ultimate horizon, we worked at making sense of the world. Now we experience the transmissions of mind directly, *outside* all mediums. All emotions are transcended, even the higher ones, yet nothing is dull; we are not disengaged, just released. At the previous horizons we strove for some sort of gain or result whereas here, no longer seeking facts or producing fictions, we experience the pure, unencumbered truth. In the early stages of our ascent, life evolved into a competitive search for personal survival and success. Since then separation has been revealed more and more as the passing phase, the key distraction. Now we no longer have the need to experience 'other' as distinct from us. We realize that our relationships and ourselves have always been one and the same, inseparable; everything is nothing more than its interconnections. Now we live within a vivid yet effortless experience of the whole, dwelling in the one while doing many things.

Across this boundless horizon we exist in a sustained and continuous state of selfless awareness. This is a state of spiritual wakefulness in which life operates beyond wilful effort and beyond the confines of causes and the impacts of effects. Life, while effortless, has become most effective. Fully connected, limitless and whole, we find absolute peace. We can now recognize God's true face and see our original reflection in everything. With this original experience, there is no longer any need for teachers, or faith in empty images. By living as the silent host – tuned in and greeting all that comes and goes in this endless moment – we enter the access-all-areas, perfect incarnation of the highest spiritual freedom.

Knowing others is intelligence; knowing yourself is true wisdom. Mastering others is strength; mastering yourself is true power.
Laozi

We have seen the different levels of awareness available to us, depending on our spiritual vantage point, and the attitudes and behaviours that identify and accompany each horizon, from mindless selfishness all the way to breakthrough consciousness. Remember that it is these attitudes and behaviours that also maintain us at each horizon; change these and we help change our horizons.

Disrupted connections at any horizon always affect our psyche, an effect often revealed in us as a particular sense of loneliness, distance or longing specific to that horizon. While a sense of stillness can be healthy, loneliness never is.[241] Until we heal these disrupted or ignored relationships, in the form of re-energized connections, we are prevented from attaining true spiritual integrity and health. The transformational process of spiritual evolution, becoming more potent as we progress, therefore involves reactivating this ever-extending network of connections at each of the eight horizons.

It is now time to think about how we operate within these horizons on a daily basis, before going on to discover the science and practices that can open us to the experience of true spiritual integration. We began the process of expanding our horizons by looking at the different faces of love at each elevation. Now let's consider its opposite: anger. The importance of anger for both personal and group survival has already been discussed.

If someone angrily or selfishly hurts us by behaving at the spiritual level of the second or third horizon, we need to respond appropriately – not necessarily sword-for-sword and blow-for-blow, but also not at some soggy, obsequious or self-righteous pretence of the eighth horizon either, or in some situations we will get annihilated. A healthy immune system may need to respond in its extreme only rarely, and only when challenged past a certain point, but it still needs to respond. No immune response at all ultimately means extinction. Full spiritual fitness is not for the fainthearted. Turning the other cheek is not a matter of strength or weakness, or a matter of being right or wrong: it is a matter of keeping our eye on the horizon.

Without an horizon measurement matrix to assess them by, despots and other inappropriate leaders are able to overcome our social immune system by masking their self-serving corruption with calls to loyalty and a thin veneer of civic-mindedness. This allows them to appear to be at the higher horizons and so keep their popular authority and retain power; they have their image 'air-brushed' to appear a high-minded, humble servant of the people. Hitler, Stalin and Mao masqueraded at these advanced horizons, assuming mystical status while designing schemes that murdered millions. Today, many of the spiritual and ethical positions assumed by our religious authorities, political leaders and other public figures are measured against the accepted background of their stated belief systems, rather than against their actual behaviour on the job. Matching an authority figure's behaviour to the horizon at which they usually operate gives us the means to get beyond political rhetoric, corporate ritual and religious dogma. It allows us to measure, empirically and behaviourally, the true level of spiritual fitness and personal development of those in authority and power, enabling us to spot those who masquerade at higher horizons.

Horizon testing and matching not only helps us measure our personal spiritual fitness and identify our preferred spiritual position, but it also has the potential to allow individuals more success in partner selection, relationship compatibility and personal communication. Moreover, it would be invaluable in public office and business today to help with such things as recruitment, team-building, management, leadership and strategic planning. This would allow the creation of better businesses, better public institutions, and a fairer, more interconnected and enlightened society.*

However wide our range of horizons, we can experience a number of these levels in any one day. One moment you are with a friend dodging traffic and jumping for your life onto the kerbside, the next you are brushing the experience off and walking into a nearby gallery to quietly absorb the surrounding beauty.[242] We can even be in more than one horizon at a time, assertively brushing away a mosquito while sitting in quiet meditation for example, or absorbed in the appreciation of beauty while also making plans for what we will do with it.

Having understood the *concept* of these levels of awareness on an intellectual level, through the metaphor of the eight horizons, it is important to realize that this is an *experience*, not a theory. The horizons represent a continuum of spiritual connectedness that is effective, measurable and actionable, helping us to consciously make a difference within our lives, moment by moment. In the unruly and exciting world we have around us – a world of cause, effect, unexpected influences and outcomes, where we need to make constant adjustment and nothing is certain – our horizons must of necessity be lived and experienced as a sliding scale. This is because life is lived at many levels, from ordinary survival to extraordinary spiritual significance. Limited horizons mean a limited life, while a significant life has free access across all horizons. With *limited* horizons we are at the mercy of the unknown; we often assess a situation incorrectly, act inappropriately, are unable to predict important consequences of our actions and become our own worst enemy. With *unlimited* horizons at our disposal, all options are available.

* Horizon matching that supports the needs of modern corporate culture by predicting and selecting for a desired set of corporate values, streamlined personnel recruitment, efficient team development and the creation of compatible alliances is being researched and made available. More information is available on the website: www.mindbenders.com.au.

You have been shown each of the horizons in detail, and have also seen beyond them to the infinity. Identifying which horizon matches each of your day-to-day situations helps you manage your own process of spiritual reintegration. We now know that the process of spiritual healing is as possible as it is personal. To effect our spiritual recovery, we are strongly supported by the findings of modern science. Research in apparently unrelated fields such as quantum physics, holistic health, cosmology, neuroscience, evolutionary theory, and consciousness studies shows that these disciplines form part of a much greater reality to which we all belong. Above all, the mysterious frontiers of science today challenge the limiting boundaries of common reality while substantiating the ultimate experience mythologized in ancient teachings and still sought by spiritual aspirants and meditation practitioners worldwide – breakthrough consciousness that allows us the unifying experience within everything.

For notes and author contact information, please see website on page 385.

WAKING UP TO THE DIRECT EXPERIENCE OF THE INFINITE

CHAPTER 17

Discovering the science for why the impossible is possible

The drive for unity is certainly to me one of
the deepest elegances of physics. ... But
ultimately science is also an act of faith –
faith that we will be capable of
understanding the way the universe is put
together...

Sylvester James Gates, Jr[243]

This chapter is about uncovering evidence for the existence of the
infinity and ways into the liberating experience of that state. From
the frontiers of science we will uncover evidence of mechanisms
within space and within ourselves that combine to interlink the smallest
part of creation into the infinite whole. In the process we will get to the
essence of existence and reality itself. The discoveries presented here
reveal that there is indeed some greater reality and essential unifying
experience surpassing our current understanding, just as philosophers and
religious scholars throughout the ages have argued.

The French philosopher Jean-Paul Sartre once said that essence
precedes existence. Essence – whether we call it 'infinite energy in perfect
balance', 'the source', or 'God' – is pre-existing, and in dimensions other

than time and space. We have already seen the dysfunction that occurs in our lives when we fail to recognize this infinite essence, or forget that we are not separate entities called 'me' but are in fact connected beyond ourselves to every other thing in the universe. Yet if we are ever to get a grip on what this connection means for us, or what this infinite unity is, we first face a seemingly insurmountable problem. One of the characteristics of the energetic state of infinity (or divinity or eternity) is that it cannot be described and understood on a theoretical level, because the moment that you think about infinity, it stops being infinite – it becomes just another concept in your head, another word, another idea with a beginning and an end.

So, what do we have available that is more powerful and immediate than ideas and descriptions? The only thing that can take us to a timeless dimension that supersedes ideas and description is *experience*. Experience is the only thing that happens to us instantaneously; anything other than experience takes time. Experience is the only thing always present in the present, and the only way we really and fully grasp anything. Infinity cannot be understood; it can only be experienced.

One way into the stillness of infinity is through meditation, as we will see later. If the energy of infinity is all-pervasive (and we have already deduced that it is), there should also be some hard evidence of it that satisfies our need for direct experience as well as an understanding on a scientific and intellectual level. Otherwise, as philosophers such as A.J. Ayer have argued, we are left with the problem that 'it is impossible for a sentence both to be significant and to be about God'. In this view, statements about infinity – whether as a supreme dimension or an infinite being – are meaningless and unusable in any practical sense, in that they do not tell us anything except that the person uttering them has faith that something exists. In other words, statements of faith reveal nothing about God and everything about the believer.

But here comes the exciting part: science is now starting to find evidence for what religion, spirituality and philosophy have each sensed, yet all argued over, for centuries – that infinity and eternity (timelessness) are real. At last we are able to demonstrate through science that there really is a lot more to reality than the created, physical and finite. In fact, in one sense science and religion have been looking for the same thing, only from different perspectives. While religion and spirituality have given us one way to get to the experience of the infinite state to which we are all connected, science now gives us another: the observation and demonstration of subatomic, biological and cosmic phenomena that all point to there being levels of reality other than those with which we are familiar in our limited, created world.

It must be admitted that the new age of science – with its quantum physics, string theory and neuroscience – is hard stuff for most of us to get our heads around. But no matter how difficult to follow, it's worth hanging in there because the infinity, whose infinite field of energy in perfect balance supports all of creation from the point where time begins, leaves a fingerprint, if we care to look. Read the signs and we are better prepared to unlock the experience. Just as police and forensic experts can read small signatures of evidence collected from past events and then tie these fragments together into a complete picture, the infinity impresses its own signature on all of creation since the time when the Big Bang blasted 'within' it. We will see that the energized state of infinity, intangible but not imperceptible, is undoubtedly and eternally present.

These discoveries bring us to a new stage of evolutionary possibility, an era of informed spirituality – spiritual realism that is evidence-based. In this we have superseded superstition, gone beyond blind belief in the supernatural, declined unquestioned ritual and opened up to an experience of spirituality that is substantial and therefore truly *significant*. Its significance emerges for us as we directly access the infinity of energy through the personal experience of breakthrough consciousness. To allow this awakening, all we have to do at this point is enquire beyond our old assumptions and open our minds to the evidence supporting new possibilities.

True knowledge exists in knowing that you know nothing.
Socrates

We are afloat on a sea of unknowing. The human story is filled with unique and uncanny events that stretch our understanding of the possibilities available to us. According to legend, the ancestors of Pacific islanders crossed vast expanses of ocean using celestial and terrestrial aids that included a mystical undulation in the ocean, dismissed as folklore until modern satellite images revealed ocean swells many kilometres apart with consistent wave patterns.

At first glance our body appears to be fairly solid and stable, but look more closely and we see a torrent of microbiological changes as unceasing and turbulent as the Niagara Falls. An estimated 300 trillion trillion reactions are taking place in our body every second,[244] making it impossible to set down a comprehensive list of these reactions and their interrelationships. Yet our life depends on this flood of chemical interchange never stopping or slowing down long enough for us to measure and understand more than a fraction of it.

The point is, before we can entertain new and challenging ideas, we must first acknowledge that it's impossible to know everything about anything, and that wherever there is knowledge, there is also ignorance. All of the knowledge we carry around in our heads is either incomplete, outdated or wrong – an accumulation of 'realities' and intepretations guided by our experiences, shaped by the dictates of a wider community and bound by our habits of mind. To borrow from Shakespeare, there are more things in heaven and earth than we can ever dream of. If we want to get beyond self-limiting habits and open up to new possibilities, we need to treat new ideas and information with an open mind, rather than contempt and scorn before investigation.

However, most of us will do almost anything to avoid showing our ignorance, even though, as Leonardo da Vinci put it, the person 'who has no doubts will achieve little'. The words 'I don't know' can sound self-critical. Yet, paradoxically, the moment we acknowledge our ignorance and inexperience can be the very moment we give up the fear of being caught out. Accepting the extent of our ignorance is a powerful moment of liberation, not humiliation. The full release of our creative power is imminent the moment we allow enthusiastic curiosity to acompany our honest sense of uncertainty and 'not knowing'. When our minds are open to new possibilities, much more creative thinking is available to us.

The absolute impossibility of knowing everything can even be demonstrated. The mathematician Gregory Chaitin, for example, has shown that there exists a completely unknowable, random number that he calls Omega.[245] The discovery of this number demonstrates that there is both a limit to logical reasoning and a limit to that which can be calculated. Imagine something – in this case a number – that is real but must always remain completely unknown! There will always remain a great deal of mystery in life and in the wider universe.

In the early chapters we learned that our fragile senses scarcely give us any worthwhile grip on reality. The exciting thing is that, by fully opening our minds we may be in a position to progress towards the answers for some of the truly difficult questions facing science today, including:

- What is consciousness?

- What is the universe made of?

- Can the laws of physics be unified?

- How does any physical thing keep its form and not drift apart?

- How does a single (somatic) cell become a whole plant?

- How and where did life on Earth arise?

Nobody has come close to solving the mysteries of mind, consciousness, the self, free will or personality – or even something as basic as the origins of life. In fact, even our assumption that life originated either on Earth or in outer space is now being challenged by a third option that is quite astonishing. For a long time, science has shown us that subatomic energy particles 'pop' into existence from nowhere, appearing spontaneously from infinite energy rather than assembling from any precedent parts.* Now it has been found that particles of *life* (in the form of mycoplasmas, the smallest autonomous organisms we know of) may also form on the edge of reality – where space-time meets infinite energy and where atoms can exist in several states or locations at once.[246] This is an exciting discovery because it allows the possibility that, like particles, life itself may also not come from somewhere in time and space, but instead may emerge spontaneously out of infinite energy as mysteriously as the quantum particles that are known to bubble up almost anywhere in space.[247] It's just possible that the immaterial essentials of life, along with mind and the creative energy of intelligence, operate across more than one reality, in all the multiple dimensions that quantum studies predict.

Mysteries also surround our perceptions of space, light and time – vital building blocks of our reality. To illustrate the immense scale of our ignorance, picture the following scenario. You are blindfolded and have been led into a room of 20 people. You are told that these 20 people control your whole life and everything that happens to you – absolutely everything, both good and bad. However, before your blindfold is removed, you are also told that you will only be able to see and communicate with *one* of these people. Though the other nineteen remain to play their part in your life, you will be completely out of touch with them and can only hope 'everything goes okay'. Even worse for you, the communications you have with this one-person-in-twenty are minuscule, only a few inadequate moments every day. In this situation, wouldn't you be very, very curious to know something more about this person, as well as anything at all you could glean about the other nineteen people 'out there' in your territory? You might think that if you could only get in touch with *any* of them a little

---

* A subatomic energy 'particle' can have either an exact position or a definite speed, but not both. A particle can disappear into this uncertainty, and reappear just as spontaneously. As astonishing as this may be, we now know that this 'uncertainty' is not confined to the subatomic quantum world: Leonard Susskind – a physicist at Stanford University, California, and one of the inventors of string theory – has shown that this phenomenon of uncertainty and spontaneous translocation can exist on a massive scale, even with something as big as an elephant! (*New Scientist* 28 October 2006). Caslav Brunker and Johannes Kofler reinforced this possibility of massive translocation with their discovery (see Chapter 4) that the laws of quantum physics are not quarantined from our reality and can cross over into our dimensions and change the way our world works.

more directly you might have a greater sense of what is going on, and perhaps develop more of a say in what happens to your life.

Well, this is exactly how we are living today. Although space scientists have calculated that there are about a trillion trillion trillion trillion trillion tonnes of material in the universe, this and other known energy constitutes *only about 4 per cent* of creation. Meanwhile, 96 per cent of created 'stuff' exists as either dark matter or dark energy lost somewhere in the disappeared territory around us. Because we can't see it (it emits no light), the existence of dark matter or energy can only be inferred and its position speculated: it may be out in space, or at the end of your finger. If science is able to detect a lot of matter from the benefit of distance (and it has, discovering that there is a lot of dark matter around large bodies of 'normal' matter such as galaxies), then it stands to reason that, proportionately, there may also be a little dark matter around a little matter (such as us), but which we are as yet unable to detect because of our proximity to it. Remember, we learned in Chapter 4 that there is no separation between quantum reality (with its strange goings-on) and the classical reality in which we exist. The point is, given what we already know about the way the universe is totally interconnected, if we accept the existence of dark matter, then it must also be associated with us in some way – perhaps even surrounding us and interacting with every one of us – just as it surrounds the galaxies in outer space.[248] Like the other nineteen people in the room, although we can't see it, dark matter is inextricably linked to us – a part of us that we do not yet understand and perhaps may never understand. All we can do initially is open up our minds to the possibility that it is there.

And if that's hard to bend your mind around, try bending it around space. Although we usually think of space as being empty, it isn't: it is full of all kinds of phenomena. For example, throughout the immense distances of space, the gravitational fields of suns, planets, moons and solar systems merge endlessly into unthinkably vast hills and valleys, ridges and channels. Some gravitational fields span galaxies and may even reach back to the Big Bang. These waves of energy are substantial enough to affect the arrangements made for space missions today. But this isn't the whole story. Studies on dark energy (thought to be the energy behind the acceleration of the universe's expansion)[249] suggest that even if the universe froze and all movement stopped – including even the movement within subatomic particles – vibrations of energy would still be coming from 'empty' space.[250] This indicates that space *itself* has some type of inherent energy. But amazingly, even this doesn't solve the mystery of what space is, because we know space can be bent – and we can't bend energy.

So if space is something more than emptiness and more than mere energy, then what is it? On the tiniest scale – at the microscopic quantum level – particles of energy (electrons, positrons, photons, and so on) are popping in and out of existence in space all the time, as we will see below. We could therefore perhaps think of space as an active liquid from which particles can be produced – or a mysterious and invisible power-grid where substance is created as easily as it is reabsorbed. However, whatever space is, it is unlike anything else we know of, as it is not made of atoms and common subatomic particles, nor is it merely energy. (If you have the complete answer, get ready to collect a Nobel Prize.)

Light gives us as much trouble as space. For us to be able to see anything, scientists have deduced that there must be particles of light (which they call photons) that first move from the object, then pass through space and into our eyes. Yet recent experiments suggest that this is incorrect, and that photons, which are considered the source of light, may not actually exist as a distinguishable particle[251] – leaving us with the realization that, even today, we still have no certainty about what something as fundamental as light really is. And if this isn't perplexing enough, we also know that light acts in a way that is so weird as to be impossible: as *both* a wave of energy and a particle of matter. Yet ordinary thinking says that matter and energy are different and separate things. If you accept this logic, light should not exist at all. But it does.

Other sacred tenets of quantum physics are also being questioned. These are the so-called constants: unchanging principles that govern the operation of the universe. The inherent assumption is that these principles cannot change – they are constant – because they are the foundations on which everything in existence can theoretically be explained. Yet evidence is mounting that at least some of these constants *are* changing. Research by Victor Flambaum and John Webb of the University of New South Wales, Sydney, suggests that one constant of science – the Alpha constant (which governs the interaction between light and atoms) – is not fixed and unchanging at all. This has implications for the 'constant' speed of light, which may in fact have *slowed* since its early appearance within our space-time dimension.[252] Moreover, Lene Hau of Harvard University has succeeded in coaxing photons of light into a mysterious 'dark state' where these photons slow to a near-standstill.[253] And light has even been brought to a *complete* standstill in the laboratory for more than a second.[254]

Just as excitingly, not only can the speed of light be slowed, it can also be exceeded. Speeds faster than light have been proven in the laboratory,[255] and we already know that warp speeds (multiples of light speed) are achievable. For example, the Big Bang took a mind-bogglingly short period of time – between 10 trillion trillion trillionths of a second and 10 billion trillion trillionths of a second – to inflate 100 trillion trillion trillion trillion times its original size, which is much faster than the present speed of light. They don't build real estate as fast as that any more.

Along with the uncertainties regarding the speed of light comes a threat to another core scientific constant: *mu*. *Mu* governs nothing less vital than the force that holds together the very core of every atom. Yet even this fundamental 'constant' is turning out to be neither fundamental nor constant. Researchers in Amsterdam have discovered evidence that *mu* has changed over time.[256] This suggests that while *mu* underwrites the stable workings of nature and the universe, the universe and its constant laws of nature are also evolving, with *mu* no longer able to provide us with a reliable answer to what holds the universe together. If *mu* has changed, some other underlying force must have changed it – there must be a deeper stabilizing force at work.

Our normal sense of time is also being challenged. Einstein, who was the first to theorize that *space* could be bent (a theory now proven via experiments with light coming to us across deep space), also theorized that *time* could be bent. His proposition was that if we propelled ourselves forward far enough we would come up behind our original starting point – a theory supported by recent observations by US satellites orbiting the Earth showing that a spinning body causes space (and time) to curve. This is what Einstein called 'frame dragging', a concept that allows the possibility of time-travel.

The very concept of time seems to be unique to human experience, necessary to give depth and breadth to the moment-by-moment we are in. Yet, as we saw earlier, it is merely a very helpful and convenient structure, a feature of mind and our active brain that we use to register the way change unfolds around us.[257] In this way, time is vital to our ability to make sense of the jumble of information with which we are constantly bombarded. Its absence makes a sensible life impossible, as we see with the disintegration of mind that is Alzheimer's disease. Here is where the story of self evaporates with the evaporation of memory. As sufferers completely lose their framework of time and place and self, their experience of reality becomes bewildering, disjointed and frightening. Since our present moment is walled in between the mental activity we call past and future and is informed by them both, losing a sense of past and future also progressively locks these unfortunate sufferers out of any meaningful hold on present reality.

What we often fail to realize is that all things change at different rates. Change has a momentum, and time is nothing more than how we measure the momentum of change. Although linear time gives us our sense of past, present and future, such a time-line merely offers us convenient reference points. There is another way of registering reality and engaging with it: from an outlook that accesses timelessness, religion's 'eternity'. As we saw in Chapter 4, for one particle to appear simultaneously in two places, *timelessness must exist*. First seen at the early edge of the Big Bang, this dimension of timelessness continues as a state of pure, instantaneous change and renewal, a reality quite beyond the material world yet simultaneously part of it.

The existence of timelessness puts the significance of the present moment – and the importance of us 'seizing the day' – in a new light. There is enormous personal power in realizing that the future is always now, only more of it. The true power of 'now' is that it really is the totality of our experience, constructed from our sense of past, present and future, all of which are mere mental creations happening between our ears. (Our sense of the future is the view we create of what 'now' is becoming; the past is the view we create of what 'now' is ceasing to be; and the present is forever in a state of change.) Not recognizing the timeless present leaves us unbalanced, leaning too heavily on the past and future and so deceiving ourselves into believing we can construct outcomes (the long path). In fact, all we can do is release influences, raise our awareness, and then let outcomes unfold (the short path). Past and future exist only as powerful states of mind – navigational aids created to guide us across the eternal reach of the present moment. As the physicist John Wheeler put it:

> The very idea of a space-time continuum is a wrong idea and with that idea failing, the idea of the before and after also fails. That can be said so simply and yet it is so hard for the lesson to grab hold in the world.[258]

Like our concepts of time and space, assumptions about location and position are also being challenged. As we saw earlier, physicists at the European Laboratory for Particle Physics and elsewhere have proved that, under certain conditions, matter is capable of appearing *instantaneously* in two separate places, and that changes made to one affect the other directly and instantaneously without any obvious mechanism or connection. Furthermore, not only can two things be in two places at once, they can also move or 'tunnel' back and forwards between an immaterial state and physical reality (a phenomenon known as 'quantum tunnelling').* This even occurs outside the laboratory: Benni Reznick of Tel Aviv University and Thomas Durt of the Vrije Universiteit in Brussels have discovered that instantaneous materializations are constantly and spontaneously erupting all around us and inside us! Particles are appearing *everywhere* out of *nowhere*! Unbelievable![259]

Evidence is also accumulating that such non-local connections are not limited to subatomic particles, but also occur among 'big' things like atoms. And we also know that there is no separation between the quantum state and our familiar reality. Quantum tunnelling also allows a state of 'quantum entanglement' to exist between two or more particles of matter. Quantum entanglement describes a real connection between two or more particles of subatomic energy that links them in some intangible way so that, forever after, it is impossible to 'undo' the connection. In this way, if

---

* Quantum tunnelling is turned on and off during a process called decoherence (in effect, when an object dematerializes and no longer appears to exist). In this way, a subatomic particle can be made to migrate and appear in two places at once without physical assistance. Light, as both a wave and a particle (energy and matter), exists in a perpetual state of suspension somewhere between complete decoherence and complete materialization.

something is done to the state of one particle it instantaneously affects the state of the other, irrespective of distance. Disconnected regions are somehow connected. And it may be a real shock to know that quantum entanglement is not confined to the weird world of subatomic particles, but can produce observable effects in our day-to-day world.[260]* We don't yet know how to control these phenomena beyond the laboratory, nor is science anywhere near telling us exactly what state of mind we need to be in to consciously enter such an instantaneous and borderless reality ourselves. However, we do know that every moving object, including the human body, develops an electromagnetic wavelength (all movement creates electromagnetic waves), giving everything the essential rudiments for being both wave and particle. As impossible as it sounds, these profound pieces of scientific evidence mean that every single thing has the potential to either shift spontaneously between the material and the immaterial state, or exist concurrently in both.

These quantum phenomena provide our first scientific evidence to explain the central mystery surrounding any psychic senses: the existence of an all-pervasive mechanism to which the psychic ability could be sensitized. Excitingly, here we also have more evidence to support the existence of the spontaneous, the transformational, the creatively instantaneous. There is only one explanation on the horizon for these apparent 'impossibilities': the original power of the infinity making an appearance as only it can – instantaneously – and destabilizing our dimensions of time and space.

We already know that every action requires the use of energy. Now we have learned that particles can act in a way that disregards space and time and defies our normal sense of reality by appearing in two places at once, establishing a quantum tunnel, spontaneously materializing and entangling together. All this begs a fundamental change in our view of reality and its possibilities. Energy and matter are no longer bound in space and time. With their new independence, energy and matter can potentially appear anywhere, instantaneously.

The possibilities for tangled truth don't stop there, because space

---

* The effect of this on science is to be profound. Physicists will no longer be able to claim accuracy in determining and understanding the actual properties of anything without including the effects of entanglement in their calculations.

itself (which we have already learned has presence and energy, though not physical substance) can also be entangled.[261] Through quantum entanglement, not only can distant particles be linked without reference to space and time, and not only can particles materialize and dematerialize in space, but also *separate points of space* (in which all particles of matter have existed since space began) can also be entangled. All of this scientific 'weirdness' points to an additional aspect to reality – dimensions where entities cease to be separate, and where places that previously appeared distinct now merge into one place, one mega-position. The whole of reality is not so much lots of separate things filling space, but more like some sort of cross-linked tunnel matrix interconnected every which way. Quantum facts can only be explained by a completely interconnected universe in which there are no absolute beginnings or endings, and ultimately no local reality.

Ours is now being revealed as a world and universe where space and distance are dynamic and the speed of time variable. It is possible for energy to short-circuit space and time, and for existence to escape the mechanisms of cause and effect. With subatomic particles known to carry away information from their original position as they entangle and tunnel, there also seems to be some form of transferable intelligence (information reading) involved. And this brings us to the question of just how much influence our intelligent power of observation gives us over reality.

In Chapter 4 we saw that the act of observation changed the thing observed, confirming that mind and matter are entangled. Now physicist Wolfgang Rindler has discovered that observation can *create* subatomic particles – the building blocks of atoms and our physical world.[262] As startling as it sounds, Rindler's work demonstrates that particles can be created and destroyed by the relationship between an observer's motion and the shape of space. He shows that, at some level, matter has no independent existence from us as its observers. This phenomenon reconfirms what we learned earlier: that the mere *act of observation* is able to trigger particles of matter to come into existence, to change, and also to 'morph' into a state somewhere between matter and energy (they become dematerialized).

These facts – already measured and repeated in the laboratory – mean that intelligence (as an essential part of observation) has now been proven to create matter at the subatomic level and move particles at a distance, as well as being implicated in dematerialization. Merely catching our attention is enough to subtly change whatever takes our attention. These facts speak to the moment where the mind is caught in the act of changing the material world. They reveal again that reality and mind are conjoined, and that our acts of observation contain far more creative power than we realize in our everyday lives.

The phenomenon of Rindler particles has also led to another equally startling discovery: that at a fundamental level no particle can exist in total isolation. Nothing exists independent of everything else. *Completely independent, objective existence is now a proven fallacy.* Context creates substance! Rindler's twin discoveries – non-independent existence and the materially creative power of observation – bring us to the astonishing conclusion that mind is a necessary part of reality. Everything ultimately begins and ends in the eye of the beholder in some way.

These quantum facts of life mean that the standard model of reality – where two or more widely separated objects or localities are each unaffected by changes in the other – is now revealed to be incomplete and inadequate. There is reality outside of us, just never completely disconnected from us. Quantum tunnels can now be considered as another instance where the state of infinity reveals itself by breaking through the 'surface' structures of physical reality. Not only is our old view of reality crumbling, but a new view of observation and intelligence is emerging. Physical reality is inseparable from observation, and as observation requires intelligence, we can now see that ours is an intelligent universe shaped by the energies of observation, including self-observation.

These are completely new concepts for many of us, with ideas that contradict common sense. Yet these phenomena are facts; it is only the mechanisms for their implementation that remain a mystery. The discoveries presented here are merely fragments gleaned from the frontiers of science, but enough to keep an enquiring mind engaged. These discoveries are not some hypothetical abstract of philosophy or religion. Even if we never manage to solve or fully understand the new mysteries they present, it is exciting just to know that there is a much greater reality that escapes our present grasp. This evidence, first appearing across the field of quantum science, supports the philosophical insights and spiritual intuitions that have been handed down to us through the ages: that there really is a substantial and all-encompassing unity to creation.

Now is the only time available to change our perceptions and look at the mysteries of our universe as if with new eyes, from a new vantage point. Indeed, the very act of acknowledging these mysteries begins to turn the key to the doorway of our perceptions. This excites our sense of wonder and propels us, unrestrained, beyond the locked-in certainties of form and into the marvellous possibilities created by less structured dimensions.

Having come this far, we now appreciate that not only is absolutely everything part of a greater whole, but also that each greater whole is in turn part of others. Through a multitude of seen and unseen dimensions, not only is everything influenced by its background but everything is *continuous* with its background in some real and substantial way, until we end up face-to-face with the boundless infinity. The awe-inspiring conclusion to be drawn from this is that everything is directly connected with everything else through the infinity, and that through multi-dimensional networks of connections and relationships everything is forever influenced by everything else from everywhere.

We stand on the threshold of resolving the mysteries of mind, matter and transformation. This is where science, philosophy and religion meet. Welcome to an age of new and significant possibilities.

What lies behind us and what lies before us are small matters compared to what lies within us.
Ralph Waldo Emerson

What we now need to do is find evidence of entry points that give each of us real, direct and conscious access into this realm of infinite possibilities. We will look for these mechanisms within ourselves and wider afield. To begin the search, let's take a look at some of the more challenging contemporary scientific questions, and think about how they might be answered from our new vantage point.

For example, what is the X-factor that maintains any network to keep it working and keep every single thing within it whole? Astronomers have been seeking just such a 'glue', the gravitational glue that holds all the galaxies in place and stops them simply flying apart., We also need to find the glue that makes *anything* keep its shape down at the smallest micro level. For instance, what keeps your body intact when every structure within it and everything around it is constantly changing? Some force or field is stabilizing every changing thing, from the largest galaxies to the smallest body-cells. This bonding 'energetic' first appeared at the time of the original Big Bang and continues to stabilize every single thing in existence today.*

Related to this question is research on the whereabouts of the 96 per cent of matter and energy 'gone missing' since the Big Bang, as we saw earlier. This is an almost unimaginably huge per centage of 'stuff' that we just can't find – yet in theory it should be as easy as finding a haystack hidden behind a needle! How can it be possible for so much to have gone missing? Is the missing matter and energy still 'in touch' in some way with the material stuff of the universe that got left behind?

Certainly, galaxies have a lot of 'dark' or missing matter or energy concentrated around them.[263]** This is important to grasp in our search for universal coherence and cosmic connectedness: we know conclusively that any huge mass (such as a galaxy) is linked to a large amount of something immaterial.[264] Armed with our new understanding of the essential indivisibility and connectedness necessarily running throughout the whole of creation since its beginning, it follows that much of that missing 'something' must remain in some association with every material thing in the known universe, no matter how small. We could expect this

---

* The workings of the universe as we know it are explained within the strong and weak nuclear forces, the electromagnetic force and the force of gravity. Each of these forces is powered by subatomic 'particles' of energy: the electromagnetic force by photons, the strong and weak nuclear forces by gluons and bosons, and gravity by the yet-to-be-found gravitron. (Several laboratories report breakthroughs in the search for any one of the five Higgs Bosons.) But these forces don't capture or explain the force of observation, the power of love, the energy of life, or the power of mind. Perhaps the weird goings-on we see in subatomic particles when they entangle with our attention and are affected by it, bear witness to an original quantum power fuelling consciousness and observation.

** Research suggests that much of the missing matter or energy has also been absorbed by black holes (cosmic phenomena so dense that anything coming too close to one cannot escape the pull of its gravitational field, not even light).

juxtaposition to be too fine to see close at hand but to be detectable within and around a galaxy-sized mass, because at great distances it would appear in concentration.

This associated 'quasi-matter' seen concentrated around galaxies is the best candidate for the universal glue that science has been seeking – the cohesive force or 'energetic' that bonds all structures including our bodies, supporting them in their state of constant change that has persisted since first existence. If this is the case, then we could expect this quasi-matter to be present at *all* boundaries, surfaces and points of separation in and around all things since creation, mediating at *all* points and moments of change.[265] This binding presence would explain why the unrelenting forces of change everywhere do not quickly culminate in a random demolition through destructive effects: *quasi-matter helps maintain order and stability.* This 'morphed' energy-cum-matter would then be supporting every entity, form and structure – from selfish genes that hold together and co-operate within cells, to solar systems and galaxies that don't fly apart. This bonding agent is forever linking the two realities – original reality (the actual infinity of balanced energy) and created reality.

Biological science also has its mass of unresolved questions, some of them regarding structure and how we maintain the physiology that supports consciousness and communication at all levels. To help us in our search for mechanisms supporting the universal unity evident within universal change, as well as allowing consciousness and awareness to exist, let us continue by looking into an anomaly within our own nervous system. The human body has over 45 miles (72 km) of major nerve fibres supporting a haze of nerve endings. Relatively few nerve endings – which include the numerous lumps, bumps and other physical irregularities that occur along each fibre – appear with specialized receptors. The majority of these nerve endings and protrusions do not have any clearly defined function – certainly not the common uses, such as for muscular stimulation, physical sensation or any other identifiable purpose.

Most medical textbooks still diagram sensory nerve fibres with only specialized, receptive end structures. Yet in any sensory nerve pathway supplying our limbs and body (for example the medial cutaneous nerve in our arm), two-thirds of its total fibre population have simple, non-specialized – and apparently redundant – nerve endings. Indeed, the greatest number of these non-specific nerve endings are clustered in the digestive tract. Which raises the question: what are they there for? If there is no such thing as 'life-force' in food, what is so much of this 'redundant' electrochemical wiring doing in our gut?

Nature is too intelligent and too efficient to allow 90 per cent excess and waste in any of its systems – 'use it or lose it' is a well-proven law of life and evolution. For example, what was once our tail has now shrunk to a small stub called the coccyx at the base of our spine. Also, our apparently useless and often troublesome appendix is all that is left of what was once a second stomach. Moreover, we know that our body is a mass of electrochemical pathways, yet it is difficult to imagine any electrical circuitry, or any other system at all, fulfilling the promise of its design and producing its best work with only ten per cent of it turned on and useful. This, along with nature's drive for efficiency, would imply that *all* the body's nerve endings have a use, not just the high-profile ten per cent. So what is the body doing with so many nerve endings that have no clearly defined function?

Let's look for clues, and a good place to start is to see just how much electrical activity in many forms is buzzing throughout us. Our body is made up of atoms, and atoms are electrical circuits. This makes us each a composite electrical circuit, living on a planet that itself rotates in an electromagnetic field. The cell division and migration happening throughout our entire body is influenced by electromagnetic fields. When our naturally-occurring electrical fields are interrupted, cell division and cell repair are altered; boosting this natural bio-field boosts our body's rate of healing.[266] Bio-electrics is even suspected of playing a key role in the chemical make-up and molecular migration within our genes. We are a supercharged, bio-electrical phenomenon interconnected and affected by other electrical circuits and fields. For a similar reason, every house fitted with electricity must be 'earthed' – to electrically connect it into the Earth's greater polarity.

The human body displays a continuous process of electrical transfer, with electrically charged ions constantly flowing in and out of every cell. Not only do cells run on a charge of ions, but so do nerves. And just how much of everything around us is also humming with electrically charged ions? Well, in fact almost *all* matter created in the universe consists of an *ionized* (electrically polarized), gas-like phenomenon called plasma, a quasi-material substance distinct from solids, liquids and gases and believed to make up more than 99 per cent of the universe. This is an *electrical and electromagnetic* universe more than a material one. Plasma filaments weave and span the vastness of intergalactic space. Plasma-like ions are also forever moving throughout our body and being channelled through its membranes, and many of our non-specific nerve endings are known to also be involved in ion channelling. Even some of our sensory nerve fibres – such as the A and C fibres in the skin – provide channels for these ions to be collected.

In other words, almost the entire universe is composed of ions that we are also alive with. So we now need to ask, is there some link between the extensive, dormant, bioelectrical network of nerve endings running throughout our body and the rest of the electrical universe in which we find ourselves? If we truly are connected to everything beyond ourselves in anything like a material, quasi-material, biological, psychological or spiritual way, then any search for a bio-mechanism that allows such super-connectedness could be expected to feature ion channelling in some way. As we are known to transfer electrical charges (and information) in and out of ourselves through ion channels, and the universe is primarily electrically charged ions, then here we have just such a sympathetic mechanism for connecting us by direct transference to the whole of the universe.

And the exciting possibilities don't stop there. The neurons in the outer layer of our brain (cerebral cortex), which are known to respond to changes in the electromagnetic field surrounding our head (and are also key to human consciousness),[267] tend to have their information-gathering nerve endings pointing *outwards* and their information-transmitting endings pointing *inwards*. What would attract the receivers to evolve with an outwards orientation? Wouldn't we expect, in the interests of biochemical efficiency, that the distribution of both transmitter *and* receiver endings to be either inwards towards the source of their biochemical stimulation, or at least be distributed randomly in our head? Could the reason be that not all the information to which our brain responds originates exclusively from *inside* the brain?

Let me make a bold speculation: the 'undifferentiated' nerve endings of our body and the 'aligned' neurons in our brain are evidence of a bio-mechanism forming a part of a multi-dimensional network that integrates us, balances us and keeps us healthy and fully connected within the mysterious whole of creation. Just as the brain's recently discovered God-spot facilitates spiritual experiences and transcendent sensations, so the meridian lines of the Chinese healing tradition (used to balance *qi* energy) may be an early discovery of another part of this bioelectrical distribution network. Within this network, the bulk of our nerve endings act like ion-channelling 'lightning rods' to attract an electrical charge and connect our bodies into a multi-dimensional, holistic matrix. These power-sensitive nerves then function as a biological maze of electrostatic transmitter/receiver pathways working to plug us in to super reality and the infinite whole in ways we barely understand.

Just as neuropeptides are known to link mind to matter and help information exchanges between our different parts,[268] I believe that our whole brain and nerve network links the known reality to the unknown; the internal with the external; the separate self with the infinitely connected self. We are wired for bigger things than we realize.

Not only do medical texts consider 90 per cent of our nerve endings and protrusions to be worth only passing reference, but we are told that a similar percentage of the substance in our DNA has almost no direct biological relevance to us.[269] In addition, though we use all regions of our brain, cognitive scientists tell us that in terms of mental capacity our brain is idling. Again, how can all this excess be cluttering our body, when we know that nature *removes* excess? Could these seemingly redundant capacities have some unforeseen yet collective use? To answer this we need to look again at how we sense the reality around us.

We already know how our five senses select their information from the meagre four per cent of created reality remaining in the infinity of energy around us. Is the obvious inability of our five senses to get us in touch with so much of reality (as we saw earlier), coupled with incomplete activation of our electro-spiritual circuitry throughout our brain and body, the source of our eternal discontent, psychological imbalances and spiritual yearning? Does such suspiciously unnatural redundancy throughout our body signpost dormant or deactivated networks as the answer to why we intuitively hunger for connection while blindly creating an excess of separation and division in our world?

As we develop spiritually and awaken to higher aspects of our self, we begin to tune in to the whole of reality, both the created and the uncreated, and 'turn on' our whole nerve network in both body and mind. It may well be that the role of the undifferentiated nerves and other biological 'redundancies' that persist within us is to help lift our access into the missing 96 per cent of creation needed to take us beyond separation and on to full connectedness. Seen in this light, our attachment to separation and the *created* reality – supported by our five senses, along with our protective instincts, negative attitudes and defensive outlook – would certainly help explain why so much of our electrophysiology remains deactivated and functionally redundant, and why any unifying, holistic experience is left to scientific fantasy or the religious idea of the afterlife.

At the physical level we are separate individuals. Yet we are also an integral part of the natural whole, as is everything else. Based on this knowledge, it is entirely possible that our *full* network of nerve endings can assist us to become plugged in and connected to the experience of the infinity, becoming perfectly balanced, spiritually integrated and transcendentally healthy. If this was true we could then expect that ageing would be accompanied by a shrinking in the number of these ion-channelling and other 'free' nerve endings, as our mitochondria (energy cells) begin to fail and our *qi* energy or vitality withdraws inwards in favour of vital organs and other bodily functions needed to preserve basic life. And, yes, this appears to be borne out by research: important findings suggest that damage to the region of the brain responsible for artistic ability, creativity and empathy (the corpus callosum), is accompanied by the shrinkage (atrophy) and loss of a significant diversity of neural connections.[270] We don't simply lose our artistic and creative abilities; rather, we lose the bioelectrical modem along which they form, operate and inspire.

The whole of created and uncreated (original) reality has many dimensions and perhaps many entry points. For instance, the conventional view of the death-bed is that the so-called babbling and ranting of the dying comes from dementia or the effects of drugs. Yet anyone who cares for the dying knows that some appear to become 'sensitized' and start talking with people in the afterlife, as if communicating across a bridge from which we observers remain excluded. If we have fully developed our three fundamentals of integrity, we realize that death is merely a shift of dimensions and nothing to fear. Just as we create intimate connections with our physical world even before we are born (where we respond to such things as music and the sound of our mother's heartbeat), we can activate a circuitry of connections linked to the 'after' world while still alive. Death is a brief moment of transition, a mere moment of mind in the eternal present.

As the poet Rabindranath Tagore wrote, 'Death is not extinguishing the light; it is only putting out the lamp because the dawn has come.' The moment of death is the point where what made us 'us' transitions back into a state of pure energy. In this sense physical death is more a discharging of power, a lessening of the vital flow of universal energy through our physical circuitry, as the individual re-emerges fully into the energetic state of infinity. Seen in this way, physical ageing and decay become nothing more than a sign of the fading of that light as our essence diffuses into the infinity beyond the boundary of our bodily separation.

To what various religions call 'gone to heaven' and spiritualists might call 'returning to the source', science has now also given a name: quantum tunnelling. At last, science and religion are running on the same track. Science finally has an explanation to offer for the viewpoint championed by the strongest religions throughout human history: that nothing has a complete ending or a beginning, that all things are essentially connected, and that death is a passing phase. Just as in the astounding situation where a particle is able to cross dimensions and change into a wave of energy before rematerializing elsewhere as a charged particle of matter, we too cross dimensions, transforming from energy into matter at birth, and then back again at death through the quantum gateway to re-enter the field of infinite energy in perfect balance.

As we are beginning to see, every moment of our lives is made possible only because we simultaneously interact with multi-realities – both created reality and original, uncreated reality. The early explorers of our planet crossed unknown horizons and changed our view of the world. Early space explorers then went further and changed our view of the universe. Now the final exploration is the most far-reaching – into our own psychological inner space, where our well-chosen viewpoint can empower us to directly change reality itself.

We are all lying in the gutter, but some of us are looking at the stars.
Oscar Wilde

We have looked within to find evidence of possible mechanisms giving us direct access into the infinite; now it is time to look to the heavens and beyond. In doing so, it helps to reconsider what sparked off our existence in the first place.

In 2001, astronomers discovered light from a super-cluster of galaxies so far away that they are older than our Big Bang and therefore older than our universe. It is as if today's universe is part of an endless cycle of booms and busts, with each cycle lasting about one trillion years,[271] during which time the energy is slowly reabsorbed into the infinity. Cosmologists now tell us there may be other universes, other meta-dimensions, other creations beyond ours – governed by different scientific constants, unknown forces and weird laws. There is even some evidence to suggest that our universe began with the explosion of a collapsed megastar,[272] meaning that our reality eventuated from within another star that itself had arisen from an earlier creation.* We live less in a universe than in a multiverse, with our universe just a microscopic part of mega-reality. There is no reason except fear or self-absorbed arrogance for presuming that life exists nowhere else but here on Earth,[273] and no reason except vanity for presuming that all life is like us: carbon-based and needing water, amino acids and other familiar elements for survival.

The Big Bang gave us evidence of the first flash of creativity, yet cosmologists tell us there may be many more Big Bangs happening elsewhere right now, pulses in an unfathomable cosmic heartbeat. These creative bangs may be big enough to create a universe, or small enough to fit between our ears – and yes, let's consider our personal existence no less a creative flashpoint than the original Big Bang.

Evidence is accumulating that life exists beyond Earth, and may have

---

* This allows the earth-shattering possibility of worlds within worlds, realities within realities – multiple creations beyond the reach of every known law of nature (the fundamental forces that order our universe and inform our very existence).

had its origins there. The British medical journal, *The Lancet*, reported that a tonne (1.1 tons US) of bacterial material falls to Earth from deep space every day![274] This is along with 90 tonnes (100 tons US) of space dust and debris. Earth's outer stratosphere unexpectedly contains large quantities of viable organisms. No one knows for sure if they came up and out from Earth or in from space.[275] Astrobiologists calculate that rocks, many of which have been ejected from Earth since its beginnings (and, by implication, from any other planet in the universe), could cocoon living microbes for millions of years.[276] In 1994, radio astronomers discovered amino acids in outer space that are basic to life;[277] other complex organic molecules are also common there.

Some of the essential substances in our body (cobalt, for example, an essential part of vitamin B12; or selenium, incorporated into proteins to make selenoproteins, which are important antioxidant enzymes) have been made exclusively in the crush and cosmic furnace of long-collapsed stars called supernovae, and carried here from deep space on intergalactic winds – the small pressures on Earth are not enough to create these molecules. Revelations from the *Stardust* probe that returned to earth on 15 January 2006 show that space objects – asteroids, comets, planets – amass material not only from their 'local' area but from almost anywhere and everywhere in this vast yet interconnected universe.[278] Moreover, even our local thunderstorms have a cosmic trigger; it would be impossible for a storm's lightning to strike without cosmic rays from distant galaxies spraying every square metre of Earth's atmosphere and detonating the storm cloud's ionized electrical charge.[279] Our solar system is blasted with cosmic winds, carrying particles flaring from the sun and roaring past our planet at 500km (300 miles) per second, before eventually fizzling out and merging with interstellar gases sweeping past our fragile planet. All this serves as evidence that we are made from stardust – we are, as the cliché would have it, children of the stars.

Indeed, some of our genes are conveniently designed to travel as stardust. Researchers at the University of California have discovered that some forms of DNA would survive without water in the freezing vacuum of deep space, and could perhaps survive forever.[280] Life as we know it needs amino acids, and at least one amino acid, glycine, is quite common in deep space. Moreover, in 2004 the NASA Martian rovers *Spirit* and *Discovery* found conclusive evidence that running water once existed on Mars, allowing the possibility of life there, though not necessarily life as we understand it.

The oldest fossils ever discovered are not animal or even biological, they are cosmic microwave radiation and light captured from the earliest stars, and even close to the Big Bang when time began. However, there are other fossil tracings of an inheritance from another source that pre-exists creation, from the infinity of energy that supports our creation and the created universe. If we have inherited our personal looks from our parents and forebears, our collective genetic building blocks from the earliest carbon-based life (with much of life's gene-pool still shared in common), and the hydrogen so fundamental to us from Big Bang's swirling, explosive cauldron, then what *else* could we be carrying forward that is imprinted in us from the original, infinite background? What specifically came in to us and our reality through the point where original creativity and the infinite first meet the finite and the physical? Let's briefly become forensic detectives and compile a list of possible suspects along with the supporting evidence…

The infinity: What happened to the infinity *after* the Big Bang? By its very nature, the actual infinity of energy in perfect balance had no surface-edges that could be separated, or points that could be blown apart. So it must still exist, retained everywhere and in everything, including us. We are therefore suspended forever in the infinity as it continues unchanged.

Silence and stillness: All music is as much the arrangement of silences between the sounds as it is the sounds themselves. Speech also makes no sense without silence. Certainly, the infinite field of energy in perfect balance was very quiet and undisturbed without the Big Bang. Everything else created on a grand scale since then – including the stars, the moon, the sun and every moment of life – still moves within the infinity's original silence. Every action we make and connection we create is born within its own brief moment of silence and stillness and is sustained there. Silence and stillness clear a path for action, releasing us into a creative and connected frame of mind. The silence and stillness we drink in when we take time out in nature or practise meditation originated in the infinity of energy in perfect balance.

Balance: Balance bestows life with the qualities of harmony, continuity, equality and equilibrium. The infinity was the original energy in perfect balance and it remains so today. The peace we need in our lives is built on balance. We seek a life in balance, maintain our body's chemical balance, balance a budget, make balanced judgements and decisions, retain mental balance – all created from the original balance within the infinite energy.

Creativity and transformation: Creativity is a 'force' that organizes or reorganizes energy and transforms matter. Here, transformation means the instantaneous creation of a new whole.

In our human experience, creativity, composed as it is from flashes of insight, is a force or field, not a thing. Creativity is the quality of original manifestation, without which nothing can exist or be transformed. All matter is organized energy, and all matter is an original outcome of creation (original creativity). Our own conception and birth was the second creative genesis, following the original creative impulse that spawned the Big Bang. Our lifetime of creative acts can also be seen as microscopic extensions of the original creativity with its larger power of cosmic genesis. On a personal scale, our individual spark of creativity makes relationships, organizes solutions to problems, flashes with insights and then facilitates their expression and development. Personal creativity, as an extension of original creativity and retaining those attributes, transforms the way things are and the way we perceive them. All objects and entities within creation remain the work of the original creative power arising from within the infinity of energy.

Coming from before or outside time and place, creativity transcends time and space. The creative process is retained within us from the original creative moment of the Big Bang and lives on within the biochemistry of our molecules every instant. Just as the original creative event gave rise to the universe and everything within it, only our personal creativity can give rise to a personal experience of the complete whole.

Intelligence: Intelligence is neither matter nor energy as we know them. Yet intelligence is a force we can identify through the qualities of observation, transference, communication, learning and organization. There can be no creativity without intelligence; intelligence and creativity are interchangeable; and both bypass time. Like creativity, intelligence is needed to organize or reorganize energy. Creativity and intelligence work hand in hand: intelligence reads the information for the arrangements, creativity applies the intelligence and gets the work done. In reality each requires the other, an arrangement needed *within* the Big Bang where energy was first organized. Just as the existence of intelligence does not mean a separate creator did it, our particularly complex, biological hold on intelligence should not blind us to the more simple intelligence in other species, nor should we ignore inorganic intelligence.

Transformation and change: Here, 'change' is used to refer to the cause-and-effect alterations we commonly see in the physical world taking place over time. However, change also has an infinite, timeless aspect, which I shall call 'transformation'. This feature refers to the origin of change: the Big Bang, occurring without recourse to time and space, was the first *instantaneous* transformation in our universe. Since then, this creative force has been available to us only as change – our familiar cause-and-effect alterations that take place within the dimensions of time and space. Our experience of transformation in its finite form – change – gives us a link between the infinite and the limited dimensions of time and space. Whenever change is observed to happen instantaneously, without reference to time, it reverts to its original state, which is transformation.

To understand the dynamic omnipresence of change is to move towards understanding the immediate power of transformation and instantaneous transition. Despite how change might appear to arrive from the outside and be delivered onto something – say, arriving as a hammer onto a nail – on closer inspection it is seen to be change being released within the hammer (and within the arm holding the hammer) and making the hammer change location before it contacts the nail, within which more change is released! The point here is that change doesn't arrive and happen to something; change is a characteristic of everything, inside and out. Change cannot be played forward or backwards; there is no rewind button. Change just 'is'. As the Zen Buddhists say, 'You cannot enter the same stream twice'. Another important point to realize about change is that once change is triggered – as it is by everything we do, say, think or feel – it often continues unfolding in its own way, seemingly out of control and with unexpected consequences for our position in the world.

However, with further scrutiny the mystery of change deepens. Allow me to make what will seem at first an absurd statement: change never happens; only endless transformation happens, from the beginning to the end of every event in the transition of time. Stay with me for a moment and let me explain. Everything in existence is complete as it is and in whatever condition. In that sense, everything simply 'is'; beyond our evaluations, everything is neither good nor bad, fat or skinny, high or low, it just 'is'. Now let's choose something – this page of the book, for example – and imagine changing it by tearing it in half. What may appear to be a change to the page is, on further inspection, in fact the instantaneous disappearance of the original single page and the simultaneous appearance of a tear which continues on to eventually become the appearance of two half-pages. My point is that we do not have a constant page that has suffered tears and changes. From the instant the first tear began there is no longer a page, pure and simple; it has completely and entirely gone, not a bit gone or half gone. The original page continues to exist only in our memory. In other words, reality is not something static and distinct that change visits: *reality is the proof of change as well as its repository.* Anything 'solid' only exists because at the subatomic level it is constantly moving and therefore changing.* Existence is an unbroken process of creative change.

---

* Because all matter is made up of atoms; an atom is made up of separate bundles of energy; and energy is synonymous with movement.

From this view, reality can only be the observation and expression of change itself – it has no separate substance or permanence. What we call reality is what we make of unending change. Because transformation is presently expressed and witnessed in our classical reality of time and space as change, we think we see change being caused around us and turned on and off at will. But what we see as change is endless instantaneous transformation, exposed to us across the dimensions of time and space; we observe the way things are now, remember how they were, and from these observations draw conclusions about change. Despite our usual preconceptions, change is in fact out of our control, independently occurring everywhere, always. Change, being eternal and uninterrupted, means that all our individual efforts to cause particular effects and completely control outcomes are undone sooner or later.

When we look to the transformational roots of change and how these might be uncovered to enhance our spiritual life, we come to realize how shallow our view of reality and change really is. In truth, we can only ever see the *surfaces* of anything, nothing more. We *deduce* depth; our senses only give us length and breadth, only surfaces and externals. Break open anything to see inside and there is a new surface – another edge, border, boundary. The appearance of physical reality could therefore be called the surface view of creation; a view of borders, surfaces and edges that began with the Big Bang and physically define the universe as we know it. Change emerges through every point of these surface-edges to constantly regenerate them as a collective whole, operating wherever every single thing begins and ends. Each surface, no matter how massive or minute, is an interface between one thing and the next, a network that eventually connects seamlessly into one complete, unbroken whole. Through this dynamic mechanism of continuous surfaces and edges, when we change any point or part, the whole changes. We now see just how completely change affects everything, at every known point, ceaselessly and always. This fact alone unmasks change for what it actually is: original, spontaneous transformation filtered through our five senses, and the dimensions of time and space.

The existence of intelligence, observation, transformation and change – all of which combine to create our sense of reality and give power to choice – are what we have available to make our personal existence meaningful and *significant*. Intelligent and creative free choice liberate us from the rigidities of certainty by creating completely novel possibilities and guiding their implementation, however impermanent the results. In this way, the uncertainty principle liberates us into the power of creative transformation and its possibilities.

I think a future flight should include a poet, a priest and a philosopher. [That way] we might get a much better idea of what we saw.
Commander Michael Collins, Apollo 11

This is an intelligent universe. Of all the features of original reality (which is the infinity of energy in perfect balance) that carry over into our created reality, intelligence is the most important and the least understood. In reading further, we will discover the extent to which our universe is intelligent. In the process we will come to realize that intelligence is less something restricted to individual minds, and more an organizing force that exists outside form and beyond the organic. Although our egocentric outlook on reality has us assume that our intelligence also originated with our birth, there is evidence indicating otherwise. Intelligence is not individual or singular, nor is it a separate thing inserted into us by an independent creator. Intelligence is universal – a feature of the universal background. And, as we will see, the evidence we now have indicates that the source of this universal intelligence is the infinity of energy in perfect balance to which we remain inseparably linked.

If we are to fully understand how intelligence and creativity appear and function within our integrated universe, we need to take a new look at what intelligence and creativity are, and uncover where they arise and operate. The tremendous power of transformation to which our lives are forever linked – the creative power that comes *through* us in direct proportion to our openness to the infinity – can be freely accessed depending on how well we understand and use the tools of intelligence and insight.

Intelligence precedes creativity and is immobile without it; creativity is how intelligence declares its existence. On the other hand, without intelligence, creativity doesn't exist. Creativity requires intelligence, and vice versa. We know that the Big Bang was the beginning of creation, and as any creation must, by definition, be accompanied by creativity, creativity was necessarily involved as the first creative 'pulse' accompanying the Big Bang. And it follows that if the Big Bang was accompanied by this pulse of creativity, it must also have been accompanied by some original, if formless, intelligence. Though this conclusion challenges our common sense, we will see that its implications are empowering. Again, this is no confirmation of a separate God or creator, only confirmation that intelligence is much more than mere thought and something locked in our head.

So, if we are to understand intelligence as a force that exists beyond the confines of form, we need to start by understanding both creativity and its antithesis, randomness. Anything random is completely without order, whereas chaotic sequences, while appearing disordered, actually follow specific and detectable patterns. Randomness is the name given to a completely unorganized mess, while chaos marks the beginning of organization (though, as we saw earlier, chaotic patterns are often hard to detect except by a gifted few, and may be passed over as random). Creativity brings order to the random, and this progression from randomness to orderliness begins by giving us chaos. Then, if uninterrupted, creativity continues to organize chaos until it is no longer chaotic, but instead transformed into a whole new organized, complex entity composed of many similarly patterned parts. A bit like baking a cake. We start by gathering the various (randomized) ingredients and implements from a variety of shops and other locations. These disparate parts then begin to be organized in the (chaotic) kitchen and finally sent off into the oven. Presto! A new creation; a transformation of parts. The point here is that creativity (organization) starts with envisaging an outcome (however simple) within a random disorder of separate (energetic) parts, then organizes this random mess into chaos and increasing order, on its way to a new creation. This new entity (cake) is the incidental result of the chaotic connections previously created.

One glance up into the star-clustered night sky reveals two pieces of evidence of something mysterious involved in the early stages of creativity's original progression from nothing, through chaos, to something as vast as our cosmos. If the Big Bang was completely random, as you would expect if there was no original organizing principle to interrupt randomness, we would be without our familiar, untidy heavens. This is because there would have been nothing to interrupt the 'mechanical' and uniform distribution of this explosion as it appeared within 'empty' infinity on this first occasion.[281] In a random universe that began with an uninterrupted explosion and spread, we would now be seeing a uniform (though unorganized) distribution of stars and galaxies. Astrophysicists conclude that the reason galaxies and stars swirl and cluster, and are not distributed evenly across the skies and throughout the universe, is because some extra influence interrupted the randomly smooth (and mechanical) spread of the Bang. Yet in an 'empty' infinity of energy, the Big Bang should have been alone – there should have been no other influence present!

This interruption – built into the mechanical and random spread of the Big Bang to make it uneven – gives us our first evidence of creative organization in the universe; something *other* than randomness cannot be more randomness, and the only other option is *organization*. And organization, as we have seen, is evidence of creativity. The uneven spread of stars and galaxies in the night sky is evidence of the original organizing presence of creativity, a force that continues to bring increasing measures of order to our chaotic universe.[282] 'Interrupted' created existence is evidence of intelligence afoot in the universe – where organization exists, creativity exists; and where creativity exists so does intelligence.

What other indications do we have to support the unlikely notion that there may be a universal, unstructured intelligence? Well, physicists at Cuza University in Romania have produced a low-temperature electrogaseous plasma that can grow, communicate and replicate like living cells by splitting in two.[283*] In other words, an inorganic gas composed of nothing more complex than a set of electrically charged ions has displayed signs of rudimentary intelligence. This gives us new pause for thought, since it is

* Plasmas – the dominant state in the universe – are electrically charged ions, the same stuff that is constantly moving almost at will through our skin and throughout our body.

also known that 99 per cent of all matter in the cosmos is electrically charged plasma, controlled by the forces of electromagnetism rather than the force of gravity. And if plasmas, which are found throughout the cosmos, can show signs of intelligence, this would suggest that intelligence may indeed pervade every corner of creation.

As we deepen our understanding that this is an intelligent universe, the more open and sensitive we become to the connections that inspire a direct and intelligent experience of infinity. The scientific leads we find here bring us face to face once more with the most profound teachings of philosophers and religious scholars: that, by superseding form, intelligence reveals itself to be omnipresent.

The creation of a thousand forests is in one acorn.

Ralph Waldo Emerson

Have you ever wondered how a seed becomes a tree, and how a single cell becomes a whole plant? We know the acorn grows into the oak, so from where does the acorn acquire its *intention* to become the big oak tree (rather than, for example, an elm or a eucalypt)? And where does it then store this intention? It must have at least some intelligent registration of future becoming, since intention (the imagined future) displays intelligence. Again, the implication is that intelligence exists at levels other than just the human or animal, and that there must be some organizing force operating here that we cannot identify but which exists outside the physical structure of the acorn.

As we saw in Chapter 6, the Darwinian theory of evolution misses the full implications of intelligence. The power of intelligence is key to evolution, spiritual development and creation in the universe. Our intelligence allows us to make creative choices that affect safety and survival, with even the simplest free choice having the potential to make outcomes uncertain. Many creatures, from the biologically complex to the simplest, make choices, and to that extent they are intelligent. Admittedly, most choices are little more than reflex responses, and early life's rudimentary powers of choice did little to challenge the Darwinian principles of fitness and survival. But, as we saw earlier, even simple choices retain an element of variability and unpredictability: the moth that opted to either to land or fly away, made a choice that changed the rest of its life, anything from escaping a predator, to winging towards a mate and a whole new generation. As more complex intelligence evolved, decisions and choices began to look less and less like reflex responses until, ultimately, evolution reached its present complex potential in humans – selfless choice, transcendent insight and transformational creativity. Intelligence has always carried purpose and choice: like a radar transmitter locking onto an aircraft, intelligence has always affected the evolutionary process by facilitating the moment-by-moment transfer of information and choices made within any species, anywhere from the smallest cell to the larger forms of life.

Intelligence takes many forms and has many applications, but its primary use is to make sense of information. Information and the exchange of information – whether written, carried as vibrations through the ground, or transported as chemicals in a nesting bird's brain – becomes meaningful only when picked up by some form of intelligence and understood or made use of. The health of every living thing, no matter how huge or microscopically small, depends on the exchange of information both within itself and with the external environment. Even down at the micro level, all living cells exchange information with their particular surrounding environment.

We might assume that if information is exchanged, it is exchanged from one place to another. Yet, as we learned earlier in this book, there is no specific, identifiable location in which consciousness or intelligence can be found – all atoms and molecules within us (including 'memory molecules' deep within the brain's DNA) shift their position every two minutes or so. Also, though we constantly make new brain cells, we lose about 100,000 neurons (out of 100 billion) every day, and most of the molecules within our surviving brain cells are completely replaced each week. We could expect all this movement to really mess up the communication connections that exist between the molecules, yet these connections are renewed along with the molecules themselves. How? There must be some process whereby intelligence *crosses the gap* between departing molecules and the new arrivals. And this means that memory must exist *outside* matter.

No one is entirely sure where the entry-point is located at which mind becomes matter and stores its intelligence as biological memories in our molecules. The reason for this is simple. *There is no entry-point!* Like space, intelligence is everywhere. No one can say at what point perception connects to the physical to combine as one intelligent whole. One thing is for sure: intelligence creates organization and complex networks. For example, South African naturalist Eugene Marais has described how the death of the queen termite in a colony caused an *instantaneous* reaction throughout the mound, ruling out smell or 'messenger' ants as communicators.[284] What instantaneous networks and connections are operating there? Is the ant's nest itself almost a living entity that has not yet learned to move, an energized quasi life-form with the queen acting as its brain and the worker ants and soldiers the equivalent of its red and white blood cells? Seen in this light, a healthy forest of trees can also be viewed as a single, intelligent living organism that has its own complex, interwoven chemistry of living parts. Just like us, any organic whole – whether an ant's nest, a forest or even a whole planet – is an intelligent organism awash with circulating nutrients, particles and biochemical communication pathways. And if all of life is an interactive network of complex connections, it makes sense to say that all life has intelligence.

The existence of intelligence across the whole of life can be seen everywhere we look. For example, research shows that all genes store memory of some sort somewhere in their chemistry, and that this deep memory affects their future and the future of the whole organism to which they belong; in fact, all genes are chemical memories that show the whole of life how to behave.[285] In the same vein, the almost miraculous ability of stem cells to transform into other cells suggests some kind of chemically sponsored intelligence, some cellular memory, some intangible interconnectedness, some attraction that chemistry serves – perhaps even some sort of *intention* at the cellular level. Any cell that can be transformed into another type of cell in the body begs us to look at intelligence in an entirely new way. If all genes and cells have intelligence, and we know that all life forms have genes and process information, then again it stands to reason that *all* life is intelligent. In fact, not only is all of life intelligent, life is an ongoing *expression* of intelligence. We can infer intelligence by observing life. Life, as a creative force, is a display of intelligence.

- Nature is awash with intelligence. Right across the entire natural world we see evidence that intelligence is not a human monopoly:

- Alex Kacelnik at Oxford University has video proof that birds can learn to make and refine tools to solve problems. (*Animal Cognition* (2006) 9:317–34.)

- Keith Kendrick, a neurobiologist at the Babraham Institute at Cambridge University, has shown that sheep recognize other sheep from photographs taken at unfamiliar angles, and that they can recognize the faces of more than 50 sheep and at least 10 humans (suggesting a degree of social sophistication not usually associated with sheep). (*Nature*, 8 November, 2001.)

- Culum Brown of the University of Edinburgh has discovered that fish form mental maps of favoured feeding grounds and resting sites they learned about from other fish in their shoal – an example of cultural transmission. Brown has also trained fish to escape through a hole in a net, a feat they remembered and could repeat the instant they were retested 11 months later! (*New Scientist*, 12 June 2004.)

- Using selective attention and recalling locations, a spider (*portia labiata*) remembers a variety of rhythms to selectively pluck at the edge of another spider's web and so lure the resident spider to its death. (*New Scientist*, 27 May 2006.)

- Koko the gorilla at the Gorilla Foundation, California, is famous for her extensive sign language – including being able to indicate the severity of her toothache on a scale of 1 to 10. (*New Scientist*, 14 August 2004.)

- Dark-loving cockroaches can be trained by another (robotic) cockroach to prefer bright light. (*New Scientist* 6 January 2007.)

- Bacteria that move around an obstacle in ways that exclude chemical or other triggers, can only be described as intelligent. (*New Scientist*, 20 November 2004.)

Even dirt may be intelligent. Compost may actually be smart (or at least something about it is). In experiments by David Wilson at Binghamton University, New York State,[286] soil samples were taken from near to one another and then each sample placed in its own container. From these containers Wilson grew plants, each in its own sample microcosm. The soil from this first generation that grew the most biomass was then selected to create another microcosm, and so a second generation of plants was begun in the same successful soil. This process was repeated 16 times – 16 generations. During the process, the selected microcosms continued to improve until, by the end of the experiment, they were producing three times as much plant biomass as the originals! It seems some feature of the whole system was being passed on to benefit plant growth, rather than responsibility falling to any feature of an individual organism. This feature is most likely to be something to do with interactions *between* organisms in the group rather than the organisms themselves. Once again, we have evidence that even down to the smallest level, intelligent transference exists. While many questions regarding intelligence and creativity remain, there are no miracles or magic in this intelligent universe, just laws and principles that we don't fully understand.

Now that we are seeing evidence for intelligence existing beyond matter at the micro level, what about the possibility of also finding it at the macro level and beyond? If we find intelligence not only 'outside' both the large and small, but also everywhere in between, this would mean we have uncovered universal intelligence. Once the genie of intelligence is physically 'out of the bottle', the possibilities for intelligence become infinite. Perhaps space, which we already know has energy and is not nothing, is another word for intelligence, or information. If intelligence is universal, it would have to exist not only across all life forms, but also outside structure or boundaries. And yes, we do have evidence of this, already revealed where we saw intelligence transferred between incoming and outgoing atoms and molecules in our bodies. It is also indicated with the germination of plants, and the unusual properties of water.

Water, and in particular the hydrogen within the water molecule, is deeply implicated in the mysterious goings-on of intelligence. It appears as the one 'secret' ingredient that inspires the intelligent organization of matter into what we call life. From the simplest cell to the complex life and intelligence that have evolved into us, life would be impossible without water; the amino acids fundamental to all life would not curl up into their right shape without it. Water is a combination of two firmly bonded gases (hydrogen and oxygen), but whose separate molecules are loosely held together by weak electrostatic hydrogen bonds that give water its fluidity. Water is almost as old as time itself, and hydrogen bonds were among some of the first bonds ever created – at the birth of the universe. The hydrogen bonds within water today exert a controlling influence over the functioning of life's DNA – and DNA is the underlying code that controls the whole of life. Water's fluid bonds are therefore vital to life; they create the difference between us and a skin bag of cheap chemicals.

We also see links between water and intelligence in other ways. For example, work by Rustrum Roy, a materials scientist at Pennsylvania State University, has shown that water retains some kind of memory or impression of the compounds previously dissolved within it.[287] This stored information is most likely retained within water's swirling combination of fluid electrostatic connections. And since 'memory' molecules have been detected within our DNA (as we saw earlier), we can now infer an electrostatic link between water, life, intelligence and the whole of creation traceable back to the beginning of time itself.

To help us understand more about intelligence, we need to stay with water for a few moments and look further into its power and influence. Water's flexible electrostatic bonds, while making water fluid, are also so powerful that they are even capable of altering the very core of an atom – the fundamental structure of our material world. Water's powerful but loose bonds conspire to trigger a chain of events that actually moves protons (subatomic particles at the very heart of an atom) between one atom and another.[288] This means that the energy of water has the power to rearrange the building blocks of the physical universe itself!

And now to the grand finale regarding water, its place in our search for the organizing energy of the universe and our intelligent connection to it. We know that hydrogen made an early appearance in space, and (as we saw earlier in this chapter) we also know that if we lowered the temperature of the cosmos to absolute zero (-273°C) all movement and energy-transfer in the universe would cease, except for the 'zero point' vibrations of 'empty' space (remember, space has an energy of some sort).

An incredible discovery has recently been made: water has the capacity to detect these unworldly and original energy vibrations running through space.[289] Remembering that infinity and space are energetic states and not indications of direction or location, we are now beginning to see that there is something within the deep mystery of space that vibrates and connects with something in the water. When considered together, the combination of this residual vibration that we call space and water's ability to detect it suggest we have early evidence of some original transference, some original energetic connection linking the hydrogen in water to the infinity of energy running throughout creation and all of life.

In an interconnected universe, some mechanism is needed to make that connection, however immaterial it may be. And this universal connection must include the intelligence of the universe. Something is being exposed within the mysterious properties of water suggesting that we are close to uncovering a mechanism linking our intelligent material universe into the original infinite *source* of that intelligence. We already have water implicated in a mysterious and fundamental transfer of information affecting the very core of biological matter, able to rearrange the nucleus of atoms and connected to the mysterious energy 'behind' space; and hydrogen, a component of water, is also found everywhere across the deepest reaches of the universe. Could the energy-sensitivity within water be a primal recognition, an indication of original communication throughout an intelligent universe?

We have made our intelligent appearance within this infinite field of energy. We are not alone as the only intelligent life, and there is mounting evidence that even the infinite field of energy itself is intelligent. In a fully networked and interconnected universe where there is no local reality, there is nothing stopping the ubiquitous energy of intelligence from reaching between self and the original, uncreated and perfectly balanced infinity of energy. Our personal spark of creativity is a tiny fragment of an infinite, intelligent, creative reality. We can picture intelligence as an overarching field or force – an energy – having each and every life plugged into it, rather than it being plugged separately into every life. In this way, we live *within* intelligence rather than intelligence living within us. Life did not evolve intelligence; intelligence evolved life. The human brain accesses intelligence rather than possessing and controlling it.

Supporting this view, Oxford physicist Rodger Penrose observes that the brain's network of neurons is vastly underpowered to account for even the simplest of mental tasks – our brain just doesn't have enough detectable power to do the things it does. In fact, so-called autistic-savants are known to solve certain mathematical problems, such as complex calculations involving more than six digits, faster than the most powerful computers. These feats involve speeds only possible in the dimensions of quantum physics where energy and matter transform and intermingle, and where space and time are disregarded. The way brain cells network, as presently understood by neurologists, no one should be capable of working out 10^{20} different possibilities simultaneously.[290] Yet here we are, alive and well and unbelievably capable.

So, if the workings of the human brain and intelligence allow access to more power than our brain alone can account for, where else can we look in the infinity of reality for a power source or linkage that has the capacity to allow our brain to do what it does? To help us answer this question, and at the same time make a most powerful personal breakthrough into the unifying experience of everything, we need to reconsider some of the mysteries we looked at in Chapter 4 that arise from discoveries in quantum science:

What medium allows a photon to split and end up kilometres apart, allowing no distance to exist between somewhere and somewhere else? What medium allows an effect (whether it is the spin of a photon or a psychic experience) to be transferred instantaneously (timelessly)? What medium allows instantaneous communication between two widely separated locations? What background medium or ultimate power source allows the existence of spontaneous creativity and instantaneous change, something that happens both within the brain's mind-body link and throughout the world? What medium allows the background microwave radiation from the Big Bang to be the same temperature everywhere across the cosmos, even though there is no known mechanism for heat radiation to travel fast enough throughout vast space and so become standardized? What medium or force is causing the expanding universe to accelerate at all points within it, instead of decelerate?[291]

The answer to these questions lies within *the power of the infinity* itself.

There is no joy in smallness. Joy is in the infinite.
Chandogya Upanishad

Picture this. We are way back beyond time, before space and distance. There is not yet any before or after, and no up or down. Without any points of reference, we are completely without direction. Whatever is about to happen, one thing is for sure – at the moment of the Big Bang, this momentous event must occur across a background, because one implicit rule of existence is that *everything* in existence must have a background in order to exist. This background to the Big Bang is what scientists refer to as the infinite energy in perfect balance.

So let's look and see what all this means. We have an infinite field of energy in perfect balance that gets punctured by the Big Bang. After a cool-down period, the energy at the puncture site converts and condenses into spiral galaxies to become the unevenly distributed (and surprisingly flat) universe we know today.[292] However, because it's local, the Big Bang can't fracture the infinity. Instead, the Big Bang can only enter some lesser dimension or dimensions that must still find some way of allowing the infinity, which is unrestricted and limitless and remains so, to be connected up at all times and at every place, because that's what 'infinity' means and does. Meanwhile, the infinity, because it is infinite, remains unchanged. Welcome to our universe.

This background of infinite and perfectly balanced energy is what the Big Bang went off in. All creation remains suspended in this background, including every one of us on Earth at this very moment. The energy 'field' of the infinity remains intact. As the mother of all backgrounds, the infinity is with us at every point within creation, accessible wherever mind and matter intermingle. Though deep space is often assumed to be something that exists 'way out there' past the planets, *all* space – distant, personal and inner – is one and the same, with us suspended in it. Similarly, we are also taught that infinity is some impossible state 'out there' or (when described as heaven) 'up there', which means that infinity remains at a distance and unattainable. In a scientific sense this is also where it remains – conceptually distant. However, with spiritual maturity, we realize that infinity is *also* eternally present and right here – with us, through us, above and below us, in us and all around us.

We have evolved to the exciting point where the laws of physics, the aspirations of religion and the insights of philosophy *can* be unified. When Einstein gave us the general theory of relativity, he acknowledged we were still missing a unifying theory that covered everything. However, as discussed in Chapter 1, maybe this search for a theory misses the point. What we are missing is not a unified *theory* of everything, but an emerging experience of infinity that eventually must include both every single thing *and* every single background (context). Throughout the book, this ultimate state of wholeness has come to mean the infinite context in which every single context or part exists. This is the ultimate paradox: an apparent 'something' without recourse to anything; beyond everything. Whether we call it 'infinite energy in perfect balance' or 'God', this infinity is not a 'thing', not physical or created or measurable or finite. And it is this ultimate understanding that reveals what we should be searching for: a unifying *experience* of everything, an outlook that engages the infinity; an enlightening realization that becomes our living experience of the infinite connection between every finite thing in the created universe; the connection that is the infinity within us, through us and around us.

To achieve this breakthrough in our consciousness, it is important first to recognize that the reality we sense around us can only ever be a surface impression supported by a much deeper reality. What we consciously call 'the real world' is created at the very point of time and place where the infinity of energy endlessly emerges through mind and awareness to become the material world. However, with breakthrough consciousness, we now see that surface reality has been misunderstood; in fact it is nothing more than a porous membrane through which communication and influence (change) are transferred, a medium of communication between inside and outside. Boundaries have blurred to reveal that inside and outside are different facets of a single continuous reality. Now that the individuality of each and every thing has been surpassed, the wholeness of everything is revealed.

This transcendent and transformational 'experience of everything' – called enlightenment, heaven and a variety of other names – is available to us as a direct experience of the infinity. Reality is one unbreakable continuum, unbroken from here to infinity and eternity. It is both our significant purpose and ability to live in the conscious experience of this reality. This breakthrough experience marks the unleashing of the boundless power of creative intelligence within us.

But what is this infinity of energy? And while we're at it, how big is the 'whole' in holism? Science has already discovered that we cannot reach any formula for the infinity through a process of multiplication, reduction and mathematical deduction. Einstein searched fruitlessly for the unified field

Einstein's final passion was for a unified theory of everything, and string theory has come closest to claiming that title. In 1991 J. Richard Gott, an astrophysicist from Princeton University, proposed the existence of cosmic strings, and string theory was up and running.[293] String theory claims that the fundamental particle of energy forming the basis of matter (within the protons and neutrons at the nucleus of atoms) is not a quark, as generally believed in scientific circles, but an infinitesimal vibration of energy only 10^{-33} centimetres across.

However, the fundamental deficiency keeping string theory from being the unified theory of everything is that it is 'background dependent', which means that the theory is ultimately only able to handle a finite amount of reality in a finite region of space. This allows whatever reality is remaining outside the theory's admittedly vast conceptual reach to stay beyond the edges of it and escape out into the infinity. Because string theory fails to take full account of infinity, it cannot be a truly unified theory.

This problem is fundamental to all theories – they fail to capture both the vantage point of the observer who is observing the theory, and also the energy expended in these acts of observation. (Remember, observation changes matter and therefore it releases energy.) The ultimate vantage point is infinity. The only way beyond any best *theory* of (almost) everything and into the direct experience of infinity is breakthrough consciousness, allowing us the unifying *experience* of everything.

through the medium of mathematics, but even the most precise mathematics falls short of capturing the direct *experience* of unity – and theories that can't be verified remain mere commentary. In fact, no theory can lead us to direct experience, any more than we can find God within one exclusive religious tradition only, or via any blind belief, however strong our conviction or devotion.

So if mathematical formulae and scientific theory won't do it, what will? Remember that the infinity also provides the ultimate conceptual viewing-point from which the observer, the act of observation and the observed are conjoined in the form of direct experience. Personal experience is where intelligence and reality unite and become inseparable – a quantum entanglement. Therefore, the only way that the infinity can be directly engaged and experienced is from a position where the observation point is also infinite; nothing less comes close. Infinity can only be experienced from infinity; a creator ultimately only has eyes for their works of creation. This is the outlook onto the universe from every position within it – the ultra-position – and it is a point of view achievable only by a truly opened mind. In effect, this is a mind that has let go of self-limitations, and without becoming unhinged has become unlimited. Therein lies the unifying experience within everything. This is the eternal state of enlightenment, *nirvana*, heaven; the ultimate homecoming.

Earlier, in the eight horizons, we began to see how this vantage point can be gained spiritually, through the art of letting go. In addition, we have also discovered that infinity can be demonstrated directly through science, with its presence concluded through the new discoveries being made in cosmology and quantum physics. No longer mere theory, science can now demonstrate that there are points throughout the greater cosmos as well as the subatomic world that are entry-points to the state of the instantaneous, eternal present, the energy field of infinity.

One such entry-point is found within the evidence for black holes – finite amounts of mass that are infinitely dense and infinitely small. It is agreed that at the core of a black hole there would be a singularity, an infinitely small point of reduction, meaning that created matter is so infinitely reduced that it merges with the original background of infinity. In black holes, just as with 'dark' energy or matter, time and space eventually become completely suspended and infinitely compressed. Cosmologists and quantum physicists tell us that in such a place time no longer exists as past, present and future, and space no longer exists as separate points of distance. And by no coincidence this is also an effective definition of infinity! At the centre of a black hole there is a 'singular' point that is also infinite. This is the ultimate paradox within science, a point as hard to get our head around as Zen Buddhism's sound of one hand clapping. Whatever else happens in every black hole, the singularity at their centre means that there are points in space where the limited dimensions of our created reality have again been crossed, allowing access to the infinite field of energy in perfect balance.

Incidentally, remembering (as we saw in Chapter 8) that everything in existence can be seen as one big relationship struck between its component parts, and in the light of how Rindler particles disprove objective existence, there can be nothing that is ultimately objective and separately solid to even be crammed down into this impossibly small singular point that science has calculated at the centre of a black hole. Rather than this singular point being a point of impossible compression, every singularity at the centre of every black hole can also be seen as nothing more or less than a site of absolute and original emergence for time and place, a point where the Big Bang can still be found connected to and emerging from 'within' the infinity of energy. Singularity is one place where existence and the infinity can be seen woven together as one whole, in the ongoing and eternal relationship of creation.

This 'singular' effect where place and time are transcended is not just confined to astronomical phenomena in deep space, however. A state where reality as we know it can be suspended has now been observed at the subatomic level here on Earth, within the atoms of super-conducting crystals (used in computers). The spin of the crystal's electrons can be 'impossibly' slowed down to a standstill and enter a new phase, as if time itself has stopped or effectively becomes eternal. In other words, timelessness is not just a mathematical calculation, like the complex models that infer the existence of dark matter and dark energy. The timelessness of eternity is real, and has been demonstrated in the laboratory.

Because we are ourselves created finite beings, we can only understand and experience this unusual uncreated reality (infinity) at the interface or zone where it meets our familiar created reality. So let's review the evidence for there being such a 'space' where our created reality and the infinity conjoin. We have seen the subatomic particles of laboratory crystals entering a fundamental state of change – a phase transition – that effectively *suspends or supersedes time*. We also have masses of intergalactic matter being influenced by dark energy, dark matter and black holes – with the 'darkness' being caused by the fact that time and light get lost in them and enter another dimension! In fact, dark energy, dark matter and black holes may even be different views of one and the same missing or 'dark' force: a team led by George Chapline, a physicist at the Lawrence Livermore National Laboratory in California, and Nobel laureate Robert Laughlin of Stanford University, point out that black holes, dark energy and dark matter can be explained by a phenomenon they have called 'dark energy stars'. These may be stars whose fuel has been expended and so have collapsed, then exploded with such a force that both time and space are suspended at the accelerated extreme outer edge of the explosion. This 'dark force' would appear as dark matter or dark energy, depending on how we tested for it.[294] The interesting point for us in all this is that our universe behaves as if it is itself a dark energy star, seen by us from the inside looking out as a universe awash with missing matter and missing energy throughout and extending to the outer edge of the energy star's Big Bang.

In other words, our universe and everything within it are surrounded by an 'edge' of suspended time and space, an unseen force that is co-existent with matter rather than separate from it. (Remember that this edge that gives everything definition is also the same original edge that arose with the Big Bang to give definition and boundary to every single thing in existence today, big and small.) All matter can be seen to be coexistent or in combination with infinity and timelessness.[295] The universe is awash in a timeless mystery.

A 'dark energy star' universe would account for why some of the most distant galaxies observed by our astronomers appear older than our universe. We might ask how a dark energy star the size of our whole universe could come into being? The answer is that size doesn't matter when compared against the energetic state of infinity. In that state and from that infinite position, all sizes are the same, and all distances are one.

Let's see where today's science has positioned us. From what we read in the early chapters, we now know that the act of observation changes the thing observed, so there must be some real connection whose mechanism remains unknown. We also know that one thing can be in two places at once, making simultaneous appearances in space and time. This means that in some state of reality there must be a super-connecting shortcut across space that suspends all time and distance, penetrates matter and makes every place the same place. In addition, we know that an event in one place can simultaneously occur elsewhere, confirming that there must also be a shortcut through time to the instantaneous. And not only can particles 'materialize' as if from nowhere, the rules governing their unbelievable behaviour in the subatomic quantum world are transferrable to our classical reality of time and place. Finally, at both the macro level and the micro, dimensions can distort: not only can miniscule subatomic particles slow to a timeless standstill, but also massive galaxies have a mantle around them in which time stands still. Eternity and infinity appear at every point around us and inbetween.

We are left to ponder these historic times we are in, the age when science, religion and spirituality collide. We live and breathe the combination of two realities, the finite and the infinite, a combination that is no longer mere philosophy or mathematical theory but is now supported by evidence reflected in the timeless halo of eternity that surrounds all matter and energizes it. What the religious have alluded to in the afterlife, and advanced meditation has offered us in this life, science is beginning to uncover all around us. When the right mix of both realities is fully accessed and fully activated within us, what then happens is more than just a breakthrough concept or a scientific view from the outside. Breakthrough consciousness becomes a living reality, and the unifying experience within everything becomes our experience.

This may not be as far off or as way out as it seems, because the angel's eye view we should have from infinity is already a daily routine for us, though much dimmed. Stay with me and let me show you. Science tells us that our galaxy – the Milky Way – rotates once every 200 million years. From what viewing-point has that particular measurement been made? If the intergalactic carousel that is the Milky Way is viewed and measured from the galaxy's centre, then to complete the measurement we still need a fixed reference point *outside* the spinning Milky Way – some unmoving reference point – to measure the galaxy's rotation *against*. But we already know that nothing is fixed in our ever-changing and expanding universe; the whole universe is accelerating, with each part moving away faster and faster from the other. Every galaxy and every single conceivable thing in the universe is forever moving, changing and expanding. So where can the astronomer's *second* steady and unwavering point of reference be located to help measure and observe the rotation of our Milky Way? There is none out there! The only knowable unchanging point of reference in an ever-changing physical reality is the infinity accompanied by our consciousness of it. The astronomer's brilliant imagination has been projected *outside the galaxy* to look back at the central fixed point. By doing this, the astronomer's point of view has ever so softly entered the infinity, which is the only ultra-position from where our mind can possibly pass over all changing boundaries and complete the measurement beyond every ever-changing, false reference point.

The powers of insight and creative transformation implicit in higher states of consciousness are not just limited to dreamers, stargazers and Nobel Prize winners, however. Full-blown breakthrough consciousness can be accessed by every one of us the moment our fixation on separation is cast off, and our outlook turns on to higher, more intimate connections. It can happen anytime, anywhere. The actual infinity of energy, with all its original and creative possibilities, is as omnipresent and omnipotent today as it was at first genesis when the universe began. Though not composed of matter, this original infinity is nonetheless eternally present; it is what our 'higher' or 'spiritual' senses have always adjusted for. The infinity also accounts for the omnipresent and omnipotent attributes that religion has sensed and personified as God. Yet whereas a religious interpretation of the infinity can leave us vulnerable and fearful of a separate, all-powerful supreme being, the holistic view of infinity shows that we are supported, rather than exposed, within the universe. In this way, a truly holistic state of mind is accompanied by the experience of what religion calls 'being at one with God' – only we don't have to adopt a sectional faith or die to achieve this unity. On the contrary, this experience is available all the time, everywhere we are.

It is possible to be a master creator reactivating our own connection to original creativity by tuning our minds first to non-judgemental awareness and then to empty awareness. This is the art of knowing nothing, the nothing that is the deep and original emptiness from which everything arose. This emptiness and deep silence is more than the absence of sound. Seeing beyond the limited reality of causes and effects, we enter the point of view beyond living and dying. This is where every possibility begins. This is the point of infinite divinity and godliness.

Life is a quest undertaken within infinite energy. Out of the state of infinity, all things are created and all possibilities arise, from the vastness of the cosmos to the breath of a newborn baby. Accessing the infinity through the science of self-observation and mindfulness (non-judgemental awareness), then empty awareness, allows us the ultimate experience of everything. This is meditation at its best, a methodical awakening to enlightenment.

CHAPTER 18

Show me the path and I'll continue my progress

Go as far as you can see, and when you get
there you'll see further.

Iranian proverb

Now that we have an *understanding* of how our life and our ability to make a difference are affected by our spiritual capacity and awareness, it is time to explore the ways in which we can step beyond the limits of our intellect. It's time to welcome the ultimate conscious experience. This chapter eases us beyond our limited range of perception, and steps us into the power of pure perception and unlimited awareness.

Here we begin to experience the unity within all diversity. The meditations given here are integral to our spiritual development, and are designed to prepare us to step out of the psychological mindset of separation into the ultimate state of linked-up experience. Meditation traditionally has four areas to focus on: our body, our feelings, our consciousness and the physical world. For all the true prayers, meditations, chants, incantations and formulae practised around the world and developed down through the ages – and from which the four meditations in this chapter are distilled – the common thread running through all of them is self-observation leading to the liberating 'loss of self', and creative transcendence. Rather than this being seen as an altered or heightened state, let's see it as an *optimizing* state – a capacity of mind that releases us (and our full potential) from the sub-optimal condition we call normality. There is nothing wrong with normal; it's the subnormal that has got in the way. The meditations given here are key to spiritual development and our accompanying psychic facility, a way to ensure that the subnormal is no longer allowed to hold sway over our lives.

Meditation is not evil, a fad, or a nice idea 'if we only had time'. It is spiritual exercise, essential for spiritual fitness, and a stepping-stone to spiritual maturity. Some people say that prayer is most often used to tell God what God can do for us, while meditation is best used to ask what we can do for God. Either way, the wiring of the brain not only reflects many different types of intelligence, it also reflects our spiritual evolution. We may not be able to control our future at call but we can control our mind and what we allow in there; our mind is our passport, our border control, between where we are now and where we are going. At the very least, mastery over the mind creates a wonderful sense of freedom. The brain can be rewired voluntarily – that's exactly what learning does. This rewiring evolves faster in some than in others, given local conditions and internal predispositions. Like physical exercise, at the very least meditation helps restore our mind-body balance; at this level, meditation provides the psychological 'reset' position and stress reduction so supported by doctors.[296]

However, meditation is also much more than relaxation, or even brain training to decrease anxiety and depression; it can also be enlightening. Meditation allows us to voluntarily regulate attention, the key to learning. And as meditation advances, different and more powerful brainwaves come into play, as a collaborative study of meditation between the Dalai Lama and Richard Davidson of the University of Wisconsin has shown.[297] This East-West study, which has been running since 1992, has identified the presence of unusually powerful gamma waves that are better synchronized in the advanced than in the novice meditator. Intense gamma waves play a part in linking up different brain circuits, and are associated with superior mental activity and heightened awareness. The further we enter this highly alert state of mind – in which we remain psychologically present and 'in touch with' whatever happens in and around us without adding to, subtracting from, holding onto or denying any of it in any way – the more we experience the true nature of ourselves as emphatically non-individual and fluid, not grasping, stuck or separate. Meditation helps us effectively penetrate the deeper issues of life.

Meditation does not only affect the psychology of mind, it also affects the physiology of the brain. Sara Lazar, a research scientist at Massachusetts General Hospital, has found that the brain's grey matter is thicker in people who meditate (giving favourable meaning to the term 'thick head').[298] All spiritual training is consciousness training, and advanced consciousness is the foundation of all outstanding achievement across every field of human endeavour. From ignorance to enlightenment, all religious and spiritual experience begins and ends as levels of personal observation culminating in breakthrough consciousness – an elevated outlook that leaves us fully integrated, wholly connected and spiritually free. However, a major difference between meditation and prayer is that prayer is the application of an individual to their sense of an external being or entity, while meditation opts for direct communion. In this way, meditation is more ego-free and can open us to more powerful transmissions than some forms of prayer. This issue of being ego-free is an important point: our powers of observation subtly change the things we observe, so the moment we break off our prayer to look for any desired effect from prayer while still praying, or even do this too soon after completing the prayer session (instead of staying in the heightened connection and free of ego), we move from a truly prayerful state into a disconnected, ego-driven one.[299] This untimely pattern of judgemental interference undermines the power of most prayer and other psychic influence, and must be accounted for in any effective study of the power of prayer and meditation.

In general, all meditation techniques are about focusing and elevating the mind. Practitioners achieve this by either focusing down to one chosen point (allowing us to let go of all distractions), or alternatively by diffusing their focus onto nothing in particular (again allowing us to let go of all distractions). These techniques can be either active (moving) or passive (seated or standing). One vitally important thing to remember is that you have to stay open to the moment; when you meditate, there must be no projected anticipation. Seek, in other words, and you *won't* find, as the act of seeking is itself a distraction. Instead, you must relax and let the experience come to you. Psychic forces are rarely effective when our intention is self-serving. In all meditation techniques, the less selfish our intention the more fields of energy we can access. The key to mastering these meditations and attuning them to psychic application is therefore not only the intensity of the bond that you create and sustain during the process, but also the 'cleanness' of the moment of cut-off when we release from the free-state process back into the outlook of ego. This moment of transition is to be such a perfect and instantaneous 'letting go', it is as if you have a moment of severe amnesia as you move out of the meditative state. Our self-interest always keeps its calculating eye on the long path, with all its distractions and resistance, but selflessness frees us into the clear energies of the short path.

We are not practising these meditations to seek a reward or an outcome, but initially just to have a go and see what happens. There is no right or wrong experience, and what arises need never be frightening or weird; it's no more mysterious than what is involved in the experience you are already having right now, reading this page. So if you've never done it before, just give meditation a go, slowly; and while you are trying it, pay attention and really notice what you are feeling. Take it one point at a time, without reading ahead or anticipating the next step. Your own experience is the issue, and although at first what happens may not seem very great, your experiences will grow and accumulate into something more wonderful with each practice. So take it slowly – and when you want to stop, stop. That's all.

Humanity – you – can achieve mastery. Spiritual mastery is not only possible, it is the only game in town. The following meditations have been designed to incorporate the core training at the heart of the most advanced religious practices, spiritual capacity and mystical training. Repetition is essential to break old habits of mind and rewire our psyche for change and lasting improvement. However you do it, you eventually experience the most advanced spiritual states by practising techniques that progressively elevate and expand the scope and reach of your attention while overcoming distractions by internalizing your point of control. Like any fitness training, it takes consistent practice and repetition to bring change within range, though benefits appear early. Here in this chapter, I have combined the best aspects of many techniques from many disciplines to allow the greatest possibility of awakening breakthrough consciousness in you and across your life.

If beautiful blueberries are the single most valuable food we could eat (and nutritional research suggests they are), then consider the following series of meditations to be the blueberry training for spiritual health and transformational awareness. If you have any pre-existing health issues that you think may cause you difficulty during any of the meditations, seek professional advice – and take the good doctor some blueberries while you're at it.

Distant Vision Meditation

This technique is the first step in developing a penetrating and unwavering attention. The ability to develop and maintain a relaxed yet firm control over your attention is essential for controlling the contents of your mind and the trajectory of your life.

1 As with all of these techniques, arrange for no interruptions.

2 Sit with your eyes closed, preferably with quiet music playing (no vocals). Lean slightly forward but with your back strong and upright, not slouching. This posture is easy to maintain for long periods.

3 Maintain relaxed and steady breathing throughout your practice.

4 Now pay attention to whatever you 'see' with your eyes closed – whatever appears to move across your mind and behind your closed eyelids. Usually there is nothing special or significant, just colours, shapes and a kaleidoscope of disconnected images and ideas.

5 Look into the distance of these images, look for and find the most distant point possible. Each time you think you've found the furthest point, look even further into the distance. Push way out to the outermost distance of this 'blind' field of images, and then keep your attention looking even further out…

6 Maintain this search for deep distance for up to 20 minutes, then longer as you progress.

7 Once you have gained some competence with this one-pointed

concentration, practise with your eyes open, as if you were searching through or seeing through the visual field out there in front of you, expectantly waiting for something to emerge. Remain seated.

8 Now stand and repeat what you have just done with eyes open, only this time do it while walking.

Now you will be more relaxed. You will be feeling as if the world around you is a little quieter. It seems as if the edges and surfaces of things are softer somehow, as if by looking into the distance that passes through everything you had loosened up the boundaries of the physical world. This meditation helps us loosen our mental grip on separation, our fixation on surfaces and seeing everything from the outside. Though this is just a mental exercise, some say this meditation is where they first sensed the possibility of mind penetrating matter – the possibility of the impermeable becoming permeable.

Having completed this first meditation, you are now ready to combine the distant vision training with steps towards 'empty awareness' meditation.

Directed Awareness Meditation (leading to empty awareness)

This meditation allows you to isolate your attention. Here you practise moving and directing your attention to different points. Throughout this meditation keep your head relaxed but motionless.

1 Sit with your eyes closed, preferably with quiet music playing (no vocals). Become aware of your easy and relaxed breathing for a few minutes. Let all thoughts come and go without you giving any one of them particular attention.

2 Using your imagination, pay attention to something directly behind you for a few moments.

3 Shift your attention to something you remember seeing in front of you a few moments before you closed your eyes.

4 Next, move your attention to a point on the left…

5 …then the right. By now you have spent some minutes paying attention in four directions – behind, in front, left and right.

6 Repeat each of the previous four directions of attention, only now imagine you have a pencil (with the pointed end out) either in each of your ears alternately, on your forehead or the back of your head as the case may be, and imagine writing your name in the air successively in each direction.

7 Put aside the imaginary pencil and draw small circles directly above your head, using the top of your scalp to directly scribe circles in the atmosphere above you.

8 Now, pay attention to *all five directions simultaneously* (behind, in front, left, right and above). Keep your attention relaxed. Become immersed in this for a few minutes while this 'surround-view' attention develops and settles in.

9 Finally, let go of all effort and just let impressions come. Observe them. Do nothing with them, just observe. Don't push them away or hold onto them, don't change them or try to avoid them. Just let them be, let them come and go. Your attention will become empty. Maintain this. You are now making yourself aware of awareness itself. By giving your attention to nothing but attention itself, your conscious mentality is becoming aware of the immaterial. This is also called 'formless attention'.

You may come away from this technique feeling a little giddy or tingly and warm in the head. This is not a problem and will pass.

With these first two meditations you have begun to range your attention around your inner and outer worlds. Becoming aware of awareness itself has prepared you for the following technique – 'power point' meditation.

Power Point Meditation (also called the 'Knights Move' Meditation)

In Chapter 2 we first learned of a multi-dimensional universe arranged between two realities – an original and a created reality. This meditation 'positions' your mind in both realities simultaneously. Here we discover our multi-level mind, with its enlightened capacity to observe the observer at many levels. Part of the divine paradox is that by observing self we have the possibility of suspending ego, letting go of the self and opening up to spiritual mastery. Suspending the chase, we claim the trophy.

Now that you have mastered moving your attention freely around you and through you, let's pay attention to attention itself. Paying attention to attention is the art of observing your mind. Your awareness can be observed operating at different levels. Only four levels of observation need to be described and consciously practised here. By stepping progressively further back and back and observing each of these four successive levels of awareness in turn, your power of higher consciousness becomes increasingly transformational, until you enter breakthrough consciousness. (You were introduced to the dynamics of this process in Chapter 16 when you were invited to let go of letting go of letting go of thinking of an elephant.)

Each level of awareness creates its own 'presence' or 'existence' in your mind's eye, and this is what you step away from and observe. With practice, each subsequent level becomes clearly identifiable from the previous one and appears to be above it, so that you learn to step up through each 'level' and on to the next.

- **You begin** by sitting comfortably, in a quiet and peaceful environment. Eyes open. Pay attention to your breathing, letting it flow easily and calmly. As always, arrange for no interruptions during your practice.

- **The first-level** observation is what you do normally every day – be mindful of your surroundings; simply use your five limited senses to pay attention to whatever is around you, listen and get a sense of reality from your separate position of self. None of the observation skills required at this first level are uniquely human – any animal or insect does their version of this every moment; it's one of the ways we manage to survive. This basic sense of the world informs your emotions and your responses to your surroundings. From what you have learned in this book, you know that this limited five-sense view you have of the energetic world around you is, in effect, a miniscule observation of the infinity picked up through indirect and fragmented means. However, you are also capable of a supremely direct experience. Although at this level you are picking up on reality from the outside, which is the long path wavelength, eventually it is possible to have an insider's experience. This happens in part by seeing *yourself* from the outside. To do this you need to ascend the higher levels of observation.

- **The second** level of observation is made when you take notice of what you are doing in the first level and observe the fact that down there you are conscious of the created reality around you – at this second level you become aware of being aware. This is where self-observation begins, as if you were looking at yourself from the outside, or having a low intensity, out-of-body experience. This is called 'observing the observer'. This is the start of your observable progress into breakthrough consciousness and transcendence.

- **The third** level is simply the conscious act of observing the second level.

> Here, you observe (3rd level)
>> the observer (2nd level)
>>> of what you sense as the world
>>> around you (1st level).

This third level is the platform of mind where wisdom begins. This level is somewhat more difficult to maintain for any period than the previous two. Also, while the second and third levels are easy enough to 'see' momentarily (and easy enough to understand), maintaining all three and dwelling in this multi-level perception for any measurable period takes more practice.

- **The fourth** level is observing (4)
>> the observer (3)
>>> of the observer (2)
>>>> of your responses (1) to what you sense as
>>>> the world around you.

During practice, this fourth level gives some new practitioners the feeling of actually wanting to turn around and look behind themselves. With practice, that feeling of disorientation goes and true transcendence begins. This fourth level takes considerable practice to achieve for more than the briefest moment. However, the benefits of the practice itself are many.

You might well ask, 'Why stop at four? Why not go further?' Though this is a good question, it also reveals something about you the questioner: you show that your mentality is working at the second level where you are observing yourself being the critical observer. Even though your question is about higher levels, its existence actually restricts your experience to the second. Remember that, as we just saw, it is vitally important to not calculate and evaluate the experience while in it, but rather just immerse yourself in the practice. The first real breakthrough in your meditations comes when this fourth power point can be maintained for more than a momentary flash before you slip back into merely filling your head with an *idea or opinion* about having awakened four (or more) levels of active observation. Your meditative effectiveness is developing when the total *experience* of these four horizons of observation can be sustained for longer and longer periods. A high level of mastery has been achieved when you can stay in this observational state, relaxed and at will, for longer periods each day.

Before reading on, read the previous paragraph again to see if your question has been answered; then decide if you need to read it a third time. Until you get beyond your question you disallow the experience. (And thank you, Charles Luk, for the transmission of mind…)

Let's come back down and analyse this power point technique. The fourth level means you become aware (4) of being aware (3) of being aware (2) of your responses and reactions to the energy you sample and make sense of (1) in the infinity around you. This is transformational super-consciousness, the intangible point of infinite awareness. In effect, here you are moving through Zen's gateless gate and experiencing the infinity directly. You have stepped out of the elevator and found the short path outlook that is key to the highest three horizons of Chapter 16.

The one state or field that cannot be defined by deep space and anchored by time is infinite energy, formless and in perfect balance – the ultimate background and context. The highest experience that reality-consciousness makes available is this 'emptiness' that exists beyond or aside from all things. Maintaining this state of mind within your active day-to-day life is the art of dwelling in the one while dealing with the many calls on your time and attention. This experience of enduring balance provides you with the spiritual channel that allows all the best possibilities to flow into your life.

Unlike other aspects of the meditations given here, we need no preparation or planning to enter this self-observing state. It is spontaneous – self-observation can be practised anytime, anywhere. Your degree of transformational consciousness comes as an expression of your *level* of attention – the height of your observation-point and how long you maintain it. The ability to maintain advanced levels of observation comes with practice. Ideally, there should never be a conscious moment when you are not paying attention and observing your mental generator. You can easily observe your state of mind during whatever else you are doing moment-to-moment in your life.

You are now ready to apply your powers of breakthrough consciousness to everyday experiences.

Transformational (or Three-pointed) Meditation

This meditation is the direct application of the idea that mind affects matter, and can eventually be used not only to train your mind, but also to benefit the subject of your meditation in some way. With this meditation you learn to create and contribute to positive outcomes more directly, rather than through the long path of causes, effects and unexpected outcomes, which is where the possibility of resistance is strongest. This meditation is where you can begin to answer your own true prayers. By practising this technique and the later ones mentioned, you advance your spiritual integration via the three fundamentals (see section 3) and move your life up through the eight horizons. With this technique, as novel as it is (and others like it are), you can begin awakening the transformational abilities that accompany advanced spiritual development.

However, it is important to remember the point we made earlier in this chapter: once you begin a practice session, do not allow yourself to be distracted by thinking of the outcome. The idea is to learn to focus on a single subject, whether a person, an object or a desired event or outcome, and see what happens – not so much what happens to the subject (at least not at first), but the effect that the practice has on you. This meditation is not a party trick; to begin with we are not so much trying to move something as to practise the mental disciplines necessary to eventually influence it. If you stay at the practice from the standpoint of mind-training, the rest will follow without a thought.

Remember, you can effect change by using the power of your mind only when it is used selflessly – when your reason transcends the ego and the separate self, to be applied purely to the benefit of others. This is because completely letting go of the psychology of separation (including the separate self) is the only way in which holistic, healing connections can be fully engaged.

Although this technique has superficial similarities with structured prayer, it is actually very different. Unlike prayer, effective meditation is not an application to a separate deity, but more an opening up to engage with a connection that is forever present, and so manifest an outcome directly, on the short path, through ourselves.

This meditation is completed in three stages. First, we get familiar with the three points in question and their placement around us, using a static object. Then we learn to apply these points of attention to influence a movable object. Finally, we begin to apply attention to a person or overall situation we wish to help or positively influence, rather than restricting ourselves to something inanimate.

Stage one

1 Sit comfortably and become aware of your easy and relaxed breathing for a few minutes. As always at the beginning of each of these meditations, let all thoughts come and go without selecting any one of them for particular attention.

2 Gently pay attention to any object of your choice, perhaps a vase on the table in front of you. This is your first point of attention.

3 Develop two other points of attention – one behind the vase (visualize a point in the space behind it) and one in front of it (a

point in the space between you and the vase). You now have three points of attention operating simultaneously.

4 Remembering the earlier 'distant vision' meditation technique where we looked further and further into the imaginary distance: now imagine that the point in the space behind the vase is an opening through which you can see out beyond it to nothingness, to some 'infinite emptiness'. This is what the children did with me during the walk in the forest, when they could 'see beyond everything' (see Chapter 9). In fact, imagine this point as being where all points and pieces of physical reality meet the infinity.

5 Maintain these three points – the point between you and the vase, the vase itself and the infinity seemingly 'beyond' the vase – simultaneously for as long as possible.

As you practise this meditation and its variations, notice that at first the middle point is a solid, real object to which you give your attention, while the front and rear points are merely projections from your consciousness. However, as you become more proficient, this middle point of attention will also become a projection or visualization, like the other two points. This means that the object of your attention will no longer need to be physically present with you in order for you to be able to influence it.

Stage two

Now we prepare to apply these three points to an active situation, using a movable object as the focus of our attention and trying to create an outcome by influencing the object. At the point that lies between you and the object, you will be learning to project or 'see' this outcome. Later, the outcome can be anything you want to create around you, but for now we are just playing with the idea of trying to move an object using simply the power of mind. Remember that this is something we already do quite easily to the physical molecules of our brain each and every time we have a thought.

However, once you begin, again remember that the more you look to see if the process is working, the less it will be working. Just concentrate on using your powers of attention and observation to maintain the three-point structure as a meditation technique, and leave seeing what happens until later.

6 Suspend a small object, such as a key, from a thread in front of you, and make that the first point.

7 Visualize the outcome you want (for now, let's make it some movement of the key) in the position between you and the key.

8 Now open up the third point of attention – the infinity position – behind the key.

9 Maintain this three-pointed arrangement for as long as you can, without falling into the familiar trap of evaluating your progress while doing the practice.

Stage three

After initial practice with inanimate objects, of more interest will be learning to use this technique selflessly in your interactions with others. This third stage will enable you to read people with something even stronger than heartfelt empathy; to gently enter their world from the inside, as if you were them – holistically in fact. With mastery of this technique (and further training) you will have connected with them at a level that allows you to bring alignment and balance into their lives in the form of specific physical or psychological healings. This technique is at the heart of psychic, diagnostic and healing abilities. It is also empowering, equipping you to gently register and engage all forces that influence the world around you and through you.

This is not the place for gullibility, or for negative preconceptions. At some point as we approach practice, we need to abandon cynicism and suspend scepticism. Once we've decided to practise any one of these techniques, lingering scepticism or cynicism diminishes any release or transference of power by withholding and diverting the power of our psyche into ego and the separate self. Equally unhelpful is blind faith or absolute certainty. In all this, openness and the simplicity of innocence are essential. What is needed beyond all resistance is the state of the unlimited mind in which we selflessly let go into the infinity of possibilities.

To practise this personalized version of the technique, at first you will need a friend or family member to be present. Eventually, practise this technique without anyone being physically present, just by visualizing the person or the situation you wish to influence.

10   Begin by establishing the three points of attention as you did in the steps above. But this time the subject occupying the middle point of your attention is a person in front of you.

11   Now, as before, visualize the immediate outcome that you want for the person, at the point of attention between you and them – something that is for their benefit alone, and not yours in any way. (It is important at this early stage that you do not tell the person what you are aiming at, at any stage in the practice; this saves you from the distractions of scrutiny, praise, criticism, embarassment, personal rewards and vanity.)

12   Then open up the third point of attention, the infinity position, again as if it is behind the person. Visualize this point of infinity expanding and extending until it completely surrounds and envelops both the person and the intended outcome. Maintain this three-part fusion as a sense of oneness for a number of minutes.

13   Now turn off and let go completely. To do so you must give up on both creating the meditation and any desire to check the outcome. This means you remain deeply silent and still, empty of everything. Only after some time in this stage (and many weeks of practice), when there has been a prolonged suspension of observation for a minute or two, might you care to lower your horizon and review how the meditation went up to that point.

14   Repeat steps 1–13 again and again and again.

15   Advance this technique further by practising it without the person being present. Try it first with a photograph of the person; then perhaps with one of their belongings, such as an item of clothing; and ultimately without any material prop at all, just by visualizing them in your mind.

Remember, if you stop to look for results you immediately drop out of the transformative state (your selfless, egoless mind). While you are absorbed in the meditation, it is vital to 'let go' and surrender completely to the moment. This is why a master-key to effectiveness in all psychic matters – whether for healing or any other outcome – is selflessness. Unselfish attention is less likely to bring up distractions at the instant of letting go, whereas a self-centred point of attention withholds a little or a lot from full connection and engagement at this subtle and heightened level.

Also, the less selfish the *content* we place into the third (or closest) point of attention – the projected outcome – the easier it is to maintain all three points simultaneously without distraction; seeking the winning lottery numbers this way has never been known to work. Self-interest pulls us back down further into the mindset of separation, with its causes, effects and reactions. On the other hand, the more selfless we become, the more potent the results.

Congratulations! With the development and extension of this technique you are integrating yourself convincingly within the sixth and seventh horizons. These two creative and psychic horizons of spiritual evolution are seeing you move your influence and effectiveness from the long, material path to the short, direct, spiritual path. Be warned again: selfishness (ego) is what holds us on the long path. However, if moved by unselfish motives, desirable outcomes will begin to develop around you as if by chance or serendipity. By maintaining these three points of attention, you can progress beyond the attitudes and outlook that accompany your separation and sustain it. Instead, you are letting go of cause-and-effect and beginning to access the mind's control-panel for transformational consciousness.

Repeat this visualization process until it becomes spontaneously and easily sustainable for you. Later, feel free to experiment, turning this technique of applied meditation to any combination of situations and outcomes. In all situations, maintain right practice until perfect. Be creative and have fun.

You must be the change you wish to see in the world.

Mahatma Gandhi

With these and three more advanced techniques – Advanced Transformational Meditation, Advanced Psychic (healing) Communication, and Absent Psychic Communication* – you are well on the way to opening complete access to the timeless power of the short path outlook in your life.

The ultimate reason why any meditations have been included in this book is to offer you the means to cultivate the gentle mental discipline that will help release your enlightenment – the breakthrough consciousness that is beyond living and dying. Out of this comes your active participation in the holistic process of life and spiritual healing. Any specific psychic effects are an incidental aside. The art of 'getting out of the way' and becoming selfless allows balance into your life like never before. This 'letting go of self' is the absolute key both to these meditations and to the art of creating a spiritually free and awakened life.

With mastery of these meditations, you have direct access to reality beyond the material dimensions – access to the seat of transformation and the origin of all change. We know that change is affecting any and all points within our material world long before and after any change we might think we cause. Because the source of uninterrupted and unavoidable change is the infinity from which all phenomena arise, the most significant thing we can do is let go of our separate selves and surrender ultimate control to the omnipotence and omnipresence of infinite change. In this blissfully open

---

* With Transformational Meditation you bring a wider transformational spiritual experience into your everyday interactions. With Advanced Psychic (healing) Communication you suspend time and place, with a state of mind so empty yet focused and open that it cleanly registers the infinity. This is one of the healer's forms, used in diagnosis where we totally empty our minds to become the open or passive receiver of impressions. With Absent Psychic Communication, the subject is physically absent and therefore the whole process is completely 'internalized' within you – there are no external anchors or stimuli in this transference technique. These additional techniques and other training are available through www.mindbenders.com.au.

state – the released state of mind in which created reality harmonizes and merges with infinite reality without collision or friction – we at last begin to directly experience the infinite oneness. With this enlightenment, infinity is rediscovered as eternally present; we are fully awakened and actively engaged through our unbreakable, conscious connection to that state. In that moment we are doing nothing to distort or diminish the whole-health and wellness of others or ourselves. We have become free enough to leave well enough alone and allow the healing wholeness to be within us again.

This enlightened position sees us operate in the world as an engaged witness, active but not interfering, connected yet not controlling, letting events unfold. Only then have we entered the short path to creating heaven on Earth rather than staying on the long path to a personal hell of uncontrollable outcomes and wild disappointments, where we presently excuse our ignorant excesses and wait for some heaven elsewhere.

At their highest expression, these meditations release us into the unifying experience within everything – the missing link in religion's search for heavenly eternity and in science's search for the unified theory of everything. Effective meditation helps us realize that within the infinity that embraces us all there is no elsewhere, only the deepening experience of immediate freedom and universal connectedness that comes with breakthrough consciousness.

Practise. Enjoy.

CHAPTER 19

It's time

There are no passengers on spaceship Earth.
We are all crew.

Marshall McLuhan

These are exciting times for each of us to make a positive change in our world, knowing what we now know about the nature of the universe and our place in it. It is the sympathetic tension between the growth of human awareness and the crises we now face that will create the solution – positive tension releases energy which gives us our drive towards breakthrough consciousness. We are now equipped to make advanced spiritual choices, both personally and collectively.

This book has presented you with a new way of seeing, and offers a new way of being in the world. Quantum physics has reminded us that all of our philosophies, religions and conventional sciences have not got to the bottom of the how, what and why of life and reality. For the most part we only dabble at the surface of reality, seeking to either cause effects or avoid them.

Here are the four *new* ways this book has given us to look at physical reality beyond the 'solid' way it appears around us every day:

- *Everything is a relationship.* Every single thing in existence is made up of parts – from the subatomic to the intergallactic – and is merely the interlinked collection of all of those parts, which are themselves nothing more than the interrelationships of their component parts, and so on and on… This means that any object only exists as long as the relationships struck between all of its component parts continue to exist. When we remove or change one of the parts we change some of the inter-relationships, and so the original object no longer exists. This view of reality shows that what we call 'object' is a collective mass of relationships.

- *Everything is a context.* Any physical object can be seen as the context created and shared collectively by all its component parts, the same context that is observed by us from the outside as the object. (Observing anything from the *inside* is the key to holism and, eventually, breakthrough consciousness.) Context is a collective relationship between all the parts created into their whole. Not only does everything have a context; everything *is* a context. A context not only surrounds every single thing, but context also constitutes everything, giving it existence. This view of reality says no context, no reality.

- *Everything is a surface.* Try as we might, we can never penetrate what appears as the surface of something. When we think we have broken through, all we have exposed are more surfaces. In a silent and colourless world where we add the sound and colour, we also deduce depth, but we actually sense only surfaces and externals. The appearance of physical reality could therefore be called the surface view of creation, an endless plane view, a shim with zero thickness, a front with no back that began with the Big Bang and can't be penetrated or avoided from any point within time and space, no matter how far we reduce something and break it down. From this perspective, physical reality is impenetrably shallow.

- *Everything is the unending expression of change.* We know that every subatomic particle in every atom of every 'solid' object is a dynamic point of energy rather than a solid piece of matter. We also know that every one of these subatomic particles – the building blocks of every material object anywhere in the created universe – is energy that is forever moving and changing. This means that reality (small 'bits' of energy forever moving) has no substance or permanence. From this view, reality is the expression of change itself.

There is some of reality external to us, that is obvious. What we struggle with is the assumption that external automatically means disconnected or absolutely separate. But the greater truth is that while we are not all of reality, at some level we remain connected as part of every single thing and inseparably connected into all. Discovering this point of universal connection, and experiencing it, is life's overarching spiritual quest. The old age of bias in favour of an outlook of separation and the behaviours of fragmentation is ending, and evolution has entered the new age of higher connections and super-consciousness.

It is important to understand, however, that spiritual fitness is not at the expense of physical survival, but acts as a complement to it. Spiritual development, as we saw in our discussion of altruism, is a necessary part of life, not an alternative to it; spiritual fitness and a vibrant, confident life are mutually *in*clusive. Our effective spiritual reach is more than arm's length, just as our personal environmental 'footprint' is much bigger than our shoe size. With the issues that surround us today, it is not enough for us to be clean and green. We also need a personal scope and spiritual reach absolutely in touch with the essence of everything around us. Mature spirituality is robust and alive; it is not about being submissive or disengaged and distant, since we cannot and will not survive if we do this exclusively. Nor is spiritual fitness a license to dominate. Spiritual fitness makes us the immersed and actively engaged witness. The fact that we are totally dependent on our fellow human beings and our environment to sustain us (and vice versa) means that co-operation and mutual consideration are paramount for everyone's continued survival; the forces of nature and the fundamentals of reality and creation ensure there are no privileged exceptions to that rule.

However, what is of most importance for us here is not just an intellectual understanding of our interdependence, but the active engagement with the relationships that create and maintain all. What we call reality is constantly transformed by the mystery of change at its surfaces, the meeting point at which two entities form a relationship or connection. It is the relationship rather than the entities involved that attract significance. Therefore, when we want to change things, it is not the things themselves but the connections – *the relationships between them* – that we must pay attention to and seek to influence.

Any evolution in consciousness only happens person-by-person. With reality interlinked, it cannot be changed bit-by-bit; instead, it is transformed completely and immediately, moment-by-moment, from within each of us, through the ever-present, infinite power of relationships and connections. While consciousness may create the illusion of the separate self, we also have a super-position available that extends beyond these self-imposed limitations. It is only when we recognize and experience the strength of this unified whole, accepting within us the transformative power of mind to influence relationships (and remember that relationships extend all the way from the infinity down to the subatomic core of matter) that we have the chance to bring about real change, both in our own health and also in the collective health of our society and our planet.

Remember that by turning the steering wheel of a car just a fraction, the car takes another direction to eventually arrive at a completely different destination. Every moment of our lives is a planetary turning point. Even changing ourselves just a little can go a long way. While it is very easy to remain locked in and distracted by the overwhelming weight of human misery in our world, we must remember that our ongoing spiritual development has global as well as personal implications: global change requires personal action. The future direction of life on Earth is now in human hands. What happens from here depends on the informed choices we make personally.

We haven't created a better world yet because collectively we don't really expect to. Oh yes, we are able to imagine what an ideal world would be like, but then we hear an inner voice saying, 'Be realistic!' However, the question should *not* be, 'Can we change our world?' because we *constantly* change it for good or bad with even the smallest thing we do. The question should be, 'Can we change our world *for the higher good*?' Whichever way we change our world depends on where we set our horizon, and what spiritual compass bearing we take.

Ancient Rome had its *Romanitas* – the ideals and ideas of Rome and the greater Roman identity. Today's global issues transcend historical borders, calling for a *Globalitas* – global citizens with global ideals and consciousness. This embraces the capacity to not only sense the separate self from the inside looking out, but moreso to see ourselves from a vantage point outside and looking back – beyond self, or 'transpersonally' –

supported by our new psychology extending beyond the limiting horizons of the personal to the unlimited outlook of the universal.

It is not enough for us to dream of a better world, global leadership, breakthrough consciousness and spiritual awakening; we must each become the person we need to be to create that world *from the inside out*. Are you willing to dream the impossible? If you can think it, picture it and dream it, it is no longer impossible. In fact, *because* you can picture it, it *is* possible. This is not some well-ordered world where every particle has a predetermined and final placement, where some super-science will finally measure and calculate all the possible interactions and outcomes. In our created universe, creativity keeps on unfolding and maintaining new reality while sustaining what 'is' and deconstructing the old. Within every one of our personal hopes and dreams, whole universes emerge.

Knowledge is power. If reading this book has moved one public official to take the higher ground, or motivated one concerned individual to engage further with their own powerful good, then thank you for having the courage and drive to make a difference.

All I have offered you here is a way to make the shift in perceptions from the long path to the short path. This shift takes you from being a guest *in* your world to being the host *of* your world; the rest is up to you. When you make the shift, it's like going through an open doorway – what Zen Buddhism calls the gateless gate. Everything you saw before, you continue to see. The difference is in the way you look at everything and anything, and the way your energy flows when you do. Rather than remaining attached to the form of something, your attention on the short path focuses on the relationships and connections *between* the forms. When we identify change, what we are actually seeing is changes to connections. On the short path, reality is experienced as being far more complex and dynamic than mere surface impressions would suggest. Physical form cannot be stable or permanent, because reality itself is an ever-changing relationship of parts. As there is nothing unchanging in physical reality, then there is no reality separate from change. Change and reality are synonymous, one and the same.

After your breakthrough in consciousness, you are aware of no longer looking at the things around you in the usual old way. All the separate mental attachments that previously and habitually took your attention and set your emotional thermometer on high or low have been let go and are only taken up again selectively, surpassed by a seamless field of possibilities, which you sense, choose and then effectively channel. Entering freely into that experience moment by moment is truly being in the flow.

The difficulty is that your attention will wander back off track to old habits, and lock onto the material world in the old attached way that affects your emotional thermometer once more. In a flash, everything around you once again becomes the cause and focus of your energetic actions and reactions. As we found when learning the techniques of meditation, this back-flip onto the long path also happens when you become attached to the outcome as it develops, and instead of letting go, take a peek for moral support and encouragement to see how things are progressing. Thwack! Back down onto the long path again.

To escape this relapse onto the long path with its limited access to reality, take up the process of detachment and 'letting go' again by looking at everything through your other eyes – your *in*sight. Now realize that every move we make never stops where we think it will, or when. Our power to influence is endless. So if you want to see a positive and lasting difference in the world, the first step is to recognize the seat of this power in you. You have always held your part of the beginning and end of all possibility in your hands; learn to use it wisely.

As Charles Luk showed me during those timely cups of tea years ago in Hong Kong, there is a point at which the very act of looking for the answer gets in the way of finding it. There is a point at which the answer to the question can only be experienced directly and from within; the answer cannot be adequately spoken. This personal breakthrough is the missing link to holism, and through which the whole processional effect begins arising from within your world.

We started this book with an exploration of some of the many crises, questions and mysteries facing our world today. In our troubled and uncertain times, global problems are in urgent need of solution, but how are we to go about finding these solutions? This is a question no one can answer for you but you. Action is needed immediately, and with many good people continuing the search, we may wonder why the solutions to such issues as worldwide poverty, global free trade, nuclear proliferation, environmental demolition, short-sighted sectional interests and personal unhappiness still elude us, feeling as we do at odds with our work, partners, children, family, community, environment and ourselves. The answer is simple: though the forces of spiritual immaturity and separation have less and less psychological hold on the maturing outlook of more and more of us, the spiritual health and consciousness of humanity remains a work in progress...

As we progress and activate new dimensions in our personal lives, the future of the whole world is affected. Return to Section One of this book from your newly enlightened position; consider the emergencies of survival and the environment, and consider what more you can do about the situation, in light of what you have read in these pages. I invite you to act now. All the very best work needed in the world begins and ends within you. A spiritual life involves working *on* life, not only working *in* life. We are all world leaders; we are all on the world stage, each one of us immensely significant and influential.

Science, philosophy, religion, politics or the arts cannot alone provide an answer to such questions. However, what they have given us are insights – intentional or otherwise – that share a collective theme: that everything in the universe, from the quantum particle to the most distant galaxy, shares a connection to infinity. Around each life is a link to the everlasting; around each ideology a hope; and around each creative flash a glimpse of original creation. These insights are some of our clues, our prompts. Finding the breakthrough experience that makes these insights significant within our particular life is up to us.

Ultimately it's not necessary to answer all the big questions about God, the universe and everything else in between. And it may not even be possible. Seeking *the way* is good first practice, so maintain the momentum of your present interest in these matters; the rest will unfold horizon after horizon, level of connection after connection.

There is more to your extraordinary life than staying alive. The next great wave of human potential is beginning to take shape. The ultimate truth about reality is not hiding out there in deep space or waiting in heaven; the truth is within us now. If we turn on to our possibilities, all the darkness in the world cannot put out the light of our candle, however small. In fact, one candle *dispels* the dark; a little light reveals many doorways. More and more of us realize we have only just begun. The creativity that began with the Big Bang continues with everything we do and every choice we make.

The questions and issues raised in this book, and the pathways outlined, are not here to offer a cut-and-dried solution to life's problems. The current of holism runs through the world, seeking to balance and complete the circuitry of creation. All this book aims to do is to reactivate that energetic in your life, to make you conscious of the current of holism as it runs through you. We all have the grace and power of creation within us. Unlocking this potential allows us to channel the highest of connections, to engage powerful forces for the good while we continue, as always, to change the world from wherever we are. All I have tried to do is open up the mind of each reader to new possibilities that arise with our emerging creative potential. The rest is up to you. Any flowers you have found within the pages of this book are yours; all I have provided is the vase. May we expand our horizons, help others, and be happy.

As Charles Luk would say, more tea, anyone?

For notes and author contact information, please see website on page 385.

You will find all the numbered supporting notes – including sources, comments, case studies, glossary and further information – on the *Think of an Elephant* website. The website is also a great source for interviews with experts and free downloads:

thinkofanelephant.com

More information and training are available from the author and his associates on the ideas presented in *Think of an Elephant*. This additional access includes private sessions, seminars, workshops, personal profiling and corporate consultancy.

Email: paul@mindbenders.com.au
Website: www.mindbenders.com.au

Bibliography

Achterberg, J, *Imagery in Healing – Shamanism and modern medicine,* Shambhala, Boston, 1985

Ader, R, and Cohen, N, 'Behaviorally conditioned immunosuppression', *Psychosomatic Medicine,* vol. 37, 1975, pp. 333–40

Baron-Cohen, S, *The Essential Difference: The truth about the male and female brain,* Perseus Books Group, 2003

Bragdon, E, *Spiritual Alliances: Discovering the Roots of Health at the Casa de Dom Inacio,* Lightening Up Press, Woodstock, VT, 2002

Benson, H, *Timeless Healing: The power and biology of belief,* Diane Books Publishing Co., 1996

Bernstein, P L, *Against the Gods: The remarkable story of risk,* Wiley & Sons Inc., New York, 1996

Blackmore, S, *Consciousness: An introduction,* Hodder and Stoughton, London, 2003

Boyd, R and Silk, J B, *How Humans Evolved,* third edition, W W Norton & Co., 2002

Bruer, J, *The Myth of the First Three Years,* Free Press, New York, 1999

Bunn, T, 'Black Holes', Berkeley Cosmology Group, http://cosmology.berkeley.edu/ Education/BHfaq.html

Carroll, L, 'Mind over Matter – Pet studies show a physiological basis for placebo effect', *Neurology Today,* vol. 5, no. 11, November 2005, pp. 19–21

Carson, R, *Silent Spring,* Houghton Mifflin, New York, 40th anniversary edition 2002 (first published 1962)

Chaitin, G J, *The Unknowable,* Springer Verlag, Singapore, 1999

Chapman, G, *The Five Love Languages: How to express heartfelt commitment to your mate,* Strand, Sydney, 2004

Chopra, D, *Ageless Body, Timeless Mind*: *The quantum alternative to growing old,* Rider, 1993

Cialdini, R, *Influence: Science and practice,* fourth edition, Allyn & Bacon, 2000

Cooper, L F, and Erickson, M H, *Time Distortion in Hypnosis: An experimental and clinical investigation,* second edition, Crown House Publishing, 2002

Covey, S R, *The 7 Habits of Highly Effective People,* Simon & Schuster, New York, 1989

Darwin, C, *The Origin of Species by Means of Natural Selection: The preservation of favoured races in the struggle for life,* edited by J W Burrow, Penguin Books, London, 1968 (first published 1859)

Davidson, J, *et al,* 'Long-Term Meditators Self-Induce High-Amplitude Gamma Synchrony During Mental Practice', *National Academy Of Science,* vol. 101, no. 46, 16 November 2004

Davies, P, *How To Build A Time Machine*, Penguin, New York, 2003

Dawkins, R, *The Selfish Gene*, Oxford University Press, UK, 1976

Diener, E, and Pavot, E, 'Review of the Satisfaction with Life Scale', *Psychological Assessment*, vol. 5, 1993, pp. 164–72

Dever, W H, *Did God Have a Wife?: Archaeology and folk religion in Ancient Israel*, Eerdmans Press, 2005

Diamond, J, *Collapse: How societies choose to fail or survive*, Allen Lane, 2004

Dotlich, D L, and Cairo, P C, *Why CEOs Fail: The 11 Behaviors That Can Derail Your Climb to the Top – and How to Manage Them*, Jossey-Bass, San Francisco, 2003

Dunbar, R, *The Human Story*, Faber, London, 2004

Dunn, S, *et al*, 'Psychosocial predictors of outcome IV: patients with early-stage breast cancer', *Breast*, vol. 24, no. 2, 2001, pp. 21–4

Earle, S A, *Sea Change: A message of the oceans*, Ballantine Books, 1996

Edelman, D, *The Triumph of Elohim: From Yahwisms to Judaisms*, Eerdmans Press, 1996

Eisenberg, D, *et al*,' Unconventional medicine in the United States: Prevalence, costs, and patterns of use', *New England Journal of Medicine*, vol. 328.4,1993, pp. 246–52.

Einstein, A, and Infeld, L, *The Evolution of Physics*, Simon and Schuster, New York, 1966

Eysenck, H J, 'Cancer, Personality and Stress: Prediction and Prevention', *Advances in Behavior Research and Therapy*, vol. 16, 1994, pp. 167–215

Field, T, *Touch*, Bradford Books, 2001

Foreman, J, 'Trick or treatment?', *Boston Globe*, 6 February 2006

Foucault, M, *Discipline and Punish: The birth of the prison*, Gallimard, Paris, 1975; English trans. Pantheon, New York, 1977

von Friesch, K, *The Dance, Language and Orientation of Bees*, Belknap Press, reprint edition, 1993

Gauquelin, M, *The Cosmic Clocks: From astrology to a modern science*, Avon, 1969

Goldberg, E, *The Wisdom Paradox: How your mind can grow stronger as your brain grows older*, Free Press, New York, 2005

Goleman, D, *Emotional Intelligence*, Bantam Books, 1995

Gottman, J, with Declaire, J, *Raising an Emotionally Intelligent Child*, Fireside edition, Rockerfeller Center, New York, 1998

Gottman, J M, Gottman, J S, and Declaire, J, *Ten Lessons to Transform Your Marriage: America's Love Lab experts share their strategies for strengthening your relationship*, Crown, 2006

Gould J, and Gould, C, *The Honey Bee*, W H Freeman & Company, 1988

Griffin, J, *The Origin of Dreams*, Human Givens Publishing Ltd, 1997

Grupas, A, *Creative Problem-Solving*. Missouri Association of Community and Junior Colleges. November, 1990 (ED 343 813)

Gurian, M, *The Wonder of Boys*, Putnam, New York, 1998

Hall, K, *Alter Your Life: Overbooked? Overworked? Overwhelmed?*, Oak Haven, Georgia, 2005

Hamer, D H, *The God Gene: How faith is hardwired into our genes*, Doubleday, New York, 2004

Hamilton, C, and Denniss, R, *Affluenza – When too much is never enough*, Allen & Unwin, Sydney, 2005

Hamilton, C, and Mail, E, 'Downshifting in Australia: a sea change in pursuit of happiness', Australia Institute, www.tai.org.au, January 2003

Hau, L, *et al*, 'Observation of Coherent Optical Information Storage in an Atomic Medium Using Halted Light Pulses', *Nature*, vol. 409, January 2001, pp. 490–93

Hausdorff, J M, Levy, B R, and Wei, J Y, 'The power of ageism on physical function of older persons: reversibility of age-related gait changes', *Journal of the American Geriatric Society*, vol. 47, November 1999

Hebb, D O, *The Organization of Behaviour*, John Wiley & Sons, New York, 1949

Jeans, J, *The Mysterious Universe*, Macmillan, 1930

Kaku, M, *Parallel Worlds: A journey through creation, higher dimensions, and the future of the cosmos*, Doubleday, New York, 2004

Lang, T, and Heasman, M, *Food Wars: the global battle for mouths, minds and markets*, Earthscan, London, 2004

LeBlanc, S A, with Register, K E, *Constant Battles: The myth of the peaceful, noble savage*, St. Martin's Press, New York, 2003

Libet *et al*, 'Subjective Referral of the Timing for a Conscious Sensory Experience', *Brain*, vol. 102, 1979, pp. 193–224

Licauco, J T, *The Truth Behind Faith Healing in the Philippines*, National Book Store, 1982

Licauco, J T, *Beyond Ordinary Reality: Exploring the powers of inner mind*, Solar Publishing, 1987

Lorenz, E, 'Predictability: Does the flap of a butterfly's wing in Brazil set off a tornado in Texas?', 139th meeting of the American Association for the Advancement of Science, 1972

Lovelock, J, *Gaia: A New Look at Life on Earth*, Oxford University Press, Oxford, 1979

Lyubomirsky, S, *et al*, 'The Benefits of Frequent Positive Affect: Does Happiness Lead to Success?' *Psychological Bulletin*, vol. 131, no. 6, 2005

McEwen, B S, and Norton Lasley, E, *The End of Stress As We Know It*, Joseph Henry Press, 2002

McCaig, C, Zhao M, *et al*, 'Controlling Cell Behavior Electrically: Current Views and Future Potential', *Physiological Reviews*, vol. 85, 2005, pp. 943–78.

McCormick, D J, and Plugge, C D, *If I Am an Artist, What's Wrong with My Picture?* Association for Experiential Education, 1997 (ED 414 141)

Mandelbrot, B B, *The Fractal Geometry of Nature*, W H Freeman & Company, 1982

Marais, E N, *The Soul of the White Ant*, Human and Rousseau, 1970

Maslow, A H, *Motivation and Personality*, Harper & Row, New York, 1954

Masserman, J, 'Altruistic Behaviour in Rhesus Monkeys', *American Journal of Psychiatry*, vol.121 pp. 584–5, December 1964

Mayberg, H S, Silva, J A, Brannan, S K, *et al*, 'The functional neuroanatomy of the placebo effect', *American Journal of Psychiatry*, vol, 159, pp. 728–37, 2002

Mitchell, B, Macklis, J, *et al*, 'Constitutive and Induced Neurogenesis in the Adult Mammalian Brain: Manipulation of endogenous precursors toward CNS repair', *Developmental Neuroscience*, vol. 26, 2004

Moberg, F, (ed), 'The Sustainable Development Update', www.albaeco.com/sdu

Monbiot, G, *Heat: How to stop the planet from burning*. South End Press, 2007

Moore, S, 'It's Getting Better All The Time', Cato Institute, 2000

Nasar, S, *A Beautiful Mind: The life of mathematical genius and Nobel laureate John Nash*, Thorndike Press, 2002

Nisbett, R E, *Geography of Thought: How Asians and Westerners think differently … and why*, Free Press, New York, 2004

Norberg-Hodge, H, Merrified, T, Gorelick, S, *Bringing the Food Economy Home: Local alternatives to global agribusiness.* Zed Books, UK, 2002

Odling-Smee, F J, Laland, K N, and Feldman, M W, *Niche Construction: The neglected process in evolution*, Princeton University Press, Princeton, N J, 2003

Ornish, D, *Love and Survival: The scientific basis for the healing power of intimacy*, HarperCollins Publishers, New York, 1998

Ornstein, R, and Thompson, R F, *The Amazing Brain*, Houghton Mifflin, Boston, 1984

Ostrander, S, *Psychic Discoveries Behind The Iron Curtain*, Prentice Hall, New York, 1971

Payne J, *A History Of Force: Exploring the worldwide movement against habits of coercion, bloodshed, and mayhem*, Lytton Publishing, 2004

Pembrey M, *et al*, 'Sex-specific, sperm-mediated transgenerational responses in humans', *European Journal of Human Genetics*, vol. 14, 2005, pp. 159–66

Pellegrino-Estrich, R, *The Miracle Man: The Life Story of Joao de Deus*, Lightning Source, Inc, 2001

Peters, T, *The Tom Peters Seminar,* Random House, New York, 1994

Powell, D, 'Autism and its Implications for a Quantum-Classical Model for Brain Function', conference paper, *Towards a Science of Consciousness*, Denmark, 17–20 August 2005

RavenWing, J, *The Book of Miracles: The healing work of Joao de Deus*, First Books Library, USA, 2002

Rice, G, 'Aiding behavior vs. fear in the albino rat'. *Psychological Record* 14, pp.165–170. 1964. *See also*:

Rice, G, and Gainer, P, '"Altruism" in the albino rat', *Journal of Comparative and Physiological Psychology*, vol. 55, 1962, pp.123–5

Robertson, I, *Stay Sharp With The Mind Doctor: Practical strategies to boost your brain power*, Vermilion, London, 2005

Robinson, M, *Peace Between the Sheets: Healing with sexual relationships*, North Atlantic Books, 2003

Rothstein, B, 'All for All: Equality, corruption, and social trust', *World Politics*, vol. 58, no. 1, October 2005, pp. 41–72

Ruppert, S, 'Critical Evidence: How the arts benefit student achievement', National Assembly of State Arts Agencies, 2006

Seligman, M, *Learned Optimism: How to change your mind and your life*, A A Knopf, New York, 1991

Seligman, M, *Authentic Happiness: Using the new positive psychology to realize your potential for lasting fulfilment*, Free Press, New York, 2004 (reprint edition)

Sheldrake, R, *Dogs That Know When Their Master is Coming Home, and other unexplained powers of animals*, Crown Publishing, 1999

Snyder, A, 'Autistic Genius?', *Nature*, 1 April 2004

Stanford, C B, *The Hunting Apes: Meat eating and the origins of human behaviour*, Princeton University Press, New Jersey, 2001

Steele, E J, Lindley, R V, and Blanden, R A, *Lamarck's Signature: How retrogenes are changing Darwin's natural selection paradigm*, Perseus Books Group, 1999

Strogatz, S, *Sync: The emerging science of spontaneous order*, Hyperion, New York, 2003

Sylvia, C, with Novak, W, *A Change of Heart: A memoir*, Warner Books, New York, 1998

Talbot, M, 'The Placebo Prescription', *New York Times Magazine*, 9 January 2000

Thakur, R, 'Choosing human security', *UN Update*, Issue 27, September 2003

Tompkins, P, and Bird, C, *The Secret Life of Plants*, Harper & Row, New York, 1973

Union of Concerned Scientists, *World Scientists' Warning to Humanity*, Cambridge, Massachusetts, 18 November 1992

United Nations, *The Role of International Processes for the Promotion of Sustainable Forest Management on Forest Certification*, Secretariat of UN Forum on Forests, October 2003

United Nations, www.undp.org/dpa/statements/administ/2004/april, address by UNDP administrator Mark Mallock Brown, 2004

United Nations, 'The Inequality Predicament', United Nations report, 2005

United Nations, 'Global Refugee Trends: Statistical overview of populations of refugees, asylum-seekers, internally displaced persons, stateless persons, and other persons of concern to UNHCR', UNHCR report, 2005

Verne, J, *Paris in the Twentieth Century*, Random House, New York, 1996

de Waal, F B M, *The Ape and the Sushi Master: Cultural reflections of a primatologist*, Basic Books, New York, 2001

de Waal, F B M, (ed.), *Tree of Origin: What primate behaviour can tell us about human social evolution*, Harvard University Press, 2002

Watts, D J, *Six Degrees: The science of a connected age*, WW Norton, New York, 2003

Wenger, M, Bagchi, B, *et al*, 'Experiments in India on Voluntary Control of Heart and Pulse', *Circulation*, vol. 24, 1961, pp. 1319–25

Wenger, M, and Bagchi, B, 'Studies of autonomic functions in practitioners of Yoga in India', *Behavioral Science*, vol. 6, 1961, pp. 312–23

Wilson, E O, *The Future of Life*, Vintage, 2003

Ho, Y C, Cheung, M C, and Chan, A S, 'Music Training Improves Verbal but Not Visual Memory: Cross-sectional and longitudinal explorations in children', *Neuropsychology*, vol. 17, no. 3, 2003

Zohar, D, and Marshall, I, *SQ: Connecting with our spiritual intelligence*, Bloomsbury, London, 2001

Zuberbühler, K, 'Language evolution: Semantic combinations in primate calls', *Nature*, May 2006

Index